FLETCHER STEELE, LANDSCAPE ARCHITECT

Fletcher Steele, Landscape Architect

An Account of the Gardenmaker's Life, 1885–1971

Revised edition

R O B I N   K A R S O N

For Doris Cross

with best wishes,

Robin Karson

October 13, 2004

LIBRARY OF AMERICAN LANDSCAPE HISTORY   AMHERST

DISTRIBUTED BY UNIVERSITY OF MASSACHUSETTS PRESS   AMHERST & BOSTON

Copyright © 1989, 2003 by Robin S. Karson
All rights reserved   Printed in Canada

Library of Congress Cataloging-in-Publication Data
Karson, Robin S.
Fletcher Steele, landscape architect : an account of the
gardenmaker's life, 1885–1971 / Robin Karson.
p. cm.
Includes bibliographical references (p.   ).
ISBN 1-55849-413-8 (alk. paper)
1. Steele, Fletcher. 2. Landscape architects—United
States—Biography. I. Title.
SB470.S65K37 2003   712'.092—dc22   2003016247

These publishers generously gave permission to use quotations from the following works:

The Enquirer, Cincinnati, Ohio: "Village Improvement," 8 January 1925.

The Garden Club of America Bulletin: "Plant Material," by F. Steele, September 1921; "Lisburne Grange," by F. Steele, September 1935; "A Patio Greenhouse," by Mrs. George Doubleday, November 1941; "Private Post-War Planning" (part 1), by F. Steele, June 1944; "Private Post-War Planning" (part 2), by F. Steele, September 1944.

Horticulture, The Magazine of American Gardening: "Enlightened Laziness," by F. Steele, February 1943; "When Trees Turn into Problems," by F. Steele, September 1946; "Food Alone Is Not Enough, Flowers for Freedom, Too," by F. Steele, March 1948.

House Beautiful; copyright © The Hearst Corporation. All rights reserved: "Aesthetic Principles of the Spring Flower Garden," by F. Steele, March 1922; "Gray-Leaved Plants," by F. Steele, November 1922; "New Styles in Gardening," by F. Steele, March 1929; "Mission House," by F. Steele, July 1930; "A Garden Constructed before the House," by F. Steele, August 1930; "A Dooryard Garden with Intimate Planting," by F. Steele, March 1931; "The Temple Garden," by F. Steele, July 1933; "Your Own . . . Your Neighbor's Land," by F. Steele, September 1934.

Landscape Architecture: "The Department of Landscape Architecture in Harvard University," by James Sturgis Pray, January 1911; "A Landscape Architect's Kit," by F. Steele, January 1921; "French Gardens and Their Racial Characteristics," by F. Steele, July 1922; "Color Charts and Their Use in Gardening," by F. Steele, January 1923; "Spain," by F. Steele, January 1929; "New Pioneering in Garden Design," by F. Steele, April 1930; "Landscape Design of the Future," by F. Steele, July 1932; "Fine Art in Landscape Architecture," by F. Steele, July 1934; "The Bureau and the Landscape Designer," by Henry Hubbard, and "Private Delight and the Communal Ideal," by F. Steele, in "The Landscape Architect in the Present Situation," by H. Hubbard and F. Steele, January 1941; "China Teaches," by F. Steele, April 1947; Review of *Gardens and People,* by Stanley White, October 1964.

Naumkeag/The Trustees of Reservations: "Naumkeag Notes," by Mabel Choate, 1952–1956; "Naumkeag Garden," by Mabel Choate, Summer 1956; "The Choates at Naumkeag," by Morgan Bulkeley, July 1968; "Narration," by Geoffrey Platt, July 1983.

Pantheon Books, A Division of Random House, Inc.: *Calder, an Autobiography with Pictures,* by Alexander Calder, 2d ed., 1977.

Town and Country: Interview with Fletcher Steele, 15 December 1926.

The following archives generously gave permission to use quotations from their holdings: Fletcher Steele Papers, Rush Rhees Library, Rochester Historical Society, University of Rochester, Rochester, N.Y.

Photo Credits

All photographs not otherwise identified are by Fletcher Steele.
Photographic archives are identified by the following abbreviations:

SUNY ESF College Archives: Photographs are from the manuscript collection of Fletcher Steele held at the Terence J. Hoverter College Archives, F. Franklin Moon Library, State University of New York College of Environmental Science and Forestry, Syracuse, New York. The American Society of Landscape Architects donated the collection in 1974. Funds from the Graham Foundation for the Fine Arts and Architecture were used to create the Study Print Collection of Steele's client jobs.

LC: Photographs are from the Fletcher Steele papers, Manuscript Division, the Library of Congress, Washington, D.C., donated by the American Society of Landscape Architects.

Frontispiece: Fletcher Steele at Naumkeag, ca 1930. (Courtesy The Trustees of Reservations)

I want all my places to seem the homes of children and lovers. I want them to be comfortable and if possible slightly mysterious by day, with vistas and compositions appealing to the painter. I want them to be delirious in the moonlight. . . . I believe that there is no beauty without ugliness and that it should not be otherwise. Both are capable of stinging us to live. Contrast is more true to me than undeviating smugness. The chief vice in gardens is . . . to be merely pretty.

—FLETCHER STEELE

Contents

Preface to the Revised Edition

Although I did not know it at the time, I became acquainted with the work of Fletcher Steele in 1983 on a visit to Naumkeag. (The docent on duty that day attributed the landscape design to Stanford White.) A call to the Western Regional office of The Trustees of Reservations produced the name Fletcher Steele and, remarkably, the local Amherst library owned copies of both of Steele's out-of-print books, *Gardens and People* and *Design in the Little Garden*. These volumes provided rich background for understanding a landscape that was fast coming to haunt my imagination, whose colors and shapes and excitements made immediate, almost kinesthetic, sense. But as an art historian and a new contributing editor to *Landscape Architecture*, I wanted to know where Steele's ideas had come from and how they figured in history.

Ngaere Macray, of Sagapress, learned of my interest and sponsored a trip for me to visit Steele's papers at the Library of Congress with an eye toward writing a new introduction to a reprint of Steele's last book. The one hundred thousand documents housed there—letters to and from clients, travel diaries, photostats of plans and drawings, and photographs—made it clear that Steele had been a designer of unusual talent and complexity. His accomplishments, I thought, merited more than an introductory essay. A trip to F. Franklin Moon Library, in Syracuse, New York, home of the other large repository of Steele's papers, redoubled this impression.

Ngaere was also enthusiastic about the potential for a book on Steele, but I met with blank stares and discouraging words on most other fronts. (At the time, 1985, only two American landscape architects, Charles Eliot and Frederick Law Olmsted Sr., had been the subject of biographies.) Working through the ASLA network, I began contacting practitioners and found some who remembered Steele and admired his work. Dan Kiley was most outspoken and clear in his assessment that Steele was "the only good designer working at the time," but Garret Eckbo was also enthusiastic and so were Vincent Merrill, Peter Hornbeck, and Henry Hoover. I began locating surviving landscape designs by Steele and comparing current conditions with old photos, plans, and drawings. I met many of Steele's clients, all of whom told vivid stories, some of which scarcely seemed appropriate for a book on landscape architecture. I soon came to believe that there was no way to write about Steele's landscape designs except in the context of his long and rich life.

Fletcher Steele came out in June 1989, when there was still little published scholarship in the field of American landscape history and almost no name recognition of any practitioner beyond Olmsted. The book met with critical success and found enthusiastic readers around the world. In the years following publication, *Steele* provided the basis for a touring exhibition and a series of conferences held at PaineWebber in New York City, which brought to national recognition the names of a host of American practitioners who, like Steele, had languished in obscurity. Additionally, it provided the stewards of Steele's landscapes with new perspectives on the cultural value of his designs and aided caretakers in making maintenance and preservation decisions about them.

The upsurge of interest in American landscape history generated by *Fletcher Steele* and other books published by Sagapress and a few other publishers emboldened me to imagine an organization dedicated to publishing such books for the purpose of educating broad audiences in hopes of inspiring enlightened landscape stewardship. The new program would include monographs, surveys, and reprints of classics in the field of American landscape architectural history, well designed and engaging yet grounded in thorough research that met high academic standards. Sound scholarship, I reasoned, would add to the stability of the emerging field.

I was joined in this dream by Nancy R. Turner, a former client of Fletcher Steele's and a vice president of the Garden Club of America, John Franklin Miller, Nesta Spink, Eleanor Ames, and Michael Karson, who, with me, founded the Library of American Landscape History, Inc., in 1992. The organization has slowly flourished, having since developed twelve books, including five volumes in the ASLA Centennial Reprint Series, several award-winning monographs, *Midwestern Landscape Architecture, Pioneers of American Landscape Design* (with our partners in the National Park Service and the Catalog of Landscape Records in the United States), a new edition of Olmsted Sr.'s first book, and the present revised edition of *Fletcher Steele.*

The opportunity for revising *Steele* arose last year when the initial print run of 6,000 copies was exhausted and Ngaere Macray graciously transferred the reprint rights to LALH. The generosity of LALH trustee Michael Jefcoat and his wife, Evelyn, plus gifts from many other contributors has made the project possible. In the new edition, typographical mistakes, misspellings, and errors of fact or omission in the original have been corrected, the client list and bibliography have been updated, a new index has been provided, and new contextual material has been added throughout. Carol Betsch, a consulting editor for LALH, has guided this process with great skill and wisdom. The revised edition also features a large format and a handsome redesign by Mary Mendell, more than fifty new photographs, fine reproductions, and a price accessible to general readers and students.

The projects discussed in this book were selected on the basis of their quality, innovation, and surviving documentation; they are presented in sequence according to beginning date. Discussions of projects that spanned many decades are presented in phases. Steele's own words are used extensively throughout. Quotations from letters and published material have not been edited for spelling or grammar, nor have references to plants been corrected for current usage. Common names for plants are frequently supplied; I have relied on *Hortus Third* as the final authority on current usage, both common and botanical. Latin names appear in italics, except in those few instances when the Latin has been accepted into common English use.

Whenever possible, I have incorporated Steele's own photographs since they necessarily represent the designer's point of view. Other images commissioned by Steele from professional photographers supplement them, as do photographs by clients, and a number of superb contemporary images by Felice Frankel, David Broda, and Carol Betsch. I have replaced some of the handsome color plates from the first edition (by Alan Ward, Ken Druse, and Felice Frankel) with new images that better communicate current conditions in Steele's gardens.

Naumkeag, the Mission House, and Camden Public Library Amphitheater continue to offer the general public the best opportunity to see Steele's work, and I encourage readers to visit these sites. Many of Steele's private residential landscapes are also in the hands of wonderful stewards and they, too, continue to be maintained according to original design intent, although they are not so easily accessed. At least one remarkable design in private hands has sadly fallen victim to radical revision since the publication of the first edition. The project of tracking and reporting all these changes, positive and negative, lies beyond the scope of the current edition. However, interest in pursuing such documentation continues to grow, and those engaged in this research are seeking to find print or Web-based venues for publication.

Introduction

For sixty years Fletcher Steele practiced landscape architecture as a fine art. His commitment to the notion that gardens are works of art as surely as paintings or music informed every design decision he made. Steele's gardens reflect a deep, continuing interest in experimentation. Along with his writings, they constitute a primary link between the Beaux Arts formalism in which he was trained and modern landscape design.

Steele made his first garden in 1915, his last in 1970. Many of them were, and a few remain, great works of art. Steele's notion that the garden could be a private dreamscape, "a sure prop to contentment," was also innovative and it, too, led to bold experiments with color, form, material, and garden space that helped redefine aesthetic boundaries in his field.

Garrett Eckbo considered Steele "the transitional figure between the old guard and the moderns." Eckbo said, "He interested me because he was an experimenter, he wasn't content to keep repeating the formula—which we were still being taught was the only way to do things. . . . His vocabulary was traditional but, like any good designer, he was taking the vocabulary handed him by the culture and manipulating it well. I was also very impressed with him as a human being. He seemed to possess great humanity, to be a leader."[1]

Daniel Kiley concurred. "Steele was the only good designer working during the twenties and thirties, also the only one who was really interested in new things. The others were caught up in the hierarchy, they were organization men, old fogies. Steele was the one who looked up the modern French architects to see what they were doing with gardens. The idea that a garden didn't have to be symmetrical, or static, was a revelation in the field."[2]

Steele has become known for his early modern experiments, but he also introduced many innovative ideas for suburban landscaping. "I met Fletcher Steele unfortunately all too few times," wrote George Tobey, author of *A History of Landscape Architecture*. "I knew him as a gentle, kind, learned landscape architect, but then was unaware of his seminal position in the 'functional' movement. Later investigation, however, enlightened me. Steele's book, published in 1924, titled *Design in the Little Garden*, spelled out, clearly and simply, the design principles most of us follow today."[3]

Steele was also remembered for his precision. Peter Hornbeck, who had his first job working for Steele in 1955, said of him: "Fletcher Steele was a man of authority, aplomb, and great presence. He meant what he said and said it carefully, often wittily, using anecdotes to make his meaning clear. I found him very reasonable—logic and order were everything. Mr. Steele was so incisive in his perceptions of a problem, so sure, so very elegant in his statement of an idea, his comments often seemed like the sun coming out. We felt this in the office and his clients often did too. His conviction and enthusiasm were compelling and inspirational but much more important—and the profession is better for this—he was a great artist working with great ideas as did no other of his time."[4]

"I care much for the shape, size, and proportion of the empty air spaces of my gardens and guard them jealously," Steele wrote. "Otherwise I am ready to let the client choose the enframing 'style.' Planting is chosen to bring out and enhance the size, proportions and color of the spaces. And the careful, if possible obvious relation of the garden to the big landscape features is worked over hard. Carving and modeling of the earth, building walls and masonry which in height and width are varied and curved to harmonize and often repeat the curves of mountains and valleys in the background, is a fascinating profession. I should have called myself a 'landscape sculptor' for that is what I was and am."[5] Steele first sculpted the earth abstractly in 1933. Inspired by a broad, mountain landscape and carved with bulldozers, the shape of Naumkeag's South Lawn was revolutionary for its time—"an abstract form in the manner of modern sculpture, with swinging curves and slopes which would aim to make their impression directly, without calling on the help of associated ideas, whether in nature or art."[6] The sweep of lawn constituted the first modern earthwork in the United States.

Steele's practice was almost exclusively devoted to private gardens. He claimed that he avoided public projects because "everything good is flattened by committees."[7] Steele's resolve to work within intimate client relationships reflected an art-making process that drew inspiration from his patron's personalities and character. "A garden," he once wrote, "is a token —a symbol—of what its maker cares about."[8] The project of discovery implied by this, Steele's deepest conviction, was inseparable from the more traditional goal of discovering the genius loci. Both tasks stimulated Steele's passion and, ultimately, his creativity. The garden theater of the Camden Public Library, one of Steele's finest creations, stands among a small number of exceptions to his preference for private work.

Underlying all Steele's landscape designs was a belief in the evocative, life-enhancing potential of the field that he considered the sister art of architecture. He created gardens in the context of his clients' "dreams and preferences," remaining alert to the immediate and obvious reason a garden exists—to give pleasure. While challenging the formal conventions of his art, he asked his clients questions. "Do you like to hear the telephone bell? Where will the baby-carriage go? Do you want to keep an eye on the weeds or get out of their way? Where will you put things down? Do you like supper al fresco? And where will you sit to be with the stars?"[9] He took their answers seriously, and designed solutions to accommodate them.

Of the nearly six hundred gardens Steele designed, few survive with their design integrity intact. Naumkeag, in Stockbridge, Massachusetts, is the finest and best preserved of those very few open to the public today. ("Next to cooking," Steele once observed, "gardening seems to be the most ephemeral of the arts in America.")[10] Plants and stone are fragile, as are social contexts. As lives changed, those many clients who hesitated to add wings to distinguished houses did not refrain from installing new swimming pools or tennis courts in their landscapes. Rising labor costs made maintenance of the largest gardens impossible, and the grand residences to which they were attached were often destroyed to make way for new housing developments or passed into the hands of organizations with limited funds. Steele's interest in designing in relation to the particular characters of his clients also contributed to his gardens' vulnerability. Experimentation resulted in distinctive but idiosyncratic places that left some new owners cold. More generic designs, in some cases, have fared better than Steele's, many of which required great upkeep, and so were simplified to the point of eradication.

Nor were Steele's gardens protected by professional criticism and review. Most often published in the pages of popular magazines, they received enthusiastic but superficial review and, in his opinion, were never well represented. "To be sure," he wrote in 1955, "photographs which really give an impression of more than two dimensions are impossible to take. And since space composition and its pull to the eye and the imagination are my greatest interest, I cannot expect to be satisfied very often."[11]

Over his career Steele collaborated with several distinguished talents in related fields, including Ralph Adams Cram, who was also his friend, and Alexander Calder. Steele's balustrades and jets d'eau drew little attention from the modern art world, though. His clients wanted elegance in their gardens, not challenge; luxury, not confrontation. New Bauhaus and de Stijl functionalism were also at odds with Steele's love of sumptuous materials, traditional form, and lavish, decorative complexity.

Since Steele's death in 1971, many architects and landscape architects have become frustrated by the spareness of modernism's legacy and eschewed it in favor of invention and expression—the very aspects of Steele's gardens that tended to undermine their preservation. Today, less prejudiced eyes take a fresh look at his work. They perceive a bold spirit, rich imagination, and a relentless passion for making art.

FLETCHER STEELE, LANDSCAPE ARCHITECT

Rochester and the Steeles

John and Mary Steele's elder child was never called by his given name, which was the same as his father's, and his father's before him. He was Fletcher from the first and remained so until he died. His parents were conservative, intelligent people, poles apart in their interests—she a musician, he a lawyer—but joined by a commitment to propriety and dignity in all things. Their son remembers that they also knew how to have fun. "I was born in Rochester [New York] in 1885 and had the advantage of being brought up in an old house in the friendly, stimulating atmosphere of an old-fashioned, keen environment."[1]

As verbal as he was artistic, the boy straddled his parents' intellectual worlds comfortably. J. Fletcher Steele also inherited his parents' strong code of ethics, along with a tendency toward self-scrutiny and self-remonstrance. At age eight, he felt guilty enough about hoarding peanuts from his younger sister, Esther, that he wrote a letter of confession to his mother. With chastened relief, he told her that a mouse ate the hidden peanuts and gnawed a hole in his pocket as punishment.

The family was comfortable but not well-to-do, especially by standards in the unusually prosperous upstate city. The Steeles spent their winters in a middle-class house on Rochester's Park Avenue, and summers in nearby Pittsford in a farmhouse owned by the family since 1850. "The wait for the Auburn Road train was made exciting by the chance that an express would go rushing through on the main line. . . . Finally our train would come along—everybody gave themselves good long waits for trains those days—and we would go bustling and tootling along, part of the time by the good old canal, to the Pittsford Depot, as it was called. There we were met by horse and vehicle with a flat top on four iron sticks and fringe falling down all around the edge. Once in Pittsford we forgot the city for months."[2] When Fletcher was ten, and his sister Esther eight, the family moved to Pittsford for good.

John Steele practiced law in the "Little House" that sat near the family's modified Greek revival house on Monroe Avenue. His letters reveal a lively, articulate mind and a set of values reflective of his New England ancestors. Expressions of affection for his son were shadowed by frequent criticism. John Steele's standards were high, and his capricious son did not always meet them to perfection.

Mary Steele was a loving mother, bright and insightful, and an accomplished amateur pianist who performed for friends and local gatherings. She was playful in a way that John Steele was not, and seemed to take delight, almost in spite of herself, in her son's feistiness. He later wrote her: "As I look about and see how much better educated I am than most people, and how you have always encouraged everything that made life worth while and subordinated things that could easily make life wretched, as happens with most people, I realize that I am immensely happier and luckier than most in having started right by properly selecting my parents."[3] Mary's sister, a

Opposite: The Steele family garden, Pittsford, N.Y. (SUNY ESF College Archives)

Above left: Fletcher and Esther Steele, ages six and four. (SUNY ESF College Archives)

Above right: The Steele family home, 20 Monroe Avenue, Pittsford, N.Y. (SUNY ESF College Archives)

painter and true adventurer, held her nephew spellbound with accounts of travel to Rome, Constantinople, St. Petersburg, and Peking. He never forgot his aunt's exotic example.

For a time Mary educated her children at home. The lessons naturally included music—Fletcher studied both voice and violin. At age twelve he biked eight miles into Rochester and back every day to attend Bradstreet School for Boys. Education was important in the Steele family and in Rochester. That it did not begin or end with school was not lost on Fletcher.

My impression is of decent, earnest thought on the part of the older generation, with a few enchanting exceptions.

When they read they seriously wanted to learn. They talked over ideas with each other on Wednesdays or Fridays. They wrote papers with ideas in them to read aloud and having known some of the writers, I am sure that what they said was worth knowing. . . .

Curiously enough, according to my memory, the women were wise with women and the men with men on these mysterious Wednesdays and Fridays. Wisdom in Rochester, in those days, was sexually a parallel affair, and may be yet for all I know. Whether men's wits all ran out of their boots when they looked in ladies' eyes, I am not sure. It did not look that way to playing children.

The people that I knew were good and kind and they were also prosperous. Perhaps it is more simple to be good and kind when also prosperous. Rochester had a lot of . . . desirable wealth. . . . While there were almost no rich people, there was a much greater proportion of those who had from a quarter to half a million dollars than any other small city they were able to find. People here were not only good and kind. They could afford to be graceful about it.[4]

By the turn of the century, Rochester was outgrowing its provincial roots. Soon it would have its own theater companies, symphony, and art museum.

Young Fletcher, who would spend his life in the company of millionaires, was never particularly impressed by wealth. In Rochester, he wrote, "money makers had not won any special following from the crowd, and certainly no worship. They were acknowledged to be smart and smartness was well thought of in Monroe County. But it was not enough to make a leader of any man. It did not give a rich man the privilege of having his weaknesses flattered and his faults discreetly overlooked. No amount of wealth gave him power, in those days, to stay away from church on Sunday without a whispering that he did not relish."[5]

Fletcher (standing), Esther, Mary, and John Steele (right of center) on the front porch of their Pittsford farmhouse, ca. 1900. (SUNY ESF College Archives)

Neither did Steele grow up with the type of garden that he would create for so many others. The Steeles' place in Pittsford was not grand, nor was its form particularly distinguishable from others of the time. "The fruit trees were my country club. The old Erie Canal was a better swimming hole than any modern chlorinated contraption. . . . My people before me had economically and pleasantly divided two or three acres of village land into lawns, kitchen yard, horse yard, and garden. The garden was not very logical. Flowers grew along the paths under the fruit trees. Grape trellises pushed off here and there between lines of vegetables. A stream sprung from under a big elm and meandered alongside the land. White fences ran around the whole lot and across it here and there. There was nothing grand about it—certainly no conceivable axis. I doubt if my grandparents had ever heard of such a thing."[6]

By Steele's own reckoning his vocation took root in childhood, but it was not a love of plants that lured him. "From earliest time [I] was never satisfied with the place people or nature put things or with their shapes and sizes. I suppose it was because I thought it was easier to change plants than buildings that I decided on landscape architecture because I

was not rich and had to do something. I have never regretted that decision."[7] Later he claimed, "I would have gone whole-heartedly into any of the arts."[8]

A New Profession

It is doubtful that Steele had heard the term "landscape architect" as a child—before the turn of the century there were scarcely fifty in the United States. The remarkable foundations laid by Andrew Jackson Downing, Calvert Vaux, Frederick Law Olmsted, Charles Eliot, and others had expanded the scope of the field of landscape gardening to include park and city planning.

In the last decade of the nineteenth century, economic, social, and artistic forces converged to create steady work for professional landscape architects in both the public and the private sphere. The Industrial Revolution had given birth to a class of homeowners able to afford grand homes with grand landscapes just as deteriorating urban conditions and nostalgia for nature were further enhancing the appeal of "country."

The new country estates depended on a comprehensive railway and road system to link them to city centers.

The World's Columbian Exposition of 1893 proved a milestone for the young profession. Millions of visitors marveled at the spectacular results of comprehensive planning evident in Olmsted's and Daniel H. Burnham's scheme. Thoughtful disposition of buildings, inspired placement of sculpture, and poetic and lavish use of water opened the public's eyes to new design possibilities in their dismal cities and around their homes.

The founding of the American Society of Landscape Architects on 4 January 1899 formalized the field. Among the eleven original fellows was Steele's future mentor, Warren H. Manning. The society's first acts were to establish standards of professional competence and to set procedures governing practice, thereby legitimizing the field in the public's mind. The timing proved propitious for young Fletcher, who would not have been permitted to pursue a less "regular" vocation. The formation of the society led quickly to the establishment of professional training courses in various colleges and universities, the first at Harvard University.

Steele traced the genesis of his calling to a specific episode, which he later recorded in the third person. "It was a sunny summer afternoon that seemed good to his touch, but his mood was shattered when his mother spoke: 'How beautiful Turk's Hill is today!' The long steady incline lay stretched across the eastern landscape, and then suddenly broke off so sharply as to make one wonder why. The boy's eyes were glued to the break and, to the merriment of his elders, he replied: 'Not 'specially.' He resented the way the hill was cut off, and thought it would have been better if it had gone straight on to Lake Ontario."[9]

Along with his wit, Steele's tendency to be critical would stand out as one of the dominant forces in his life. It would keep him in a stance of close, often painful self-scrutiny, while it fostered discriminating taste in food, art, and friends. By turns it would terrorize and serve him. Criticism figured centrally in Steele's definition of his profession: "That is what it means to be a landscape architect. Examining the land. Mentally dissecting it for better or worse. Planning possible changes and designing them in detail."[10]

In Steele's case, the lifelong tendency to approach situations critically—land, food, workmanship, quality of light, and, inevitably, the self—was fueled by a quest for perfection that, not coincidentally, resembled his father's. Whatever its psychological genesis, Steele's critical nature ultimately served better his professional eye than his sense of inner peace.

Williams College

On graduating from Bradstreet School for Boys in 1903, Fletcher headed east. "I knew what I wanted to do and on that account my family said I needed a decently rounded education while they could force it on me as they knew nothing ever would afterward. So I went to Williams College, joined a pleasant club and did little or nothing but grow. Although I enjoyed myself exceedingly, it was then that I decided that almost everybody was amusing but not bright. I have kept that opinion—reinforced it, rather. Also I still think that education is much overrated."[11]

At Williams, Steele discovered he had a talent for making conversation and that people were amused by his barbed and witty observations. Intellectually precocious at nineteen, he was also talented, well read, and gregarious. His poor grades at college reflected a lack of interest in his subjects (the exception being philosophy) and a taste for alcohol that would not diminish over the years. Young Steele performed in the glee club and the choir—for which he wrote humorous songs—and acted in an occasional drama. A few of his many friendships, mainly with fraternity brothers, lasted beyond college. Grahame "Grady" Wood, a wealthy Philadelphian, would prove a lifelong friend and important client.

During college Steele began to suffer bouts of depression he termed "the blues," one leading to a suicide attempt, which he recorded in his diary. A gas failure in his dormitory can be credited with saving his life. Shortly after graduating, he reported that he had conquered his depression, but early-morning insomnia, often a symptom of depression, would plague him his entire life.

At Williams College, Steele grew to love the simplicity of early colonial architecture and the gentle beauty of the Berkshire mountains. (This landscape would one day form the backdrop for one of his finest gardens.) He identified with the area's deep-rooted Puritan values that emphasized Yankee practicality. He completed nearly all his coursework at Williams in three years, but lost interest in graduating. His parents pressured him into finishing his degree in 1907. Despite parental misgivings, Steele never doubted his decision to enter Harvard's new graduate program of landscape architecture that autumn.

Graduate School of Landscape Architecture, Harvard

"I went a couple of years to the Harvard School of Landscape Architecture. The one great teacher I had there, Denman Ross, more than made up for a lot of wasted time."[12] Ross was not even on the landscape faculty; he taught aesthetic theory.

Steele's letters home during the two years of graduate school convey more enthusiasm than he later remembered. "You would be surprised at the way I seem driven to work," he wrote home in November of his first semester, "—four hours in the morning—four in the afternoon & two to three in the evening. . . . But I am very happy. It is rather strange too, for I get none of the pleasures that always seemed so necessary to me too—no one to converse with from one weekend to another—no music—no piano, and food that is frightful and accompanied by noise and smell and people painful to remember."[13] Steele was in tough financial straits, but he liked his teachers and guest lecturers and felt confident that he had chosen the right field.

Harvard had inaugurated a graduate program in landscape architecture only the year before Steele enrolled, having abandoned after just five years the undergraduate program, "which had been found to give too little time for adequate training."[14] He and his fellow students were guinea pigs and their training was based on the traditional Beaux Arts approach that characterized the work of the instructors.

Before Steele's time the program had operated under the auspices of the Department of Architecture, and it retained its strong design orientation. "It certainly was most appropriate," wrote James Sturgis Pray (eventually chairman of the new department), "that this subject should be Architecture rather than Engineering or Horticulture, since the point of view of our instruction is that of a Fine Art—an art of Design—in the practice of which the materials used are subordinated to the principles of their arrangement."[15] Steele's lifelong philosophy regarding the practice of landscape architecture as a fine art would echo that of his alma mater.

The roster of early instructors and administrators at Harvard included the most prominent names in the field: Frederick Law Olmsted Jr. and Arthur Shurtleff (later Shurcliff) were the original instructors. Henry Vincent Hubbard, the first recipient of Harvard's undergraduate degree, joined the faculty a few years later. Olmsted returned to practice full-time in early 1907, although he maintained a role of consultant in the department, and James Sturgis Pray took over as chairman. Degree requirements included courses in "Landscape Architecture, History of the Fine Arts (especially Architecture), Elements of Architectural Design, Plants and Planting Design, Surveying, Road Building, Water Works, Masonry and Foundations, Contracts and Specifications, Geology, Meteo-

rology, Physiography, Botany, Mathematics, and Languages."[16]

During Steele's stay the program increased the number of professional courses within the department from five to twelve. "We have consistently desired to take advantage of existing instruction in other departments," wrote Pray, "but sometimes this has been impossible without unduly sacrificing the point of view of our profession and the development in the student-body of a true professional esprit-de-corps."[17]

Unlike many other students, Steele had never learned to draw freehand and spent considerable time mastering the rudiments that his instructors considered fundamental to a well-rounded education in the field. Later, drawing was practically a prerequisite for admission.

The Harvard program taught a Beaux Arts approach to design, in which the notion of composition was all-important. Its precepts were based on those of the Ecole des Beaux-Arts, which had gained prominence during the nineteenth century and formed the single greatest influence on architectural thinking of the time. According to one historian, "What *composition* signified [in the French system] was not so much the design of ornament or of façades, but of whole buildings, conceived as three-dimensional entities and seen together in plan, section, and elevation."[18] In simplest terms, Ecole students composed with interior spaces and exterior volumes, arranged symmetrically, along clearly defined axes. Concerns with use, appropriateness to site, form, and dimension were fundamental to the comprehensive approach. Specific architectural ideas, *partis* (or "choices," from *prendre parti*, "to take a stand"), were not legislated. Beaux Arts came to signify a system, a technique rather than a style.

Separation of composition from style formed the basis of Steele's landscape education, and it strongly influenced his approach to design. The prominence of composition over style (also a Beaux Arts precept) was fundamental to his work. But for Steele, space-shaping was an intuitive rather than a learned process.

It is not the thing itself which affects him [the landscape architect] but its bulk and position as related to other matter round about it and to himself. Its individual virtues do not count if it is too large or too small or in the wrong place. . . . This feeling that things are in the way where he wants free space or, conversely, that an open hole would be better if filled, is a strong component of his procedure when composing a landscape. Without it an equally agreeable pattern might be contrived. . . . But for plastic quality derived from modeling the earth till it makes him feel good, fixing points of vantage higher or lower than suggested by existing circumstances and regulating the size and location of foliage masses, the landscape architect depends on a physical sense refined until it is affected by solid material and empty space.[19]

While at Harvard Steele supplemented his small stipend from home by singing in a synagogue (this in spite of being raised a Presbyterian). "As it is I think if I turn anything, it will be Jew," he wrote to his surprised mother. Steele's musings on conversion were inspired by architectural as well as theological attractions. "In the first place the new synagogue is about the most beautiful and appropriate building in the commonwealth—white marble with five low domes of gold in the eastern style, interior simple, with huge gorgeous gold seven branched candlesticks—looking vastly amusing with electric lights however—beautifully carved tablets quite a good deal handsomer than Moses could ever have received from heaven, tho' in the same style, a fine stern marble altar, used familiarly for a pulpit, the venerable spots for fire & goat sacrifice doing quite well for a reading desk and a glass of water. . . ." He finishes: "I don't see but we have about as satisfactory a denomination as we would want, for they add to good Unitarian ideas the fire & color of High Church."[20]

Rabbi Fleisher, "one of the finest men I have ever known," Steele wrote, had a philosophy of social morality that emphasized the brotherhood of men and the equality of women; he also held novel ideas concerning wealth and democracy. "To him the prevalence of the money spirit has made for democracy as nothing else in the world has ever done. . . . He admires great wealth, only instead of the vertical lines that it draws now between those who have & those who have not, he would divide with a horizontal line, and judge each man as he made a good or a bad millionaire, a good or a bad poor man. He would free and equalize women educationally and economically just as fast as the whole body demands it and no faster. 'The day when men & women can consider decently all questions of sexhood & sexuality and not be considered indecent, then will women be equals of men.'"[21]

Apprenticeship with Warren Manning

In September 1908 Steele's life changed dramatically. "You will be surprised to hear what has happened," he wrote to his mother.

Warren H. Manning, Steele's mentor. (Manning Family Association)

I went in to see Warren Manning. He gave me splendid advice about what work to do this winter. Then I told him how I was fixed for this month. He thought a minute and then said "I think the experience would be valuable to you, and if you like you may come in to work with me. I cannot promise you any pay, but you will have an opportunity to study all the problems I am working on now and see how I treat them." I leaped at the chance of course. Today was the first day and I learned more about landscape proper than I did all last winter. He gave me the data about a hospital in the west—told me his difficulties, gave me the roughest sort of a sketch of what he wanted & told me *to go ahead* as tho' I knew all about the whole business. You can wager that pleased me. [22]

So began a six-year apprenticeship with one of the most accomplished landscape architects in the country. It appears to have been a congenial match. Manning's senior status in the profession rested on his success as designer, city planner, plantsman, and teacher. Much admired by the younger professionals, Manning had been mentor to others before Steele, although never to this extent. (Manning's mentor had been Olmsted Sr., for whom he worked from 1888 to 1896.) In Steele, Manning had found an exceptional student—bright, eager, well educated, and socially adept. He would deeply influence his protégé's ideas about the profession.

In 1912 Manning wrote about residential design for *Landscape Architecture*: "Considered as elements of landscape, the buildings of a large estate are incidents of no greater importance than are the woods, the water, the open field, the sky, and the grazing herds.... The family derive quite as much pleasure, especially in the summer home, from such landscape features." The mention of pleasure, especially, reflected an orientation to the work that would take deep root in Steele's imagination. So, too, would the idea that "we regard both architecture and our own profession as among the fine arts. We recognize that a man, to be successful in either profession, must have, first, an artistic instinct."[23] In December Steele wrote his father: "Last night I went out to Mr. Manning's to dinner and had a fine time. He kindly gave me a general invitation & wants me to 'make myself at home there.'"[24]

Two months later Steele visited New York on the ten dollars his parents had sent him for the tailor. "Well, it may be quite wrong, but I'm certainly glad I did." The trip was grand. The young man was filled with enthusiasm, over the fashion scene at the Plaza Hotel, "brilliant beyond anything I remember to have seen," dinner at the New York Republican Club ("We had the center box"), an afternoon at the Metropolitan Museum of Art (which "I had never seen"), all-night dinners, and tea in artists' studios. "I felt like talking fortunately & was invited to many places before I left, as a talker seems popular."[25] Important clients would be only too happy to wine and dine the soon-to-be-famous landscape architect and "talker."

"I have just had the best news I have ever had," he wrote in July 1909.

Mr. Manning said "I have decided to make you my private traveling secretary. It will be your duty to get a good working knowledge of every job I am working on. Then to accompany me on all my trips, see what is being done, make all my engagements for me and see that I keep them. Meet all my clients so that you can represent me when it is impossible for me to be present, study the ground with me so you can carry out my plans in the office when you get back. Make all my traveling arrangements, and finish a great many projects that I have only time to start, like planning the replanting of all the barren islands in Boston Harbor. I shall want [you] to take all the literary work off my hands, such as the writing of reports; and letters when I am traveling. It will not be easy. You will work all day, get on trains at midnight where I shall keep you up giving me reports, perhaps getting to your destination at three in the morning where you go to a hotel for a snatch of sleep before you are off for work at 6 or seven o'clock. You must be ready to go at an hour's notice. You will go soon to Albany, again to Toronto, to Sea Bright New Jersey, New York and perhaps Washington. In other words be ready to go anywhere at anytime. A good man can get more out of such a life than any other, and can be most useful to me. Let's see if you're the man."

I was really more excited than I have ever been. It seems almost too good to be true . . . to get such varied experience both on all the work and in the design under the constant personal supervision of a man like Mr. Manning is enough to take your breath away. This is very much the same experience that Charles Eliot had with the Elder Olmsted. I don't suppose anyone else has ever had a like opportunity.

Steele would make the most of it. "My next step will be less to study the work than the man himself."[26] He never returned to Harvard to finish his degree.

One of Steele's first jobs for Manning was assisting with the layout of a big estate on Buzzards Bay. It involved the same tasks Steele would soon be undertaking in his solo practice: "I was down looking over [the] estate . . . planning the site for the house, the roads, farm buildings, stable and garages, the place for gardens and wharves for the yacht and boats, where to cut vistas thru the woods, planning for reservoir and saw mill and gate lodges." Steele did not find the job easy. "I have to work like a slave, driving stakes, climbing trees for the view, taking notes, meantime getting information on all the trees and shrubs and plants, writing letters, constantly ready to go to Carolina or Timbucktoo."[27]

In September Manning told Steele that "the way you are taking hold satisfies me that you will be capable of big things some day."[28] Manning raised his wages from forty to sixty dollars a month, and Steele worked harder than ever. "The affairs are so much bigger, and big things always interested me more than small ones. To be sure I am carrying out the details of his big ideas—a few of them—now, but I am given a big leeway for my own conceptions to wiggle in, and I almost feel as tho I were doing some big work myself."[29]

The next project for Manning was architectural. Steele was

to design elevations for a cluster of buildings for North Carolina State Normal and Industrial College, now the University of North Carolina at Greensboro. The challenge seemed to suit him. "It has been an interesting problem, as the plan of the buildings & their arrangement had been settled when I got back from the South . . . construction to be as cheap as possible. This means long shed-like buildings in which the interest must lie very much in the size and distribution of the windows." Cost limited Steele to using stock sizes, but by combining "half of a very tall window and over it a cellar window, it becomes a rather nice shape."[30] Steele enjoyed problem solving, particularly when many stringencies necessitated inventive solutions.

In 1910 Steele took over for Manning at a residential job for the Leigh family near Charlottesville, Virginia. He stayed at the plantation for weeks at a time, supervising work as it developed on-site. He became a member of the household, practicing the new roles—of artist, adviser, negotiator, engineer, and entertainer—with great success. But Steele had not yet decided to focus his professional life on garden design. He was enjoying his work on a comprehensive land-use map of the state of Massachusetts. "I like this sort of thing very much. It takes a sort of ingenuity to get a great deal of it and wandering around all over and learning a lot."[31]

In June Steele returned to Cambridge and paid a visit to Harvard's landscape department to see the students' new work. "Some of it is very good and all of it interesting, but I cannot tell you how glad I am that I did not go back there another year," he wrote home. "In the first place, I think that there are so many old maids there in the department and so much pedanticism that one would get after a while the thing that is always brought up as the objection of the college man— that he thinks that he knows it all and that the way that things happen to be done in the office aren't right if they are not done in the same way. In the next place I think that they spend so much time over details that it becomes puttering instead of working half the time. . . . The training there too seems to be a very good apprenticeship for becoming a draftsman in an office and that only practically."[32]

Four months later Steele reported,

The amount of work that I now have is simply colossal. And as you know, the more that I have the better I like it. . . .

You see it is this way. Always before the office has been divided into two main sections, as all architects are I suppose, namely the clerical end and the drafting end. Well,

Miss Walker, the head of the clerical end is an unusually clever woman, and that end of the work goes off like clockwork. But as a matter of fact, the head of the drafting department has not much of an executive head, and lots of things were getting behind always, as the pressure of new work that is coming in all the time is simply appalling and the last thing always seems the most important. So there was no very close connection between the two parts of the office. The new experiment is that I am interposed as the connecting link between the two parts. I have been given the desk in Mr. Mg's sanctum sanctorum, and am present to hear all his dictating and his conferences with Miss Walker about the progress of the work. All the plans are explained to me directly and are handed over by me to the drafting department—he does not have anything to do with the drafting room directly, or will not have if I carry out my part of the work O.K., except under extraordinary circumstances. I take all of his sketch plans, study them out, and make what elucidations are necessary by drawing hurried sketch plans or in writing, and then they are taken to the head draftsman who takes all directions from me about what is to be done. Of course if anything [goes] wrong, I have to bear the whole brunt of the responsibility, but I am not afraid of responsibility, you know, and never try to get out of things even if Mr. Mg is at fault himself, by telling him all the excuses, but get to work at once on getting what he wants done.

Steele's letter expressed how urgently he wanted to impress his parents. "Of course if it had been so arranged that I would simply be head draftsman and nothing else, I would not have stood it for a minute. I can see no possibility for a head draftsman to advance beyond a certain point unless he starts out for himself. But it is nothing of that sort at all. I am really an assistant directly for Mr. Mg and as such I get an insight and an oversight into the whole working of the profession that I could not get in any other way in the world."[33]

Steele continued to work for Manning, his freedom increasing with his skills and confidence, but by 1912 he was questioning how realistic the possibility was of a future in Manning's office. "I would not hesitate to stay on definitely with the idea of working into a strong position there, as Mr. Mg has suggested that I do. Such was for some time my hope. But as time goes on, I am less & less able to persuade myself that anything definite will come of it for many years, in which I would be practically marking time instead of marching." Steele was convinced that Manning would not relinquish for many years his

Travel sketch by Steele, no site identified, from "Europe, 1913." (SUNY ESF College Archives)

While it is an invaluable side, it is by no means the expression of the whole profession. And my nature, by training and choice, inclines, if anything rather to the side which he has not." Steele said that he favored the example of Frederick Law Olmsted, whom he considered an "extraordinary genius." Olmsted, Steele felt, "had unusual refinement of feeling for every thing he touched, (refinement meaning feeling for exquisite finish and consideration of the more intimate if generally unexpressed needs of people)."[35] An abiding interest in "exquisite finish" and "unexpressed needs of people" would also shape Steele's approach to landscape design.

For the time, however, Steele decided to stay where he was. He reasoned that while Manning's training was not helping him develop his artistic nature, it was the other side—the technical—that needed most work anyway.

The following spring Steele made a grand tour of Europe. Warren Manning, in effect, sponsored the trip by giving Steele time off from work, making him a gift of one hundred dollars, and offering to pay him and give him the use of his staff to write up an account of the trip on his return. The rest of the money came, somewhat reluctantly, from Steele's parents. He set sail for Portugal on 8 April 1913.

Europe, 1913

The four-month tour took Steele through Portugal, Spain, North Africa, Italy, France, Germany, and England. Besides gardens, he visited museums, parks, and cemeteries, taking extensive notes on these and city squares, fountains, street plans, and architecture. The first paragraph of the 125-page report for Manning reveals a sharp eye and almost a painter's perceptions.

> We sailed on a gray, cold day. I never . . . saw Boston Harbor more beautiful. Red ferry boats, bright green or light blue harbor craft scuttled about in the foreground of a splendid landscape, with a red purple city beyond crossed with bands of deep blue, tipped with the gold dome of the State House. Great swirls of white steam drifted lazily over it all, and beyond a dark gray sea and sky formed a clear cut background. Nowhere in Europe did I see richer color or more interesting compositions than in Boston Harbor.[36]

Color persists as a major theme in Steele's journal—on the first page of the manuscript it is mentioned thirty-seven times. Comparative criticism and formal analysis structure the writer's perceptions but not at the expense of emotional involvement. The dreamer and the evaluator coexisted harmoniously.

plan of grooming his own son, Harold, to take over the office ("At present it appears the boy is interested in other things") and was certain he would never be content working for Harold. Philosophical differences with Manning had emerged as well. "Many of his ideas I consider fantastic, of many I strongly disapprove, and while I am warmly in accord with his finest broad minded theories, and will always maintain them with thanks to him for instilling them in me, yet few of them interest me enuf to support with enthusiasm these, and no others, for life."[34]

Specifically, Steele took issue with what he perceived as Manning's "one-sidedness" concerning his exclusive concentration on characteristics of "convenience and economy and natural conditions, whence he believes beauty will follow." To Steele's eye, it did not always work out that way. "That side in which he [Manning] excels is the one which would appeal to . . . a horticulturalist [or a] park superintendent and engineer. But it is not a side which appeals to an architect or an artist.

Out of the trip came many new, specific landscape design ideas: wide paths; the powerful decorative impact of bamboo; turf as a bedding plant; gravel in place of conventional lawns; sculpture niches formed by plants; the proper proportions for pergolas (massive supports, delicate lattice); pots for maximum impact and ease of care. Most were quintessentially European. As the trip wore on, Steele also developed a clearer appreciation of certain fine American traditions that seemed, by comparison, superior to European efforts. "Too much is frequently said of what is fine and too little about what is bad in Europe."[37]

Steele's musings address the effects of landscape as well as its abstract presence as form: "The hills [of Madeira's coast] were broken with rock . . . we saw extraordinary fantastic shapes on an immense scale such as is difficult to imagine.

Great masses of mountains have more dignity and grandeur, but irregular jagged peaks are more inspiring to the imagination."[38] His early interest in emotional response to line, color, and form would prove ongoing and eventually central to his work.

Steele was particularly moved by the sight of the Bay of Naples.

[It] is all in beauty that is said of it. The keynote was given, though at a dramatic pitch of intensity which could not be maintained, by the old Castello of Ischia. Take the most imaginative castle-covered island rock that Maxfield Parrish ever put in a fairy tale, with a romantic coloring and mystery that he can but faintly approximate, see it from the blue Mediterranean on a summer misty morning, and no more

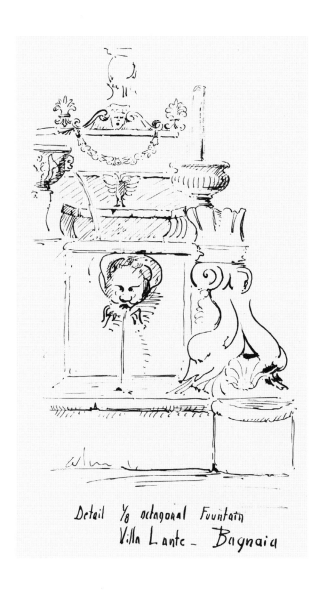

Detail ⅛ octagonal Fountain
Villa Lante - Bagnaia

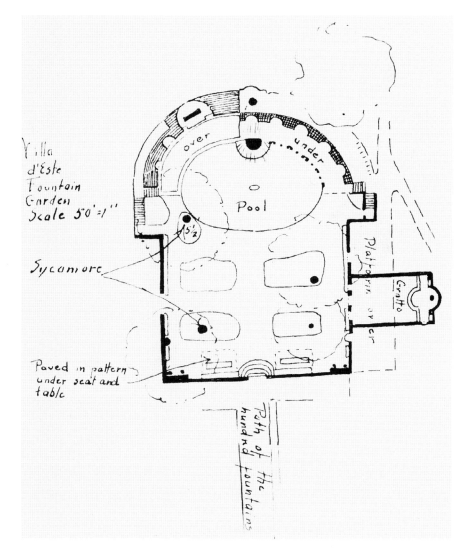

Villa d'Este Fountain Garden Scale 5'0"=1"

Sycamore

Paved in pattern under seat and table

Pool

5'2

Platform over cr

Grotto

over

under

Path of the hundred fountains

wholly satisfying introduction to the adventure of Europe could be devised. To starboard about twenty miles away was the picturesque angular skyline of Capri. Dead ahead slowly taking form in the mist which continued long to cover its summit, lay the immense bulk of Vesuvius. At first I could not believe it was real. It was so much larger than any other land in sight that it seemed impossibly out of scale. Later, when the clouds had all rolled away, save a delicate mist which concealed the summit, its lines were too perfect to be real outside of Hokusai's glorified Fuji. Even now as I look up out of my window and see it soaring up in the moonlight across the bay I wonder if it can truly be.[39]

From the miniscule and immediate to the grand and philosophical, most of Steele's observations were critical in spirit. "Rome is old and immensely interesting but seems a dead body on which only the worms live and thrive. There seems a break between the old and the new Romes. . . . But Florence is new and living, seeming to have inherited the old treasures and to be using them easily and adding to them as naturally as any young healthy person uses and enjoys his inheritance."[40]

Some of Steele's recollections were deeply sensual. He wrote: "Venice, after nearly a week, has still that peculiar intensity of seeming reality that belongs to dreams. It seems the only real place I have been in. It is a mould and into it I poured like hot wax. I seem to be—to have always been—a part of Venice. Or, to change the idea, it is as much a new sensation as if I had hitherto seen in form only, like a photograph, and suddenly the world in color had appeared." After such soul-baring, Steele recovered with a joke: "People speak of wonder in Venice. I have wondered but once and that was why nobody keeps pet ducks."[41]

Certain schemes left permanent impressions.

More than any gardens which have been built since, the Pompeiian gardens (which are merely the decorations of courtyards with sculpture, fountains, paths and vegetation) arrived at a complete understanding of their possibilities. In all cases the garden was, more than in any other western country, but one of the rooms of the house. It may be said that the patios and other small court gardens of many European countries have followed this custom and might be said to be as intimately connected with the architecture, but so far as I saw them it would seem to me that, except in Pompeii, such places have always been treated as enclosed gardens and not as house rooms. . . . At Pompeii . . . the same form of decoration was used in the garden as in the other rooms, namely, painted walls, sculpture, benches and fountains. . . . The only difference seems to have been that where it was open to the sky, vegetation was used instead of rugs or velvets as a floor covering, but as far as one could judge, the way of using vegetation and the effect which was sought were the same kind as in the use of other floor coverings.[42]

These conclusions foreshadow one of Steele's most important works, the Afternoon Garden of Naumkeag, an outdoor extension of the house in the same sense described here.

Steele seemed to learn as much from the inferior designs as he did from the superb ones. Of the Villa Aldobrandini at Frascati he wrote: "This is a very late baroque garden, very ugly and stupidly designed. Grades are bad, lines are bad and general conception is bad. The only feature of any interest is the cascade and water organ . . . which is quite amusing." The Villa Lante, on the other hand, was Italy's most "charming" garden, Steele's highest compliment. Among other sites that made permanent impressions on Steele were St. Peter's Square in Rome, the Luxembourg Gardens in Paris, and Place Vendôme, which he considered "flawless." "The Place Vendôme in Paris is perfect. It is the simplest of all in design and execution; its proportions are most majestic; its decoration superb. If it possesses some of the superhuman coldness of perfection which threatens Raphael and chills the Venus de Medici, it is in the company where each of us would wish our work to be."[43]

A Boston Practice

Returning from Europe in July, Steele spent the next several weeks sorting through his notebooks and dictating his report to Manning's secretary. By the end of 1913 he had decided that it was time to leave his teacher. Steele's post as secretary of the Boston Chapter of the American Society of Landscape Architects put him in regular contact with other practitioners and marked the first of a long, sometimes tempestuous involvement with the field's professional organizations. Steele found a small apartment on Charles Street that he rented with several other men—his apprentice wages from Manning had left no savings. The first year was lean.

Steele wrote to his father early in March 1914 and asked for a loan. Two weeks later, he sounded optimistic about his business prospects: "There are a good many odd jobs that I am doing for people. Yesterday I sent quite a long article to a magazine and hope that I may sell it for something. People are talking all the time, so I have hopes that other things will turn up before long."[44] Money—and Fletcher Steele's choice of profession—would remain heated topics between father and son for many years. Fletcher's letters home were determinedly upbeat, filled with evidence of his impending success.

Miss Houghton has just written me that she has a scheme for some rather extensive changes on her place. The Dewart job should be good for a couple of hundred. . . .

The other [letter] is from my friend Grahame Wood of Philadelphia, who says that he has just been presented by his father with fifty-two acres of very handsome land, and by his mother-in-law with as many thousands to build a house upon it. This will mean a sure job.

I do not consider all this at all bad for a professional man who has been at work less than a month, do you?[45]

Steele did secure the job for Grahame Wood's estate, Blossom Hill, the first stage of which involved laying out a long drive and plantings to enhance views across the hills of Wawa, Pennsylvania. Steele's beautifully rendered plan recalls many aspects of Warren Manning's estate work, particularly Manning's circa 1912 design for Frank A. Seiberling, Stan Hywet, in Akron, Ohio, which Steele may have known well. The spatial organization at Blossom Hill was loose and informal, as Manning's often was, determined by the lay of the land, views, and naturally occurring incidents, such as a ravine. The specific components recorded on Steele's plan also recall Manning's vocabulary: gatehouse with long entry drive, extensive vegetable gardens, arbor, orchard, meadow, rock garden, woods (marked "Deer Park"), golf course, and great sweeps of open hillside with views clearly marked.

No correspondence survives to shed light on the chronology of the landscape development at Blossom Hill or intriguing notations on the plan, such as "Fairy Ring." Steele continued to work for the Woods for many years, relying almost exclusively on plants from Upper Banks Nursery in Media, Pennsylvania. This superb nursery, owned by Fairman Funess, supplied plants for many of Steele's other jobs, too. Steele and Grahame Wood remained lifelong friends, and several other members of the family also consulted him about their properties.[46]

"Later in the month," Steele wrote his father in June 1914, "I expect to visit the Woods, my Philadelphia clients, at their

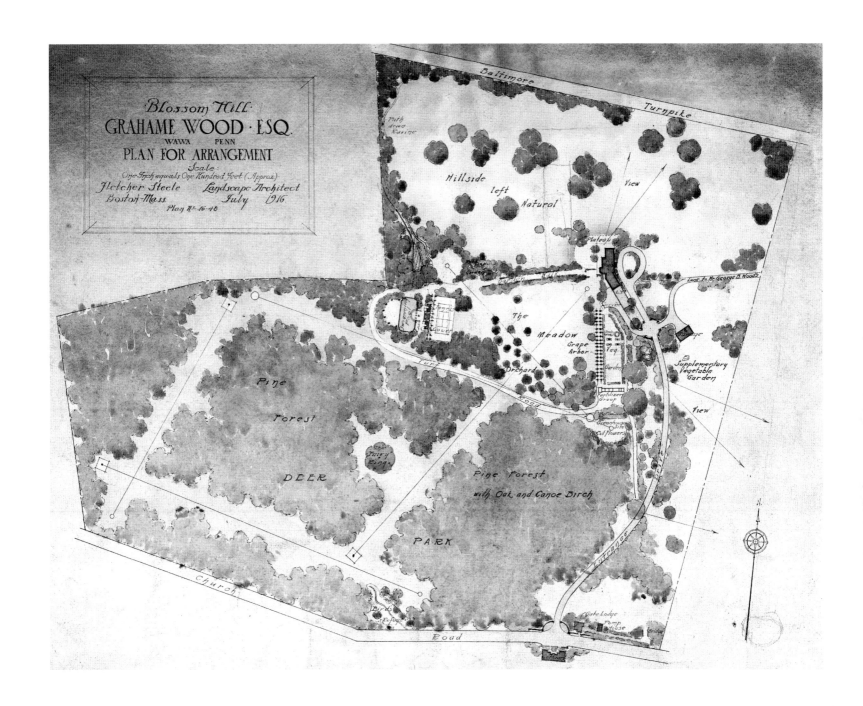

Blossom Hill plan, 1916. (SUNY ESF College Archives)

Opposite: Blossom Hill, the estate of Grahame Wood,
Wawa, Pa., design ca. 1914. (LC. Photo by Paul Weber)

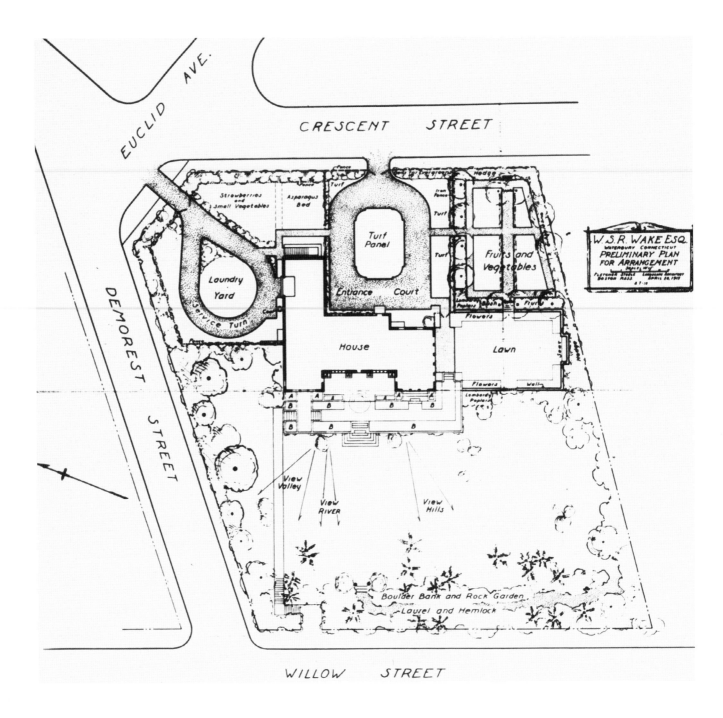

CRESCENT STREET

EUCLID AVE.

DEMOREST STREET

WILLOW STREET

W. S. R. WAKE ESQ.
WATERBURY CONNECTICUT
PRELIMINARY PLAN
FOR ARRANGEMENT

W. S. R. Wake plan, Waterbury, Conn., 1915. The layout reveals Steele's concern with efficiency, practicality, and the relationship of the garden to the surrounding landscape.

place in Newport, and to go yachting with them. This means at least two pairs of white flannels, some white kid shoes and lots of white stockings. Fortunately their automobile and yacht will do away with the necessity of carfare. As you can see this means an entire new wardrobe which will cost me several hundred dollars, and all the money I can possibly make will go into it as it is obviously bad business not to be decently dressed."[47] For Steele success would depend on meeting his clients, even those who were friends, on equal footing.

During this period, it appears that Steele was supplement-

ing his income with landscape design instruction for young women. The architect Eleanor Raymond reports to have taken classes from him and then to have volunteered to work in Steele's office without pay. Raymond wanted more formal instruction, and in 1917 she entered the newly formed Cambridge School of Architecture and Landscape Architecture.[48]

In 1915 Steele published a dramatization of the process of designing a residential landscape in *Garden Magazine*. "The Landscaping of Peridot" featured imaginary clients, the Littlefields, and a landscape architect named Russell. Steele's authoritative tone and design sophistication belie his newness to the field; he sounded as though he had been through the process thousands of times.

"Dear Russell," the client writes, "We have bought some land in Chestnut Hill and intend to build at once. You have bored me so often about people waiting till after their house is built before they call in a landscape architect that I write without delay. Come out with us Monday to look over the ground." The Littlefields are confused by Russell's revolutionary scheme: "I'll be jiggered, Russell," they complain. "The way you've got it here, the house doesn't face the street at all. It's end on to the street, and kitchen end at that. What d'you think of that? . . . Kitchen on the street where everybody can see it instead of around behind somewhere out of sight." The clients are even more confused by the fact that the garage is on the sidewalk.[49]

Through Russell, Steele explains his unexpected and novel arrangement, citing first the importance of privacy, then issues of building cost, good versus bad views, existing resources (trees, stone walls, views), maintenance (initial versus long-term costs), and efficiency in use of space. He stressed the importance of utility. "The functions of the different parts of the grounds answer fairly well to the functions of rooms of a house, though not exactly of course. . . . The entrance turn, of the landscape compartments, may be compared to the hall of a house; the service turn or court to the kitchen entry; the drying yard is kin to the laundry and the kitchen garden to the kitchen. I like to think of the tennis court as the billiard room of the grounds and the flower garden as the drawing-room."[50]

The Littlefields are finally won over to the landscape architect's plan, and the article ends, accurately enough, with a drink. In its general layout, the Littlefields' garden resembles many others Steele was designing during the period, such as that for W. S. R. Wake of Waterbury, Connecticut. Steele's fictional account reflects the same practical concerns that would occupy him his entire career, as well as the discussions he would have with so many clients, most of whom he would find amusing, and a few, endearing.

2 · First Flowering: Tradition and Experiment, 1915–1926

Ethan Allen
North Andover, Massachusetts
1915–1923

Grahame Wood's job had given Steele a professional toehold; Ethan Allen's would boost the young landscape architect into the upper ranks of the field. The genesis of Steele's work for Allen at Rolling Ridge is unclear but it likely involved a recommendation from Steele's former boss, Warren Manning, who had been commissioned to design Allen's cemetery plot in 1913. Allen, a wealthy New Yorker, hired Steele in 1915 when the house plans were still on the drawing table. He had bought a forty-acre peninsula on Lake Cochichewick in North Andover, Massachusetts, just before the turn of the century and now, nearly two decades later, was ready to build a country estate on it.

Later Steele wrote, "The owner had the gardens built first to take advantage of all trees and views; then built the house so that he could walk out on finished grounds the day he moves in. . . . In fact," Steele elaborated, "lawns, house, gardens, and garage should all be properly disposed on the plan before the house is definitely located. Each one must be properly related to the others, as, if wrong, any detail of the place, such as the house, will hurt everything else."[1] (Construction in some areas of the garden would actually stretch well into the 1920s.) The opportunity to coordinate early landscape and architectural decisions would not arise as often as Steele hoped; Rolling Ridge would stand among a small percentage of jobs to evolve this way.

Steele laid out the long, winding approach through surrounding woodland and meadow. "To make up for lack of age, it is necessary to use already existing trees and forest as part of design," he wrote later.[2] Two large (thirty-inch diameter) pines were preserved to establish the end of the drive and entry to the forecourt. A second, shorter road was made to take guests directly to a proposed boathouse and veranda on the lakeshore. A drawing from Steele's office dated November 1915 and labeled "Detail in clearing to be used for house site" may indicate that Steele was involved in selecting the location for the house.

Andrew Hepburn's Georgian revival design predated the historical work of his firm (Perry, Shaw & Hepburn) for the restoration of Colonial Williamsburg. The two-story house had two connecting wings—one for servants' quarters and a garage with second story for guests—that enclosed the geometrically paved automobile forecourt.

Rolling Ridge was one of Steele's first estate landscapes, but it did not lack maturity or conviction. The imaginative plan used diagonal views and an unusually dramatic circulation sequence. Steele's relationship with both client and design was long-lived. When Russell Tyson bought the place in 1928, he kept Steele on to advise. Ethan Allen's daughter, Katherine Russell, would later buy Hyghe Contente, a Manchester estate designed by Steele in 1932, because she so admired his work.

The garden landscape at Rolling Ridge included a shady lawn and exedra, a rhododendron-bordered bowling green leading to a circular pool and great waterspout, a cascade, a wooded fountain walk, and then, a boat house and terrace. The west side of the house overlooked an expanse of lawn and,

Opposite: Rolling Ridge, bowling green. (SUNY ESF College Archives. Photo by Paul Weber)

Rolling Ridge during construction, ca. 1919. Two large white pines determined the location of the house and the entry drive. (SUNY ESF College Archives)

Rolling Ridge during construction, ca. 1919. To the left of the cart is the exedra, to the right are the bowling green and pool. (SUNY ESF College Archives)

beyond, Lake Cochichewick. The spatial organization was broad and its impact powerful. This was a landscape to be walked—garden theater at its best.

From the south loggia two distinct spaces were visible. Nearby was the shaded lawn backed by the large curve of the exedra, on axis, and in scale with the building facade. Angling obliquely to the right (west), lay the sunken bowling green and rhododendron garden, defined by high (one-and-a-half-foot) concrete curbs. A deliberate color succession in the rhododendron planting—pink to red to violet—enhanced the already considerable distance. Steele would remain true to this early interest in illusion making. If there was a way to make a garden seem larger, he used it.

Bordering the smooth bowling green were beds of evergreen candytuft, bearberry, vinca, English ivy, box, and myrtle in a multi-textured ground-cover tapestry, while speciosum lilies and coralbells contributed mid- to late-summer color. An arborvitae hedge backed the beds, clipped shorter at the end to

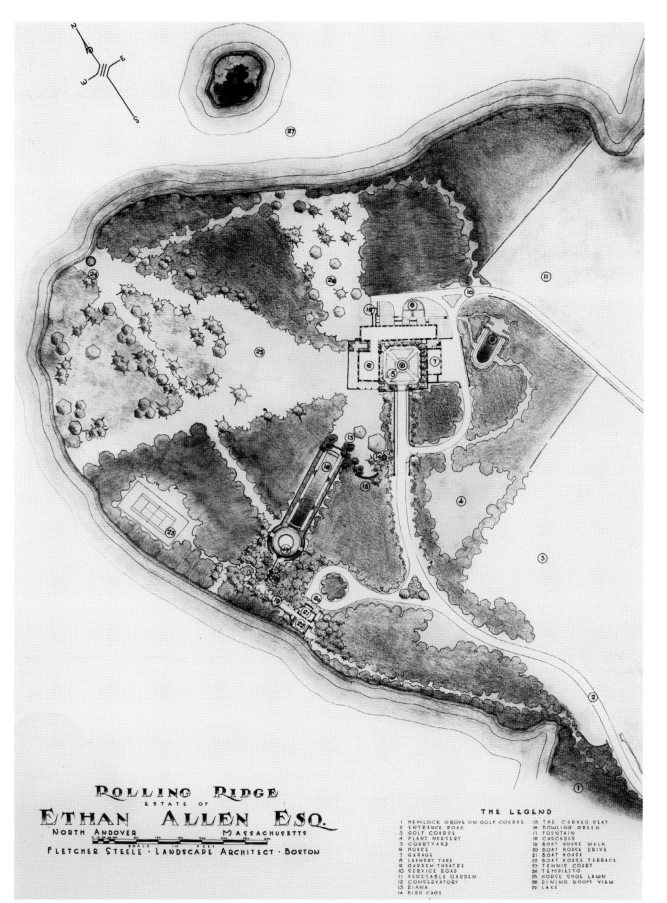

Rolling Ridge plan, 1915. (LC)

ROLLING RIDGE
ESTATE OF
ETHAN ALLEN ESQ.
NORTH ANDOVER   MASSACHUSETTS
SCALE IN FEET
FLETCHER STEELE · LANDSCAPE ARCHITECT · BOSTON

THE LEGEND

1 HEMLOCK GROVE ON GOLF COURSE
2 ENTRANCE ROAD
3 GOLF COURSE
4 PLANT NURSERY
5 COURTYARD
6 HOUSE
7 GARAGE
8 LAUNDRY YARD
9 GARDEN THEATRE
10 SERVICE ROAD
11 VEGETABLE GARDEN
12 CONSERVATORY
13 DIANA
14 BIRD CAGE
15 THE CURVED SEAT
16 BOWLING GREEN
17 FOUNTAIN
18 CASCADES
19 BOAT HOUSE WALK
20 BOAT HOUSE DRIVE
21 BOAT HOUSE
22 BOAT HOUSE TERRACE
23 TENNIS COURT
24 TEMPLETTO
25 HORSE SHOE LAWN
26 DINING ROOM VIEW
27 LAKE

Rolling Ridge, baluster and bench details near the fountain jet. (SUNY ESF College Archives. Photo by Paul Weber)

further the sense of distance. The bowling green led to the fountain circle, a distant echo of the foreground exedra. An eighteenth-century statue of the huntress Diana marked the hinge formed by the exedra lawn and bowling green, her twisting glance an ingenious connector between the two views. The circular pool (twenty-five feet across) was surrounded by a curved balustrade, the balusters cast in five slightly varying molds "to avoid the banality of mechanical perfection."[3] Some years later Steele would proudly report one visitor's reaction to the garden: "Mrs. Means without knowing that I had anything to do with the place, began at once to say that to her, although she had seen most of the great places in America, it was the only one she knew of that had the charm of the age-old garden of Europe—and that although obviously only a small part had been finished. As that was a good part of the thing I was aiming at when I did it, I am more than pleased of course."[4]

The pool's waterspout offered a compelling focal point from the loggia. The architectural feature was somewhat at odds with the Georgian house, but it resonated with the Italian spirit of the pool and fountain.

Surprise and spatial clarity are uneasy partners, but Steele's design for Rolling Ridge provided for both. Only after arriving at the fountain circle did the visitor see two broad staircases leading to a cascade. The stucco retaining wall and its flanking steps curved down past the cascade and into the woods. The color of the stucco wall—peach—was unexpected and luxurious.

Here the setting shifts from sun and vertical thrust to cool shadows and a quiet rush of water through three small pools. A hemlock woods cast dark shadows at the bottom of the cascade where the water disappears underground. It emerges again to play in six small fountains lining the woodland path. At the path's end, the lake is fully revealed. This is the garden's fulfillment, the answer to a promise announced forcefully by the big spout and then remembered in the cascade and, again, in the fountain shells: water leading to water, artifice to nature, intimacy to panorama and the world beyond.

Steele's inspirations for Rolling Ridge were drawn from many sources. Two years before, he had seen baroque water staircases at villas in Frascati, Florence, and Rome. He had visited the Generalife and remembered the tiny fountains there playing along paths. In England he had seen grand bor-

Rolling Ridge, a view of the house loggia from the fountain. (SUNY ESF College Archives. Photo by Paul Weber)

Rolling Ridge, staircase behind the pool. (SUNY ESF College Archives. Photo by Paul Weber)

Rolling Ridge, cascade and broad-leaved evergreen plantings. (SUNY ESF College Archives. Photo by Paul Weber)

Rolling Ridge. Shell fountains based on examples at the
Generalife in Spain led visitors from the cascade to the
boathouse veranda. (SUNY ESF College Archives. Photo
by Paul Weber)

ders, wide lawns, and great stands of rhododendron. French formalism had instilled in him a lifelong appreciation for boldness and theatricality.

But Rolling Ridge was no import. "Another thing that amuses me," Steele later wrote, "is to have people say 'It is a perfect Italian garden' and the next 'It is purely Spanish' and another 'It is genuinely English,' according to the European things that they have seen and liked the best. Of course it is nothing but American, although quite unlike any other American place."[5]

Steele was not troubled by the presence of foreign influence in his work. At Rolling Ridge, and elsewhere, his mind was on the genius loci. "It does not take the traveler long to find out that hills are hills and valleys valleys all over the world. In every country man has built on them both well and ill; fitted, and failed to fit, his structures onto the land. When he has had respect for the qualities of the site, then nothing in style or decoration has gone far wrong."[6]

CHARLOTTE AND ATKINSON ALLEN
Rochester, New York
1915–1926*

Steele began his work for Atkinson and Charlotte Whitney Allen (no relation to his North Andover client) shortly after

*Steele's work on the garden continued from 1915 to 1967; it is discussed in four phases.

the Rolling Ridge job started. Their home—a wedding present from the bride's parents—was still under construction on Oliver Street in Rochester when Steele was hired. They had been married only a few months. Atkinson—"Rap"—was an old school chum of Steele's from Bradstreet. It was probably this connection that had prompted the job, but it was Charlotte, not Atkinson, who would figure most importantly in Steele's life.

Tiny, fiery, elegant Charlotte Allen hated flowers. She once wrote Steele, "I believe that the secret of the most beautiful gardens in the world—such creations as Villa d'Este, Caprarola, and the Villa Lante in Italy, or the Generalife in Spain—is that they show as few flowers as possible—are indeed, almost flowerless. Green is the clue to creating a garden, and not the possession of all the hues of the rainbow."[7] In spite of these words, horticulture, in any color, did not hold much interest for her. Among her passions were literature (Henry James, in particular), travel, and good conversation. She found Fletcher Steele fascinating. The two native Rochesterians would come to share a friendship central to both their lives, especially after Charlotte and Atkinson's Mexican divorce in 1934.

In 1915 Steele had also begun a large town garden for Edwin A. Stebbins, just a few blocks away on Rochester's East Avenue. Grand homes, rare, old, lovely trees, and a sense of quiet, dignified wealth set the street apart from any other in town. Dr. Stebbins's garden would develop along entirely different—and less distinctive—lines from the Allens' but it

Allen estate, after completion of the wall and stone walkways, ca. 1916. (SUNY ESF College Archives)

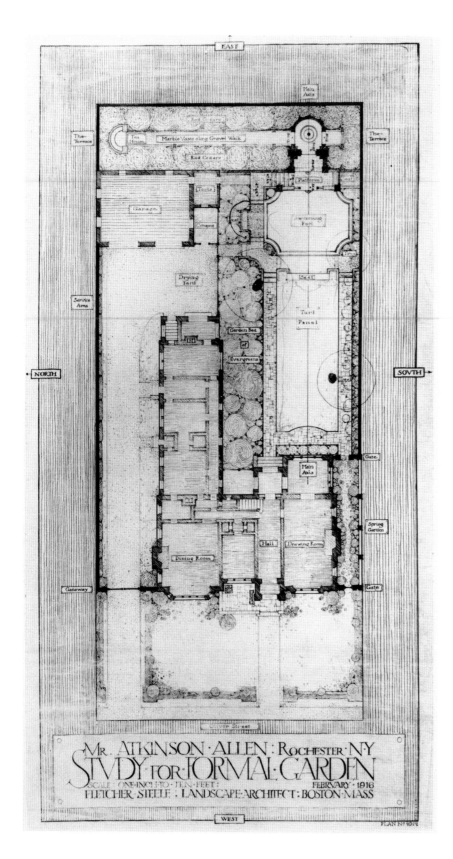

Mr · ATKINSON · ALLEN · ROCHESTER · N·Y
STUDY for FORMAL GARDEN
SCALE · ONE·INCH·TO·TEN·FEET · FEBRUARY · 1916
FLETCHER · STEELE · LANDSCAPE · ARCHITECT · BOSTON · MASS

too would occupy many years' work and involve considerable expense. Steele's reputation as a prominent landscape architect was taking sudden and dramatic hold.

The Allens' small lot (90 by 200 feet) and its suburban setting made a walled garden a near necessity, but Steele's scheme included unexpected variations on an English tradition, inspired by modern European gardens. The "rooms" of English Arts and Crafts gardens were similarly volumetric, but they relied on hedges as boundaries and were predominantly horticultural in impact. The Allens' garden would more resemble modern town gardens of the Munich School, which emphasized masonry walls, changes in level, and sculpture. Steele's trip to Europe two years before had included visits to contemporary gardens and professional exhibits where such designs were winning acclaim.

Although work on the garden would continue for half a century, nearly every important feature was represented on the original 1916 plan, even the figurative sculpture, which would not be commissioned until ten years later. A few minor alterations would occur. The small teahouse indicated for the end of the terrace walk would never be built. (A mobile by Alexander Calder would eventually occupy this spot.) Planting was originally to be wholly evergreen, except for the spring garden tucked on the south side of the house. The terrace allée was to have been red cedar (it may have been tried without success); European beech proved a durable alternative.

The handsome 1916 plan was drawn by Stanley White, recently graduated from Harvard, who was supporting himself doing "trifles" for the landscape architects John Nolen and Harris Reynolds as well as Steele. Steele's practice was not generating enough work to keep a draftsman employed full-time. Stanley—older brother of the essayist E. B. White—would emerge as one of the profession's great teachers, first at Lowthorpe School and then, for thirty-seven years, at the University of Illinois. His stylized rendition of the Allen scheme reflected period drafting conventions, but his artistry transcended the utilitarian demands of a simple plan.

The layout was not complicated. A large turf panel spreads directly on axis with the drawing room, whose French doors open onto a roofed terrace. The long edges of the lawn are defined by Medina stone walkways (quarried in upstate New York), and at the lawn's end is a swimming pool. A clamshell

Allen estate plan, 1916. (SUNY ESF College Archives)

fountain spills water into the pool. Allen told Steele to make the water "up to here," indicating a mid-neck depth, about four and a half feet on her small frame, so she could walk from one end of the pool to the other without getting her hair wet.[8] (Steele said that she looked like the little Queen Nefertiti on his mantel, copied after the famous original he had admired in Berlin.)

The garden's interest was enhanced by the raised terrace and its hidden allée. The terrace platform would also provide a setting for a sculpture (by Gaston Lachaise) directly on axis with the drawing room. On two sides the garden is defined by a high brick wall; the other two perimeters are abutted by the L-shaped house. The elaborations that took place subsequent to this plan never affected its structural logic.

In Beaux Arts fashion, the major garden axis responds to the architecture of the house and constitutes the organizing force of the outdoor space. The secondary axis stands at a right angle to the primary. The plan strikes a judicious balance between the house terrace at one end and the sculpture niche at the other; likewise, the proposed teahouse answers the sculpture on the allée axis. Marble vases at regular intervals establish a processional rhythm to the allée.

The garden was intended to be green from its inception. Charlotte's neighbors remember her complaining about the floriferous purple wisteria on one of the house walls, which Steele had assured her would never bloom in her lifetime. But the prohibition on flowers was not complete. (It was disorder she hated, not color.) Later planting plans featured a long band of Heuchera ("as red a show as we can get"[9]) and a spring garden of blossoms whose names, at least, she found "very splendid" and "entrancing."[10]

The green architecture was composed of narrow and broad-leaved evergreens including arborvitae, yew, andromeda, box, holly, euonymus, pyracantha, and rhododendron. An early watercolor by Steele suggests a less architectural planting scheme than was ultimately developed, but by 1922 the structural role of the plants was clear. Steele's pen-and-ink drawing (one of the few from his own hand) shows a low hedge at the front of the long bed and three evergreen niches holding vases. Eventually the low hedge would be doubled and the long row of red Heuchera planted inside, and the niches would enclose specimen plants of unusual form and presence. At various times Steele tried weeping dogwood and globe hawthorn. Holly, andromeda, and rhododendron offered softer

Allen estate. The 1922 pen-and-ink sketch suggests more geometric plantings than did earlier proposals. (SUNY ESF College Archives)

1922 Planting for Atkinson Allen Esq by Fletcher Steele —

40-04

Whitney Allen in Rochester, New York which in many ways is the best place I have ever done, as well as about the smallest. In fact, Mrs. Allen says that it is so satisfactory that she has sold her country house at the lake and never goes to Europe or anywhere else anymore, as her own place is so much more satisfactory than anything she ever can see abroad."[11] The link between garden and travel was powerful here and elsewhere in Steele's work. Not only did European itineraries routinely include trips to important gardens, but specific features were often integrated into owners' gardens back home to transport them to distant lands just by stepping outside.

Important additions in 1926, 1934, and 1938 would complete the garden, reflecting Steele's interests, respectively, in modernism, eclecticism, and exoticism. But the designer's successful pairing of powerful spatial impact and drawing-room charm would not be disrupted by any of the subsequent additions. Steele shared Allen's passion for the exquisitely detailed and perfectly crafted; his own garden might have resembled this one. Here was a haven for the connoisseur, a setting for contemplating beautiful things and remembering beautiful places. And more.

Steele had created a stage set for intimacy, the sort its owners (and he, too) relished. The grander, necessarily looser designs, such as Rolling Ridge, evoked larger physical dramas—exploration and adventure. This one set the stage for cocktails and the smart, sometimes titillating talk that often followed.*

Charlotte Allen would figure prominently in Steele's life. She was a feisty, self-assured thinker who loved good fun as much as he. She was also a native Rochesterian, daughter of Mrs. Warham Whitney, whose New Year's party invitations were "at once a command and a visa for the coming year in polite Rochester." But daughter Charlotte was independent, a quality that got her expelled first from Spence School for Girls in New York City and, later, from the Century Club of Rochester, of which her mother was president. Charlotte had lit up a cigarette. "Very well, Mother," she replied on being informed that ladies were not permitted to smoke. "I'll found my own club," and she did.[12]

Rochester's most ambitious cosmopolites would gather at the intersection of Grove Place and Windsor Street to drink and dine at the Corner Club. When in town Steele would drop in and amuse his listeners with anecdotes from his latest trip, and catch up on the local gossip. The heady, self-involved group was enlivened by frequent scandal. Allen's best friend,

forms between the architecturally clipped niches, while pyracantha was supported against the brick house wall.

An early sketch (circa 1916) reveals that the sculpture was planned as the garden's focal point from the first, with planting and architectural details developing directly in relation to the central organizing figure. The sculpture was originally anticipated as a more gardenesque presence than the powerful Lachaise figure, which would be installed about 1926. The young couple's budget required that the project be developed in stages.

Many years later Steele wrote: "I have done a place for Mrs.

* A planting plan for the garden appears in appendix 2.

Clayla Ward, had found a passionate admirer in the figure of O'Donnell Iselin, eventually one of Steele's clients and a close friend. Ward also had George Eastman and E. E. Cummings vying for her attentions. Certainly, Steele's trips home were not dull.

Although not traditionally handsome, the young landscape architect turned heads. Relentless self-scrutiny was yielding a set of idiosyncrasies that highbrow clients found intriguing. Primary among these was a new way of speaking, an affectation that expressed high cultivation rather than specific geographic origins. Steele's long, nasal *a*'s and telegraphic "hot potato" phrasing evoked East Coast aristocracy. "Splendid" and "charming" punctuated talk that turned on nasty gossip and sincere poetic sentiment.

Allen and Steele carried on a flirtation—through the blessings of distance—for half a century. The design of her garden both reflected and provided the setting for a determinedly gay life in which this relationship would play an important part. She was the first of many great patrons who offered the artist financial support in the context of a real and lasting friendship. Alexander Calder remembered that "Charlotte said she once received a bill from Fletcher marked '$50.00 . . . Concentration on Tree.'"[13] Not surprisingly, Steele did better and more exciting work when he was doing it for someone he liked. The impulse to experiment—which lay at the heart of his greatest work—would find fullest expression when supported by the admiration and commitment of the client.

Aesthetic Maturity

Experimentation, at the Allen garden and other early projects, was to be distinguished from invention. Steele saw no tension between originality and the use of traditional forms.

I do not hesitate to use the ideas of other people when they help me express the ideas I want to make clear. For I have always avoided the pitfall of desire to be "original"—hateful word. Either one is or one is not original, and the result will be discovered by other people. It should never be forced on their attention. Forced "originality" is but superficial eccentricity, to talk like Ralph Cram. Dr. Ross taught me one thing at least—that there is no intrinsic value in what is new or what is old from its age, but that all things are valuable for what quality is in them. In that way one escapes trying to do a thing because it is new, and tries only for what has promise of beauty. On the other hand, all fine art worthy of the name consists in a lifetime of experiments. Otherwise

there is nothing but imitation, if not of somebody else then of yourself.[14]

Ralph Adams Cram and Denman Ross no doubt exerted strong influences on Steele's aesthetic ideas. Steele may have met Cram through Ross, his favorite professor and part-time employer. (Steele had dug Ross's vegetable garden while a student.) Now he saw both men, and Cram's family, socially. Cram, "the American Ruskin," was the foremost Gothic revival architect in the United States, a respected scholar of Japanese art, critic, poet, playwright, and leading medievalist, possessing (claimed the *Boston Herald*) a "rare combination of qualities which enabled him to maintain for decades an almost unique eminence among Americans of distinction."[15] Cram's influence on Steele arose from his own deepest artistic conviction: that art need not turn its back on the past to achieve greatness. The architect's major claim to glory rested on his explorations of the unrealized potential of Gothic architecture. Although Steele's work would not be as methodically historical as Cram's, what he learned from Cram's example was profound and lasting. The architect would later recommend Steele to several important clients.

Steele also admired Denman Ross, whose Harvard lectures on design theory inspired him as no others had. Ross often invited Steele to his home for superb dinners ("vegetables fresh from France") and theoretical discussions. As an honorary fellow of the Fogg Museum and a trustee of the Museum of Fine Arts, Ross led travel groups to Europe. Ross's most important contribution, according to his student, concerned the centrality of "pure design" to great art. In Steele's words,

Pure design, in the sense intimated, would include all disposition of lines and spots in all the possibilities of color that appeal to the pleasure of sight without appealing to the intellectual or moral nature.

. . . In a Japanese print one is concerned far more with the delightful repetition of curves, the disposition of the masses and the harmonious color than with the licentious drawing of the Japanese Lady. In such works one sees the pleasure in pure design. But it is where representation of any sort is of no interest to the artist, who perhaps may use the memory of an observed object simply as inspiration or self-created design or who may break away altogether from the memory of objects seen, and using lines and spots as his only inspiration create some design that in no wise suggests any other object, that the highest value in pure design is attained.[16]

When Steele wrote this, the world's first (and the twentieth century's most famous) modern painting, Picasso's *Demoiselles d'Avignon,* was scarcely dry. The notion that painting had meaning apart from its representational or narrative role would revolutionize artistic expression in all media, including landscape design. That Steele pondered his own design decisions as the "disposition of lines and spots in all the possibilities of color" indicates how thoroughly modern his aesthetic roots were, regardless of his choice of architectural vocabulary.

Although his apartment and office were in Boston, work took Steele often to clients' homes, where business and pleasure mixed easily. He kept in close contact with his family in a role increasingly more paternal than filial, looking after household business in great detail and eventually contributing significant financial support. He seemed to thrive on the fast-paced and rather fragmented lifestyle.

He had guessed, rightly, that pleasure often leads to business but the inverse was also turning out to be true. His time with clients was enlivened with talk of politics and poetry as well as plants. He had begun to make—and spend—money almost immediately. Good food, good drink, clothes, fine books, and objets d'art satisfied an increasingly discerning aesthetic.

One of Steele's closest friends in Boston was Mary Fay, whom he had originally met in Rochester through Mary's first cousin Uhrling Sibley, of the prominent Rochester department store family; Uhrling would later marry O'Donnell Iselin, Steele's dearest friend. During graduate school and after, Steele was a frequent guest at the Fays' home on Beacon Street. Mary Fay was cultivating a career as a singer and apparently not much interested in romance, but Steele's letters convey deep affection. After hearing her perform in the summer of 1915 he wrote:

> Of course you don't want me to exaggerate. You aren't ready for that yet. But it is the promise—the promise that even I who have always loved to hear you sing more than anyone else—never understood until the other night. I declare though, I am not sure that I can be self-sacrificing enough to hope that you will leave what you have and try for the big things. After the thrill of just listening was gone the other night I felt a sadness. You seemed unconsciously to yourself to be looking down a new vista where I am afraid even you would not be able to carry us with you. . . .
>
> You don't want a long disquisition (is there such a word?) on the subject from me. But I do want to say that, while your stage presence is charming and not at all amateurish, you fail to use your remarkable personality as much as you might.

Steele's letter offers more advice—about controlling the emotions of the audience, and then about the importance of the right clothes (a subject fresh in his memory). He finishes, "Forgive me this letter. I remember what you said about my 'laying down the law' & know how loathsome it is. But I am so much interested and you asked for my impressions."[17]

The letter would be inconsequential if there were any evidence that Steele felt deep, romantic attachments to other women during his lifetime; there is none, although his journals, and several casual comments by friends and colleagues, suggest regular, passing sexual liaisons with both men and women. Mary Fay once confided to her daughter, Caroline, that Fletcher Steele had proposed marriage to her many years before and that she had turned him down.[18] Nevertheless, Steele assumed a central role in the family after Mary married Tom Dabney in 1921. He was a frequent Sunday dinner guest, a travel partner, a godfather to her first child, Lewis, and a treasured pot-stirrer.

Lewis remembers "Uncle" Fletcher's admiring comments about Franklin Roosevelt starting arguments over dinner. Fay, the Dabneys' second daughter, treasured the exotic presents Steele brought her from abroad. All the children describe him as a loving and devoted member of the adopted family. Whatever the emotional roots of Steele's relationship with Mary Dabney, it proved permanent, lasting until he died.

World War I

In response to the war, the profession recommended that teams of three—landscape architect, architect, and engineer—assist with the emergency construction of large camps for the new National Army. Olmsted Jr. was chairman of the National Conference on City Planning. Through the War Industries Board he urged the government to utilize the services of expert community planners. Twenty-six of the forty-five fellows of the American Society of Landscape Architects closed their professional offices. The remainder continued to maintain their businesses with small amounts of war-related work. Private projects ground to an abrupt halt.[19]

Steele closed a flourishing practice in October 1917 to enter the American Red Cross. He had attempted to enlist in the army at the Plattsburgh, New York, training camp but was rejected on account of his age, thirty-two at the time. He appears to have pulled some strings—trading on his visual expertise—to find a position where travel would be possible. In the Red Cross Department of Public Information he was given the complimentary rank of captain and sent to Europe to take pictures.

In London and Paris, Steele was able to return to some of the gardens and city squares that had moved him strongly five years before, although travel through the besieged European countryside must have been horrific by contrast. Steele's confrontation with the sublime and the tragic are reflected in dozens of personal photographs that record both the architectural triumphs that would inspire his work to come and the desecrations of war. Images of defoliated forests, ruined buildings, and one especially stirring picture of a shattered statue of Christ were carefully pasted into scrapbooks that also contained ideas for new gardens.

Steele soon left the battlefields of Europe for more exotic shores. "Yesterday afternoon I got a telephone call from Major Murnano . . . saying he had heard I was an expert on Russia. I denied this, but told him I was keen about it, whereupon he said 'can you be ready to go tonight?' Papers could not be rushed through in that time, but I am going tonight to London and then after that to Russia—Heaven knows quite how or why."[20] Arkhangelsk, an occupied supply port on the White Sea, left new and strong visual impressions. He wrote to his mother:

I hear that there will be a mail tomorrow, so I hasten to write something. . . . The one feature that makes the place look

Steele in Russia, holding a camera, 1919. (SUNY ESF College Archives)

Europe, site unidentified, during World War I. (SUNY ESF College Archives. Photograph by Steele)

like a frontier town gone looney are the churches, which spring up on every block. They look like the things children draw the first time they get a pencil in their hands. They are simple cubes surmounted by five domes. And such domes! The only way I can describe them is to say they look like Maxfield Parrish dreams of the Arabian Nights in toy balloons with half the air gone. They are hideous shapeless excrescences, made to look as conspicuous as possible by thick layers of solid gold and patterns in bright green tiles and gold spots. But this is not enough. On top of all they have idiotic needle point spires topped by fantastic crosses or disappearing into thin air. On the sides of the building, on all blank wall spaces, they have huge paintings of scriptural subjects which could be beaten by any second rate sign painter at home. . . .

There is so much that is curious. . . . In the first place it is never really light even when the sun shines. You see the sun is low in the sky all the time, and will get lower for some months. The sunsets last for hours, until one forgets all about them, although they are gorgeous at times—the first one I saw had brilliant color that I never saw equalled anywhere else. Especially startling is the fiery purple tinged with crimson. But you can't keep on looking at even that more than two hours and a half with any excitement. As I love gray days and colorful twilights, it is very lovely in my eyes. But most of the men were heartily sick of it even before they landed.[21]

Steele returned to Russia once more, in 1927, as part of an extensive European tour, and he wrote an article, "City Planning in Moscow," that spring, for the *Garden Club of America Bulletin*. The country did not influence his gardens nearly so much as it did his politics, which were slowly but steadily swinging from left to right. In 1925 he told an audience that during his student years he was "an out and out rank socialist."[22]

Steele was discharged in 1918 and afterward made a Fellow of the American Society of Landscape Architects. (ASLA membership in 1917 totaled ninety-three, with about forty independent offices.) He began to settle back into his work from a small apartment on Tremont Street.

Steele's war experiences left him involved and politically informed. He often wrote letters to newspaper editors, usually with a contentious point of view. In response to an article in the *Boston Transcript* claiming that Rheims cathedral had been singled out as a target by the Germans, Steele wrote to protest the American piece of propaganda—because it rendered questionable reports of true atrocities. He reported from firsthand

experience abroad: "Compared to the area covered and its great height the cathedral has suffered less than any similar structure in the whole city. . . . I feel the more strongly that the way to stop the back-fire of incredulity toward all their [the enemy's] practices . . . is to limit ourselves to those facts which are incontrovertible."[23]

Two months later he wrote with equal enthusiasm to the editor of the *Rochester Democrat and Chronicle* to take issue with an article encouraging widespread use of the ginkgo tree. "They should be planted only where a specimen is wanted which will not disturb a serene landscape by possible vegetable antics."[24]

In spite of the one-and-a-half-year hiatus, Steele's practice was intact, and his prospective clientele more interested in gardens than ever. The profession was growing rapidly (in 1920 the ASLA had 127 members). Large enrollments and new training programs nationwide produced a general lowering of standards. New complexities were forcing specialization in the field, and the splintering of the artistic from the technical—which Steele would emphatically decry—had already begun. The field undertook to codify professional practices, ethics, and education, hoping to assure the future identity of the landscape architect, with mixed success.

WINGFIELD
John and Nora Towne
Mount Kisco, New York
1921–1928

During the three years between his return from Russia and a long series of estate-scale projects, Steele was occupied with several small jobs and continuing development on some of the old work. One of his first big postwar projects was for the Townes of Mount Kisco, New York.

Mount Kisco is a beautiful village, particularly from vantage points atop its many hills, where the wealthiest residents inevitably chose to build. Wingfield commanded one of the best views to the west, "a stirring, dramatic landscape—what the old English writers called 'sublime.'"[25] The country mansion, designed for John Towne by Harry Bigelow of Bigelow and Wadsworth, was constructed in 1910. A large rose garden by Arthur Shurcliff was built shortly afterward. Nora Towne wanted to enlarge and update the garden; she and John Towne had been married only a year when Steele was hired in 1921. His design would contrast with the elaborate trelliswork and small garden areas laid out by Shurcliff, but he would retain the lines of the old plan.

Some of Steele's finest designs were overlays, gardens on top

Wingfield, Formal Garden, ca. 1920, design by Arthur Shurcliff. (SUNY ESF College Archives. Photographer unknown)

of gardens. Many of his jobs had existing landscape designs, usually in proportion to the size and architectural style of the house. Steele took pleasure in negotiating the complexities between new features (occasioned by changing tastes) and existing ones.

Steele once described the Towne garden as the "type of natural country landscape which Americans like to have created around their houses. A few years ago this was an ugly hillside which was reshaped, the trees brought in and the meadow planted, to get the results shown."[26] Steele's caption, written for a slide show given in Paris in 1930, scarcely does justice to the garden's inventiveness.

One aspect of Wingfield's plan came from work Steele was completing for Ethan Allen. In both designs, a long passage was laid out to bring visitors from the house to an apparently distant circle. Each circle constituted a nexus for other garden areas and paths. But while the passageway at Rolling Ridge doubled as a bowling green (necessarily rectangular), the Wingfield path had no such constraints and Steele leaped at the opportunity to work a little perceptual magic. He used a French trick of perspective that lengthened space through foreshortening. Weeping willows on either side of the path closed the passageway, so that, viewed from the house terrace, the circle appeared farther from the house than it actually was. (At Rolling Ridge, the diminishing height of the arborvitae hedge and the blue-tinged plantings at the far end of the rhododendron beds enhanced the illusion.) At Wingfield, Steele may have been inspired by Watteau's *La Perspective*; the spatial configuration in the painting bears a strong resemblance to the garden's willow-lined vista. The painting entered the collection of the Boston Museum of Fine Arts at about the same time that Steele was creating the Mount Kisco garden, in 1923, and he had a reproduction of it in his files.

Pots of hydrangeas and lilies lined the gravel steps at Wing-

field, contributing color and fragrance to the walk down the hill. Opposite the gravel path, a flight of turf steps led the eye (if not the foot) up to a parapet with two columns and a small jet d'eau. The view was carried higher and farther still to a grotto. The arched entrance to the "cave" was crowned by a pediment and flanked by a pair of columns echoing the proportions of the nearer pair. It was a stage set of strength and simplicity.

A stucco exedra (of nearly the same peach tone as that at Rolling Ridge) defined the circle's edge. Tufa reliefs decorating four large pedestals suggested Italian prototypes; each supported an elaborate cast-concrete ornament that marked the garden's main axis (house to path to circle to stairway). Steele

fashioned them after an English form gaining popularity through Gertrude Jekyll's widely read book *Garden Ornament*. Vines softened the geometry and linked the forms with the glistening foliage. Steele's sensitivity to texture and surface in plants was everywhere evident. Mattie Edwards Hewitt, one of the best known garden photographers of her day, was commissioned to photograph the estate for the Paris Exhibition of 1930. Her images glimmer with drops of light reflecting from shiny-leaved willows, rhododendrons, lilies, and vinca.

The circle opened at either side to paths leading into surrounding meadow and woodland. "The flowers," reported one newspaper, "grow on uneven slopes and finally disappear in the trees."[27] To blur the edges between the formal garden and

Wingfield, path, after planting, 1923. (SUNY ESF College Archives)

surrounding wilderness, Steele continued the same plantings throughout. The mountainous woodland beyond the garden was made accessible by these meandering meadow-like paths, which become more rustic as they moved away from the formality of the garden proper. The experience of wilderness and mountain views at Wingfield and elsewhere were critical to these designs. The gardens led visitors to these more informal settings where the experience of nature became a private communion. As did his mentor, Warren Manning, Steele looked to the genius loci for guidance in his gardenmaking. One of the most profound purposes of his gardens, despite their architec-tural trappings, was to help his clients make contact with the spirit of the place.

Steele's work at Wingfield continued. Over the next two decades, the Townes regularly consulted him on opening views to the woods.

Opposite: Wingfield, steps to the Circle, after planting. (SUNY ESF College Archives. Photo by Mattie Edwards Hewitt)

Wingfield, steps to the Circle, ca. 1921. Steele's concern with the organizing force of axis is made clear by the stake at the center of the Circle. (SUNY ESF College Archives)

Wingfield, Circle and view toward the fountain. (SUNY ESF
College Archives. Photo by Mattie Edwards Hewitt)

Wingfield, view from the Circle to the meadow. (SUNY ESF College
Archives. Photo by Mattie Edwards Hewitt)

Wingfield, flower-lined meadow and surrounding woods. (SUNY ESF College
Archives. Photo by Mattie Edwards Hewitt)

Opposite: Wingfield, path in the woods. (SUNY ESF College Archives. Photo
by Mattie Edwards Hewitt)

LISBURNE GRANGE
Samuel and Katherine Sloan
Garrison, New York
1921–1937

As Steele's reputation grew and his technical mastery deepened, his gardens came to express a spirited playfulness. The distinctly lighthearted borrowing from venerable old traditions that dominated his work during the 1920s was as much a sign of the times as of a personal artistic development. Steele's clientele—most of them wealthy—were looking for fun in their gardens. They wanted to swim, to stage dramas and comedies, to play croquet and lawn tennis. Vague undercurrents of nineteenth-century cultural insecurities persisted among the wealthy, but the broad historicism dominating residential architecture and landscape architecture was motivated by a less weighty task than gaining cultural legitimacy.

Steele's designs were affecting the same whimsy as elegant movie theaters of the period. Indeed, their purposes were not so different. Theater architects giddily incorporated florid Re-

naissance and baroque details, and Italian and Spanish courtyard layouts into their schemes. The Italianate pool at Lisburne Grange grew out of a similar, almost cinematic impulse—to play at being someone else, somewhere else.

The Sloans' estate sat high on a ridge in Garrison, New York, about twenty miles north of the Townes' Wingfield. Katherine and Samuel Sloan had inherited the Victorian Italianate house from Samuel's father; in 1916 they hired J. Gamble Rogers to transform it into a more convincing palazzo. Samuel Sloan was a railroad industrialist, well traveled and wealthy. Kitty Sloan was an important member, committee chairwoman, and soon-to-be president of the Garden Club of America. They had no children.

The burgeoning Garden Club of America provided Steele with lecture bookings, publishing opportunities, flower show jurying, society, good friends, and—the focus of much of the ancillary activity—clients. But Steele also wanted to make an impact theoretically in the field, and he realized that the Garden Club of America and horticultural societies were determining the state of the art as much, if not more, than were the

Lisburne Grange, terrace and view east. (SUNY ESF College Archives)

Lisburne Grange, terrace and view northeast. (SUNY ESF College Archives)

professionals. By 1920 he had become the club's "most faithful male member"; his attendance at that year's (the seventh) annual meeting was undoubtedly noted by Mrs. Sloan. Steele was recorded as urging "war on the nuisances of sound and smell," encroachments from the world outside the garden wall.[28]

Lisburne Grange was approached from the north by a long winding drive that separated meadow from the broad, tree-covered lawn, planted seventy years before in the romantic style of many Hudson River valley mansions. Steele wrote admiringly of the great scale, "the grandeur of the now full-grown trees," and "the breadth of the naturalistic park scenery."[29] Across the rolling lawn fine old lindens, great purple beech, twisted Japanese maples, magnolias, false cypress, and ginkgo cast giant shadows as the sun set across the meadow to the west. Steele thought it one of the finest of all such nineteenth-century Hudson River landscapes to survive.

On the south side of the house, a tremendous terrace bounded by low box hedges was joined to the house by an open veranda. Four ancient sugar maples formed a square in the big lawn; Mrs. Sloan had designed a round mirror pool

between them to mark the space's center. A summerhouse stood at the end of the axis that ran south from the house piazza through the pool to the edge of a ridge. The long east-west axis was less articulated, and it was here that Steele first worked, "for both ends of the Great Terrace were haphazard and uninteresting."[30]

To the east some irregularly rising land, which hid an old (but still useful) reservoir, "stuck up in a queer bumpy way." The problem lay in connecting this mass, which lay to the south of a central cross axis, with the symmetry of the Great Terrace. Existing and important trees on the lower, north side made filling the area out of the question. Steele wrote: "The necessity of creating symmetrical balance with most unsymmetrical objects seemed to Mr. and Mrs. Sloan to demand professional advice, and I joined forces with them. . . . We finally resorted to swinging the axis on the center of the Great Terrace circular pool up flights of turf steps some eleven feet at the uppermost terrace . . . making a separate composition of the reservoir, accenting it as an enframement of the central feature rather than trying to screen or forget it." For this

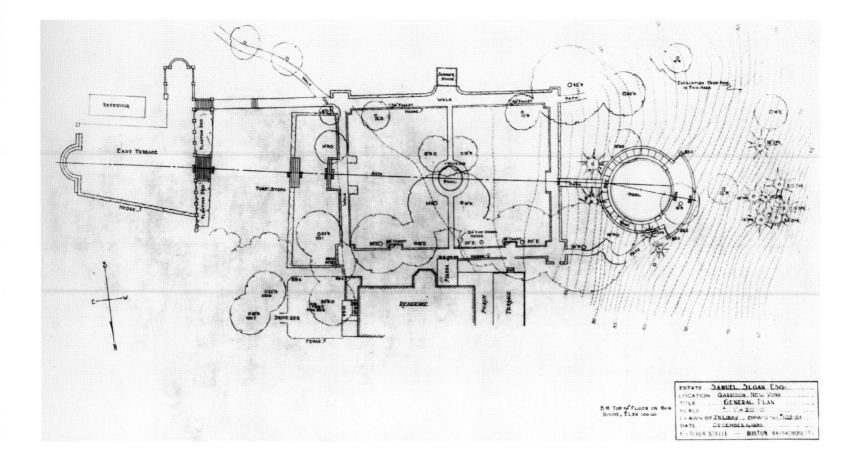

Lisburne Grange plan, 1930. (SUNY ESF College Archives)

enframement, Steele continued, "we indulged in a bit of straight theatre decoration, treating the reservoir like an old garden mount on which a templelike feature would have been built."[31] Steele had recently used a similar feature to finish an axis at Wingfield.

"At its foot we put a statue pedestal and ran an overlook platform well out over the hillside on the south to give our fantasie a solid base. Mr. and Mrs. Sloan brought a suitable deity back from Paris to grace the pedestal and marble columns from Tunis with which to arrange the false front of our imaginary temple."[32] Steele sent many clients on overseas shopping expeditions to choose their own garden ornaments and sculpture, with itineraries of important landscapes intended to educate his patrons.

The work, completed about 1922, resulted in a view that took the eye up the hill and to the "temple." A parallel view, from the mirror pool, revealed a dramatic mountain silhouette, which Steele framed with two groups of cedars. He advised limiting flowers to the old borders at the lawn periphery and favored "holding the rest of the place to composition in green foliage picked out by a few bright jars, garden furniture, and potted plants."[33] Certainly this would have been in keeping

with the original intentions and Downingesque celebration of the native landscape.

"While this work was under way," Steele related, "we would sometimes cross the terrace at sunset and walk westward into the meadow to a certain spot commanding a fine view. 'Sometime we must do something here' was the universal opinion. During hot days the idea of a swimming pool was tempting to dally with. There was no suitable termination of the Great Terrace axis at this lower, west end. Thus three factors inspired plans for a pool to use all the advantages."[34] The twenty-five-acre meadow ("the finest feature of the place") sloped down to the west and offered a bucolic aspect, untouched for three-quarters of a century—a pleasant place for a swim that would not interfere with the grand design in back of the house.

A few large trees formed a rough circle whose center was slightly off-axis from the center of the Great Terrace. To keep the trees, Steele bent the axis so that the pool and lower terrace were rotated to the south, "following the procedure of many an old garden."[35] (That Steele felt it necessary to defend the bend in his axis is an indication of how rigorous the appeal of symmetry had become in American garden design.) He sunk the circular pool into the slope and constructed turfed ramps

Villa d'Este, from Steele's office files. (SUNY ESF College Archives)

Lisburne Grange, Mrs. Samuel Sloan (?) about to dive into her swimming pool, ca. 1930. (SUNY ESF College Archives)

Lisburne Grange, swimming pool, southeast view. (SUNY ESF
College Archives. Photo by Paul Weber)

around both sides leading from a balcony at the top to a paved terrace below. The sloping wall offered a variety of heights for diving, depending on skill. (Had the Sloans had any children, the precipice may have been made less dramatic.)

Steele's design borrowed details from the Dragon Fountain of the Villa d'Este, but enthusiasm outstripped Renaissance restraint as Corinthian columns were topped with fountains, balustrades added, and iron Venetian boat rings attached, ostensibly "for the comfort of bathers."[36] The gushing, rushing pool provided a baroque counterpoint to the classical serenity of the broad valley below and the Great Terrace above. Steele's vision was an insistent but ultimately discreet landscape feature, visible only to those who sought out the quiet path at the edge of the Great Terrace.

Plantings surrounding the pool eased the transition from artifice to nature: "To increase the scale and bear out the decorative effect, big swirls of hedging were planted, clipped high at the upper end and lower as they run downhill to suggest sculpture. The bays between them are filled with flat beds of English ivy."[37] Steele liked the French form and would use it again elsewhere, often with privet. A wooded buffer between the Great Terrace and the pool was planted less formally with trees and shrubs of unusual character. The feathery foliage and late-season blooms of *Aralia spinosa* contrasted with the wide, glistening leaves of rhododendron; sweet bay magnolia flanked the entry from the Great Terrace and the path.

In 1933 Steele unsuccessfully proposed an elaborate belvedere and pleached aerial hedge, probably for the south edge

Lisburne Grange, swimming pool, northwest view. The meadow is visible on the left, under the large maple. (SUNY ESF College Archives. Photo by Paul Weber)

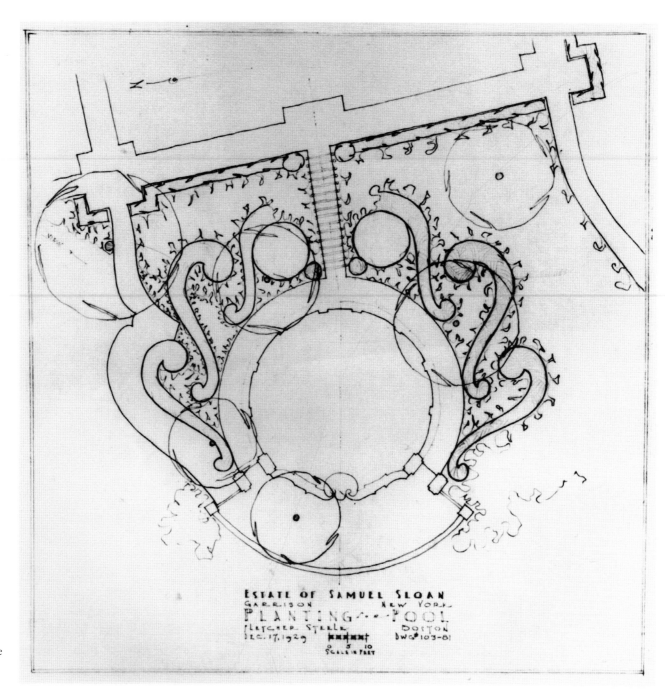

Lisburne Grange, plan of the plantings in the swimming pool area, 1929. (SUNY ESF College Archives)

ESTATE OF SAMUEL SLOAN
GARRISON   NEW YORK
PLANTING · · POOL
FLETCHER STEELE   BOSTON
DEC. 17, 1929   DWG 103-81
0   5   10
SCALE IN FEET

of the Great Terrace. Four years later a design for a fountain and pool for the uppermost terrace on the mountain-view axis would also languish unbuilt. Steele was a frequent guest at Lisburne Grange during the decade and may have generated a new design idea every time he saw the place. His patrons were willing to pay for drawings but were not sufficiently enthusiastic to pursue construction. It was a pattern in many of Steele's relationships with wealthy clients.

Steele's last piece of work for the Sloans was a replacement summerhouse for an existing, probably deteriorating structure that sat at the north end of the piazza axis. His 1937 design resembled the little pavilion he was concurrently building for Mabel Choate in Stockbridge, Massachusetts. Both structures were based on reminiscences of Steele's trip to China in 1934, particularly the curving roof lines. The Sloans' was a larger

building, cantilevered over the steeply sloping hill and pond below. From a distance, the sculptural roof seemed to float as the decorative ironwork trellis disappeared against its foliage backdrop. It was a striking terminus to an important view, exotic but not so overbearing as to compete with the monumental trees and lawn.

Steele planted the steep hill below the summerhouse with white birch, which merged gradually with an indigenous forest of hemlock, maple, chestnut, and laurel. The edge of the ridge along the perimeter of the Great Terrace was planted with azaleas and pink and white dogwood. The place retained its quiet grandeur, in harmony with the river valley below and the rolling hills above. Samuel Sloan's death in 1937 marked the end of the garden's development.

Lisburne Grange, privet hedge. The swimming pool ramp is visible on the left. (SUNY ESF College Archives)

The Influence of France

In 1922 Steele published "French Gardens and Their Racial Characteristics" in *Landscape Architecture* magazine. The essay foreshadowed Steele's second book, where gardens would be interpreted as expressions of "race" and culture. It also clarified his push-pull relationship with French design tradition, which had greater influence on him than any other. Steele celebrated the structural logic of classical French gardens and incorporated many elements into his own work, especially bosquets, allées, forced-perspective vistas, parterres, and radial circulation. Steele also admired the French tradition's emphasis of vision over the other senses, and yet he expressed ambivalence as well.

"Versailles is the grandest of the works of Le Nôtre or any other Landscape Architect," Steele wrote. "The wonder of the place is a revelation of man's imagination and handiwork. The immensity of nature is there laid under the constraint of man, directed and adorned. Order is personified. Unity is felt. Beauty is unavoidable. The absolute in gardening is there made concrete. Why does one turn away from it at times with relief?"[38]

Later in the essay Steele allows himself to "boldly find fault" with some of Le Nôtre's design: "the West Terrace is too wide and too high, cutting off the lower part of the building from a large part of the garden. The unsatisfactory terminus of the great axis is thus still further diminished. The Grand Trianon is ill related to the North arm of the canal, and one feels that a magnificent possibility was lost." Steele also criticized French landscape classicists (both designers and critics) for ignoring lively sensual pleasures in favor of a "beauty which unfolds entirely in the serene domain of logic."[39]

The dichotomous tension Steele identified in the 1922 article—between architectonic impact and sensual delight, logic and expressiveness—is evident in his own work. His best gardens would achieve a strong balance, in archetypal terms, between Apollo and Dionysus. That his parents so dramatically represented these poles—his father, the lawyer, his mother, the musician—gave the dichotomy early and vivid significance.

Of greater interest to the professional reader was Steele's review of new books on French garden design, which included discussion of J. C. N. Forestier's *Gardens* (originally published in 1920) and André Vera's *Les Jardins* (1919). Steele applauded Forestier's designs for tropical gardens (Steele was also interested in adapting traditional forms to new climates), and he liked the "useful horticultural lists." Forestier's statement on the changing style of gardens paralleled Steele's own ideas, which would first be articulated in 1929. "It is difficult to express conditions of modern life artificially by special forms or orders. This expression of the growth of life is accomplished by a practical solution best adapted to our needs."[40]

André Vera's book "of cubist-dada influence" was "decidedly worthwhile," but mainly on account of "the droll woodcuts by M. Paul Vera with which they are illustrated." Steele's dismissal of Vera on the grounds that he "seems to glorify the curious and original rather than the beautiful"[41] reflects a resistance to experimentation that was soon to change.

Top: Garden design by J. C. N. Forestier, from *Gardens: A Note-book of Plans and Sketches* (1920).

Middle and bottom: Garden designs by André Vera, from *Les jardins* (1919).

Lectures

In 1923 Steele decided to raise his lecture fee to one hundred dollars, "otherwise I shall be swamped and don't intend to become merely a lecturer."[42] His considerable oratorical talents were the subject of frequent comment. In 1925 the *Cincinnati Enquirer* responded with great enthusiasm to a talk Steele gave to the local garden clubs there.

Mr. Fletcher Steele, of Boston, should give up the White Man's burden of being a mere landscape architect, eminent though that be, and travel about cheering people up rather than devoting his entire time to the aims and wishes of a large clientele of millionaire garden owners.

For yesterday . . . talking on the general topic of "Village Improvements: American Towns, Old and New," he told so many truths in so delightful a fashion, that the members of this organization, which boasts an ensemble of 19 separate garden clubs in this vicinity, not only had a wonderful time being brusquely jolted out of any smugness which may have been theirs, but also in learning things about gardening as a fine art, which no one else had ever been honest enough, or clever enough, or had had sense of humor enough to tell them.

He talked in a most engaging conversational fashion, bringing to his aid a fund of dry humor that kept his audience in a gale of laughter while it enabled him to send home his thrusts, always softened by the "bonne bouche" of "from my point of view" or "so far as my experience goes." . . .

"In gardening," said this frank iconoclast, "it is first necessary to get rid of the enemies of beauty. I mean the horticulturists per se, the tree butchers, the endless specimen hunters. Horticulturists are indispensable; one can not garden without them, but if you listen to them alone, instead of having a garden which is useful and comfortable, qualities that make up beauty, you have merely a place to grow flowers and to leave to enter the house as quickly as possible.

". . . The trouble with Americans is that they will not give the time or the pay necessary to insure that the work of the garden is properly done, nor will they do this work themselves. They lay out far too large a plan, look at it hopelessly—and then go to the movies."[43]

Steele also lectured at the Cambridge School of Architecture and Landscape Architecture and at the Lowthorpe School of Landscape Architecture, Gardening and Horticulture for Women (both professional training programs for women) between 1915 and the schools' closing during World War II. He was also an occasional guest lecturer and critic at Harvard.

Steele, ca. 1925. (Courtesy American Horticultural Society)

Students were most impressed by Steele's iconoclastic imagination and his untraditional use of plants, based on an abstract understanding of their specific qualities, especially color. He urged his listeners—and readers—to overthrow tradition by relying on their own eyes and an expanded sense of the potential of a garden, from ornamentation to art. Underuse of peculiar, out-of-fashion varieties was a favorite topic. "The subject of abnormal coloring in plants is not easy to handle," he wrote in one essay. "Anything strange was popular in the old carpet-bedding days. That is probably the reason why everything of the sort is now deprecated by connoisseurs. . . . In more than one case I have seen fit and pleasing use of these more or less unusual objects."[44]

Steele's use of the word "object" for plant (and his frequent reference to "plant material" in his office memos) documents his design orientation to horticulture.

Plants are the materials with which to paint [the landscape architect's] compositions in terms of living things. Two flowers that enhance each other are apt to be more lovely than one alone. . . . But in the garden, one seeks more than combinations of flowers, more than pattern beds, more than the trees and shrubs that enclose, more than any one part that goes to make up the whole garden. One cannot stop short of the whole, the living compositions from the tallest tree to the tiniest flower that must be related, combined or separated, so that in every direction, from every angle, near or far, one sees a picture that makes one long for the power to fix the thing forever with paint and canvas.[45]

Steele's criticisms grew out of a mounting dissatisfaction with the state of the art. Nearsighted horticulture and bland acceptance of weak design conventions had given birth to thousands of bad gardens during the early decades of the century. Prim symmetry, sentimental statuary, and excess in the number of plants, individual garden features, and diversity of styles contributed to the widespread malaise. One contemporary critic identified "promiscuous planting" as the single leading contributor to the bad design evident throughout the countryside.[46]

Steele was traveling a great deal between clients. Work continued for the North Andover Allens, Rochester Allens, Townes, Sloans, Woods, and several others while new jobs got under way: a French formal garden for an Ardmore, Pennsylvania,

chateau and the redesign of a garden for Mrs. J. A. Maxwell of Rockville, Connecticut, originally created by Charles Platt. Steele had entered the ranks of the country's most expensive landscape architects. "For the first time I am boosting my fees way up this spring and people don't seem to think them too high," he wrote his mother in March 1923.[47]

Steele returned to Europe in 1924 with his old teacher and now friend, Denman Ross, visiting Paris, Venice, and Lausanne. Over the next decade Steele's annual travels would include new places along with the old favorites. He routinely booked first-class passage on luxury steamers, nearly always in the company of clients and friends. His pockets filled with letters of introduction, Steele continued to discover Europe, public and private.

A Growing Practice

MR. AND MRS. CHARLES SCHWEPPE
Lake Forest, Illinois
1923

In 1923 Steele started thirty-four landscape projects, all but four of them for residential settings. In Lake Forest, Illinois, he

Schweppe estate, swimming pool. The waterfall and hillside are visible on the far right. (LC. Photo by Perry-Atlas, Chicago)

began gardens for three residents, including Mr. and Mrs. Charles Schweppe.

The Schweppes' enormous Tudor home was surrounded by broad lawns and traditional, box-bordered flower beds laid out by Henry White. Steele's work would be confined to a large forecourt with reflecting pool and a swimming pool with adjacent areas; the latter revealed the same sort of theatricality and whimsy expressed in his gardens elsewhere. Steele took his cues for the pool house architecture from the main house but added curving roof lines to the two square cabanas and a strip of decorative crenellation. The results were a bit of frank historical sport.

A contemporary newspaper account documented the recent surge of interest in recreational pursuits, evidenced by Chicago's 143 golf courses ("crowded from dawn until the last throb of twilight"), the popularity of tennis and horseback riding, and the fact that swimming pools had become the "favorite rendezvous for young and old." The article continued:

The most recent of these pools is that which the Charles Schweppes have added to their Lake Forest place, a delightful and spacious affair . . . perched almost on the brink of the bluff in what might be considered a challenge to the smiling and blandly indifferent lake. The approach to the pool is one of the charming landscape features of the place. From the front door one looks down a long, green vista to a distant fountain, a stone basin sits high on a rocky eminence, a steep embankment embellished with every imaginable species of close growing greenery that delight to hug and creep over bleak stone and crags. A spray of water leaps from the basin, falling back into it and overflowing down a picturesque channel until it falls into the swimming pool many feet below.[48]

A naturalistic rock garden and slide occupied one end of the Schweppes' pool, while the formal terrace continued across the other short end on axis with the house's front door. The possibilities of mixing formal and informal elements occupied Steele's imagination for many years, although eventually his design approach transcended the Beaux Arts–inherited dichotomy.

Steele was concurrently working on a garden for Samuel Fuller in Port Chester, New York, which also included a swimming pool and terrace; a retaining wall of rough-hewn stone held fountain reliefs (in the form of lions, fish, and Greek gods) that spurted jets of water into the pool. An elaborate, multileveled pergola covered the large terrace area. The ingredients were specific to the site, but the special quality of fantasy and play were becoming characteristic of Steele's 1920s work.

In Lake Forest, Illinois, an enclave of generic medieval houses had been given a strong communal focus by Howard Van Doren Shaw's 1913 market square. It was an old European idea put to use in the setting of the emerging American suburb. Shaw based his design on Austrian village prototypes where pitched-roofed arcaded buildings frame a central park. On the ground level, stores and offices opened to the street; the upper stories housed apartments. During his several trips to Lake Forest, Steele would have taken note of the model village—city planning and community life persisted as topics of interest for him in spite of the lack of opportunity for work of this sort.

SAMUEL T. BARBOUR
Bloomfield Hills, Michigan
1924

In 1924 Steele began a project for Samuel T. Barbour, a wealthy Detroit businessman who had introduced colored stoves to

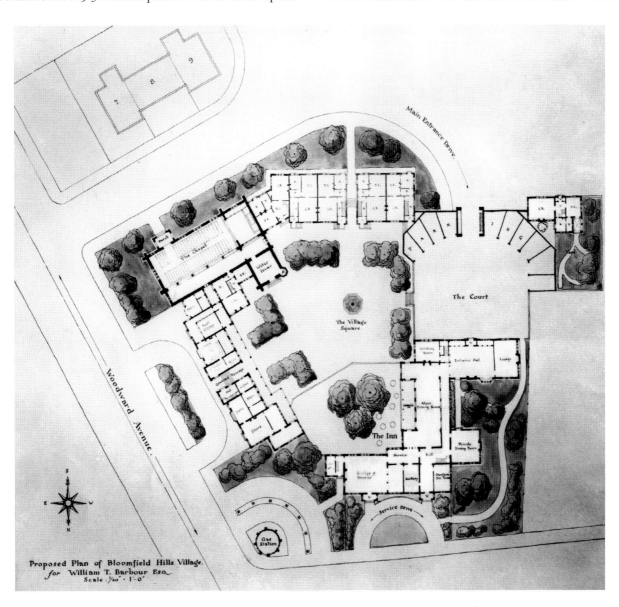

Bloomfield Hills Village plan, n.d. (LC)

Bloomfield Hills Village, presentation drawings, n.d. (LC)

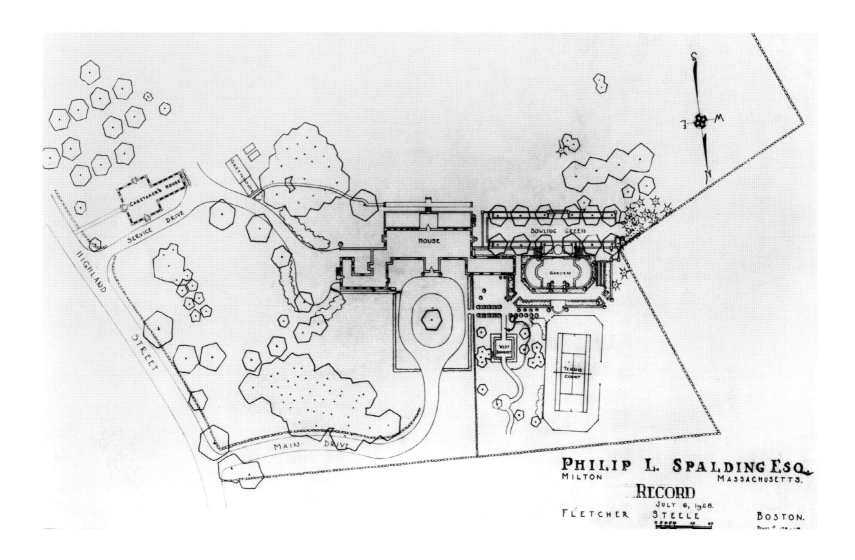

the American housewife and made a fortune. Around the turn of the century, Barbour had purchased 48 acres of rolling ground outside Detroit called Trowbridge Farm. He gradually increased his holdings to 205 acres and called on Steele to help him develop an idyllic village center for Bloomfield Hills. It was Steele's first planning project since his early work on the Arapaho Indian Mission. Barbour's wealth and great interest in the project created an ideal situation for the landscape architect.

Steele designed an eclectic, Georgian-influenced constellation of shops, chapel, inn, post office, water tower, and filling station to cluster around a village square—much as he had recently observed in Lake Forest. The buildings combined historical forms and modern usage: the water tower was disguised as a medieval steeple, the parking garage as a stable, and, most incongruous, the filling station as an English dovecote.

KATHERINE AND PHILIP SPALDING
Milton, Massachusetts
1924–1932

Steele's garden for Katherine and Philip Spalding was not typical of his work at the time. The Spaldings' new Georgian revival mansion was built on twelve acres of meadow and forest outside Milton, Massachusetts. Steele had worked in Milton as early as 1916 and would do so many more times as word spread of his unusual designs. This was a particularly important commission, for the town's grandest estate and an important client. (Philip Spalding was president of New England Telephone and Telegraph; Katherine was a member of the local garden club, a Garden Club of America affiliate.)

The Spaldings' garden differed from the Townes', Sloans', and Schweppes' in its sobriety and lack of historical reference.

Spalding estate plan. (SUNY ESF College Archives)

The design was primarily architectural, an extension of the proportions and material of the house into the surrounding landscape. Its restrained character was abstract, almost industrial.

Steele's layout included a bowling green, terraced rose garden, tennis court, forecourt, and bosquet arranged to form a tight jigsaw of interlocking parts. He relied on 8-foot brick walls to define the bowling green and rose garden. Decorative patterning relieved the strict geometry of walls. The rose garden sat at a slightly higher grade directly adjacent to the bowling green. Plantings echoed the clarity of the architectural geometry: regularly spaced elms underplanted with rhododendron enclosed both edges of the bowling green; box hedges reiterated the apses of the rose garden. A tall taxus hedge defined the big square forecourt. (Steele soon abandoned forecourt islands in favor of a sparer, unrelieved European treatment whenever space was available.)

The formal garden areas were confined to the northwest quadrant of the property so that the house's rear elevation looked out over a broad lawn and meadow, a gentle contrast to the insistent geometry of Steele's design. It is unlikely that the Spaldings asked Steele for the kind of clarity and volumetric spatial treatment that the garden exhibited. His 1924 European trip (taken the same year he began working for the Spaldings) included yet one more visit to France, where there was considerable interest in modern gardens. By the end of the decade, Steele's involvement with modernism would deepen, and his gardens would become less historically derivative and more experimental as a result.

Design in the Little Garden

By 1924 Steele had devoted many articles and lectures to middle-class homeowners which diagnosed anachronistic conventions shaping American neighborhoods and invented alternatives to many of them. Steele found the complexities and challenges of suburban landscaping compelling. His book *Design in the Little Garden*, published by the Atlantic Monthly Press as part of Louisa Yeomans King's Little Garden Series, brought together all his ideas on the subject, which had developed since his article on the same topic, "The Landscaping of Peridot," nine years before.

Critics hailed Steele's book for its readability, inventiveness, and common sense. "His pungent statements and unconventional observations," wrote one critic, "cause the book to stand out quite apart from the average rule-of-thumb manual."[49] Steele was well known in Boston before the book appeared, thanks to his frequent lectures and upscale clientele, but the book helped make him famous with the gardening public.

In *A History of Landscape Architecture*, George Tobey credits Steele's book with "prophesying the age of functionalism. . . . Four years before Stein and Wright showed their Radburn scheme, Steele advocated the reversal, in housing, of the common practice of living-room-facing-the-street, kitchen-facing-the-rear of the property. Steele recognized the change in life style from one of homecraft self-dependence, to an interdependent, mass-production economy."[50] Tobey has hypothesized that the book was not endorsed even more widely because its tone was too down-to-earth for landscape architects interested in maintaining a professional mystique.[51]

Steele considered most suburban landscaping abysmal.

The suburban house on the lot which averages 50 to 75 by 100 feet is usually curiously isolated from the land around it. One feels that a giant might come along any night and change the houses about without making any alteration in the appearance that would be perceptible to the stranger the following day. Most of them would seem to fit equally well on the foundations next door. This is carrying democracy in homes altogether too far. It certainly leads to monotony, which in turn leads to the movies and the automobile-infested roads. But why stay at home in good warm weather when there is nothing but a covered front porch to sit on and no place in which to forget neighbors and public?[52]

Steele took up the theme of privacy in gardens many times in his writing, arguing that American middle-class prejudices against privacy undermined successful gardenmaking.

Our traditions are curiously mixed up and lacking in common sense in respect of these things. Tradition says practically that it makes no difference what is done on a place if only there be an open front lawn on the street side. Thousands of people put almost all their gardening work on the effort to keep the front yard clipped and neat, while they let the side and rear yards run to weeds and trash. . . . A decent respect for the public is incumbent upon us all. . . . But our work and thought should go to improving and maintaining those parts of our grounds in which we can live in privacy and comfort.[53]

Design in the Little Garden took the prospective homeowner through the process of selecting land, planning the house, and then designing, planting, and maintaining the surrounding yard. Steele made use of the same dramatic devices in the Peridot article: an imaginary couple, Mr. and Mrs. Brown, must decide among three identical homes that received varying landscape treatments. Steele's narrative voice combined authoritative advice with amusing, mostly sympathetic philosophizing, his tendencies toward extravagance tempered by practicality.

In the spirit of William Robinson, Steele made extensive use of bad example. "Too many flower-gardens become slave drivers. Their owners never dare sit down in them. Weeds spring up while the back is straightening . . . they have a dangerous tendency to resemble the White Queen's condiment in Through the Looking Glass, 'Jam tomorrow and jam yesterday—but never jam today.'"[54]

Steele advocated that prospective homeowners find a "street laid out to be awkward to use rather than an easy shortcut for the peripatetical iceman and grocery-boy." He advised gardeners to bring shovels to test the soil, not too solemnly warning of the moral dangers that lie ahead if the result is deep rich loam. "Either pride or indifference is then all too apt to overcome the gardener. He will never learn restraint. He will never know true humility or hope—the sweetest lessons of the garden. Only great ascetic souls, with the never satisfied ambitions of artists should be given deep rich loam on which to begin their experience."[55]

Philosophically, Steele addressed the relative merits of imagination. "Frankly, imagination is the only resource that can save economy from being drab, or at least pathetic. It can create a little paradise with the weeds of the field . . . out of a place that would remain stiff and ugly in spite of a score of gardeners without imagination." But fantasy, like good loam, is a two-edged sword: "There is, to be sure, a danger in willful, undisciplined imagination. It leads to discontent where lack of money or other circumstances prevent the achievement of pre-conceived ideas. The imagination that is helpful first makes a survey of available material and then says, 'Here is my land—my tree—my house—my rose bush—my garbage. Let us set about making the best of them.'"[56]

Some of Steele's criticisms would be equally apt for the suburbs of the late twentieth century. "American lawns rarely invite one to linger. They are usually indeterminate areas covered with grass, into which house, drives, and gardens are dropped down like a few fishballs on a large platter. . . . A good lawn must be enclosed by buildings, walls, or planting, as a general thing."[57] Steele recommended views out of the garden only if strictly controlled, but thought, in any case, that a strong demarcation between the immediate garden space and the open landscape is necessary to protect the intimacy of the former, and to make the garden a haven from the world outside.

Steele suggested boundary planting as the most economical way to achieve privacy—at a time when shrubs and even trees sold for a few cents apiece.

Overplant everywhere, mixing up varieties of many things, with a preponderance of two or at most three varieties from among the many used. . . . More explicitly assume that a narrow boundary-planting two hundred feet long is being planned around a lawn. Plant one hundred trees and shrubs (far more—perhaps ten to twenty times more—than can develop to their individual advantage). Assuming that a sunny area is wanted, not more than three trees can be permitted to grow large. Plant six to ten of one or at most two varieties. There is a permanent place for six small trees, such as hawthorns, flowering crabs, Japanese tree-lilacs or flowering dogwood. Plant ten of one variety, three of a second, and two of a third. From year to year one or more of the superfluous trees can be taken out, when they have had time to show unmistakably which will be the best specimens.[58]

Steele's reflections on the then unpopular geometry of Victorian bedding out sheds light on an evolution in his private work, which would often rely on regular, highly stylized patterns.

Because carpet-bedding was bad, the world jumped to the conclusion that all planting done with regular patterns must necessarily be ugly and stiff. It took a long time for people to realize that under certain circumstances nothing but this type of design was appropriate, especially in formal gardens which had any flavor of the French style. During the long discussion of carpet-bedding and formal design versus herbaceous borders and informal design, the French have gone their own way. They have followed their own genius for order even when dealing with our familiar herbaceous plants. As a result the French flower beds are chic and almost inimitable. . . .

As time goes on I believe that the development of honesty among gardeners—which means always a growth of individual taste—will reveal the fact that many people are really fond of this classic sort of garden design, just as many people are fond of classic austerity and fine proportion in houses, even where it can be gotten only at the expense of coziness. Gardening will be the better for the development of all sorts of ideas in garden design.[59]

Some of Steele's ideas about turf proved more prophetic: "grass is used far more than necessary. A curious notion prevails that sowing grass is the only way to cover the ground except where there are beds of shrubs or flowers. . . . Close examination usually shows that grass is only one and sometimes a scarce plant in lawns. It is rather silly to keep up the old delusion, under the circumstances. There are a host of plants which make admirable groundcovers."[60]

Garden club flower shows (which Steele often judged) were ubiquitous. *Design in the Little Garden* cautioned Steele's flower-crazy audience against the overuse of bloom in the landscape: "The flower garden, to be a garden, must have a good background on at least three sides, eye high. . . . Many, many flower gardens are spoiled because they have too many flowers. A series of beds of flowers alone is a monotonous sight at best, though they may be astonishing as bright floricultural 'stunts.'"[61] Steele's arguments for good architectural composition echoed those in *The Spirit of the Garden* by Martha Brookes Hutcheson, which was published in 1923.

CHARLES AND EDITH CLIFFORD
Milton, Massachusetts
1925–1937

Steele's first goal was often to enhance space through illusion and, next, to screen sights that interfered with the character of the garden. Often this character was fictional, an invention of client and designer. For example, Charles and Edith Clifford's handsome colonial revival house nestled in a wealthy

Clifford estate, forecourt
fence detail. (SUNY ESF
College Archives)

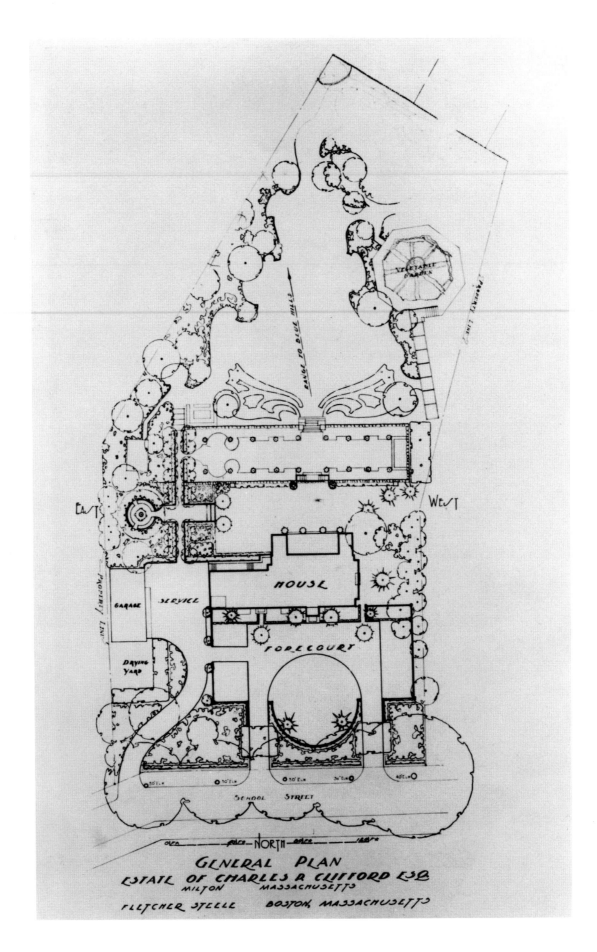

Clifford estate plan, with the central view marked. (SUNY ESF College Archives)

but suburban Milton neighborhood; yet "the main task," wrote Steele, "was jealously to guard and intensively supplement the impression of real country."[62]

Steele's plan for the Cliffords' property included a formal half-court turnaround (more, he said, would have "destroyed the village atmosphere"), an adjoining service court, a shaded fountain garden, densely planted wall garden, grape arbor, and a large terraced lawn with geometric rose beds leading to the mountain vista.

This site's greatest asset was a view to Great Blue Hill. By introducing trees and large shrubs in carefully selected spots, Steele was able to squeeze the perspective in the foreground and frame the hill in the distance. He was not sentimental about removing trees that did not fit his plan: "The best of the view was already hidden from the house, and conditions got noticeably worse each year. Rigorous, almost ruthless removal and cutting back was the only hope. It is hard to destroy what one has planted and nursed through infancy, especially when it is a fine specimen in itself. Most people are too cowardly. When anything hides a finer feature than itself, however, it must go."[63] (Twelve years later Steele wrote: "Curiously enough, the finest tree on a place is all too often the landscape architect's greatest handicap. . . . So he learns to harden himself

with the definition that any plant, little or big, is a weed when growing where it is not wanted."[64])

Steele was much concerned with "garden rhythms and balances" in the Clifford garden, particularly since the off-center view made it impossible to develop the elements of the picture symmetrically. So he established "opposing varying interests." "Rhythms were achieved by the repetition of similar forms in varying sizes and colors; by change from one dominating color to another; by checking or enhancing the untouched forms of nature with geometrical objects [the shaped beds] which are always conspicuous."[65]

A wrought-iron rail marked the edge of the house terrace. The lawn, surrounding trees, and view appeared through and over the geometry of the railing and its handsome central ornament: three birds holding a chain garland aloft, hovering above a stylized *Fritillaria imperialis* and sheaf of leaves. A tiny lion head spurted water into a small pool below.

Steele filled the dry walls with plants to create three-season color and interesting textures. In addition to the expected rock garden plants (houseleeks, *Aubrieta,* candytuft, saxifrage, and thyme), Steele included gray-green yarrow, pale blue and 'Blue Starry' bellflowers, 'Brilliant Alpine' pink, 'Shirley' and 'Fiery Red' coralbells, and creeping and woolly speedwell.[66] These

Clifford estate, retaining wall with plantings. (SUNY ESF College Archives)

Clifford estate, detail of
plantings in the wall.
(SUNY ESF College
Archives)

Opposite: Clifford
estate, fountain. (SUNY
ESF College Archives)

were ordered in quantities of five or ten apiece (160 plants were ordered at a cost of $52.80—less the 10 percent discount Steele regularly passed on to his clients).

The beds set into the lawn were predominantly rose-filled; the planting scheme was arranged according to color. The long beds shaded yellow to orange; the small teardrop beds were pink; the curved beds flanking the stairway contained flame-red roses. "One contrariety of artists," Steele wrote, "is to prove the absurdity of mediocre rules of thumb, such as the dictum that rose gardens must be isolated. Here we disproved that notion by laying out formal beds for roses as an integral part of the lawn planting and general garden ornament. They are tucked under the lower wall to be accessible at the foot of the garden steps. They are shaped to the curves of the lawn, yet definitely formalized. In June these beds, against a ten-foot

bank of mixed species roses and brilliant climbers, are one heap of gorgeous color."[67]

The shrub and tree boundaries defining the irregularly curving edges of the great lawn were composed of strong-charactered, flowering sorts and "coarse herbaceous things" that would provide bloom from spring through autumn. In addition to many varieties of rhododendron, Steele planted sweet bay magnolia, smoke tree, Japanese snowbell, white fringe tree, *Photinia*, star mock orange, *Tamarix, Stewartia,* fragrant epaulette tree, red-vein *Enkianthus,* and broad blue leaf honeysuckle. More common varieties—sweet mock orange, Japanese andromeda, fragrant viburnum, juniper, and arborvitae—filled in the remaining space. Daylilies, *Echinops,* and white mugwort are listed among the perennials grown.

Contrasting with the openness of the lawn was a shady

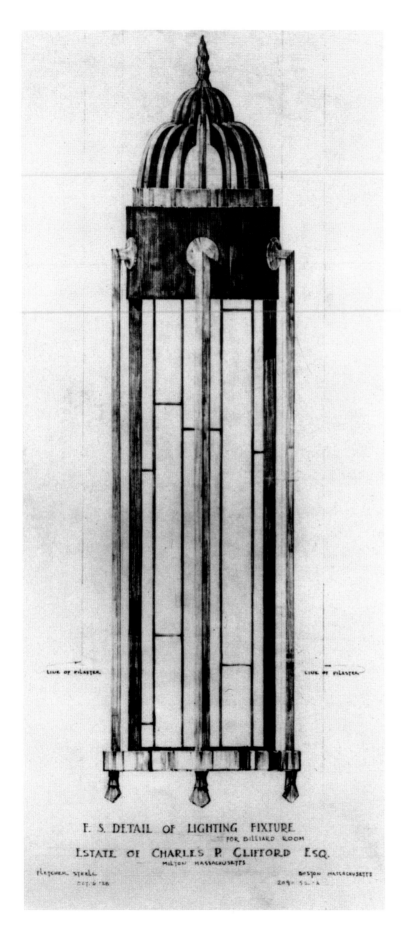

F. S. DETAIL OF LIGHTING FIXTURE
FOR BILLIARD ROOM
ESTATE OF CHARLES P. CLIFFORD ESQ.
MILTON MASSACHUSETTS

FLETCHER STEELE   BOSTON MASSACHUSETTS
   OCT. 6 '28   209-52-A

LINE OF PILASTER.   LINE OF PILASTER

nook east of the upper terrace. Here Steele curved a low brick wall around a fountain and planted a circle of lindens to provide enclosure and definition. An octagonal vegetable garden and long grape arbor were tucked in behind thick plantings to the west, invisible from the formal garden areas.

Mr. Clifford was not as enthusiastic as his wife about the extent of the garden's development—between the time he left for work in the morning and when he returned home in the evening, the garden could, and often did, change dramatically. Steele's passion for experimentation often proved contagious, but not always equally so among couples.[68]

Still, Steele liked working for the Cliffords. When he finished the garden in the mid-thirties, he began a design for the billiard room that included lighting fixtures, cork wall covering, and billiard counters. Later he wrote: "Sometimes when I have been planning architecture or furniture or picture frames or billiard room light brackets or any of the odds & ends that have taken my time and care in the past, I have wondered why I chose the professional title of landscape architect."[69]

JOHN S. ELLSWORTH
Simsbury, Connecticut
1925–1966

The lure of Europe was widespread among Steele's clients, but John and Eleanor Ellsworth proved exceptions. The Ellsworths' farmhouse and barn nestled into the hilly countryside outside Hartford, Connecticut. Steele's landscape additions and architectural adaptations for his new clients would stretch over the next forty years, always honoring the integrity of the colonial house and setting. The Ellsworths wanted a farm, a beautiful American farm.

Steele particularly admired the family, who he thought managed their wealth with discretion and wisdom. "The Ellsworths are not like the usual run. They have gradually made their own conventions over the years. . . . They work in the garden and on the farm much harder than the hired men— tend the sick cattle and cut the hay. They also have a musical life in New York where they go once or twice a week. Eleanor has run the canteen service of the Red Cross through two wars, then rushes home to get down on her knees to plant roses, then goes in to dress for dinner and appears with sapphires. . . . It is a pleasure to see the interesting books they have about and

Clifford estate, billiard room, detail of a lighting fixture, 1928.
(SUNY ESF College Archives)

study. Not the faintest trace of fashionable life about them, though they have loads of friends in every rank of life."[70]

Steele's first project on the rural property developed an idea from *Design in the Little Garden.*

If the designer insists that a verandah does not belong on a colonial house, remind him of the old arched woodsheds all over New England, which are one of the most picturesque appointments of the old farm, and can easily be turned into particularly comfortable outdoor living-rooms.

These woodshed-rooms are desirable for two reasons. They are more comfortable than a verandah because they have much more headroom. . . . They can easily be made with a large air-chamber between ceiling and roof, which goes far to keep a place cool in hot weather. And since they are on the ground, they are paved with brick or stone built

on the cool earth. Not only are they picturesque in themselves, but they serve as an excellent way to "bring the house down to the ground" and thus to make it an intimate part of the landscape design.[71]

Steele followed this advice in siting an outdoor living area among the Ellsworths' old farm buildings. His design connects the old barn with the garage by means of a covered alcove that served both aesthetic and utilitarian needs. A flagstone floor and pitched roof defined the L-shaped area, and it included space for wood storage on one side and a small seating area with built-in furnishings on the other. While a convincing traditional feature, the alcove design was also a modern three-dimensional creation, a product of Steele's increasing awareness of spatial volume.

Steele designed two more outdoor areas in the first phase of

Ellsworth estate. (SUNY ESF College Archives)

Ellsworth estate, courtyard. (SUNY ESF College Archives)

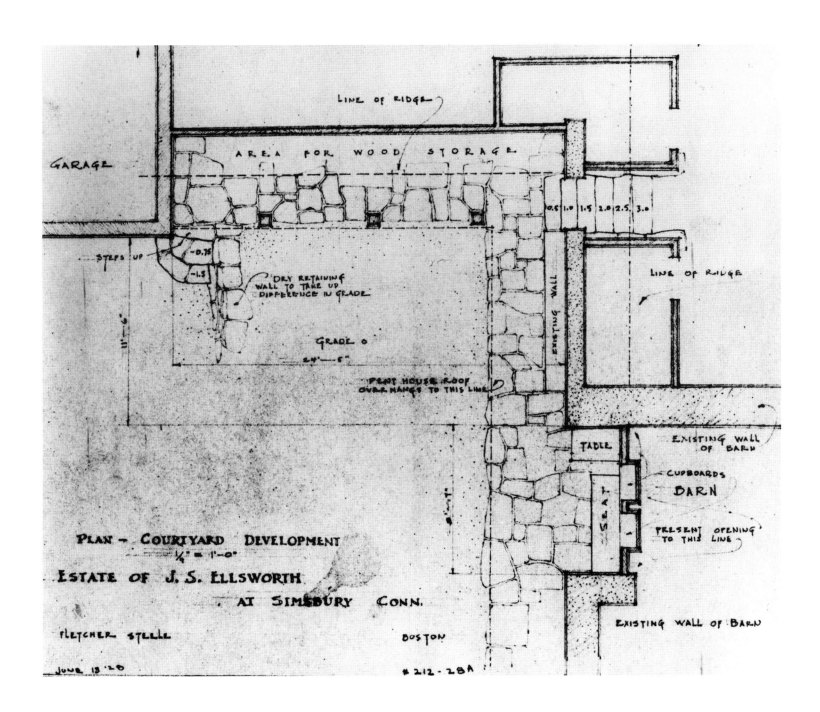

Ellsworth estate, plan of the courtyard development, 1928.
(SUNY ESF College Archives)

his long relationship with the Ellsworths. A dooryard garden bounded by a white picket fence had both strong spatial and geometric integrity and also served as a transitional architectural space from drive to house. In it Steele laid out flower beds and brick walks in modern curves. A rectangular terrace tucked between the end of the main house and an addition was covered by a grape arbor, "in accordance with tradition."[72] Here, too, the increasing clarity of Steele's space shaping could be felt.

One of Steele's handsomest designs for the farm estate took

Opposite: Ellsworth estate, view from the Dooryard Garden. (SUNY ESF College Archives. Photo by Paul Weber)

Above: Ellsworth estate, gates, silo, and barn. (SUNY ESF College Archives. Photo by Paul Weber)

the form of a gateway into the barnyard. Acorn-turned finials were the sole decoration on the simple picket fence and generous double gate, but the enormous, supporting stone piers cleverly echoed the cylindrical form and conical roof of the barnyard silo.

HOPKINS MEMORIAL

Williams College

Williamstown, Massachusetts

1925

In 1925 Steele returned to Williams College to create a memorial for World War I veterans. (Steele's very first job had been landscaping St. Anthony's Hall at Williams College in 1914; he had been back in 1923 to lay out athletic fields.) His design for the memorial was a response to what he identified as the restrained "country" elegance of the campus, an eclectic amalgamation of the sort that would continue to characterize his work into the 1930s. In developing the Hopkins design, Steele combined two large masonry piers and a delicate wrought-iron arch as dominant vertical elements. The same features appear in unidentified photographs mounted side by side in one of Steele's photo albums—it may have been this serendipitous arrangement that led to the combination in the Hopkins design. (Steele kept a large inventory of photographs and an extensive library for design reference.)

A few years later, the arrangement would turn up again, this time with the arch sitting atop the piers, in the form of an entryway to the Camden Library Theater in Maine. The urns featured in the original photo would later be adapted for a Rochester garden. In each design quotation Steele altered proportions and details as seemed necessary. At Camden, the masonry would be replaced by brick, to visually tie the supports to the main building.

In 1926 Steele began twenty gardens, including two of his largest ever. He returned to Europe and spent time in Italy, France, and Sweden. *Town and Country* magazine ran an interview with Steele alongside features on Princess Achille Murat of Indochina and Osbert Sitwell, "the most brilliant young man in England."[73] The landscape architect was living in high society now, befriending clients as well as working for friends.

Right: This ironwork arch provided a model for the arch in Hopkins Memorial. Photograph from Steele's client file. (SUNY ESF College Archives)

Below: Piers and urns in this photograph provided models for Hopkins Memorial. From Steele's client file. (SUNY ESF College Archives)

MARY SCHOFIELD

Peterborough, New Hampshire

1923–1935

It was not unusual for Steele to design more than one property for the same client, but Mary Schofield's nine separate projects between 1923 and 1935 was a record. Among these were two church landscapes; the Peterborough, New Hampshire, railroad station; a teacher's lodge; a factory site; and three family-owned homes, one of them a 120-year-old cottage in Quebec. The most interesting cluster of work took place on the shore of a millpond in Peterborough. Here Steele used old factory foundations and new retaining walls to create a system of terraces adjacent to the Schofields' main home, Beside Still Waters, which sat at the pond's edge.

Steele integrated brick and wrought iron with native stone-work to produce a two-tiered lawn on the precipice of the falls. The plan made brilliant use of the dramatic site without interrupting the village atmosphere. Steele's angular, almost constructivist treatment of the site was eventually softened by indigenous trees, shrubs, and vines.

For the Schofields' country home at East Hill he designed a swimming pool over an old outbuilding foundation. Steele's design suggests the deck of a luxury liner, his use of the white rail also functioning as a powerful decorative element (a civilized counterpoint to the surrounding birch woods). White birches, superb in conjunction with the white rail, may have inspired a similar treatment at Naumkeag, one of Steele's largest, most important gardens.

Waterfall Terrace, dam.
(SUNY ESF College
Archives)

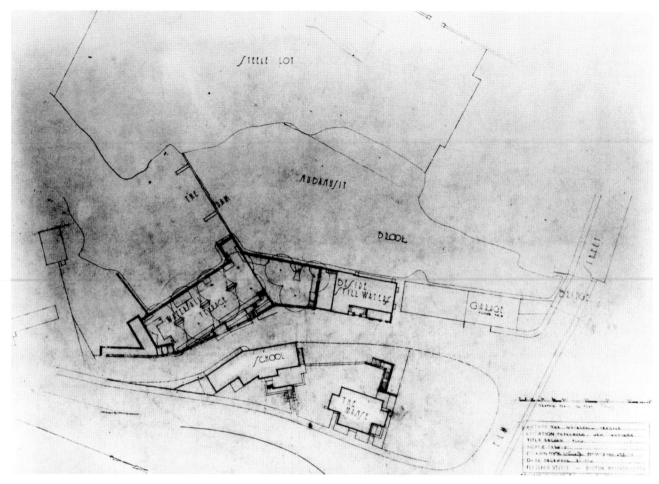

Waterfall Terrace, plan, revised 1932. (SUNY ESF College Archives)

East Hill, swimming pool. (SUNY ESF College Archives)

CHARLOTTE AND ATKINSON ALLEN
Rochester, New York
1926–1934

In 1926 Charlotte and Atkinson Allen commissioned the sculpture that had been intended as their garden's focal point since its inception eleven years before. It was probably Steele who suggested Gaston Lachaise for the job. Lachaise lived in Boston from 1906 until 1912 and may have known Steele there. He later worked in New York as an assistant to Paul Manship, with whom he shared an interest in Indian art. Manship's use of stylized drapery and smooth, rounded masses of flesh had clearly influenced Lachaise's style. By 1926 Lachaise's forms emphasized curvilinear volume and strong handling of form.

Steele worked directly with the sculptor in determining the size of the stylized, monumental nude. Scale was important to Steele and a frequent topic in his writing: "Only people and cats stay the same size indoors and out," he observed. "A house chair on the lawn dwindles and looks overdressed. The daintiest lilac bush in the garden would be a white elephant in the parlor. The cellar hole, minute when dug in the meadow, grows big when the house is built over it. Magic gets in somehow and changes the size of any object as it goes through the garden door."[74] Lachaise's seven-foot, cast-stone goddess would make her presence felt even from inside the drawing room. (In physical bearing the amazon could not have been more unlike slim, birdlike Charlotte Allen, who purportedly posed for it.) Visible from just about everywhere in the garden,

Allen estate. (SUNY ESF College Archives)

she seemed ready to slip out of her robe for a plunge in the pool. The terrace was transformed into a stage. The enframing pair of obelisks and balustrade sections marked the boundary of the now separate space, visible from house, patio, or pool, yet distinct (by virtue of its elevation) from the lawn area. The sculpture gave the garden excitement, drama, and a focal point.

The transformation might not have been as dramatic had the figure been less commanding in a purely plastic sense, or less convincing in a human one. Recent evolutions in modern art had provided Lachaise with new means of managing the tension between abstraction and representation. That more of Steele's clients did not commission modern sculpture was a matter of taste, and relative expense.

A rustic trellis of unpainted wood shored up the space behind the figure without competing with her strong, white silhouette. Lacy foliage and shadows played behind the trellis, adding the life and movement that Steele had admired in European sculpture niches. In front of the figure, a small bubbler splashed in a semicircular basin. This emptied, via a pebble-lined trough, into the shell basin and swimming pool below. The exact shade of blue for the pool, extremely bright and darker than traditional turquoise, was arrived at through experiment.

The garden had reached a new level of resolution, and many would have considered it complete—certainly Atkinson did. But Steele still had almost half a century of work before him on the place.

ANCRUM HOUSE
Angelica Gerry
Lake Delaware, Delhi, New York
1925–1948

Steele was working concurrently on his smallest garden, the Allens', and what would be his largest, that for Angelica Gerry. The Gerrys were a prestigious and wealthy political family. Elbridge Gerry, Angelica's great-grandfather, was governor of Massachusetts in 1810 and 1811 and served as vice president of the United States under James Madison. (His creative use of land—termed "gerrymandering"—rivaled Steele's own.) Angelica's brother was Peter Gerry, senator from New York. In 1820 the family purchased a thousand-acre tract of forest, lake, and pastureland in the Catskill Mountains and built a house at the edge of Lake Delaware. A second, enormous family house, also on the property, was finished at the turn of the century.

Shortly after her parents died, Gerry decided to build her own house. In 1925 she hired Cram and Ferguson to design a Georgian mansion and village church. Steele began to work for her that year, almost certainly on Ralph Cram's recommendation. Ancrum House garden would be the most extensive landscape project Steele ever designed, spanning a twenty-three-year period and ultimately requiring over five hundred plans and drawings.

By 1925 Steele's mastery of traditional architectural vocabulary was well established, as was his ability to create powerful volumes of space and to manage relationships between them. The views he created were compelling, his axes sure, his planting schemes lively, and his management of circulation ingenious. Steele was ready to try something new (and would, soon enough) but it would not be through Angelica Gerry's inspiration. She would be a client but not a close friend, a patron but not a partner. Their correspondence would focus largely on questions of finance, rarely on aesthetics.

The Ancrum master plan was on paper by 1928, but references to specific areas as much as two years earlier show that Steele had begun plotting the garden's layout soon after he got the job. Still, the plan was determined in an unusually short period of time and no major changes took place after 1928. Steele's work at Ancrum House during the thirties and forties would be in refining and actualizing what had already been decided.

Shortly after visiting the site for the first time, Steele wrote, "I feel sure you will agree with me that a garden of long shady walks with open sunny areas here and there, and flowers in simple borders, much more as in England than one would see in this country, is going to be the most interesting way the place can be developed and certainly the simplest to be maintained afterward."[75] In general, Steele remained true to his original idea, which provided his client with extensive opportunity for flowers, while the series of outdoor rooms and walks evoked logical and compelling movement through the landscape. The views were spectacular.

Inspiration for the garden's architectural vocabulary came from Elizabethan England, but Steele took cues for the axes, views, and interlocking spaces from the house and the site. Only the Flower Garden, with its geometric patterns and converging walks, borrowed its layout from the seventeenth century. His client provided many of the architectural elements and statuary.

The first two years of work at Lake Delaware were devoted to constructing power and water lines, drives, grades, and

Opposite: Allen estate, allée. Figure by Gaston Lachaise. (SUNY ESF College Archives. Photo by Paul Weber)

Ancrum House. This plan was created after the estate was completed to hang over the fireplace. (SUNY ESF College Archives)

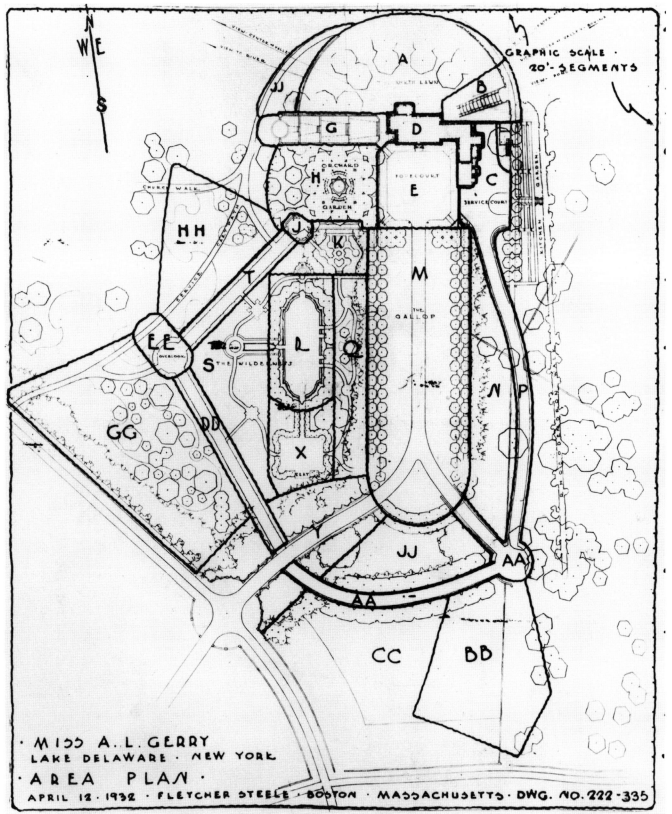

Ancrum House, canton plan, 1932. Features labeled with double letters are informal, such as service drives and cart paths.

A. North Lawn
B. Ramp
C. Service Court
D. House
E. Forecourt
G. West Garden
H. Orchard Garden
J. Octagon
K. Flower Garden
M. Gallop
N. Screen Planting
P. Service Drive
Q. Screen Planting
R. Lilac Garden
S. Wilderness
T. Overlook Walk
X. Drury Seat
Y. Entry Drive
(SUNY ESF College Archives)

Ancrum House, Gallop under construction, with beeches (left), ca. 1929. (SUNY ESF College Archives)

Ancrum House, Gallop. (SUNY ESF College Archives)

completing major planting, in the woodland and on the formal lawn. One of the earliest and most ambitious projects involved tree planting on a massive scale. Steele's plan called for two long, double rows of trees on either side of the Gallop, the drive that led to the front door. Seventy-five beeches, each tree 30 to 45 feet tall, weighing 2 to 4 tons, were dug and balled. (The balls were 6 feet in diameter.) Steele urged his client to buy motorized tractors to move the trees, but she insisted that horsepower would ultimately be less expensive. So Steele had special "steel tree moving machines" constructed at $650 apiece. It took five or six double teams to haul each tree. The same system was employed to plant the big elms on the North Lawn and the apples (transplanted from the neighboring village) in the Orchard.

The labor force was assembled from local men and high school boys. Steele and the superintendent, Thomas Wallis, oversaw the purchase of every piece of equipment used on the job; ropes, wrenches, handsaws, and dozens of other hand tools arrived in quantity. Salary sheets recording hours of workers and foremen were cleared through Steele's office in Boston before going to the client. Steele and Wallis were, in effect, running a construction company and nursery as well as designing a garden.

The location of underground pipes was coordinated with the placement of certain landscape features. The main water tank was located under a ramp dividing the large retaining wall, designed to provide a view to the new pond; in this location the tank would not have to bear weight and would be accessible for repair. As at Rolling Ridge, Steele's early involvement in the project facilitated a systemic approach. The design challenges were complex—utility, comfort, and aesthetics were all to be managed simultaneously. Steele provided the

Ancrum House, ramp and view toward the house. (SUNY ESF College Archives)

customary separation of residential and service areas; a service drive (planted with apples and lilacs) paralleled the Gallop and led to a basecourt on the house's east side.

The house sat atop a hill that Steele shaped to form a curving lawn on its north (rear) side with a retaining wall and balustrade. The curve was emphasized by twelve American elms planted to frame views, five of which were identified by name on Steele's plan. The turfed, stepped ramp emphasized the most important of these, a quote from Powerscourt, in Ireland, an image of which Steele kept in his Gerry file.[76]

In 1927 Gerry bought an old stone seat from Hardwick Hall, Derbyshire, which came to be known as the Drury Seat. The seat would be an important focal point and terminus for the axis of the Lilac Garden. But it also established a design vocabulary—characterized by a peculiar combination of massiveness and delicacy—that influenced the development of architectural detail throughout the garden. Steele found the Elizabethan period amusing but not particularly inspiring: "Ostentation," he later wrote, "was fun in the time of Good Queen Bess, a time when England was nouveau riche and gloried in it. The magnificence of that day delights us, because it was childishly sincere. Montacute and Longleat [in Somerset and Wiltshire] are tinged with adolescent dreams, and we are lenient."[77]

Even within a rigorous historical scheme, Steele mixed influences. His 1935 design for the north lawn balustrade com-

Powerscourt, Ireland. Photograph from Steele's client file. (SUNY ESF College Archives)

Opposite: Ancrum House, view toward the pond. (SUNY ESF College Archives)

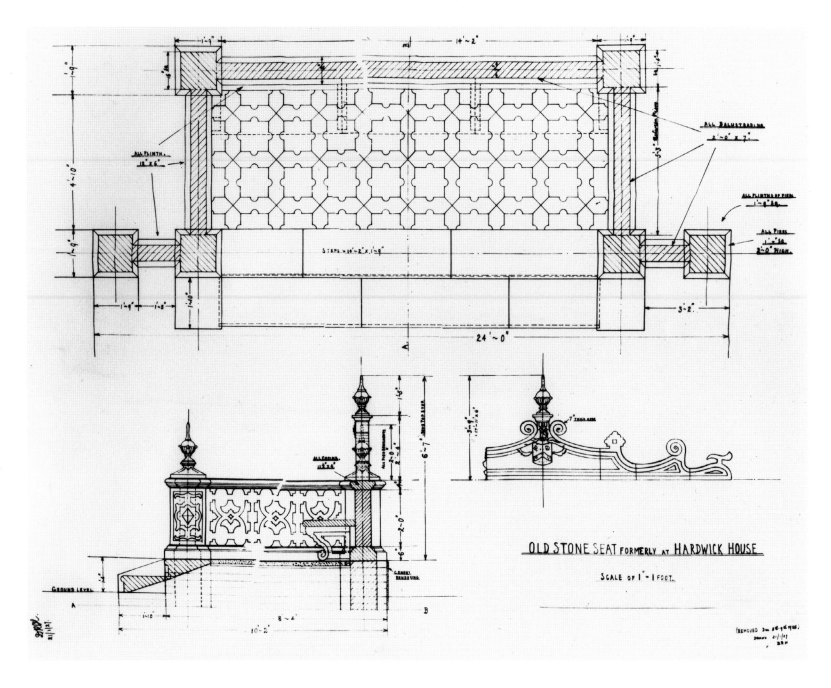

OLD STONE SEAT FORMERLY AT HARDWICK HOUSE

SCALE OF 1" = 1 FOOT.

Ancrum House, Drury Seat, measured drawing, 1927.

bined sources from three different Elizabethan country mansions: the balustrade itself came from Uffington, the pier came from Syon House (by Robert Adam), and the console (inverted in Steele's scheme) was from Wilton House. An image from *Country Life* (June 1934) featuring North Wyman's Park, Hertfordshire, inspired the parapet on the West Garden wall.

Steele's design for the garden's Octagon Seat (1931)—an important axial and transitional feature—quoted almost directly from the architectural detail of the Drury Seat and included stonework seatbacks imported by the owner. In situ, the seat's proportions appeared weak. The finials were too tall and thin,

the surfaces precious. Pale gray stone cast into overly ornate features shrank against the bold mountain setting and strong space. Many of decorative embellishments at Ancrum House (the undistinguished statuary and the ubiquitous flowerpots, particularly) tended to undermine monumentality.

The spatial configurations of the garden were powerful, though, and the plan an intellectual tour de force. Steele's use of diagonals recalled his work at Ethan Allen's estate, but here the diagonal thrust became a prominent theme, played in several variations. Approach was made via a diagonal road, parallel to the garden's most prominent axis to the northwest. The

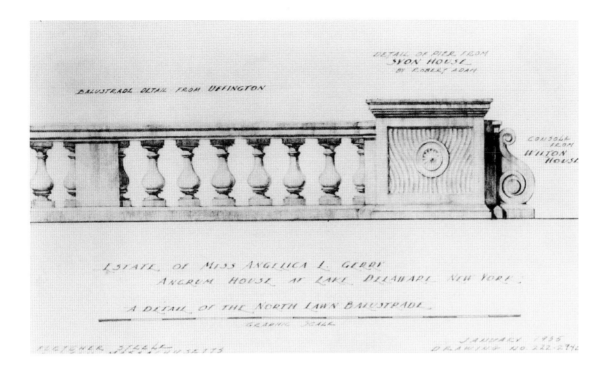

Ancrum House, balustrade, North Lawn. (SUNY ESF College Archives)

Ancrum House, balustrade, North Lawn. (SUNY ESF College Archives)

Ancrum House, retaining wall, North Lawn. (SUNY ESF College Archives)

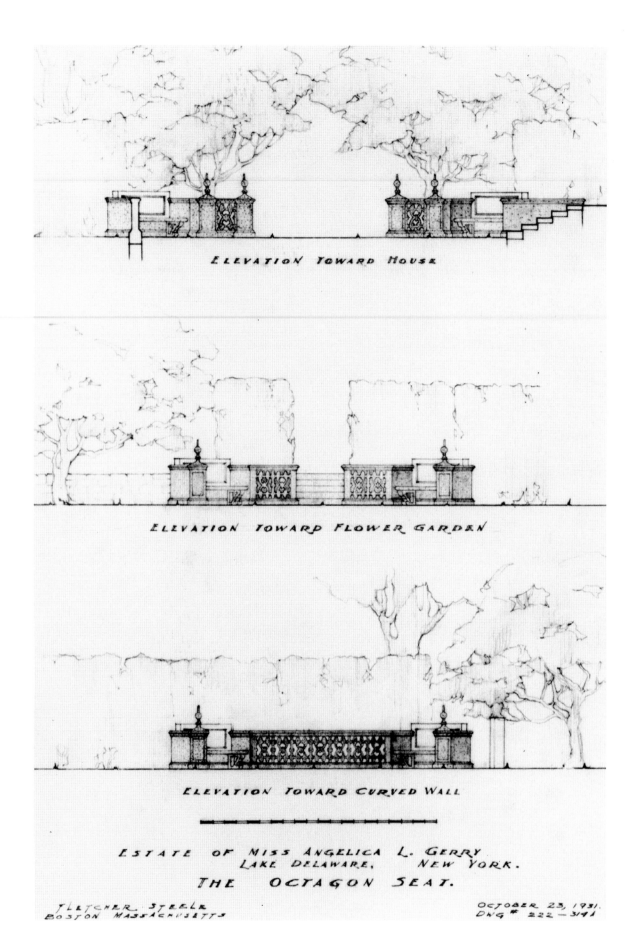

ELEVATION TOWARD HOUSE

ELEVATION TOWARD FLOWER GARDEN

ELEVATION TOWARD CURVED WALL

ESTATE OF MISS ANGELICA L. GERRY.
LAKE DELAWARE, NEW YORK.
THE OCTAGON SEAT.

FLETCHER STEELE
BOSTON MASSACHUSETTS

OCTOBER 23, 1931.
DWG # 222-3141

Ancrum House, Octagon
seat, drawing, 1931. (SUNY
ESF College Archives)

drive, a dark red crushed stone, was Y-shaped, becoming a straight avenue through the formal lawn. A large forecourt (twice the area of the house) gave ample introduction to Cram's distinctive facade.

Entry to the garden from the house came through a west door opening onto a small terrace on the main diagonal axis—the Overlook Walk—visible through the Orchard and the Octagon Seat. The play of diagonals and right angles was repeated in the design of the Flower Garden, a small area south of the Orchard. The lawn terrace's most important view, over the pond, was also a diagonal. It extended (roughly) the Overlook axis on the other side of the house.

The system of interlocking diagonals and grids was announced schematically at the garden's entry. Here, on a small terrace, an elaborate paving pattern graphically introduced the linear play that guided the interior of the plan. Sweeping

curves (of the North Lawn retaining wall, the Overlook, and the Orchard Garden wall) occurred on the perimeter of the garden proper, yielding views of the monumentally quiet landscape beyond.

Hemlock hedges bordered many of the individual garden areas including the Overlook Walk (bordered, in turn, with mountain ash), the Flower Garden, and the West Garden (a forced-perspective feature that prefigured a more spectacular version in Michigan). The Lilac Garden was backed by a hedge of *Syringa vulgaris*; rarer French hybrids grew inside. A small wilderness occupied the triangular area formed by the Lilac Garden and the two arms of the Overlook Walk. A nut orchard was planted to the southwest of the lower arm. Plant lists occupied hundreds of pages.

The pergola, constructed in 1932–33, provided a backdrop for the Flower Garden and a route from the Overlook Walk

Ancrum House, Octagon, through the orchard. (SUNY ESF College Archives)

into the Flower and Lilac Gardens. The stonework piers supported a fountain niche on the north side—the terminus to the Drury Seat axis—visible through the Lilac Garden. The pergola was realized along traditional lines: massive stone supports and delicate, hand-hewn timber poles. Roses grew on the posts; lattice on the back (south) supported annual vines and ivy.

The Flower Garden's geometry was determined by flagstone paving and large beds, in June filled with towering delphinium, the client's specialty. A wellhead and elaborate wrought-iron arch formed the garden's centerpiece. Other features on the 1931 plan of the Flower Garden were a wisteria umbrella, two large clumps of ornamental grass (*Erianthus ravennae*), a birdhouse, and a dog pool. Small beds of annuals surrounded Swedish juniper specimens inside the centermost square.

Gerry had purchased ten lead gargoyles for Ancrum House, possibly as early as 1927, as Steele had noted that "the lead figures sound splendid. They are all exactly in line with the dignity and interest of your place."[78] These were mounted atop pedestals on the curving wall of the Orchard Garden. A seated Diana, also the client's purchase, was placed at the terminus of the West Garden, her presence increased by a tall pedestal. (The drop in grade from house to sculpture site would have made the statue almost invisible from the intended vantage point.) Some of the garden's most dramatic interludes were spatial: for example, the surprise of discovering the Diana looming overhead after descending a spiral staircase in the Orchard Garden.

The prominence of the Drury Seat was also noted in Steele's early letter: "I am much thrilled at getting photographs and drawings of the seat and am making all sorts of studies as

Ancrum House, Octagon, view toward the pergola (under construction). (SUNY ESF College Archives)

Ancrum House, pergola. (SUNY ESF College Archives)

to where you will get the most pleasure out of it when placed in the garden. My first thought was that it certainly should be in the Overlook, from which you get the splendid valley view at the end of the long walk to the house, but there are difficulties here. At any rate it deserves the very best place that we have."[79]

By the following year, Steele had decided to create a special area for the seat deep within the garden. A small turf panel directly before it was surrounded by paving and, in the corners, four little fountains. The view from the little room was to

the fountain niche of the arbor (through the length of the Lilac Garden), about 250 feet distant.

Steele would be a guest at some of Angelica Gerry's house parties, along with other clients of his, some of whom she knew through his introduction. One of the purposes of the society rituals at Ancrum House, and at the other big estates on which Steele worked, was to display the house and the gardens, kept in more or less subtle states of evolution so there was always something new to see. Steele considered most Americans provincial in their search for permanent designs

Ancrum House, staircase with a gargoyle. (SUNY ESF College Archives)

ESTATE OF MISS ANGELICA L. GERRY
ANCRUM HOUSE, LAKE DELAWARE N.Y.

THE OCTAGON

FLETCHER STEELE   JULY 12 1931
BOSTON MASSACHUSETTS   222 · 311

and encouraged his clients to keep changing theirs—advice that often resulted in better gardens, as well as more business. Whatever their design, magnificent houses and gardens were important assets in the never-ending jostle for social position and power.

More than a twinge of indignation must have visited Steele on reading in the *Delaware Republican* that "Mr. Fletcher Steele of Boston, an expert landscape gardener, assisted Miss Gerry in laying out and beautifying her grounds."[80] The tone and wording of the brief article (and others like it, some of which omitted mention of Steele altogether) reflected a widespread attitude that merged design with gardening. While the word "beautify" connoted a narrow purpose to the work, the term "expert" was even more insulting, a direct contradiction of the idea that the landscape architect was an artist. Fletcher Steele, and his more imaginative colleagues, were subject to continual misunderstanding about what they did for a living.

Ancrum House, overlook. The railing was adapted from a grill salvaged from a New York City apartment building. (SUNY ESF College Archives)

FRITH HOUSE
Edith and Peter Gerry
Asheville, North Carolina
1926–1928

A few months after Steele met Angelica Gerry, he was hired by her sister-in-law, Edith Vanderbilt Gerry, to design a garden for Frith House, adjoining Biltmore estate in Asheville, North Carolina. The garden would be less elaborate than the Lake Delaware estate and more compressed, in response both to the climate and to the Spanish architecture of the house.

Steele loved Spanish gardens and borrowed from them often. The geographies of his practice usually made it impossible to pursue the specific indoor-outdoor quality that characterizes the tradition, but Asheville's climate made the choice appropriate. "The Spanish garden is built up of several walled units, each one private and complete. The parts are compactly fitted together in a closely knit pattern like the rooms of an American house and quite unlike our gardens."[81]

Steele's plan relied on walls and tall hedges to define small, sheltered spaces enlivened by tile patterns and fountains. In them any bit of shade or breeze might be enlisted to relieve summer heat, while the walls offered protection from cold winter winds. Indoor and outdoor areas were closely related— the dining room had both a dining and a breakfast terrace so that full advantage could be taken of the garden.

Frith's garden rooms adhered more closely to an axial arrangement than Spanish tradition would dictate. Steele fit the rooms together neatly, and lines of sight begun inside the house continued through separate areas. Regardless of style, he generally approached the problem of relating separate garden areas with the soul of a Frenchman; his commitment to spatial

Opposite: Frith House, forecourt with glorieta. (SUNY ESF College Archives)

Frith House, drawing, elevation of south tank. (SUNY ESF College Archives)

ELEVATION OF SOUTH TANK
SCALE ¼"=1'-0"

ESTATE OF MRS. JAMES G. GERRY

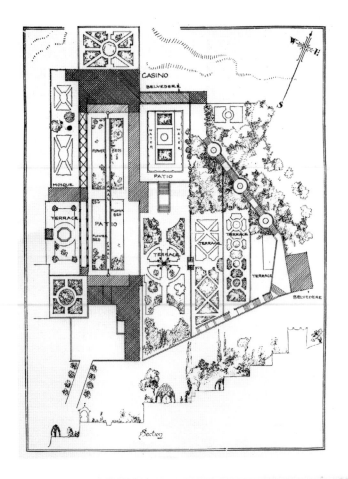

clarity and architectural logic lay deeper than any other aesthetic belief shaping his work. "Although it [the Spanish garden] generally has axes of sorts on which the balance is arranged by hook or by crook, they are never taken very seriously, as they are in France. . . . Where geometry in France would stress a panel or prove a line with urn or statue, such obvious exactions are neglected in Spain. Decoration is set up here and there to build a picture, never to announce that two and two make four."[82]

For the centerpiece of Frith's forecourt garden, Steele covered a small fountain with a *glorieta,* a traditional Spanish arbor made of trained evergreens, usually cyprus or aborvitae. Historically employed as a bower in the center of a garden, Frith's *glorieta* was purely decorative. Steele's largely visual relationship with tradition is epitomized by the new use of an old, once functional form.

Specific inspiration for Frith's design came from Steele's

Generalife, Granada, Spain, plan, similar in graphic style to the plan for Frith House. From Steele's office files. (LC)

Frith House, plan, n.d. (SUNY ESF College Archives)

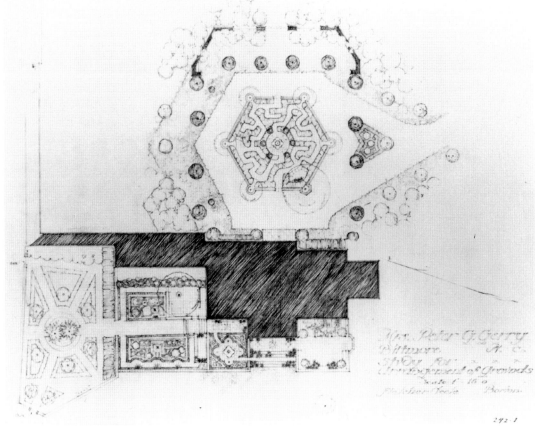

memories of Cordova in 1926: "The little places are far more fascinating than I had ever dreamt of, and quite different. Over and again I was reminded of Pompeii and of the way life was lived in ancient Rome."

RALPH ADAMS CRAM
Sudbury Center, Massachusetts
1926

Cram estate. (SUNY ESF College Archives)

The little patios are quaint out of all reason. From the street one enters by a sort of vestibule with tile floor and walls. The further side has an iron grill or heavy doors which are closed only in the large, single houses. Then there is a rounded arch and beyond, open air again with ever different glimpses of charming detail which, fairly soon, resolve into a fairly simple arrangement in the diagrammatic sense. . . . I don't know when I have seen so much accomplished on a similar area. Potted plants are everywhere. There is not a sprig of grass to be found. There is a wealth of vegetation and yet a simplicity that is rarely found with us. I would like nothing so much as the chance to try for similar results.[83]

No correspondence survives between Steele and Cram on the subject of Cram's garden, but it seems likely that the architect had a hand in its design. The garden reflected strong vernacular influence and respect for the history of the site—an old apple orchard. Steele's photo caption written for the Paris Exhibition of 1930 (where he also showed images of the Towne garden, Allen garden, Grahame Wood's place, the Hopkins Memorial, and others) referred to the "typical American stonework" that defined a system of low terraces. Although photographs show some classical elements, including a sundial, columns, and a pool, the strong, generous design reflects a commitment to working within a traditional, site-responsive framework.

3 · Deeper Dreams, 1926–1935

For the first ten years of his practice, Steele had specialized in eclectic, Beaux Arts–inspired gardens that offered distinguished settings for his clients' homes. His tolerance for repeating design solutions had always been low, and as more were tested, his search for ideas turned more consciously toward art and to his own and his clients' unexplored realms of imagination—their dreams as well as their preferences. He was coming to regard deep and real "private" satisfaction as an important artistic goal for design.

"It does not take the artist in the landscape architect," Steele wrote for a Westport, Connecticut, lecture,

> to figure out the number and sizes of the areas needed by his client. That is at most the problem of the engineer, picture puzzler and compromiser. And to decorate the areas which have been determined by his client and him requires little more than the talents of a nursery planter or at most, commercial artist. Why, then, does the landscape architect consider his work to be a Fine Art, along with sculpture and painting and, indeed in some respects, more exacting than either of those two—more near in human values to that of music to the average man?
>
> The reason is that, on condition that he be a true artist, of course, he strives to bring to other people's lives a suitable inspiration for their contentment, even he hopes their happiness. To reach this sensitive achievement, he must first study the personality of the people for whom the place is to be created. He refuses to be turned out in the front yard like a dog while his client holds him on a leash demanding "What would you do here? Make me a pool under that tree."

Instead he wanders into the house to see what kind of books she reads, what kind of furniture and bric-a-brac she gathers about her. He gets her talking about her travels and the places she likes the best and ones she does not like. He probes to discover, not what she has, but what she dreams of having: not what she does but what she would like to do.

Steele's thoughts then turned to the quintessential purpose of a garden. His words reflect a sharp awareness of the daily routines of women, in particular.

> In other words, he [the landscape architect] is frankly skeptical about the obvious, whether manner of life, possessions or expressed ideas. He knows all too many people whose daily life and daydreams do not correspond. And what he aims at as a sure prop for contentment is to furnish the best available background for the clients' daydreams. He says to himself: "In business, in charity, clubs and family life, this person is tied down in a thousand ways necessary to decent communal life. Those obligations have become habitual until they have come to believe that their real and genuine selves [are] bound up in living for others and with other people considerately. If that were so in fact, they would not be good wives and mothers. They would be nuns. Every human being keeps to the end a personality which is private, with its own private desires and satisfactions often quite unrelated to the every day life they lead, which, indeed, they do not want to change. These unspoken desires and satisfactions come to life in daydreams. Daydreams hurt nobody. Often they help to keep us steady in the whirlpool of

Opposite: Naumkeag, Afternoon Garden. (SUNY ESF College Archives. Photo by Paul Weber)

events which push us on every side. Dreaming enables us to withdraw into ourselves for brief moments and rests us. It is good and if the garden makes it easier and pleasant to dream, then it is a good garden."[1]

Other forces were at work on Steele's artistic development, too. In 1925 he visited the Exposition Internationale des Arts Décoratifs et Industriels Modernes in Paris, where he met J. C. N. Forestier, whose book, *Gardens: A Note-book of Plans and Sketches*, Steele had reviewed a few years earlier. Some visitors to the exposition were disappointed at the lack of modern architecture there—Art Deco dominated the displays—but the garden section better represented the avant-garde, owing largely to the influence of Forestier, who had overseen its installation.

The Garden of Water and Light, designed by Gabriel Guevrekian, featured a rotating, mirrored globe that reflected the spray of the fountain and strong hues of the bedding plants. Steele wrote appreciatively of the three-dimensional sensitivity in Guevrekian's design: "Water in the pools lies at different levels. The beds are not flat, but pyramidal or tilted at various angles, so that the usual loss of interest in a flat pattern in perspective is minimized and a way indicated by which vertical dimensions may play a major part in future garden design." Steele also admired Robert Mallet-Stevens's garden of concrete trees (by the sculptors Jon and Joël Martel), for the "marked vertical elements in his garden beds."[2] Steele soon came to include hand-colored slides of many of these gardens in his public lectures.

Two other aspects of the modern gardens Steele saw in Paris had a strong impact on his gardenmaking. The frankly unsentimental use of plants evident in many of them left a lasting impression: "Horticulture as such is important, not for the love of plants, but for what one can do with them," Steele later observed.[3] He soon began to approach planting design from this more abstract perspective. Steele also admired the manner in which the traditional organizing role of a symmetrical axis had been abandoned by Guevrekian and others. This, too, prompted experimentation in his own work.[4]

From top to bottom:

Exposition Internationale des Arts Décoratifs et Industriels Modernes, *Rapport Général,* vol. 11 (1925).

Garden of Water and Light, by Gabriel Guevrekian, from the Paris Exposition. Hand-colored glass slide in Steele's collection. (SUNY ESF College Archives)

Garden with Concrete Trees, by Robert Mallet-Stevens, sculpture by Jean and Joël Martel, from the Paris Exposition, *Rapport Général,* vol. 11 (1925).

Steele's gardens after 1925 would continue to borrow on historical vocabularies, but color and form would be increasingly bold, and abstract space-shaping would emerge as an important area of exploration. Designs for the next decade would be more idiosyncratic, more vibrant, and ultimately more original than those preceding.

NAUMKEAG
Mabel Choate
Stockbridge, Massachusetts
1926–1929*

In July 1926, Steele lectured to the Lenox, Massachusetts, Garden Club. Steele's reputation was growing and so was his practice—ten major gardens and several small ones were initiated in 1926; his new book was a critical success; his income was substantial and steadily increasing. The European trips had become annual events and important sources of inspiration.

Steele enjoyed the podium, but he also spoke to drum up business. Horticulture was an increasingly popular pursuit, particularly among the wealthy. "Gardening," he had told an audience three years before, "is the fad of the moment. Everybody has a garden. Indeed, more and more people actually go out into their gardens from time to time, even when there is no company to show about. If this habit increases, gardens may in time have charm, which can only come with use."[5] Garden clubs were forming everywhere and Steele was one of the most popular speakers on the circuit, his sharp-edged wit, worldliness, and charm offering a combination that audiences (mostly female) found irresistible.

"I spent that night with the de Gersdorffs who had a dinner for me," Steele wrote his mother on 8 July, "where I sat next to Mrs. Montgomery Sears. She was staying with Miss Mabel Choate, daughter of the late Joseph Choate, who is charming. Mrs. Sears promptly persuaded Miss Choate that night to give me a job."[6] Steele would have been surprised to learn that he had just met the woman who would soon be his best client and one of his best friends.

Mabel Choate was strong-willed and proper but full of fun, with a taste for adventure. She was fifty-six when she met Steele (Steele had just turned forty-one.) Choate read, she collected, she painted, she gardened. She was not afraid to speak her mind. "Experience had taught her that Jacobean settees, modern pianos, Flemish tapestries, oriental rugs and up-to-date French paintings

Mabel Choate in the recently planted arborvitae allée, Naumkeag. (LC. Photographer unknown)

could all be harmonious if well arranged. So she had no fear that Chinese garden ornaments, Gandhara sculpture, ancient English metal tubs and Vermont troglodytical rocks could not be pulled together in her picture."[7]

Joseph Hodges Choate had had a long and illustrious career in law and diplomacy, culminating in a six-year ambassadorship under McKinley to England, during which time the family lived abroad. (While in London, the Choates rented Naumkeag to the Marshall Fields, whose children played baseball in the mansion's spacious front hall.) When the McKinleys came to lunch at Naumkeag in the summer of 1897, Mabel Choate was witness to an unusual event: "The President was affable and attractive, and everybody was in good spirits and all went well—nothing could have been more satisfactory. Suddenly in the middle of lunch the President rose from his chair, walked around the table and in the most dignified

*Steele's work on the garden continued from 1926 to 1958; it is discussed in four phases.

manner placed a napkin over the head of Mrs. McKinley (large napkins were then the fashion) and returned to his seat, saying 'my dear wife is sometimes afflicted with seizures.' The conversation was continued, and after a few minutes or so, Mr. McKinley got up once more, crossed the room and removed the napkin and Mrs. McKinley was herself again. It was all done in such a simple, gentle fashion that the President must have endeared himself to everyone forever."[8]

Joseph Choate successfully prosecuted the Boss Tweed ring, handled many famous antitrust cases, and argued the unconstitutionality of the newly proposed income tax law before the Supreme Court. It was his idea to call the estate "Naumkeag," an Algonquian word meaning "fishing place," and the original name of Salem, Massachusetts, his birthplace. His wry sense of humor—and Yankee practicality—were appreciated by his Stockbridge neighbors. Once, when asked to donate money for the town cemetery fence, he refused on the grounds that "nobody inside can get out, and no one on the outside wants to get in."[9] The family was tested by a series of tragedies.

Mabel's brother Ruluff died suddenly while home on vacation from Harvard, just before the Stockbridge house was built. A second son, George, was diagnosed schizophrenic and, after much soul-searching, sent to live in a sympathetic sanatorium in Boston. Mabel's sister Effie died a few years later at Naumkeag after a long struggle with then-untreatable colitis. Mabel's mother, Carolyn Sterling Choate, was an energetic and dutiful wife though not, apparently, a particularly warm mother. An amateur painter, she wore a ring inscribed "Wedded to Art" until she married Joseph. She insisted on art instruction for her children; these summer lessons gave Mabel a lasting appreciation for fine art.

When the family decided to build a summer home on their cherished Stockbridge hill, "there was no need to choose an architect," remembered Choate, "for Charles McKim was an intimate friend," and plans were soon begun. "Probably at his suggestion the Olmstead [*sic*] Brothers were called in . . . but when they insisted that the house should be located half way down the hill near the oak tree, to this my parents could not

Naumkeag, Lower Garden, design by Nathan Barrett. (LC. Photographer unknown)

agree. So then Nathan Barrett of Boston was summoned and he approved of their favorite spot where they had so often sat and there the house was to be." But McKim soon became engaged, and "with the day of his marriage fast approaching he turned us over to a promising young man in his office, Stanford White."[10]

"From almost the beginning of the building of the house, Mr. White took my mother shopping and they went all over New York and visited every antique decorator and kindred shop." (Mabel Choate's memories of her mother in the role of enlightened patron may have provided a model for her relationship with Fletcher Steele.) "If my mother ever became impatient and thought the house was not getting on fast enough Mr. White would say 'Why Mrs. Choate, you don't weep and tear your hair enough—that is the way people get things done."[11] From all the evidence, Mabel Choate never wept or tore her hair at Steele, though she probably had cause to.

The house was demure when compared with scores of other estates under construction throughout "the inland Newport."[12]

The forty-four-room, shingle-style mansion was designed for gracious comfort, in contrast to the prestigious formality reflected in the Italian palazzi and Stuart manors nearby. The massive structure was broken into bays, turrets, gables, niches, and porte cochère. The forms counterbalanced one another while playfully recalling historical prototypes. Strong horizontal emphases related the house to the mountain setting. Naumkeag was soon furnished with treasures from family travels, an idiosyncratic mix of the exotic and fine.

The sloping, forty-nine-acre site "was a pasture with close clipped grass and occasional boulders scattered about and bare of trees except for one large oak and a few thorn-apple trees," according to Mabel Choate.[13] Barrett must have been inspired nonetheless, for the garden he created was beautiful. "He had vision at a time when most landscape designers merely fumbled," Steele would later write appreciatively of his predecessor's work at Naumkeag.[14] Even so, Barrett's vocabulary left the younger members of the family mystified. Mabel Choate later wrote that he "confused us children by talking of the 'features' of the place—we having always thought the word meant noses, chins, etc. and were astonished, but we soon learned and 'features' became one of our best family words."[15]

Two large flower gardens sat on terraces to the north of the house, "each shield shaped and divided into sections by graveled paths. The corner one was very Victorian with beds of geranium, heliotrope, etc. with a long formal path just above it running from the [north] end of the property to the house and bordered with evergreens."[16] After a family trip to Germany a few years after the house was built, a linden walk was planted near the south end of the property. Athletic fields, a summerhouse, a large greenhouse (to supply the Choates' New York City house with year-round flowers and vegetables), an orchard, barns, and pasture were maintained by a large staff.

"Every moment of the building of the house and the laying out of the grounds was watched with excitement by the family and with curiosity by everyone in town. I suspect that my father's old partner, Mr. Southmayd was voicing public opinion when he asked, 'What all the gimcracks were for' and said that 'his women folks would be the ruin of him yet.'"[17] Scarcely any changes took place after the initial flurry of construction. Mr. Choate died in 1917; Mabel's mother, ill for the last years of her life, died in 1929.

As Choate and Steele toured her gardens the day following his Lenox Garden Club lecture, she explained her wish for a pleasant place to sit close to the house. She had seen outdoor rooms in California and wanted one too. The job was beginning just the way so many had.

"Together [Miss Choate and I] agreed that the bones of what had been first done were good and should not only be preserved where possible but that the old spirit should be followed in all that was to come. The 'feeling' of Victorian elaboration must be continued. Design should be clarified and modern ideas of fitness inaugurated. . . . Nothing must look 'up-to-date.'"[18] With this general guideline in place, design for the outdoor room began—but not before Steele had designed a new service courtyard. "I couldn't possibly work for anyone whose back door looks like that," Steele said as they walked toward the house for the first time.[19] "Looking at it with new eyes," Choate later wrote, "I saw that he was right. It was dreadful."[20] So Steele planned a new service court that would be screened from the front drive. His lack of protocol seems not to have offended his new client, and perhaps she was stirred by his candor. By 1926 she seemed eager to assume ownership of Naumkeag, having been a dutiful daughter for half a century.

The only suitable location for an outdoor room, Steele reasoned, was the south end of the house, adjacent to the library,

where it would receive afternoon sun. A wall would be constructed to define the second (east) side and provide privacy from the drive. "Shall we include the big elm or keep it outside the wall?" wrote Steele. "A tree behind a wall, rising and stretching out huge branches, would hold our garden in eternal embrace. An agreeable gesture. . . . It's not unpleasant to have the fine 3' tree trunk an ornament inside the garden. For one thing, as soon as the wall is finished, it will seem as old and inevitable as the tree. That's a way that trees have. They make their environment look as old as they are themselves."[21]

How best, then, to establish the remaining walls to create an enclosed space without obscuring the fine mountain view? Recalling the happy blend of containment and openness within a colonnade, Steele solved the problem by using columns to build the two remaining sides of the room. Not only would columns not obscure the view, they would frame it. "Now it happens that south and west open onto a serene vista of valley and distant mountains. Since the breadth of view is better controlled from the west house terrace, there will be no harm in cutting this panorama into sections by planting or posts. It must not be forgotten nor obliterated, however, nor should the fine silhouetted skyline be nullified by a strong horizontal band such as a flat vine roof would be."[22]

Old oak pilings recently dredged from Boston Harbor were purchased. Archangelo Cascieri was hired as the firm's sculptor that year and instructed to carve the posts in a "Norwegian" style "because woodcarving in Norway is always bold yet not without elegance," Steele wrote. "Their shape must be good yet a touch of nonsense would do no harm. Why not put Venetian gondola posts, rising out of the sea, up on the top of a hill? Why not follow the color of medieval trappings seen in medieval manuscripts which are both strong and gay?"[23] Heavy ropes were festooned between the posts to provide support for woodbine and clematis. An early drawing, by Butler S. Sturtevant, Steele's office manager and chief designer from 1926 to 1927, shows an elevation of the room with the vines and the pots with which Steele anticipated edging it. It also shows the location of the sculpture, Frederick MacMonnies's *Boy with Heron*, which would determine the dimension of the new garden.[24]

MacMonnies was one of a group of young sculptors specializing in garden sculpture and a favorite of Stanford White, who recommended him to the Choates to fill a niche at the front of the house. Steele admired the work, later writing of "its handsome agitated silhouette and finely shaped lights and shadows."[25] But, he argued, the sculpture could hardly be seen where it was. Mable Choate agreed to moving it to a site where

Naumkeag, Afternooon Garden entry. (SUNY ESF College Archives. Photo by Paul Weber)

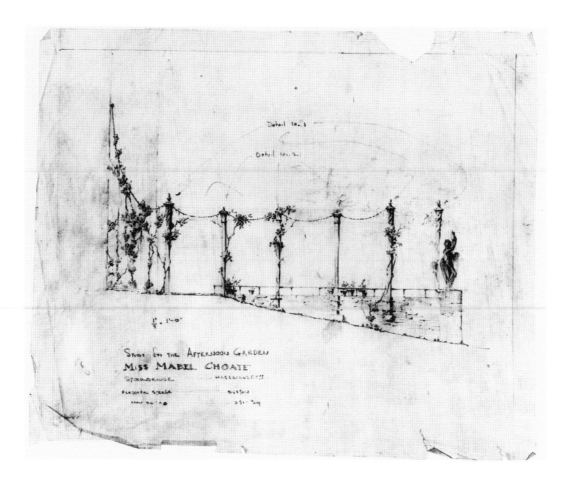

Naumkeag, Afternoon Garden, sketch by Butler Sturtevant. (SUNY ESF College Archives)

it could provide a focal point for the new room. Steele first imagined placing the sculpture in the middle of the new garden, but there it would spoil the "well-shaped volume of air" he so valued. He then asked a local boy to step in for the bronze and moved him about on a ladder (to represent the pedestal), until a spot was found where the sculpture might be admired from all angles.

Quick, drive in a stake. There's the right place for the statue! But it's not in line with anything. Put the spot on our survey. The centre is 18" from the projected west line of the house. Just enough to allow for flapping wings. There's the third line of our garden—and the fourth. Let's put him on the corner, by all means. The garden traverse is closed . . . 45' in length away from the house. 35' wide. After all, there was no Fine Art in that. Just common sense and Mr. Crighton with his step ladder plus a statue, green trees and the sky. . . .

Next, we must plan for shade. The big elm in the southeast corner throws long shadows across the area until noon, blazing sunlight then until nearly dinner time these daylight-saving June days. Shall we cover the whole area with a vine roof? That might be done in Italy or Spain, and would be pleasant on hot days. But a bit gloomy to look out on in the rain. And what of the night sky stars and moonlight? They're

the ideal roof. Vine covering part of the garden? Why not. Next the house, certainly to keep the sun out of the windows without need of awnings or shutters. A roof wide enough to count. We put up experimental boards, and find that 11 feet will be neither too narrow nor too wide. Along the wall, where it is hottest, will be another roof. . . .

Then [we] paused to lounge in our imaginary garden. Dark brick and stone walls: brown floor: heavy shade from vines and trees: posts and statue colorful but dark in tone: rich red purple beech crossing our vision away from the house: dark green banks of foliage beyond. All rather dark. Only the dipping, changing sky for gaiety and cheeriness. We check off the means of raising the color values and enlivening our garden room. We can bring the sky to our feet in a mirror. We can use plants with silver foliage and bright flowers: we can paint the furniture as we please. Lastly and best we can bring merry jets of water, the more the better. . . .

The garden room must have a giddy carpet. To please both eye and ear, four little fountains, memories of the Generalife, were set to start a pattern.

The "carpet" pattern was elaborated by a French knot design defined by an edging of box. First blue *Lobelia erinus* (the color

Naumkeag, Afternoon Garden. "Potted plants, chairs and tables give it a livable look, and one can sit there with a friend, and talk. Or alone, and dream. and never have a sensation of loneliness, or feel that it is necessary to find something to do." Mabel Choate, *Garden Club of America Bulletin* (July 1939). (SUNY ESF College Archives. Photo by Paul Weber)

Naumkeag, Afternoon Garden, ca. 1930. (SUNY ESF College Archives. Photo by Paul Weber)

of the alternate high posts), yellow *Calceolaria* (later, *Santolina chamaecyparissus*), and pink crushed marble filled the knot. "Without thinking we planned these beds of necessary dirt to be level with our flagstone," Steele wrote. "In fancy, subconsciously almost, I felt myself stumbling over them as over a rug that is wrinkled. What more natural than to continue the analogy: Why not have a rug that is flat? Why not sink the beds so that the top of the flowers is level with the flagging? It worked out very well."[26]

In time, the lobelia was mulched with coal, Steele's answer to Choate's observation that the plants seemed to be suffering from the heat.[27] The lobelia prospered but, in time, was eliminated altogether because the shiny coal mosaic was more attractive to Choate's eye than the plants. A shallow, black-glass "Claude Lorraine" pool in the center reflected the sky. "The eye is sufficiently satisfied and the contemptuous horticulturist can look away to dozens of pots of fuchsias, yellow callas, agapanthus, and bamboo," Steele wrote.[28]

A bed in the corner contained ferns and Turk's-cap lilies, "native plants which are encouraged to go their own way within reasonable bounds, [giving] the impression that nature is content."[29] *Arenaria* grew like green velvet between the brown flagstones, chosen over formal paving to suggest country rusticity. Water dripped into an old lead cistern. Red-purple, blue, and white clematis and Virginia creeper climbed the Venetian posts and the rope garlands strung between them. Ironwork pot holders inspired by memories of Seville provided space for still more flowers. Choate's collection of fuchsia expanded and thirty varieties filled the bench-back holders.

Ironwork chairs inspired by Pompeii were purchased and meticulously painted, and yellow tile tables made to catch the brilliant hues of *Calceolaria*. Roman "thrones" and matching footstools were constructed of pink concrete according to Steele's design. Choate was a large woman, and after thirty years of sitting in these chairs she once remarked to him how horribly uncomfortable they were. "But Mabel," he replied, "you're not supposed to sit in them, you are supposed to look at them."[30] Originally named the "Temple Garden" by a facetious workman who "thought it must resemble King Solomon's," the outdoor room was renamed the Afternoon Garden to avoid confusion when the Chinese Temple Garden was constructed years later.[31]

The design drew on eclectic landscape traditions from Italy, France, and Spain, responding to Choate's taste for sumptuous, even contradictory textures and faraway places. Steele later wrote, "Should the gardener follow the game of styles? By all means that depends on personal taste. On condition that the general design is good, the details interesting, that the

natural landscape setting receives due homage, and that one goes ahead wholeheartedly, then the style can follow any sympathetic lead. These general limitations hold one in fairly sharply, however. The end of sympathetically following the landscape setting in itself is severe."[32] Steele felt a special concern to pay "due homage" to the natural landscape when the view had such character as this.

The Afternoon Garden was the first of many developments at Naumkeag that stretched over the next thirty years. Decades later Steele wrote: "To me its real interest lies in the fact that it shows a place which was developed, one thing from another, with only a vague overall scheme in mind in the first place.

Naumkeag, Afternoon Garden, view from the library, ca. 1930. (SUNY ESF College Archives. Photo by Paul Weber)

Naumkeag, Afternoon Garden, bird's-eye view, by Henry Hoover, 1930. Steele exhibited this drawing in Paris in 1930. (SUNY ESF College Archives)

Growth of this sort has a sort of life of its own that never comes when everything is planned in the beginning."³³

Steele included a model of the Afternoon Garden in an exhibition held at the Louvre in 1930. He commissioned, in his words, "the best model maker in the country" to create the 3-foot replica, which included "exact reproductions of the carved and painted posts, the elm tree and in fact . . . all the details of the garden." He searched for a painter to create a panoramic sweep of the Berkshires to form the backdrop. "Then I would put a ground glass over the top through which the light would come, and so fixed that everybody would have to look at it through holes pierced in the sides. In this way one would get a normal aspect rather than an exaggerated bird's eye view from which most models ordinarily suffer."³⁴ No photos of the ingenious model have been found.

Henry Hoover and the Office

Some share of the success of the Afternoon Garden and others that followed in quick succession (for Naumkeag and elsewhere) should be credited to Henry Hoover, Steele's "hand" for fourteen years. Hoover began working for Steele part-time in 1925 while still an architecture student at Harvard, and when he returned from a two-year travel fellowship in Europe in 1929, he joined the office full-time. It was then that Steele fully defined the role of the drawings in the practice. They would show clients the intended character of their gardens.³⁵

Steele once wrote: "In works of art . . . in homes and gardens, we want significance—character—underneath the pattern, something deeper than surface eye attraction to pull on our minds and our sentiments. Without the help of pattern, to be sure, the inner revelation is obscured. Character and meaning alone cannot make a work of art. Pattern alone is not enough. Both must be present and they must fuse."[36]

The scope, quality, and quantity of Hoover's drawings were notable even for the period and, according to Hoover, they marked a change in Steele's office procedures. They were accurate enough that the general draftsmen could reliably use them as bases for their working drawings. Best of all for Steele's business, the pencil sketches were also compelling. Thanks to Hoover, clients could hear water splashing in unbuilt fountains, smell roses on imaginary trellises. Hoover's skills more than compensated for Steele's shortcomings as a draftsman.

According to Hoover, Steele ran his office with a firm, even compulsive hand. Pencils were sharpened every evening before closing, books returned to shelves, half-finished drawings piled out of sight. All ran according to plan—Steele's plan. Hoover occupied his own tiny cubby well apart from the general working area where the other draftsmen (usually one or two) drew alongside those working for architect Charles ("Chud") Loring. Although Steele and Loring shared the office at 7 Water Street for close to twenty years, they worked together only once, on the Camden Library project. Still, it was a congenial arrangement. Hoover remembered that the single tension between the two staffs centered on the humidifier. Steele turned it on every time he passed through the drafting room to his office; Mr. Blair, Loring's chief draftsman, turned it off as soon as Steele was gone. No one ever said a word about the ongoing struggle.

Steele's office was elegant. A glass screen from Paris covered the window's drab view onto Water Street. A broad, three-inch slab of black marble formed his desk, which was always meticulously neat when visitors arrived. The filing cabinets were constructed of stainless steel and bronze, the bookshelves filled with fine old volumes. Steele relied heavily on his library when initiating a new design with Hoover, pointing out specific images to be adapted for use in the new schemes.

George Campbell was Steele's general manager between 1925 and 1935. Campbell oversaw the operation of the office and acted as superintendent on important jobs, such as Ancrum House. Once he traveled to Europe with Steele, which, according to Hoover, raised subtle questions in the office about the nature of their relationship. The staff, including Hoover, knew little about Steele's private life but were well aware of his intimate and usually flirtatious involvements with many female clients. Secretaries were often asked to make dinner reservations or order flowers for women friends.

Virginia Cavendish, Steele's plant specialist during the pe-

riod, had one assistant to help with quantities of plant orders. Cavendish communicated directly with local nurseries and landscape contractors about orders, made planting plans, and kept in contact with owners. Steele stepped into some of these roles with important clients, but he was often unable to satisfy the demands for contact. His near annual trips to Europe, often undertaken spontaneously, provided relief from the tension that his intense working style generated.

Each new job began the same way: with a visit to the site, "black bag" in hand.[37] Steele sensed the theatrical potential of these meetings and took advantage of it, plotting his presentations carefully. Hoover was charged with the responsibility of folding plans so that the newly designed areas could be presented to clients in proper sequence. Secretaries were to keep the camera loaded and supplies in order, and Steele's standards were exacting. Hoover reported that they "lasted between two hours and two months. They cried a lot."[38]

Steele's behavior was based on an aristocratic view of station and an unforgiving, tyrannical perfectionism. He was regularly curt with servants, waiters, and field workers, and when his standards were not met, he became aggressively rude. With senior members of his office staff, respected colleagues, and clients, he was unfailingly cordial. Hoover remembers only one blowup during the fourteen years they worked together. "Mr. Steele wanted me to spend some time in the south, overseeing an important job, immediately after my wife had our first baby and, of course, I refused. He was furious but I wouldn't go. Finally he just dropped it, without really understanding why I wouldn't do what he wanted me to."[39]

Steele's black bag, with compass, measures, grading stakes, string, camera, film, and notepads. (SUNY ESF College Archives)

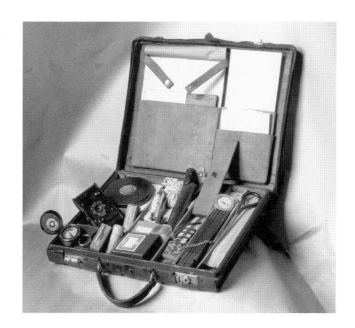

Initially, Steele gave Hoover specific instructions for his drawings, based on images from the library. But the architect proved a good designer as well as draftsman, and Steele soon looked to him for new ideas based on more general suggestions. The thirties—Steele's "primitive period" in Hoover's view—were characterized by a spirit of experiment and a gradual abandonment of historical precedent. The process became more extemporaneous, with more decisions made on-site. Steele placed few time restrictions on his chief draftsman. Clients, who were expected to foot the bills, seemed willing enough to comply.

Mission House, door-yard garden with a mix of herbs, flowers, and shrubs. (SUNY ESF College Archives)

MISSION HOUSE
Mabel Choate
Stockbridge, Massachusetts
1926–1932

Shortly after Mabel Choate and Steele began working on the Afternoon Garden, they began restoring the Mission House, Stockbridge's oldest building. The collaborative project drew on their shared passions for American history, architecture, antiques, interior design, and gardens. The house museum and grounds were to be a memorial to Choate's parents, of whom

she wrote in the dedicatory plaque: "The character and fortitude of the early settlers lived again in them."

Steele supervised the relocation of the building and designed a new setting for it on Main Street, just down the hill from Naumkeag. He also advised on preservation and interior decoration. The furnishings would be authentic to the period, and more: at Steele's insistence they were to be without even "a hint of restoration"[40] and within the specific character of the house. The latter consideration was exactly the same guideline Steele used in "furnishing" a garden.

Steele often criticized contemporary American culture, but he admired colonial design, "the dignity and simple beauty of the past." He based the designs of his parents' gravestones on those of John and Lucinda Adams and modeled his reading glasses after those in a portrait by John Singleton Copley in the Boston Museum of Fine Arts. Steele's photo albums contain dozens of pictures of seventeenth- and eighteenth-century buildings he encountered on the road between jobs, elements of which were often incorporated into current landscape projects. He wrote on the subject of colonial gardens many times. Despite Steele's concern about the authenticity of the Mission House interior, however, he designed the outbuildings and gardens "for general effect only."[41] In his own field, Steele's delight in invention ran deeper than the impulse to truth.

Steele was adamant about paint, though. Inside and out, it was to be authentic to the period, and so was the egg tempera base. Henry Hoover was sent to Stockbridge to supervise the mixing of the paint in fifty-gallon drums. (It had been concocted from hundreds of dozens of old eggs bought at discount from local farmers.) Paris green, brick dust, ashes, and iron oxide were used to tint the base. Almost immediately after the paint was applied, swarms of flies arrived, attracted by the stench, and became stuck to the tacky surface. The project had to begin all over again.[42]

"There is a subtle quality that pervades the homes and gardens of the colonial period that we should be able to catch and transpose to our own use," wrote Steele. He particularly admired Washington's Mount Vernon as a model colonial garden and had some of its qualities in mind when designing the Mission House setting. He praised the usefulness of colonial garden plans. "Neat rows of vegetables, bush fruits, and fruit trees, when prettily arranged and edged with flowers, are capable of giving strong esthetic satisfaction to the seeing eye." He thought the yard especially evocative: "Wood chopping in one corner, sun-cooking preserves in another, linen bleaching in the middle, churning under a grape arbor at one side,—a hundred forms of industry were carried on here. . . . Our Colonial

Mission House, grape arbor. (SUNY ESF College Archives. Photo by Paul Weber)

forebears knew that use and beauty can and do go hand in hand."[43]

The "old fashioned garden" of the Mission House, Steele wrote, had "its straight walk lined with fruit trees and flower borders, its vegetable plots, bush fruits, and casual rose bushes and beds of striped grass."[44] The dooryard garden there recalled the one Steele had done for the John Ellsworths' garden in Simsbury, Connecticut, where decorative brickwork was interplanted with ornamental herbs and flowers.

Steele also endorsed the economy of land use and ease of maintenance in colonial gardens. Compact, neatly joined

Mission House, front
gate. (SUNY ESF College
Archives)

flower gardens were traditionally located near the house where water was available. All land was put to good use. "Too often one sees some land back of the garage or beside the house or between garden and property line which is, strictly speaking, neither part of lawn or garden nor put to any definite use. This is wasteful.... People who live in their gardens must be able to retire in them as to the walled-in rooms of a house. Many of us in these democratic times have forgotten this fact which was obvious to George Washington."[45]

In *Design in the Little Garden*, published two years before he began the Mission House project, Steele had argued passionately for privacy in all kinds of gardens, urging readers to be guided by colonial gardenmakers, who "put their houses close to the street, largely to avoid the stupid and needless care we put on our uninteresting front yards today."[46] At the Mission House he designed small outbuildings to provide an enclosed yard, bounded on the fourth side by a fence.

Steele also praised the common sense of colonial gardenmakers like Washington who laid out simple geometric beds but "adjusted their forms gracefully to existing objects: used them as opportunities to create changes and varieties in designs that otherwise might have been too prim." His advice to contemporary homeowners was "if the garage gets in the way, yield the design to the inevitable. Get around as best one can, and then go on again. Instead of unsightliness, the result is fairly sure of having unexpected charm."[47]

By 1932 the work was largely done. "So was the old house brought to life again after a long sleep."[48]

Mission House, yard and barn. (SUNY ESF College Archives. Photo by Paul Weber)

Camden, Maine
1929–1941

In 1928 Mary (Mrs. Edward) Bok hired Steele to design a landscape for the new Camden Library. Steele had been recommended for the job by Charles Loring, who was the architect for the building, an elegant brick colonial structure. "Little did they know," remembers Loring's daughter, Alice Pickman, "that the garden would end up costing more than the library."[49]

Mary Bok was a patron of the arts both in Philadelphia (where her father had founded the Curtis Institute of Music) and in the coastal village of Camden, where the family summered. In 1928 Mrs. Bok presented the town selectmen with a large parcel of land on the corner of Main Street and Atlantic Avenue, one of several belonging to the family. "All she insisted on," remembered Steele, "was that the library grounds should be designed to serve in the broadest way all activities suitable to a town library. . . . It was this last remark that led me to designing a garden theatre. Of this she heartily approved."[50] Hoover

remembers some conflict between patron and artist over the specifics of the design. Mrs. Bok wanted something more "delicate," perhaps more "French," than the bold rock treatment Steele proposed. He refused to compromise, and eventually she gave in.[51]

The wooded site for the garden was sharply sloped: "Behind the building the land was more than a story lower than in front. The basement was used for bookstacks which needed light. And any door above would open on midair, thus calling for a high staircase. Now it also happened that there was a favorite statue which must be located. Whatever was done would be conspicuous from the theatre below. The only solution seemed to be a double staircase set out from the wall (thus letting in light between steps and windows), and curving out around the statue which could then have its own semi-isolated garden."[52]

Design for the amphitheater responded to the local environment both in its layout and in its plantings. The small brick library faced squarely onto Main Street, but rather than orient the amphitheater on axis with the building, Steele laid out the curve of tiered seats in relation to the harbor across Atlantic

Camden Library
Amphitheater under
construction, ca. 1930.
(SUNY ESF College
Archives)

Camden Library Amphitheater, view to the harbor. (SUNY ESF College Archives. Photo by Paul Weber)

Avenue so that the apex of the horseshoe-shaped depression sat about 45 degrees clockwise from the axis of the library. With this arrangement any production on the stage would have the harbor as backdrop. The theater bowl could be entered from the library's back door via a flight of steps and this stairway was matched by another across the theater that led to a path and playing field. Steele constructed a model of the library and landscape to work out the unusual bent axis and resulting spatial relationships.

His scheme (still in the planning stage) met with disapproval from Frederick Law Olmsted Jr., who was concurrently designing Harbor Park across Atlantic Avenue, also under the patronage of Mary Bok. "I am strongly inclined to think," Olmsted wrote in a report, "that the best axis for the theatre unit is not at right angles with Atlantic Avenue, as shown on Mr. Steele's first rough study, but (roughly speaking) about 15 degrees to the eastward." Olmsted thought that the orientation of the garden should "be made normal to the axis of the build-ing, establishing a pleasant and simple relationship which is very desirable."[53] Olmsted's concern with a more "normal" and "simple" design relationship sheds light on how iconoclastic Steele's approach had become.

Mary Bok, however, overruled Olmsted's suggestion and permitted Steele's design to develop according to his first ideas. (Steele actually seems to have rotated the axis even farther in the opposite direction from Olmsted's recommendation.) About three weeks later, he came forward with a criticism of Olmsted's scheme across the street. "My only real difference of opinion with Mr. Olmsted is my desire to keep the hillock across Atlantic Avenue southwest of the Library much as it is, rather than to cut it down as he suggested. I like its quaint picturesque quality and outline, and find it useful in framing the harbor view which lies farther south, as seen from the Library. I should miss the enframement if it were removed."[54] In fact, the grade was overly steep for a park, but nearly everyone attending a meeting in July 1929 agreed with Steele, including

Olmsted's own representative, Mr. Zach. Mrs. Bok, who was "on the fence," according to Zach, suggested that Olmsted meet Steele on the grounds to hear Steele's viewpoint and "to review the situation personally."[55] The hill was not regraded.

Steele limited plants for the garden theater to those which grew "within five miles of town."[56] With a keen sensitivity to abstract visual possibilities, he arranged maple, spruce, and white birch to soften and accent the curving ledges of rock. Large existing elms evident in construction photographs of the site provided structural anchors for the terraces. The birches were a spectacular choice. Their white trunks stood in sharp contrast to the soft green of the turf and surrounding hemlock forest, providing vertical rhythm to offset the strong horizontal curves of the tiered stone ledges. Steele would incorporate birch often into his gardens, always with great visual impact.

Steele's use of plants for their abstract, decorative qualities began to evolve after 1925, largely as a result of new ideas he had encountered at the Paris exposition. The Camden scheme (circa 1930) represents one of the first instances of bold plantings intended for specific architectural and decorative impact. The four- or five-year lag between Steele's first seeing the new style and his finally making real use of it was likely a lack of opportunity. Naumkeag's Afternoon Garden afforded no real chance for modern planting, although the parterre scheme was certainly abstract. Subsequent clients—Edith Clifford, John Ellsworth, and Angelica Gerry—were heirs to what Steele identified as the "romantic Victorian tradition, which encouraged what one might call a compulsory love of nature—and this nature of a variety seen through the eyes of a limited number of artists. Corot and the Barbizon school among painters, Frederick Law Olmsted and Charles Eliot among landscape architects, not to prolong the list, were enormously influential in forming the definite traditions of the leisure class."[57]

Although he, too, identified their work as modern, Steele

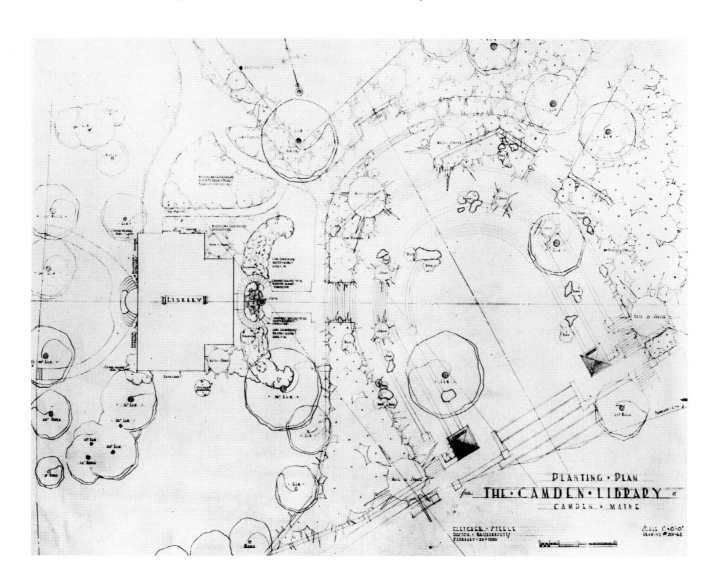

Camden Library Amphitheater, planting plan, 1930. Axial relationship between the library and the theater is "bent." (SUNY ESF College Archives)

Camden Library Amphitheater. (SUNY ESF College Archives. Photo by Paul Weber)

thought that the group of French practitioners who showed in the Paris exhibit actually continued a centuries-old French tradition. "In certain ways the French are in a good position to see materials impersonally and clearly. For French landscape architects appear to have had but little real affection for horticulture at any time. . . . A tree to them is not good in itself, but for what can be done with it, as with brick or a thousand gallons of water."[58] Later Steele wrote, "If [the landscape architect] be a true artist, he will never let his love of flowers persuade him to make a colored border where his overall picture would be better off with a bed of pachysandra."[59] The birches at Camden trade on a Victorian view of nature at the same time that they strike unforgettable white silhouettes. The two purposes enhance rather than detract from each other. Large Camperdown elms that framed matching ticket pavilions on Atlantic Avenue struck a more exotic note. The small brick structures and

wrought-iron arches recalled Steele's design for the Williams College Hopkins Memorial (1925), which had, in turn, been adapted from English prototypes.

Large rocks were incorporated into the terraces to relieve the rigidity of the regular curves as well as to evoke the nearby presence of dramatic coastal ledges, serving both formal and poetic ends. Henry Rice, Steele's rock expert, constructed convincing geological forms. Teams of horses hauled in the enormous stones and trees at great expense.

Keen on historical meaning as well as style, Steele designed tripod lights for the outdoor theater. (A popular decorative accessory during classical revivals in the eighteenth and nineteenth centuries, the tripod saw duty as sewing basket and washstand, table and lamp.) Steele's tripods not only evoked the splendor of past civilization but also helped establish a human scale and presence. They offered an unexpected counter-

Camden Library
Amphitheater, view to
the library. (SUNY ESF
College Archives. Photo
by Paul Weber)

point to the big, lichen-covered boulders and millstones that provided bases for them.

Although it was open to the public, the Camden project very much resembled Steele's typical private garden. The pull between the land, function, and a repertory of distinguished architectural forms had led to a fresh vision. The harbor provided a wonderful view and an inspired backdrop for theater productions. The gentle stir of marine activity was a pageant in its own right.

In 1942, a decade after the theater was completed, Mrs. Bok approached Steele about designing an orchestra shell for the theater. He responded by combining what he called "a niche suggested by the work of Robert Adam and a couple of Piscataqua porches!"[60] The handsome design would have enhanced an already spectacular place, but the onset of World War II prevented its realization.

NAUMKEAG
Mabel Choate
Stockbridge, Massachusetts
1929–1935

With the completion of the Afternoon Garden, Mabel Choate and her guests (Fletcher Steele now among them) had a place to sit, but their view had disappeared. The silhouette of Bear Mountain, once visible from the library windows, was being consumed by a clump of trees planted by Choate's mother many years before. By 1929 Steele's interest in relating foreground to background had emerged as a primary aesthetic goal. And, as his relationship with Mabel Choate grew, so did the opportunity to experiment.

"A major operation was called for. An army of tree men was trucked in and telephone communication established from garden to woods. Strong field glasses were glued to the eyes which directed the cutting from the garden. The curve of Bear Mountain was repeated by topping the wood to a similarly curved line. Sometimes twenty feet had to be sawed off the trees. Thus the strongest design line furnished by Nature was brought back and made the major motive of the future landscape design."[61]

Steele worked at Naumkeag through the thirties. The house terrace was enlarged according to plans begun in 1931. An earlier proposal for a circular pattern of paving stones was never realized. Two thirty-foot elms were brought in to shade the west-facing terrace. A clump of trees, including *Magnolia*

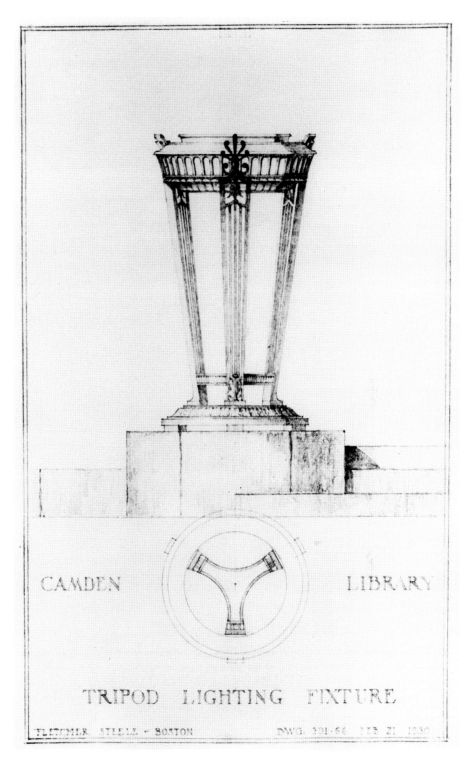

Camden Library Amphitheater, tripod detail, 1930. The final design was different from this one. (SUNY ESF College Archives)

Naumkeag, terrace construction, early 1930s. (SUNY ESF College Archives)

ESTATE OF MISS MABEL CHOATE
NAUMKEAG STOCKBRIDGE MASSACHUSETTS
THE PERUGINO VIEW

FLETCHER STEELE
BOSTON MASSACHUSETTS

NOVEMBER 1931
DRAWING NO #251 91A

tripetala and buckthorn, were planted at the southern end. The pale, warm leaves of the near-tropical magnolia contrasted with the delicate silver tracery of the buckthorn. A luminous Russian olive at the terrace corner was visible even from the distant end of the big South Lawn. The "Great Seat" that Steele constructed at the terrace edge provided a spot from which to watch the sun set. The seat's retaining wall was embellished with elaborate details: small marble insets recalled decorative stonework from the porte cochere at the house front and applied pilasters alternated with sections of brick. A vista was planted to evoke an Italian landscape painting by the fifteenth-century artist Perugino (with arborvitae instead of Italian cypress), and the view, southwest from the terrace, was maintained through careful pruning.

In 1932 Steele met Choate at the Elysée Park Hotel in Paris after visiting Vienna and Constantinople with other compan-

ions. From a window on the Place d'Etoile, they conceived a new plan for the small area near the beginning of the Linden Walk. It is not difficult to imagine them looking out over Paris's busiest intersection while reflecting on the Stockbridge garden. Either one may have pointed suddenly out the window and said, simply, "Let's do that." Like its Parisian prototype, Naumkeag's Rond Pointe was a nexus for converging ways; it also provided a stage for concerts and other musical entertainments.

Steele had become a frequent summer guest in Stockbridge, where Miss Choate entertained more or less constantly—neighbors, friends, friends of friends, and relatives. She loved music and sometimes organized her house parties around it. After one particularly musical weekend, Steele wrote to Charlotte Allen, "Stockbridge was fun, though I don't need to hear any more Mozart for quite a while—say 82 or 3 years."[62]

Naumkeag, Perugino View, drawing, 1931. (SUNY ESF College Archives)

Geoffrey Platt, who married Mabel Choate's niece at the peak of Steele's work at Naumkeag, retained a vivid impression of his aunt: "It appeared that Aunt Mabel believed that multiplying doctors' prescriptions by four or more would speed recovery. Argerol had been prescribed, with a resulting blue tinge to her slightly gray complexion.... Her majestic presence overwhelmed the blue tinge. She was tall and well built, had a lively manner, full of laughter, was interested in everyone and everything."[63]

A large and apparently devoted house staff kept the near-constant flow of guests happy. Meals were prepared from homegrown vegetables, milk, and butter from the farm. Occasionally Mabel Choate offered a beginning course of bowls of tender new peas to be eaten with spoons. ("Is this all we're getting?" Steele complained the first time.[64]) Tomatoes were grown year-round in the greenhouses, which also provided plants for the house, fuchsia and agapanthus for the Afternoon Garden, and, later, bamboo for the Chinese Temple Garden. Margaret, Miss Choate's kitchen maid, mixed particularly memorable martinis, served on the terrace as the sun sank behind Monument Mountain and the sky turned from blue to orange to purple. This was the garden at its best: the onset of dusk, in high summer.

"We saw a great deal of Fletcher Steele," remembered Platt. "Very lively and entertaining—outspoken. He was great company. He and Aunt Mabel had a marvelous time together, with much laughter and private conferences.... But never did they give us the slightest inkling of what they were planning to do, nor afterwards, any reasons why."[65] Not all the relations were thrilled with the extent of the new garden work. Choate's brother, Joseph Jr., saw his children's inheritance evaporating in the spray of tiny, expensive fountains. When she announced that she planned to leave the house as a museum for the public, he was outraged. But peace eventually prevailed, in part because her other investments proved lucrative.

In 1933 Miss Choate noticed a line of dirt-filled trucks passing the house. She stopped a driver and learned that fill from a new house foundation was headed for the dump but she could buy it for 50 cents a load if she wished. (Steele had told her that the big sweep of South Lawn would need more dirt before grading could begin.) By phoning Steele immediately, she was able to

Place d'Etoile, Paris, 1932. (SUNY ESF College Archives)

Naumkeag, Rond Pointe, view from the Linden Allée.
(Photo by Carol Betsch)

Naumkeag, new fill on the South Lawn before grading, early 1934. (SUNY ESF College Archives)

tell the drivers where on the steep lawn it should be dumped. So began the first modern earthwork in this country.

"The vital importance of curving form," wrote Steele, "which was begun on the south lawn here at Naumkeag, generated by the curve of Bear Mountain beyond and made clear in the curve cut in the woodland, was a satisfactory experiment. So far as I know it was the first attempt that has ever been made to incorporate the form of background topography into foreground details in a unified design."[66] The "satisfactory experiment" resulted in a lawn that curved and sloped in frank imitation of the distant mountainscape, now made visible by the woodland pruning. The scale was enormous, the impact extraordinarily bold. Steele recounted the process by which he eliminated traditional alternatives and arrived at the abstraction:

Neither the client nor her Victorian house: neither Bear Mountain nor the hillside itself wanted a so-called naturalistic affair with a path meandering downhill. A range of terraces in the Italian Garden manner was unthinkable because neither the line of view toward the Mountain nor the shape of the hilly lawn bore any architectural relation to the Temple [Afternoon] Garden. Besides, Italian Gardens do not fit Victorian wood houses.

The only recourse was to create an abstract form in the manner of modern sculpture, with swinging curves and slopes which would aim to make their impression directly, without calling on the help of associated ideas, whether in nature or art.

To do this took a lot of work; cutting and hauling and scraping; then doing it all over again, because it was necessary to learn what to do while doing it. Most of all it took unbelievable patience on the part of the client, who had to watch men interminably raking a few inches off a ridge for a week or more after the work appeared finished.[67]

The curving edge of the lower lawn, defined by a Japanese-inspired fence, repeated the contours. (To some extent, the root system of the old oak also determined its perimeter.) Brick service tracks reversed the outward swing and led the eye to fulfillment in the rock promontory. A row of globe locusts (*Gleditsia robinia*), "like glorified lollypops on sticks," threw "swooping shadows across the modelled earth, marking the minor changes which would otherwise flatten in the harsh light." (Choate identified these trees as pollarded larches—the more exotic variety may have been tried first without success.) The trees were practical as well as interesting. "The place can get torrid in the sun. So there must be a way to get down across

Naumkeag, South Lawn after grading, ca. 1940. The roof-line of the garden structure mimics the spruce. (SUNY ESF College Archives)

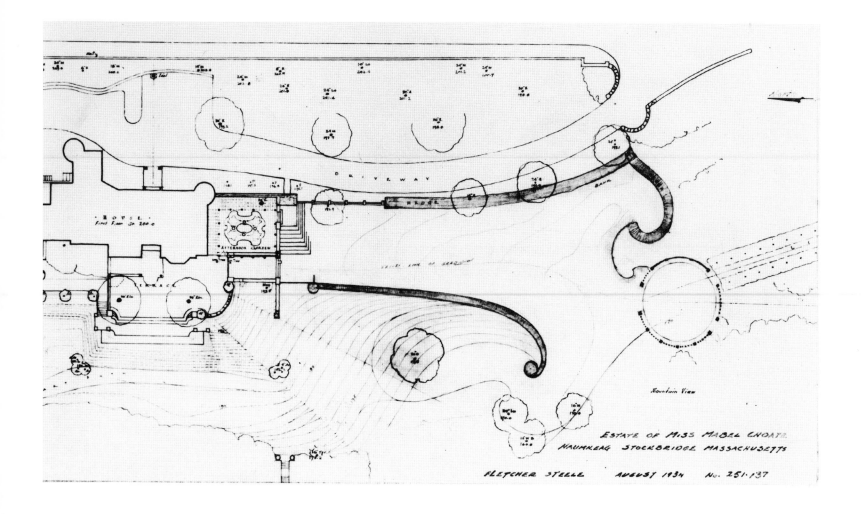

the lawn in shadow. A hedge would hide the view and squeeze
the upper lawn area."[68]

A hedge of red Japanese maples defined the uppermost
finger of the lawn, which curves out of sight behind the end of
the double hemlock hedge. "To screen the drive on the upper,
eastern side, a hemlock hedge, beginning rather low toward the
house, is clipped higher and higher as it recedes," wrote Steele.
"This complements and accents the modeling of the earth. The
idea was all right, but at first it was thin. It was the client who
perfected it. 'Why don't you double it on the inside?' she asked:
'I saw a double hedge in France and liked it.' No sooner said
than done, as is the rule when a good proposal comes from a
client. Now the frame of the lawn picture has a vigor and style
which it lacked before."[69] The great swooping, curving lawn
seems to go on and on, its impact sudden and insistent and vis-
ceral. Once-distant mountains, appropriated by the new contours, participate in the garden magic.

It would be a few years before Choate and Steele found

the focus that they felt the South Lawn lacked. "What finally
developed was dipped out of the American melting pot, like so
many other things on the place," Steele recorded. "A cast iron
grapevine verandah support, originally from an old house in
Washington, was cut down to make a small square structure. It
was roofed with curving slats and set up on an obvious little
eminence which had developed as part of the grading." Choate
painted the curious little house with the same deliberate gar-
ishness as the iron benches and Venetian poles. Later they put a
sacred rock and her Ming pedestal inside. "Like all good Chinese garden decoration, it appeals strongly to the imagination
without any obvious reason. It is just a rock, but makes one
think of all sorts of romantic things." The collaborators con-
gratulated themselves on the effect. "It attracts the right
amount of attention without competing with the bronze statue
near the house. Without any forced attempt to be odd, it is yet
sufficiently unfamiliar to seem appropriate in the slightly unexpected aspect of the lawn."[70]

Naumkeag. View to house terrace. (Photograph by Carol Betsch)

Naumkeag. Afternoon Garden with *Boy with Heron*. (Photograph by Carol Betsch)

Naumkeag. View to South Lawn. (Photograph by Carol Betsch)

Naumkeag. South Lawn, view southwest. (Photograph by Carol Betsch)

Naumkeag. House terrace, view northwest. (Photograph by Carol Betsch)

Naumkeag. Chinese Garden. (Photograph by Carol Betsch)

Naumkeag. Rill to Blue Steps. (Photograph by Carol Betsch)

Ancrum House. North Lawn with planting of pink phlox. (Photograph by Thomas Wallis,
prior to 1960, courtesy of Mr. and Mrs. Elbridge Gerry.)

Rocklawn. Stylized border planting of begonia, yellow canna lilies, ornamental grasses, and other varieties. (Photograph by Fletcher Steele, SUNY ESF College Archives)

Charlotte Whitney Allen estate. View from house terrace. (Photograph by Felice Frankel, 1987)

Seminole. Primrose garden, spring. (Photograph by Fletcher Steele, ca. 1960, SUNY ESF College Archives)

Richard and Nancy Turner estate. Vista, spring. (Photograph by Felice Frankel, 1987)

Grosse Pointe Shores, Michigan

1928–1931*

Steele was at his artistic best with opinionated clients whose non-negotiable demands stimulated his imagination. If the client was interested in the design (as many were) and had some artistic sophistication, so much the better. A lively dialogue would ensue. "The work of the landscape architect," Steele wrote, "is to balance three tensions. The pull of the land. The pull of the client and the pull of the professional designer himself. His job is to make a pattern of the three. If the balance never wavers and the tensions never turn into a tug of war, then the outcome is apt to be a pretty spiderweb."[71] Standish Backus would prove an able partner in creating one of Steele's most elaborate and artistically successful webs.

Steele probably met Backus through his friend Ralph Cram, who, in association with Robert O. Derrick of Detroit, was designing Backus's new Grosse Pointe Shores home. The development of Backus's garden would parallel that of Angelica Gerry's in many respects: both were constructed during the 1930s from comprehensive master plans, both relied on an English design vocabulary for their architectural elements, both involved a great number of plans and drawings. Both would also cost their owners extraordinary amounts of money. (The *Detroit News* reported that the Backus house cost nearly $1 million. The tulip bill for one of the twelve flower gardens on the estate one year came to $328.48; it bought 5,300 bulbs.)

Standish Backus and Steele immediately liked each other. The two men shared a lively, offbeat sense of humor and a passion for excellence in art and architecture. Steele discovered that they were distantly related. When he joined the National Society of Puritan Descendents in 1931, his lineage search turned up one Lieutenant Joseph Kellog (ten generations before) who was also an ancestor of Backus's.

When he was a boy, Backus had traveled through Europe with his parents and filled his diaries with sketches of English castles as he dreamed of becoming an architect. Instead he had become a lawyer, engineer, and successful industrialist, organizer of the Cadillac Motor Car Company, general counsel for General Motors Corporation, and president of Burroughs Adding Machine Company. But he had never lost his love of design. The new house and property would prove an outlet for his long-dormant dreams. Dorothy ("Dottie") Backus was a gardener and she took a more active interest in the horticul-

*Steele's work on the garden continued from 1928 to 1941; it is discussed in three phases.

tural proceedings, but plants were not discussed in nearly the degree of detail that architectural features were.

Concurrently with the Grosse Pointe project, Backus asked Steele to design a garden for his summer home in Manchester. Backus's fortune was not immediately affected by the Great Depression, and business, apparently, was good for Steele too. "All of our clients," he wrote to a colleague in 1930, "seem to have made money in the recent stock market break and to be determined to spend varying sums of it immediately."[72] The impact of the Depression on private landscape development was paradoxical in that those who still had money were able to buy more with it. The major expense in building and planting any garden—labor—had become dirt cheap.

Steele worked closely with both architects and client in laying out the design for the Detroit property and was consulted before construction began. The size and shape of the lot exerted considerable impact on the scheme. The narrow five-acre parcel was set on a busy street in a wealthy but essentially suburban neighborhood opposite Lake St. Clair. Cram and Steele sited the house so that its length ran east-west on the lot, at right angles to Lake Shore Drive. (Because the street was a major thoroughfare, the house was set back on the property.) This unusual orientation proved crucial to an integrated development of the surrounding landscape. A more traditional front-facing arrangement would have cut the property in two and created an especially difficult problem of relating front to back. Steele wanted to avoid the conventionality of a front yard/backyard scheme anyway; he wanted the land to suggest the

Standish Backus and Steele at Backus's Grosse Pointe, Mich., estate, 1933. (SUNY ESF College Archives. Photographer unknown)

grand distances of an English country manor, a tall order on five acres.

Another constraint on the design was Backus's preference for early English architecture. At his instruction, Cram's forty-room mansion took Gothic form, although massive limestone elevations yielded to Tudor half-timber construction at the structure's western, service wing. No expense was spared in creating the fine mantels, doorways, friezes, and paneling for the interior or in furnishing the house, which required frequent shopping trips abroad. Modern conveniences were incorporated throughout. An elaborate telephone system connected rooms. The eight-car garage had electric doors. A walk-in vault protected the family's silver service. In the basement a small plant generated power for the house.

The canton plan for the estate was laid out by 1930, but architectural and planting elaborations evolved over the next decade. Steele altered ornamental details after walls or balusters were in place and new visual cues emerged. Beaverboard maquettes provided important information about scale and impact. Standish Backus's approach differed from Mabel Choate's and that of most of Steele's other clients. Backus wanted to establish the whole garden—from the ground up—

rather than develop complete sections in sequence. He was also confident that he could afford the finished product. Most of Steele's clients began their gardens with little notion of just how big, or how expensive, they would eventually become.

Steele's mandate to consider the separate garden areas concurrently led him to relate them forcibly, fitting them together like an ingenious jigsaw puzzle. The requisite expansiveness of the garden's character and the limited space made Steele think hard about how to squeeze the most into five, then, with an additional purchase, seven acres. The big house acted as the organizing principle: each garden part related directly to it as well as to other adjacent areas.

During the first stages of design deliberations, Steele warned Backus against "keeping too much to one era" and thereby robbing the garden of some of the interest and vitality it might otherwise have.[73] Backus, in general, preferred the simple, massive, and even primitive qualities of medieval and early Renaissance forms to later, more delicate elaborations. Steele, of course, loved complexity and fine surface detail. The artistic tension between artist and patron persisted during the decade-long project but both men thrived on the arguments it provoked. Letters and telegrams about the project passed between

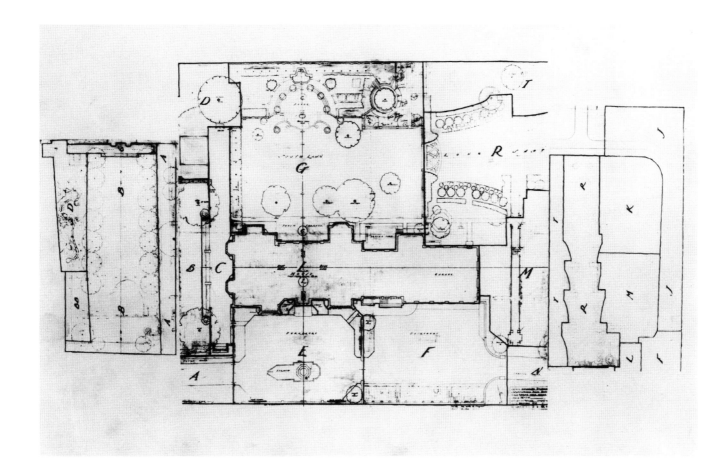

them, sometimes daily. Steele visited Detroit frequently and met Backus in New York, as Burroughs's business took him there often.

Despite the attention to architectural detail throughout, no attempt was made to create an authentic English garden. Steele approached the project as a Beaux Arts problem: discrete garden rooms would intersect according to a strong, axial plan. Architectural elements and plants would define these rooms, each having its own ambience and use. The garden as a whole would reflect a character based on the historically evocative house and the more personal idiosyncrasies of the family. Backus probably never realized how French some of the garden areas actually were.

One of Steele's earliest schemes (from 1929) had the house in its final location but placed a moat at the structure's east end. An irregularly shaped basecourt was pushed to the extreme west end of the house, one wall of which was established by a large, ovoid herb garden. The scheme was abandoned in favor of a more formal and ultimately more rectilinear one (and the moat disappeared).

In the final version, a long driveway paralleling the South Lawn led to a forecourt, which abutted a large and formal basecourt with herb gardens and the eight-car garage. (Visiting chauffeur quarters were located over the garage.) A service road gave access to the property from the north. Two terraces extended the house interior: the larger South Terrace overlooked a formal lawn and Stage area, while the East Terrace provided a view over the sculpted "front" lawn to Lake St. Clair. A small, densely planted wild garden defined the South Lawn to the east and abutted the Stage area—the nexus of the garden compartments. Here putti frolicked in a cascade pool against a beech hedge backdrop. The estate's most splendid and original feature, the Long Shot, constituted the axial answer to the wild garden.

Steele's assistants, who tired of their boss's airs, referred to it as the "Big Shot."[74] The long lawn was forced to a narrow end in a French trick of perspective that made it appear longer than it was. Six pairs of bays enclosing lilac-backed herbaceous borders were hidden by tall arborvitae hedges. From the Gothic stonework tracery at its head, the Long Shot appeared as a tunnel of green. The colorful flower beds appeared only to those who walked the length of the lawn. "Really Fletcher," wrote Butler Sturtevant, Steele's former employee, "it is swell . . . the nine feet between the last group of evergreens in the vista

Backus estate plan with Steele's canton system.
A. Drive
B. East Lawn
C. East Terrace
D. Wild Garden
E. Forecourt
F. Basecourt
G. South Lawn and Stage area
K. Orchard
L. House
M. Kitchen Garden
N. Service drive
R. Long Shot
T. Boundary planting
(SUNY ESF College Archives)

Backus estate, forecourt with a thyme bed and the obelisk. The basecourt lies immediately beyond, to the west. (SUNY ESF College Archives)

Backus estate, basecourt under construction. (SUNY ESF College Archives)

Backus estate, Long Shot, stone tracery and the first bay with lilacs. (SUNY ESF College Archives)

Backus estate, Long Shot, view toward the house into the second and first flower bays. (SUNY ESF College Archives)

looked like twenty. You are a thoroughly dishonest person."[75] A grape arbor led from one bay of the Long Shot to the kitchen gardens, drying yard, orchard, and nursery.

House and drive construction were under way when Virginia Cavendish was sent to Detroit in August 1931 to make a complete report on the state of existing plants, including those that had been purchased the previous year in anticipation of major planting efforts the following. She worked with Nicholas Reding, the Backuses' gardener, cutting, root pruning, espaliering, and moving plants as she took notes and recorded locations and conditions. "Nicholas, the gardener, seems to be an unusually intelligent person for the job," she noted in her report to Steele. "He handles the plants easily and carefully and seems to grasp ideas and carry them out unusually satisfactorily. He put the most beautiful ball on the little ginkgo he moved that I have ever seen anywhere."[76]

Because Steele was not operating on familiar ground, one of the first challenges was to locate good plants. "Some little research along the lines of moving large specimen plants from the east to Detroit has brought to light the fact that losses are very high with such material so I made a fairly thorough study of nurseries adjacent to Detroit and the material that they had to offer that might be available for our work there," continued Cavendish.

The nurseries north of Detroit . . . were very unsatisfactory. They have no large size evergreen stock and their small size stuff is poor in color and texture. . . . The soil in this entire area is very sandy and would probably make poor balls.

South of Detroit, however, the result was much more encouraging. Mr. Backus made a trip with me to the Westcroft Gardens on Grosse Ile where we found some splendid big specimens of taxus, some nice large cotoneaster horizontalis in pots, cotoneaster divaricata, foveolata and francheti in fine large field grown plants and other miscellaneous material. We also found there Mr. Stanton, a soil expert, who promises to be a mine of information as to soil conditions and treatment in that country.[77]

The nursery at the Backus estate was vital to the garden's success. A large parcel of land adjacent to the kitchen garden was set aside for holding small plants until they matured. One plant order from April 1913, marked "Additions to Nursery," listed 105 shrubs in twenty varieties, many of which were not considered hardy in the climate. *Mahonia* (hollygrape) and *Taxus baccata* Hibernica (Irish yew) were among those with risky prognosis for the long Michigan winter. The Long Shot presented especially complicated maintenance problems as the arborvitae were to form perfect, architectural niches of flat walls behind the flowering beds. Natural maturation and lower limb loss necessitated continual infilling with small plants.

Steele recommended humus "everywhere to get the maximum healthy plant growth after these things are once in the ground." In preparation for the 1932 planting season, he ordered 105 tons of it at a cost of $1,575 (delivery additional). Plants were to be mature specimens, "as this is such a conspicuous place that I believe you would not want to wait for effect."[78] Steele figured transportation, preparing soil, and planting to be roughly equivalent to the costs of the plants themselves. In 1931 a mature *Pinus cembra* sold for $100 (four were to be planted at the entrance to the drive), an espaliered apple was $125, but roses and clematis were a dollar each and Japanese anemone were only $12 per hundred.

Hoover was charged with preparing many of the working drawings for the garden along with those for client presentation, since Ralph Cram's involvement and the job's high budget lent a formal cast to the proceedings. Steele's instructions to Hoover were more often delivered in person than written out, but his schedule during the period often found him away from the office. Concerns with form, function, and historical appearance color Steele's directions. A handwritten note from Steele to Hoover suggesting new design guidelines for a pair of sentry boxes—the great gateposts at the driveway's end—offers a glimpse into the Water Street office process. Backus had objected to the first drawings: "I would much prefer to have these posts of an earlier period than the Georgian which they seem to be on your drawings. . . . I feel that these posts are the first thing of importance which one sees on approaching the house from the lake shore drive and I would rather that they gave the impression of an earlier period than they seem to under their present design. . . . As you know, I am not overly fond of Georgian architecture, and I have a strong desire to have these piers give an impression of primitiveness as an introduction to the house proper."[79] On 19 August 1932 Steele wrote Hoover:

Dear Harry,

Try a sketch of Backus piers in form of very shallow sentry box—no door—on as near old pier design foundations as possible. Just big enough opening for man to stand in out of rain. Tudor feeling gotten by buttresses, perhaps or suggestions of battlements or little carving like entrance door of house. Perhaps top of little gate to service could be hinted at in opening or something of same period. Don't want to work that motive too hard or will spoil gate. Flat arch like windows probably better. Stone back on Basecourt side. Suggestion of dovecote over if you want it, though probably too gardenesque, though carrier pigeons & falcons were kept somewhere, surely.[80]

Steele's trips to Detroit often resulted in revised designs: "I have been studying the balustrade and had a board put up to lean on and look at. While I hate to admit it, I am convinced that I made the Forecourt and East Terrace Balustrade just 6" too high. It should be a bold height. 3'3" is higher than the ordinary domestic scale, but just right. 3'9" as I had it before would be just plain cheeky and not comfortable to have about. Hence the revisions which only took a few minutes to make."[81] And two months later:

There is nothing like a visit to the grounds to give one a fresh point of view. The reason why you have not before received all the information about foundations was that wandering about the new place gave me some new, and it seems to me, important ideas of slight revisions of summer house locations and environment which I am enclosing. The result is simpler and less expensive than before. More spacious and convenient. . . .

The second fact noticed on the place was that the fairly definite line of trees almost in the middle of the east and west length of the Wild Garden naturally will throw the apparent axis northward to lie between the trees and the south boundary should be filled with trees and shrubs to make a screen. Locating the summer house in the middle would be undesirable.[82]

The grammatically ambiguous phrasing was a problem intrinsic to Steele's busy schedule, especially when letters were "Dictated by Mr. Steele but not read as he had to go out of town before the notes were transcribed"—a frequent notation on his letters.

In December 1931 Steele wrote to Backus in excruciating, characteristic detail about a paving pattern he was working on

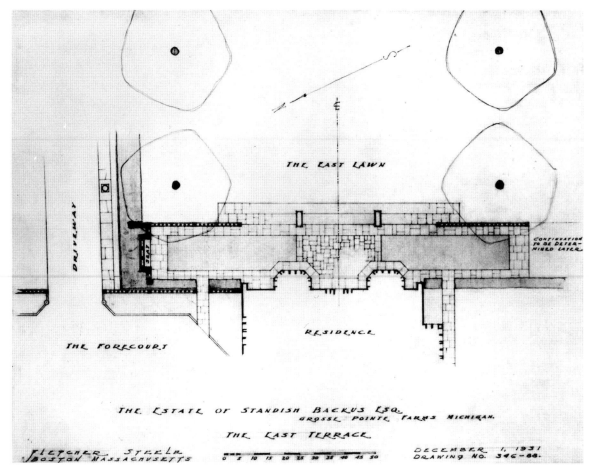

Backus estate, East Terrace plan, 1931. (SUNY ESF College Archives)

Backus estate, paving pattern for East Terrace, 1931. (SUNY ESF College Archives)

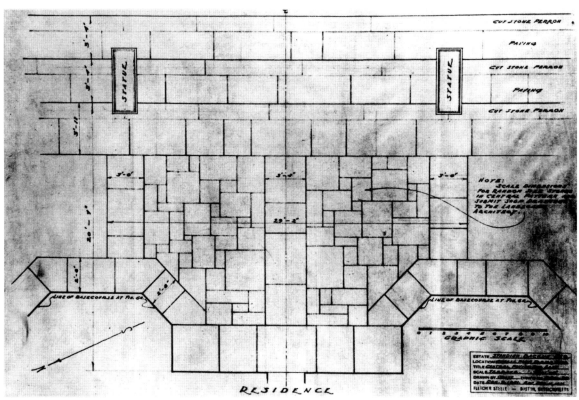

for the East Terrace. Steele seems to have relished the chance to expose the usually invisible lines of reasoning to an appreciative client: "Don't think it is any happy-go-lucky division into rectangles. I have changed every line on it at least four times. Now I think it is cunningly, not quite symmetrically balanced. The view is carried away from the door to the wider angle quite unconsciously by the sizes and arrangement of the stone and diagonal patterns. And the eye is enticed to wander about from one part to another without weariness or sudden arrest, as in a good painting." Steele concludes, "I believe I'd make a good cubist."[83]

The paving plan shows Steele at his obsessive best. Only careful study reveals the subtle deviations that may or may not have "enticed" the eye to wander "without weariness or sudden arrest." A second letter, received by Standish three days later, further describes how the material, crab orchard stone, "would cover very quickly with a darkish moss,"[84] toning down the brilliant color, but also one might assume, obscuring many of the lines that had been so painstakingly laid out. This attention to detail was absolutely typical. In some cases it made the difference between a mediocre design and a superb one. In other cases it was an exercise in eccentricity.

The letter goes on: "I am perfectly certain," Steele promised, "that your final result would have the warm, rich, comfortable look of English things, in marked distinction to the average American paving which is either too cold and gray and smooth on the one hand or else too rough and nondescript on the other." This was neither the first nor last time Steele would warn his clients against being "American" in their tastes.

Steele then turned his attention to the South Terrace, which opened to the small formal lawn and raised stage area. "I look on this terrace rather as attached closely to the house interior than from the garden inwards, so to speak. It would be practically a garden-room of the house." Steele suggested a marble floor with a brass inlay of a zodiac pattern. "Good for dancing and an excellent background for rugs, furniture and plants at other times."[85] He enclosed a sketch (uncharacteristically in his own hand) and continued to coax Backus; but the zodiac project was finally rejected in 1932.

"Since I last saw you business conditions seem to have been getting worse rather than better," Backus responded, "and there have been a good many necessary items of additional expense in connection with the house which are unavoidable at the present time, and therefore we think it necessary to abandon—

Backus estate, proposed South Terrace, with a zodiac design, 1932. (SUNY ESF College Archives)

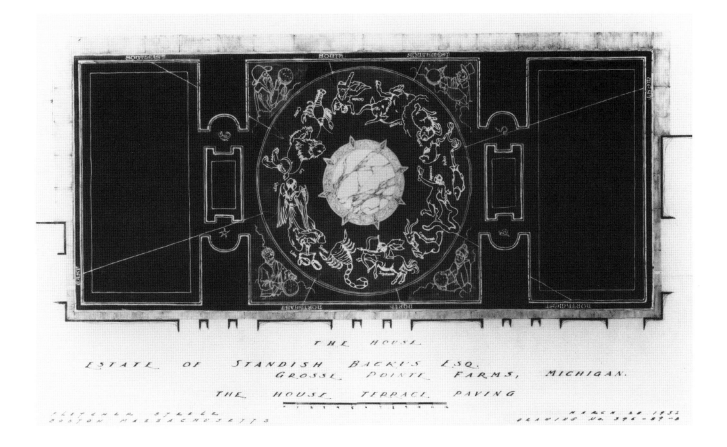

THE HOUSE.

ESTATE OF STANDISH BACKUS ESQ.
GROSSE POINTE FARMS, MICHIGAN.
THE HOUSE TERRACE PAVING

FLETCHER STEELE
BOSTON MASSACHUSETTS

at least for the time being—any further thought of incurring the expense necessary to install the South Terrace as you were planning it. Therefore I think we shall have to use the ordinary flagging, as in the East Terrace, for this particular area until such time as we can feel justified in going to the additional expense necessary for the zodiacal diagram."[86]

The Great Depression

The collapse of the stock market is usually considered the end of the Country Place era and its gold mine of private commissions for the landscape design business.[87] But for several years Steele continued his gardenmaking with the same kind of clients, in the same kind of settings as before. His designs from the thirties differ subtly from those of the previous decade, but this can be more accurately attributed to personal and artistic developments than to economic influence.

"Dear Father," Steele wrote in June 1932, the darkest year of the nation's economic disaster, "it all seems rather unusual to have so much on hand to do, as I am told that everybody else's work has eased down instead of increasing. So that if I have a year like this in what is other people's bad year, it looks as though there wouldn't be very much diminution." The younger Steele was still defensive about the unpredictable nature of his profession. His letter continues, as nearly all of them did, with a brief analysis of current events. "This morning's news about Hoover signing the Tariff certainly proves him to be, as far as I am concerned, exactly what I warned you before the election would certainly be the case. . . . I think he is an abominable creature and always did." Both father and son were Republicans, but Fletcher, at least for the moment, was "utterly disgusted with the Republicans' way of running the government."[88]

Steele had fewer clients between 1929 and 1941 than in the twelve years preceding, but the volume of work did not greatly diminish because many of the jobs (Backus, Choate, Doubleday, and Gerry) were ongoing. As a result of widespread unemployment, labor costs were at an all-time low, which, ironically, made grand schemes possible for even less. In the context of the larger catastrophe, however, the scope of some of the gardens is perplexing.

In 1932 Steele announced at a meeting of the Boston chapter of the ASLA that he would "prefer to starve" than work in the public sector.[89] The display did not endear him to his colleagues, some of whom were out of work. Those excitedly (and voluntarily) pursuing the profession's widening role in the public sector were offended by what they perceived as elitism. Steele's flamboyant, outspoken style and apparent self-

assuredness had also alienated some colleagues over the years, as had his booming practice.

The New Deal marked a major turning point in the practice and the image of the landscape profession. The creation of the Tennessee Valley Authority in 1933 rescued many careers. Subtle design concerns faded before the more dramatic impact of hydroelectric power, flood control, navigation, and forest management. The lives of four and a half million people were directly affected by the TVA's new projects. During the 1930s, the National Park Service incorporated new land for parks, parkways, and national seashores, all of which required the services of landscape architects. The period also saw the profession turn its attention to the impact of the automobile. The goals of these projects were multiple, but making "art," as Steele defined it, was usually not among them.

Steele claimed that he shunned public projects because "everything beautiful is flattened out by committees,"[90] and since group approval was a necessary component of any project of national or civic stature he was, de facto, not interested. In fact, Steele did enter a design competition for Boston's Copley Square in 1936 but did not win.[91] In 1934 he delivered a paper at the thirty-fifth annual meeting of the ASLA as a response to the new, widely divergent specialities in the field. "Where beauty is sought as the dominating object of the work, where use is subordinated to this object, art becomes fine art. Not otherwise. Architecture and landscape architecture oscillate between useful and fine art."[92] Steele was determined to pursue beauty as a primary goal in his work. Personality and history had conspired in such a way that he could.

WESTMORELAND
George and Mary Doubleday
Ridgefield, Connecticut
1928–1932

Within months of meeting Standish Backus, Steele started working for the Doubledays, probably through his Garden Club of America activities. Mary Doubleday was a member of the Ridgefield Garden Club and active nationally. Her husband had been president of Ingersoll Rand Company since 1913. One of Steele's first projects on the large estate was a "patio greenhouse." Mrs. Doubleday described the evolution of the feature for the *Garden Club of America Bulletin*:

For some years, when autumn came, the question arose as to where the tall plants, such as bay tree, oleanders and hibiscus should spend the winter. . . .

With a husband who loves trees and dislikes to have the

Westmoreland,
patio greenhouse.
(LC. Photographer
unknown)

landscape marred by roofs, it was out of the question to suggest an addition to the present greenhouse. Suddenly this husband had a happy inspiration of a hole in the ground. . . . It would be a deep excavation, roofed over with glass. . . .

From the moment the idea was conceived, it grew by leaps and bounds. It would be ideal for tall plants, but why should this hole in the ground be ugly? . . . From usefulness to plants, the idea turned to the comforts and pleasures of the family. It might be made a lovely place in which to sit and rest among flowers after a long trudge in cold, snowy weather. The children added their wish for a fireplace. . . . If he [the husband] were going to sit in it, there would have to be the sound of dripping water, always music to his ears. . . .

An architect was called in to execute the fulfillment of all the family desires. He had travelled widely, he loved adventure, wasn't afraid to try all suggestions, clever in design and a genius in artistic details.[93]

From a "long, straight, grassy" walk, past old-fashioned flower and vegetable gardens (probably not Steele's design), "you will find yourself entering a small gravelled court over which a rustic arbor supports vines, hanging heavy with luscious grapes" —in Steele's records, "the wine terrace." The article continued:

From it, through an ordinary sized door, you enter a small vestibule and look through a second door, directly opposite, into the Patio itself. The walls of the vestibule are painted a strong blue color, so often seen in Italy. A small window, on your left, cut out of the eighteen inch stone wall, lets in light from the north. In the corner . . . a rough oak shelf supports a large, gay, canary-yellow Carboni bowl converted into a wash basin. Above it, Spanish tiles fill a space. . . .

Already a foreign feeling begins to take possession of you and upon entering the Patio proper, you are sure that you have been transported into a quaint old corner of Spain.[94]

Steele's memories of Cordova and Seville, first articulated at Frith House, were finding more rustic expression in Ridgefield. Two cement stairways with landings led down into the

Westmoreland, pool.
(SUNY ESF College
Archives)

patio; a ramp along the north wall connected one entry and landing with a long balcony extending the length of the east wall.

> A roof, which covers the balcony, is made of small round poles, giving an open, slat effect. Over this roof a jasmine rambles in profusion, intoxicating you with its sweet and delicate fragrance. . . . Across the front of the balcony sits a balustrade with heavy, weathered oak rail and irregular spindles, as though during many past years the original ones had been broken and replaced by makeshift odd ones. Iron rings placed at irregular intervals on this balustrade hold pots of flowering begonias, fuchsias, geraniums, nasturtiums, air plants.[95]

The room was 22 by 25 feet, and 25 feet from the floor to the peak of the glass roof.

> The three solid oak doors, the one leading into the potting shed, the one on the north wall, which is for a shallow closet, and the one opening into the vestibule, each with a picturesque gable above it, create the amusing and delightful impression of dwellings.
>
> The steps from the balcony are veritably hung into the south wall, and by grooves on their outside edges, in a mysterious way water drops slowly, falling into a pool beneath. This pool, made of cement, extends wider than the steps, and one can easily imagine people of a whole village coming here to draw water.
>
> All mechanics of the Patio were carefully hidden by the ingenious architect. Many pipes are concealed under the ramp along the north wall. . . . Hidden in the angle of the northwest stairway is an iron grill, through which more heat passes into the Patio. The gables over the potting shed door and west door into the vestibule, are so artistically designed that strangers only admire them, never dreaming that they are vital to the entire heating and ventilating system.
>
> The walls of the Patio are of plaster of . . . irregular and variegated colors, yellow, blue, pink and purple. When these walls were being painted, the distinguished architect directed the workman to bring buckets of white, red, blue and orange paint. Then, he was instructed to use first red, then blue on top of it or orange with white to make streaks. The result was a weathered, antique effect, a perfect background for plants and flowers.[96]

Henry Hoover thought it one of the office's most intriguing

projects. The penetration of the space (a near-perfect cube) by stairways, ramps, balcony, and arched entryways constituted an ingenious arrangement. In its appeal to the imagination, the patio also achieved its intended impact: in Mrs. Doubleday's words, "a foreign feeling begins to take possession of you."

The garden's major feature was a long vista that originated at a small stage (laterally adjacent to a bowling green) and ran the length of a swimming pool, an outdoor ballroom, and a pine allée, terminating at a fountain, over four hundred feet away. The planting for the ballroom included weeping dogwood in bays between small fountains, canoe birches behind the mock orange hedge (for height), and *Magnolia glauca* scattered through the background (for fragrance).

WINDCLYFFE
Standish Backus
Manchester, Massachusetts
1929–1940

Standish and Dottie Backus's Manchester summer cottage perched on the edge of a bluff. Steele's plan was straightforward, almost inevitable, in that the only viable location for a garden with an ocean view was the narrow strip of lawn behind the big shingle-style house; the garden's medieval tone was less predictable. It was as playful as the Backuses' Grosse Pointe place was solemn, as theatrical, even capricious, as the other was dignified. This was a vacation house, after all.

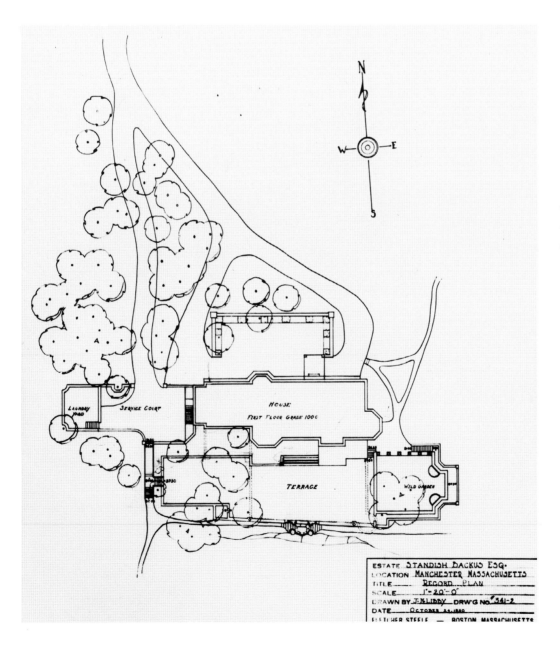

Windclyffe plan, 1930. (SUNY ESF College Archives)

Steele had a considerably freer hand in designing the Manchester place, largely because Standish Backus was less involved in the project. At the beach, he preferred walking along the shore and listening to the rocks "sing" to poring over old English sourcebooks. Neither would the Manchester garden be constrained by an overarching concern for architectural harmony between landscape and house design.

Steele's scheme was inspired by the modern gardens he had seen in Sweden just months before. He had particularly liked Carl Milles's garden at Lidingo, where the sculptor had made extensive use of ironwork architectural elements. Steele borrowed Milles's use of iron urns and railings but gave them a ceremonial twist in Manchester by installing a pair of colorful standards at the center of the railing overlook.

The rectangular lawn was bordered by a decorative railing on three sides. Two large urns (imported from Sweden rather than custom-made, for economy's sake) flanked the banner poles and a stairway that led down the steep hill to the south. Bacchanalian imagery in the form of cavorting nymphs and drunken gods—intended as a pun on the family name?—enlivened the surfaces of the big iron pots.

Steele's office designed four big torchères for the rail, using mailing tubes to construct models. Plaster prototypes were then sandcast and sent out to Ryan Iron Works, a Boston company the office had come to rely upon for custom work. The torchères were illuminated with automobile headlights; it was nearly the same feature Steele had proposed without success

for the Detroit garden. Cast-stone Chinese scrolls provided foundations for the ironwork gazebos that stood at either end of the railing. An elaborate stone and ironwork wall, with lionhead fountains and iron beasts, was never built. The design borrowed from widely disparate traditions (English, Swedish, and Chinese) but the impact was fresh. The garden evoked a sense of adventure, pageantry even.

Floriculture at the Backuses' Manchester place was confined to pots. Steele's plant list for 1931 includes 212 lily bulbs in six varieties. For the 100 *Lilium candidum* bulbs, Steele suggested "potting up 15 ten inch pots with 3 bulbs in each and 55 six inch pots with 1 bulb in each." In all, the plan called for 138 pots of lilies alone. Additionally, Steele ordered seeds, plants, and bulbs in twenty-six varieties of exotics (tuberose, begonia), hardy perennials (campanula and delphinium), and annuals (petunia, nicotiana, zinnia, and morning glory). From June to September the large bluestone terrace was a jumble of color and fragrance—all eminently rearrangeable.

Steele often recommended pots to his clients as a convenient alternative to laborious perennial culture or bedding out. In some designs, such as Naumkeag's Afternoon Garden, they constituted a key element. In other gardens, pots were integrated casually, their contents and arrangement left to the client. For patios or vacation terraces deserted during the winter months, pots made especially good sense.

In 1943 Steele wrote a persuasive article on pot culture for *Horticulture.* His timing was motivated by wartime budget

Windclyffe, north elevation of ironwork rail, standards, and gazebos. (SUNY ESF College Archives)

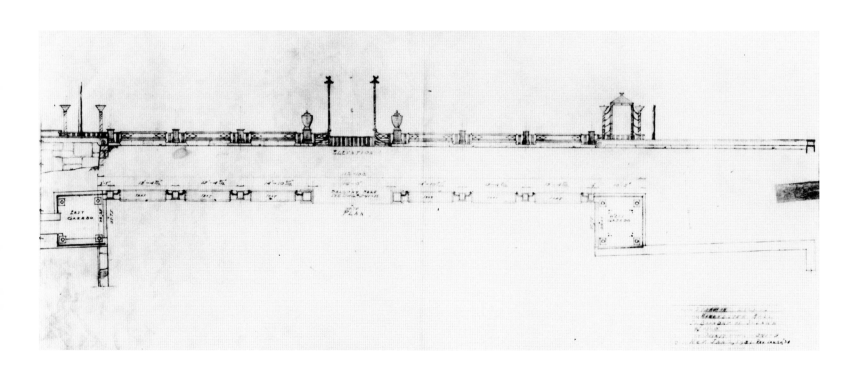

Windclyffe, ironwork
detail. (SUNY ESF
College Archives)

constraints, but Steele had been enthusiastic about the design possibilities pots offered since his European trip of 1913.

Plants are interesting from the moment the seed is put into the soil and perhaps most constantly interesting while we wait for germination and exult in the first faint tinge of green. . . . To have pot plants always around cuts out three-quarters of the work of growing them in one place, then moving them and briefly looking at them somewhere else.

. . . Any plant will grow in a pot. The common garden iris, campanulas, the maidenhair fern, and a hundred others are often prettier isolated in a pot than when crowded in beds. . . . Of course, the really lazy gardener who wants pot plants will look over his lists for things that thrive where it is hot and dry, for without continual water in our climate, a pot in the sun gets hot as a griddle and dry as a bone. He will get flowers now and again, but will rely on foliage most of the time.

. . . Of course he won't be asked to send much of his stuff to the flower show. Most of it won't be fashionable. He will, on the other hand, have his plants where he can watch them all the time, move them from place to place as they grow and the sun gets hotter. He will find continual amusement in the decorative value of the pots themselves and the minor rearrangements of his garden picture, made easily day by day when he transplants an iris or day-lily by merely shoving a pot.[97]

Villa garden by Tony Garnier. Steele's caption was "Modernism or Pompeii?" From *Landscape Architecture* (April 1930). (SUNY ESF College Archives)

The Modernists

Steele wrote two articles on modern garden design, in 1929 for *House Beautiful* and in 1930 for *Landscape Architecture*. In the first he reported on an evolution from "the romantic Victorian tradition which encouraged what one might call a compulsory love of nature," toward acceptance of nontraditional materials and forms. Mirrors, colored sand, zigzag walks, and "compositions of cubes, pyramids, cylinders, and spheres" in the work of landscape designer M. Guevrekian, captured his imagination. André and Paul Vera's two "stimulating" books (one having risen in his estimation since 1922) were recommended. "They have an important talent in adapting plant forms to achieve their patterns. And their patterns are strongly influenced by modernistic thought."[98]

In the second article, "New Pioneering in Garden Design," Steele reflected at greater length on those he considered the best among the modern designers, including Vera, Albert Laprade, Mallet-Stevens, Guevrekian, André Lurçat, and Tony Garnier, "the first and most able" of the pioneers. He credits Garnier with originating "the strong modern trend away from symmetrical axial treatment" in which "the axis is broken again and again, although rarely entirely lost. This results in a marked vibration."[99]

The attraction of the new ideas for Steele was their liberating effect. "What interests most is the expanded sense,—not a new sense but the expansion of our old sense of dimensions, space, relativity, call it what you will. Artists don't turn things inside out (though some of their results look as though they would like to). Rather they help us to imagine ourselves part of the thing they are describing in an almost abstract sort of way." He quotes Alfred Barr's description of the "expanded sense" in painting: "'While we study a Cézanne we feel these planes shifting forward and back, taking their appointed distances until after a time the painted world into which we are drawn becomes almost more actual than the real world. The grandeur of a Poussin is perceived, is read, remains as it were at arm's length. But a great Cézanne is immanent; it grows around one and includes one. The result is at times as hypnotic as listening to great music in which strength and order are overwhelmingly made real.'"[100]

Steele believed in a comparable potential for gardens and predicted its fulfillment in the near future—"we gardeners have always been behind other artists in adopting new ideas."[101] Unlike some colleagues and most of the American public, Steele believed that a great garden has life-altering capabilities, much as great paintings or music do. Steele's idea, that gardens are art, and his enthusiastic descriptions of the new gardens helped promote modern garden design in America. Daniel Kiley, one of the pioneers of modernism and an early admirer of Steele's, believes that the 1930 *Landscape Architecture* article was pivotal in his own career and of great significance in the field generally.[102]

Steele's slide lectures included works by Garnier, Pierre-Émile Legrain, Laprade, Lurçat, and other French modernists, as well as contemporary German examples. One of these images showed the Frankfurt garden that the architect Ernst May designed circa 1928, which emphasized the integration of garden and house. (Steele explored May's concept in plans for his own house a few years later.) Modern gardens such as these were considered novelties in the United States, but they were severely criticized in Germany. For example, a few weeks after Lurçat's garden was published in *Gartenschönheit* in 1930, the conservative landscape architect Wilhelm Hübotter published a redesign that featured the naturalistic plantings favored by Hitler's National Socialist Party.[102]

Two designs resulted directly from Steele's growing interest in modernism. In 1928 he began working in Seekonk, Massachusetts, for Claude Branch, for whom he designed a geometrically paved terrace. Areas of pink and black aggregate were separated by brass joint strips that also defined shallow pools. The area was flat and the scheme decorative, as opposed to the multilevel construction he was devising for James Smithwick, in Gloucester.

In Smithwick's garden, the garden's entry came via a circular stairway and curving cement wall surrounding a sculpture pedestal with fountain base. (Steele reused this design in a Rochester garden for Helen Ellwanger in 1935.) In plan, the

Villa Bomsel, Versailles, by André Lurçat. Hand-colored glass slide in Steele's collection. (SUNY ESF College Archives)

Garden of Ernst May, Frankfurt, Germany. Hand-colored glass slide in Steele's collection. (SUNY ESF College Archives)

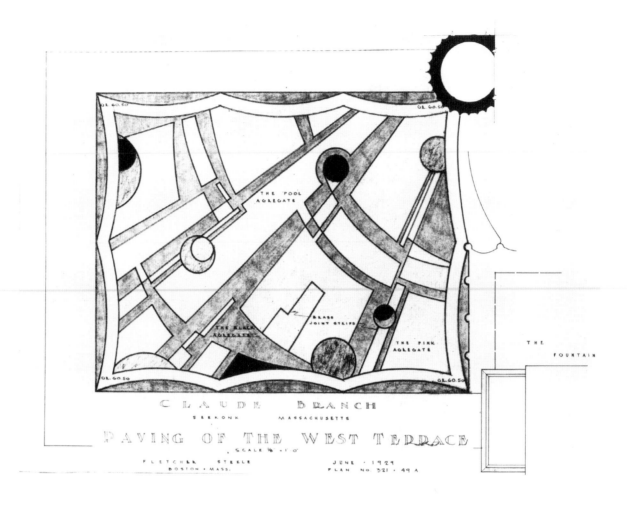

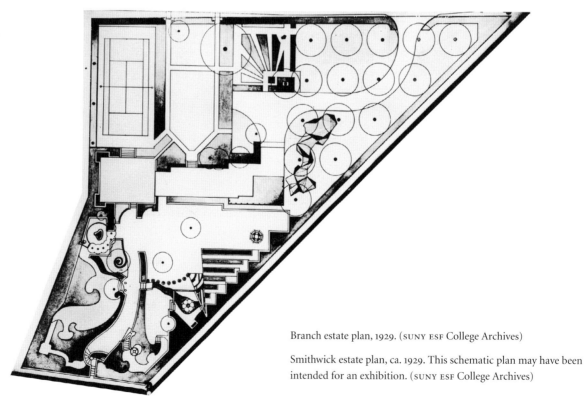

Branch estate plan, 1929. (SUNY ESF College Archives)

Smithwick estate plan, ca. 1929. This schematic plan may have been intended for an exhibition. (SUNY ESF College Archives)

DETAIL AT ENTRY
ESTATE OF JAMES SMITHWICK ESQ.
EAST GLOUCESTER MASS.

FLETCHER STEELE
JUNE 22 1929

BOSTON MASS.
308-5

Smithwick estate, entry detail, 1929. (SUNY ESF College Archives)

garden is a riot of swirls, loops, circles, and contrasting angles, seemingly chaotic, without visible logic or order. A second surviving detail (the first being the fountain entry) dissipates the modern illusion with a half-hidden summerhouse of Chinese influence, flagstone walk, and plantings, freer in growth even than Steele's typical treatment. Whatever the depth of Steele's interest in modern gardens, the new vocabulary was proving erratic.

Seyburn estate, lawn with an apple tree and pool. (LC. Photographer unknown)

MR. AND MRS. WESSON SEYBURN
Manchester, Massachusetts
1929–1932

In 1929 Steele began a summer garden for the Seyburns, who were also Detroit-based clients. Their house sat on a large but suburban and viewless lot, necessitating a contained scheme. Steele laid out the back lawn as a fleur-de-lis, using a large, existing apple tree as a central focus for the design. Curving walls of arborvitae defined the side walls of the space. A lobed reflecting pool in front of the tree was flanked by two smaller beds of annuals of the same shape. Matching sculpted privet hedges, edged in annuals, provided the backdrop for the lawn space. (Their baroque forms echoed the hedge design at Lisburne Grange.) Traffic was screened from the north side of the

corner lot by a tall, wisteria-covered, wire fence. Two concrete planting circles set into the lawn near the porch were filled with blue hydrangeas.

A steep hill on the west edge of the property was regraded to create a secluded exedra, an alternative to the exuberance of the big lawn. (Nearly all of Steele's gardens offered small-scale nooks where one or two people could find privacy.) It was a well-proportioned and elegant piece of architecture whose curves reiterated those of the big garden beyond. The hill behind the exedra was planted with mountain laurel and rhododendron, as was the adjacent wilderness area that screened the tennis court from view.

Steele's drawings included one major feature that was never realized. Either the budget was cut as a result of new financial pressures or the proposed project—an elaborate circular

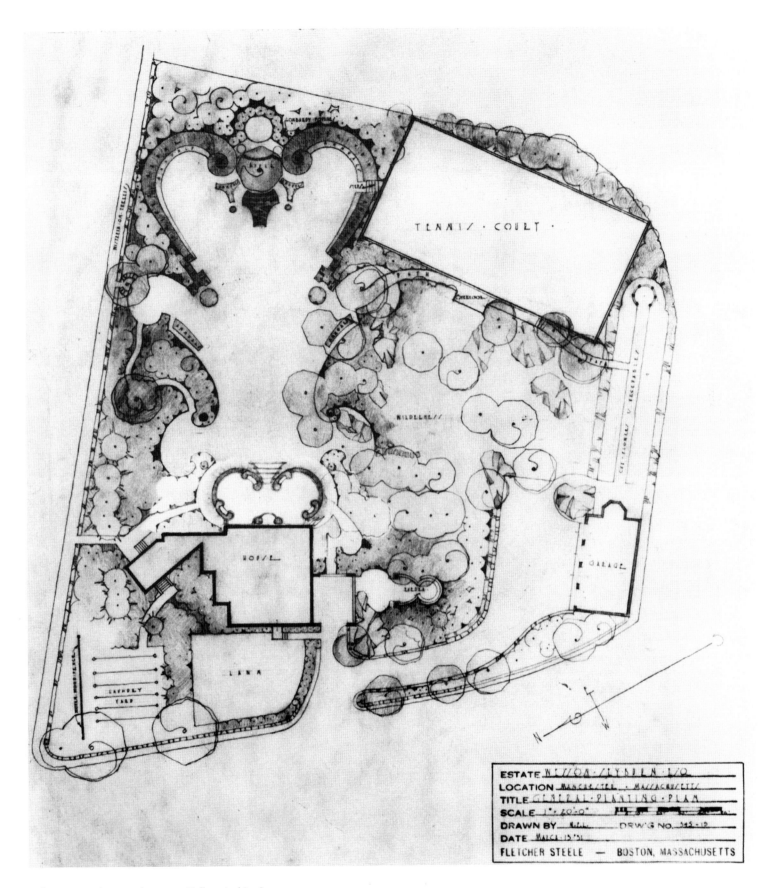

Seyburn estate plan, 1931. (SUNY ESF College Archives)

ESTATE OF WESSON SEYBURN ESQ.
AT · MANCHESTER · BY · THE · SEA · MASSACHUSETTS
THE TERRACE.

FLETCHER STEELE
BOSTON MASSACHUSETTS

FEBRUARY 1932
DRAWING No. 345-22A

Seyburn estate, terrace detail, 1932, never realized. (SUNY ESF College Archives)

terrace—did not appeal to the clients' taste. The expansive lawn design would have been more cohesive had its counterpart at the house been realized. Steele had proposed a stone terrace that, in plan, appeared as two circles. Matching circular awnings, one over each seating area, continued the motif, as did curved benches (reiterating the distant hedge shapes), and a door frame that scrolled to the floor. A flight of wedge-shaped steps was to lead down to the lawn. Two perspective drawings of the circle terrace survive, both identified as Drawing No. 345-22A. One is more architecturally substantial, with six awning supports, a scalloped roof overhang, and a low

stone wall. The other relies on a low hedge for definition, has four supports instead of six (making the structure almost ephemeral), and has a shallow conical roof instead of the flat scalloped awning.

Art Deco was an increasingly strong, though diffuse, influence on the work; Steele loved the vigorous, decorative possibilities of curved lines and sharp angles, intense, rich colors, and elegant, exotic materials and finishes. He would never abandon tradition altogether, but his interest in abstraction was gathering momentum.

MR. AND MRS. ALLAN SHELDEN
Manchester, Massachusetts
1929–1959

"At Manchester, too, is Mrs. Allan Shelden's tiny garden," Steele wrote in response to a magazine editor's query, "located perforce between street and sidewalk. I put a high wall on the sidewalk line; raised the beds around the middle to look like a sunken garden; put windows in the walls for lights at night. The public is completely forgotten and people lie sunbathing three feet from the public sidewalk and have dinner there in private at night."[104]

Summering around the corner from the Seyburns, the Sheldens enjoyed neither the spacious property nor the relative seclusion of their neighbors. A walled scheme seemed the most efficient solution to the problems of privacy and space, but the intensity of the design was unprecedented. In a reversal of tradition, nature was evoked largely through artifice: a flock of Canada geese silhouetted against the fountain backdrop, stylized metal waves lapping at the surface of the pool, and giant iron foxglove fountains dripping water into glass shells.

Extensive yew hedges reinforced the edge where garden and wall met, while hemlock (*Tsuga canadensis* 'Pyramidalis') flanked entry and backdrop and marked the rectangle's corners. A floriferous, predominantly blue-yellow bedding scheme (including *Gypsophila, Dicentra, Liatris, Delphinium belladonna,* santolina, *Platycodon,* aster, chrysanthemum, and phlox to be supplemented with petunias, ageratum, annual phlox ['Isabellina'], zinnia, nicotiana, and tuberose) was kept under tight architectural control by the concrete curbing edging the lower planting terrace.[105] Drawings for the garden show a development away from the conventional. One early plan indicates a central croquet green, double stairway from the house terrace, and statue as focal point.

Shelden estate. (SUNY ESF College Archives)

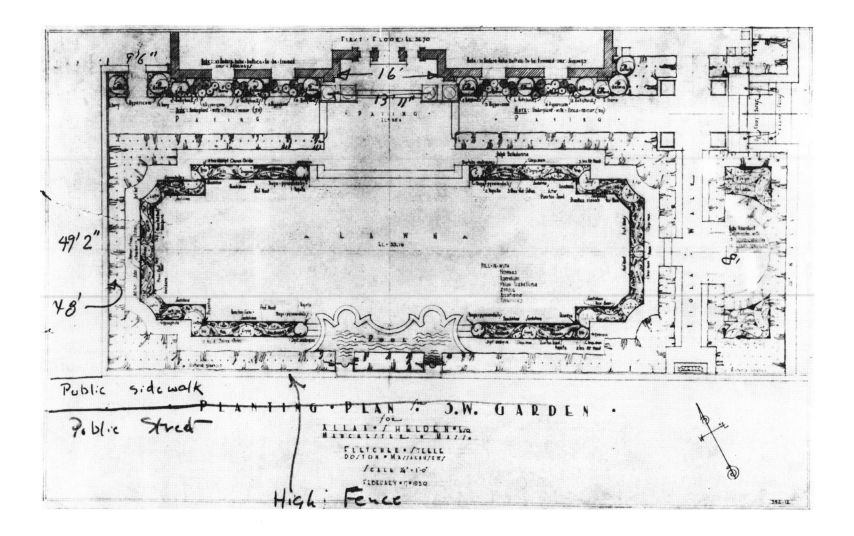

Shelden estate, planting
plan, 1930. (SUNY ESF
College Archives)

The Sheldens' tiny garden (roughly 50 by 100 feet) does not provide a very satisfactory setting for the big white house that stands immediately adjacent to it, but that particular task did not seem to have been uppermost in mind for either the clients or the designer. In 1955 Steele recommended the garden for publication along with only eight others; he clearly liked the way it had evolved.

Travel and Practice: The Finest Room in the World

The first five years of the 1930s emerged as some of the busiest and most successful of Steele's career. Life was fast-paced, filled with intriguing possibilities for travel, new friendships, and high-budget commissions. Steele had moved to a large apartment in a Beacon Street brownstone, with a view onto the Boston Common. His lecture and social calendars were crowded. In the first three years of the decade Steele visited England, France, Russia, Sweden, Germany, Turkey, Mexico, Austria,

Spain, Yugoslavia, and the American West, all the while taking on new—and big—jobs. The office staff struggled to keep on top of the dozens of projects as their boss dropped, somewhat erratically, in and out of sight.

Steele's interest in great and memorable spaces frequently led him to ponder works of architecture, probably more often than landscapes. "My impressions are still too much of a jumble to mean much," Steele wrote to his sister Esther from Istanbul on 26 January 1932.

One thing I know, that the interior of Hagia Sophia is the finest room in the world. . . . From the first one *feels* the age of Constantinople more than Rome, even. All the modern city seems but a house of cards on top of buried temples. Indeed, one of the tourist's common experiences is to go into the yard of a cheap wood house or a hole in any old garden and plunge down some steps to arrive suddenly in a vast "cistern" which runs under whole blocks of houses—

vaulted chambers with endless ranks of columns holding from three to five feet of clear cold water. . . . The vast mosques give one the same feeling of immensity as the cisterns. They are like no other interiors, because the biggest western churches are broken up by columns and piers—even Parma cathedral which seemed enormous to me till I had seen these.[106]

Office Life

In 1932 another landscape architect was added to the Water Street office, the first who had ever worked for Steele in any capacity except draftsman. Arthur Sylvester was happy to get the job, particularly in the field of residential design, as the Harvard-trained Charles Eliot scholar was primarily interested in gardens. Steele's reputation as a gifted if eccentric artist had drawn Sylvester's attention. Steele urged the young man to educate himself through travel abroad, as Steele had, and supplied him with letters of introduction to wealthy estate owners and professionals throughout Europe, in exchange for borrowing Sylvester's photographs upon his return.

During the job interview Steele asked Sylvester, "Do you have an engineering mind?" It was the same question he had asked Hoover seven years before and reflected an awareness of a gap in his own expertise. Hoover, who praised Steele's design skill, plant knowledge, and rigorous attention to detail, found him naive when it came to physics. "For example, he simply could not understand the principle of a catenary curve. When I demonstrated the contour of a swag chain by holding a piece of string, he objected that 'Chain behaves differently. It's heavier.' Once he designed a ten-foot aquarium wall that was completely impractical. I tried to explain surface pressure to him but he refused to believe that what he was proposing simply wouldn't work."[107]

Sylvester recalled that "Mr. Steele was a very dominating person and very unpredictable. One day he would be at the office at 6:00 a.m., then we wouldn't see him for weeks." The two extremes—Steele's obsessive need for routine and his impulsiveness—were both tough on office staff. Sylvester remembered his boss flying into rages, tearing up plans, when he felt he might be repeating himself. "You never knew what would happen next," Sylvester related. "We bought up iron fences, marble sidewalks, architectural fragments, then incorporated them into designs. Mr. Steele was always intent upon doing things differently. Rich little old ladies, in particular, loved him. As proper as he was, he enjoyed raising hell with people. Especially stuffy people, like members of the Boston

Society of Landscape Architects. Some of his colleagues thought he was crazy."[108] Sylvester left the office about 1936 when work began to slow down.

Steele's originality had caught the attention of other young designers as well. Daniel Kiley, who thought him "the only good designer working at the time," visited the office often during the early 1930s. Kiley was intrigued by the inventiveness and "fanciful imagination" that, in his eye, distinguished Steele from other practitioners, including Kiley's own boss (and Steele's former mentor), Warren Manning. Like Steele, Kiley admired Manning's plant and planning expertise but found him lacking in what both men identified as "art." Kiley thought Hoover's drawings superb and wanted to see some of the gardens they depicted, so when work for Manning took Kiley to Stockbridge in 1932, he phoned Mabel Choate to see if he might stop by for a short visit.

> She was immediately very receptive. I came over late in the morning and there was already a big party going on. Fletcher Steele was on the phone—to Europe—talking loudly, in an exaggerated Eastern accent that made him sound like a Bostonian. Mabel Choate lent me a camera so I could take pictures of the garden—at that time there was only the old garden, and the new Afternoon Garden.
>
> She said, "Oh, you must stay for lunch," which I did, but I was very timid then, I thought I might use the wrong spoon. It was all very formal. But she was extremely nice and we continued to write to one another for years. . . . She sent me a postcard from Egypt not long afterward . . . although I never saw her again.[109]

Steele maintained his strongest professional attachment to the Lowthorpe School of Landscape Architecture, Gardening and Horticulture for Women—as guest lecturer, critic, trustee, and, for a time, director. "Thank goodness," he wrote to his mother in 1932,

> another chore is over today. . . . Perhaps I told you that in April the impossibly spoiled child who was Director of the Lowthorpe School was made to resign. . . . Being the most conspicuous professional man on the Board they put me on as Chairman of the Emergency Committee to run things temporarily and lay out the future program. So first I was spending time at meetings & conferences to get things underway—going out to Groton, where the school is some 35 miles away—to arrange this & that. The Faculty is grand and pulled things through in fine shape.

The next thing was to make a program. Fortunately by that time I had developed some pretty definite ideas, so my schemes went down on paper without too much trouble. They were quite complicated and altogether different from anything that has gone before. However, they appealed to the Trustees. Well, I find it is somewhat dangerous to satisfy trustees. The result is that they urge one to go on to more work. At least that's what happened in this case....

That done, it was necessary to find a new Director. The requirements were really stiff. Aside from all the usual points of administrative ability, character, etc. we had to have someone with special training in our line. There aren't so many who could answer in a small profession. Those who might have the required qualities would all be successful practitioners who could hardly be expected to give up their own practice for a rather dreary educational experiment....

When I began asking questions, dozens of people were mentioned. Most of them I could weed out rather quickly. All this sort of work—I was rather high handed about (as about most things I'm afraid).[110]

Steele finally found his woman, a "proper sort," but was afraid she was too successful to consider the job. He took her to lunch at the Ritz, "where New York professional people never lunch under any circumstances. It was a good choice. She was suddenly no more in New York than in London, Paris, Madrid or Montreal. I was host and she instantly the guest. Then I worked hard." Describing his role in the affair to his sister, Steele observed: "Most people hate to be definite. I don't mind."[111]

Steele's denigrating phrase—"dreary educational experiment"—does not reflect his genuine and lasting commitment to the education of women landscape architects. Upon the dissolution of the Cambridge School of Architecture and Landscape Architecture (where he had occasionally lectured since 1915), he wrote to Henry Frost, the school's director:

I find myself deeply stirred on reading the information announcing the discontinuance of the Cambridge School....I agree with your reasoning and for the necessity of the move. None the less on that account do I deplore the fact. Nor am I reassured that the education of women is not given an unhappy blow. For it will mean a change in experience and outlook that has not been altogether an improvement in other coeducational institutions.

Concentration of the woman's point of view in a female institution has, in the Cambridge School, tended to bring to focus qualities which are essentially feminine and, because

of that, profoundly needed in the work of the world. Scatter the women and their organized interaction will be scattered. Their good influence will not lessen. But the finest fragrance of its self-distillation will be lost.[112]

Dream House

In 1930 Mary Schofield had presented Steele with two lots on Nubansuit Brook, Peterborough, New Hampshire, "in consideration of one dollar," conceivably in trade for landscape work. He envisioned building his dream house on the bucolic site and created several sketches of floor and landscape plans for it. One intriguing plan, marked May 1931, featured a rotunda.

A second, undated plan was also unconventional. It situated rooms to take full advantage of views and to create, by means of exterior walls, outdoor spaces, some fully enclosed, some finished by hedges or fences. The house's rooms were to be constructed on different levels. No elevations of it survive.

A long stretch of turf on axis with the living room terminates with a sculpture in a planting niche. A wide path cuts diagonally through the circle and finishes at the pond. Wooded buffers lay on both sides of the path and between the drive and the long, formal lawn. A second wide path intersects the lawn at its midpoint, creating a formal entrance to the garden from the drive. On the other side of the house a pergola stretches from the living room along the shore of the pond to a waterside terrace. A small courtyard is formed by the pergola and the exterior walls of the living room, dining room, and bedroom. It was a house designed from the outside in, a garden pavilion. World events, however, would conspire against Steele's dream.

EMILY AND STEPHEN SWINDELLS
Rockville, Connecticut
1931–1936

"My dear Mrs. Swindells," Steele wrote to his new client:

When it comes to the solution of a tricky imagination problem, my mind is aggravating. The right answer never comes just because I sit down and give the matter careful study. Rather it is like a name that has slipped out of one's mind. The only way to get it again is not to try to remember it, but to think of something else, and back it comes without warning.

First I tried to study the irregularity that you want (and I heartily approve), but no good ideas came. So I turned to something else and suddenly the complete picture came into

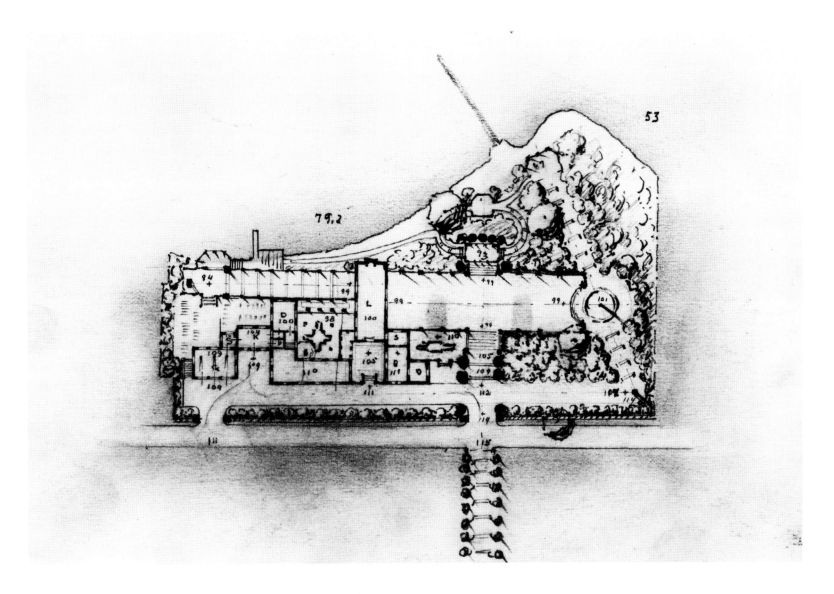

my mind, which maintained a proper balance without the symmetrical lines.[113]

The Swindells owned a high-style Victorian house in a family neighborhood on Prospect Street. The backyard, especially by Steele's standards, was small. The couple probably knew of the large garden across town belonging to Miss J. A. Maxwell, which Steele had added to eight years before. Grander than anything the couple could hope for on their half acre, the Maxwell estate had a fine rock garden, perhaps the "irregularity" that had caught Mrs. Swindells's eye.

"As I imagined myself sitting next [to] the house on your proposed terrace platform," Steele continued,

I felt the need of a small reflecting pool at my feet, and the rest came naturally. Such a pool would be at the lowest spot on the grounds, so that all the water from the Rock Garden, the two little fountains and running over the surface of the

ground after rain storms, would be caught in it and a single connection with the sewer would be sufficient—a saving of plumbing that would be considerable.

One would either step down onto the garden lawn or continue straight along . . . while the planted wall gradually changed into the rock garden. . . .

Then the trickle of water down from the rock garden, ending in the Bird Pool, would drain through a tiny open canal along the foot of this path, leading to the new pool, which would obviate the necessity of having any underground piping. Groups of flowers or bushes would be set about irregularly where the color and form were needed. . . .

This solution makes the two sides of the garden entirely different, yet keeps the right lines.

At the rear of this scheme Steele would build a treillage niche to enframe the water's source: a stainless-steel urn atop a

Sketch for Steele's Peterborough house, n.d. The grade markings document a 30-foot drop from the north (lower) side of the house to the pond (at the top of the sketch). (LC)

Swindells estate, terrace. (SUNY ESF College Archives)

Swindells estate, view from window. (SUNY ESF College Archives)

marble pedestal. The water would make a sharp diagonal cut across the platform in front of the urn, then cascade down the hill in a decorative cast-stone channel before it emptied into the large rock pool that formed the upper end of the rock garden. Heavily planted terraces and a wisteria arbor would sit at right angles to the stairway and water channels. At the writing of this first letter, Steele had not yet pictured the extensive latticework that would attach to the house by the terrace. In March of the following year, 1932, he suggested that Mrs. Swindells visit Mabel Choate at Naumkeag to see the Afternoon Garden: "The French lattice has been used there very effectively and I think would give you an excellent idea of what the finished effect would look like."[114]

"Before you can make a garden for a client," Steele instructed one young assistant late in life, "you must uncover his or her own character" (although, he continued, "you will discover that some of them just don't have any").[115] Steele seems to have conducted his initial interviews with success, his wit and sociability enhancing the investigations. His ability to form strong, early alliances ensured his clients' tolerance for what would follow: mud, inconvenience, and, inevitably, large bills.

By spring of 1934, much of Steele's design was on paper, and a model of the rock formations had been made to provide on-site guidance. One of Steele's inter-office reports describes construction techniques:

I told her that when the time came, we would move the rock as was done when building the Bartol Pool, by derrick, so that the stones could be lifted from the driveway and moved to exactly where they are wanted, without hauling them from one place to another. Meantime, she will look up one of the low field factory wagons with wide wheels, just as was used at the Maxwells', to move the heavy stones from place to place instead of trying to move them by hand, which would be a great waste of time. Mrs. Swindells is to get a lot of stones on the ground. She will pick them up and have them brought here. I told her it would ruin her lawn and she can not hope to have good grass this summer. . . .

Mrs. Swindells was really worried that the garden would be all rock and no planting. I told her we would put in plant-

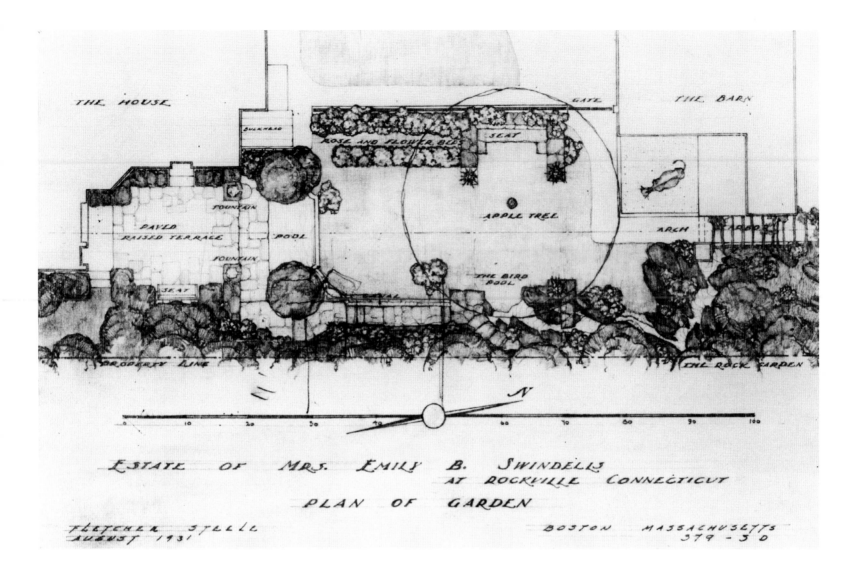

ESTATE OF MRS. EMILY B. SWINDELLS
AT ROCKVILLE CONNECTICUT
PLAN OF GARDEN

FLETCHER STEELE   BOSTON MASSACHUSETTS
AUGUST 1931   379 - 3 D

Swindells estate plan, 1931. Hoover included Emily Swindells's cow in this drawing. (SUNY ESF College Archives)

ing as we went along, consequently she would not see anything like as much rock when we get done, just as a planted wall is almost hidden by the planting.

The office is not to proceed farther than the bird bath, until that is done, no matter how ridiculous is looks beyond. It is the temptation on the part of the client and superintendent every time to start something else and try to carry everything along at the same time. Consequently, at the end, there is no one finished thing to show for the work. The office is to finish one piece before even considering what to take up next.[116]

By the end of summer the rockwork was complete and the pool filled. Steele suggested snails and oxygenating plants for the pool: "The whole thing should cost only three dollars, and be worth it."[117]

For the upper terrace, Steele suggested a circle of rhododen-dron (violet and white) and pyracantha. "In the center, after a good deal of thought, I decided to recommend one Styrax japonica. It has pale green foliage which would be a beautiful relief against the dark evergreens and rarely lovely hanging white flowers in the spring."[118]

By late fall of 1934 the pool was leaking; Mrs. Swindells had insisted on concrete against Steele's recommendations for lead. He wrote: "I am sorry of course . . . but not really surprised."[119] In January 1935 she wrote to complain about the cost of the plaster model—$259.75—for the cast-stone cascade. Steele replied that $146 covered the charge of making a plaster cast from the original plasticine. The rest was for the sculptor, Archangelo Cascieri.

Steele ordered more plants for the garden in April 1935. Wisteria, magnolia, azalea, holly, *Pieris,* rhododendron, spirea, yew, juniper, iris, laburnum, nandina, pyracantha, stewartia, and hemlock were added to the list. Steele attached an unusual handwritten postscript casting the country's deepening economic depression in a chillingly opportunistic light: "Why not look around and see if some of your neighbors haven't a big Spirea Van Houttei with branches flowing over to the ground which they would be glad to sell? There is scarcely a side yard that does not have one, and in many cases people who are short of cash are glad to sell a large plant, especially if a replacement is offered."[120]

In July 1935 Mrs. Swindells was still unhappy about the cost of the model. And the pool was still leaking. Steele canceled plans for a visit to Rockville with his sister Esther, citing Fourth of July traffic as the reason.

More plants were added to the garden in April 1936. "It always seems to me prettier to have two white to one pink dogwood," wrote Steele. "The pink is really a strong color and is well set off by a larger quantity of white. On that account I would put the pink in the middle.... P.S. I have changed one of the rhododendrons to red. A single accent of that color would be a help and it will be in the corner where it can't swear at the azaleas."[121]

Steele's design for the small property combined extremes of formal and informal elements. Its frank eclecticism and decorative extravagance may have been inspired by the Victorian house. In broad terms, he sandwiched a naturalistic rock outcropping—complete with pools and waterfalls—between two fancy pieces of woodwork: the trellis niche and arbor at the top of the hill and the elaborate lattice structure on the terrace at the bottom. Water united the scheme, falling past terraces of flowering shrubs and perennials and spilling into the pool. Two lion's-head fountains poured tiny streams into a system of channels, edged in cast-stone rope. The French lattice (as at Naumkeag) was covered with clematis, Baltic ivy, and silver fleece vine. The garden was finished. And Mrs. Swindells was happy. Twelve years later she would write: "I don't believe you ever designed a garden for anyone who got more enjoyment out of it than Stephen and I do."[122]

CHARLOTTE WHITNEY ALLEN
Rochester, New York
circa 1934

The ongoing development of Charlotte Allen's tiny garden reflected Steele's general design process. During the first phase of construction, the backyard volume of space had been defined—with walls, raised terraces, and hedges. Subsequently, architectural ornament and planting details were introduced, for color and decorative interest. Each added element brought new risks and established increasingly complicated sets of contingencies.

A photograph of a Sussex gateway likely provided the design

Allen estate model, with proposed arch. (SUNY ESF College Archives)

Allen estate, arch and
sculpture detail. (SUNY
ESF College Archives)

inspiration for the arched entablature that Steele had always envisioned for the garden. In one version, recorded in a model, Steele eliminated the central spherical ornament of the prototype and replaced it with a pediment. His final design reinstated the third ornament but reduced the ball and pediment and leveled the three obelisks. Architectural details on the applied pilasters and frieze were adapted from the house facade, as were materials, brick and cast stone. The new feature emphasized the volume between house and back boundary. The rectangular block of space had become almost tangible upon entering and the garden took on a bold, new eclecticism.

In 1934 Steele received a note and three snapshots of current work from "Sandy" (Alexander) Calder, whom he had befriended in Paris: "Am bringing the mountain to Mohammed," the note read, "but stay still a moment till I catch up to you! I'll be in Boston by Dec 15 (I think) with the *object* or *objects*."[123] Calder was talking about a sculpture he was working on for Charlotte Allen. The word "mobile" had not yet been coined.

On his way back from Chicago in 1935, Calder stopped off in Rochester to meet Allen, "introduced to me by Fletcher Steele. . . . He had been interested in my show at the Galerie Vignon in 1932. . . . Mrs. Allen wanted a mobile for her garden which Fletcher Steele had designed—this was the first object I made for out of doors. As I remember, it consisted of some quite heavy iron discs that I found in a blacksmith's shop in Rochester and had them welded to rods progressively getting heavier and heavier."[124]

The allée terminus was not well suited for a freewheeling

modern sculpture, but Steele probably did not want attention diverted from the Lachaise. He and Allen had toyed with the idea of turning Calder's mobile into a fountain, perhaps to occupy a place near the house terrace, but costs were prohibitive. If the Lachaise figure was the garden's keynote, the Calder mobile was an interesting element discoverable only by accident. The allée was hidden, found only by climbing the steps and skirting the standing nude, at the end of the walk, now planted with hostas and lined with marble urns.

Charlotte Allen may have known Calder through her (and Steele's) close Rochester friend Joseph ("Tom") F. Taylor. Taylor had met Calder in 1928 when the sculptor approached him as president of Bausch and Lomb Optical Company for information about reflective surfaces that he was considering inte-

grating into his sculpture. Calder had become a friend of the family and when in Rochester often stayed with the Taylors (for whom Steele would design a garden about 1936).

Calder also spent a lot of time with Charlotte Allen in the Oliver Street garden, creating tiny animals and jewelry from wire and pliers always handy in his pocket. One pair of earrings read "happy" and "birthday," perhaps an impromptu gift or a special order from Taylor, who greatly admired Mrs. Allen. In 1938 she bought Calder's *Flat Cat*, which sat on a table in her drawing room, "flattened perhaps," quipped one local historian, "by boredom with the muddy Matisse landscape that hung on a nearby wall."[125]

Shortly after her divorce, Charlotte Allen inherited the Clarence Smith Bookstore on Alexander Street. Every morning

Snapshot sent to Steele by Alexander Calder, 7 December 1934. Calder was proposing this mobile for the Allen estate. (LC. Photographer unknown)

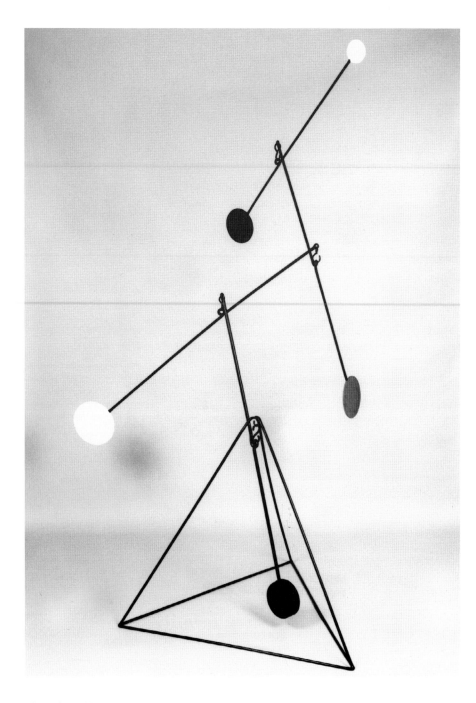

Alexander Calder. Untitled mobile, 1935, Memorial Art Gallery of the University of Rochester, gift of Charlotte Whitney Allen. (Photo by James M. Via)

at 9:30 she climbed into her 1936 Ford-Cunningham town car and rode to the store, where she sat among green velvet pillows and, according to friends, did jigsaw puzzles. To converse with her chauffeur, who was separated by a glass partition, she used a microphone. The vehicle was a rare combination of a Ford chassis and a body by Cunningham Corporation of Rochester with a retractable canopy for the front seat.[126]

CHARLOTTE AND ADRIAN DEVINE
Brighton (Rochester), New York
1931–1941

Through the 1930s Steele worked for many Rochester clients. He was continuing to experiment with treatments for suburban sites where backyard space was limited, plots were rectilinear, and screening views into neighboring yards a priority. The structural scheme at Charlotte Allen's place was providing a prototype that allowed diversity according to circumstances. The basic plan included house terrace, lawn panel, lateral hedges or walls for privacy, and a raised platform or stage.

Steele used the same plan for the Devines, who owned a modest suburban home in the small village of Brighton, south of Rochester. Unlike Charlotte Allen, Charlotte Devine was an avid and sophisticated gardener and so wanted a range of things to grow. The garden's most unusual feature was grove of fifteen locusts on the terrace. At the edge, a low wrought-iron and wood fence provided enclosure and seating on the broad wooden slats ("like fender seats around fireplaces that one sees in clubs," as Steele described them in April 1933[127]). Low brick posts repeated the white brick of the house. The Art Deco–influenced iron motif was silhouetted against a broad expanse of lawn that narrowed, imperceptibly, to squeeze the space and enhance the illusion of distance. Six sour gum trees (*Nyssa sylvatica*) were set into the edge of the lawn panel at regular intervals, three to a side. Medina stone walks bordered the panel. Arborvitae hedges and broadleaf evergreen plantings at either side of the space gradually decreased in height, also to stretch the apparent length of the area.

The raised terrace at the far end of the lawn was planted with broadleaf evergreens and arborvitae (grape arbors depicted on the early plan were never built), but interest centered on the dry stone retaining wall, which held a wide variety of rock plants. The wall was curved into a semicircle to provide more area; it held sedum, saxifrage, thyme, and other rock-loving varieties.

In 1943 a new strip of land was added along the east side of the property and Steele suggested planting a gray hedge along

Devine estate, terrace fence
detail. The rails also func-
tioned as seats. (SUNY ESF
College Archives)

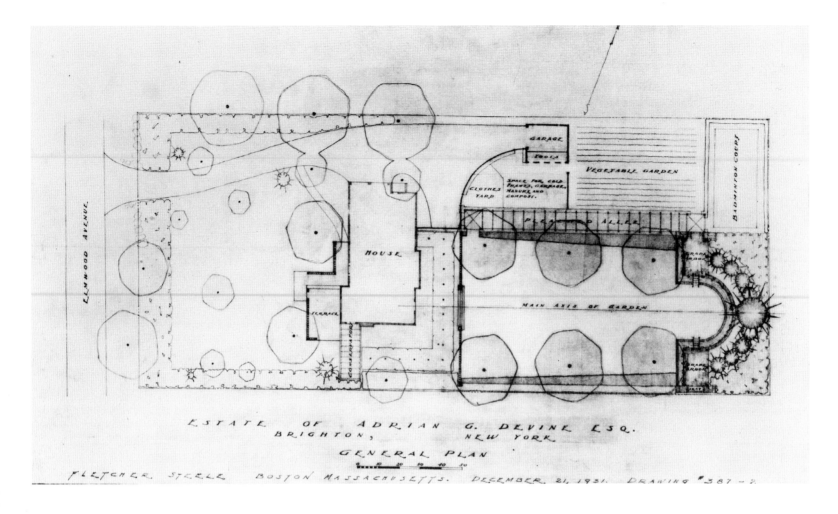

ESTATE OF ADRIAN G. DEVINE ESQ.
BRIGHTON, NEW YORK
GENERAL PLAN

FLETCHER STEELE BOSTON MASSACHUSETTS. DECEMBER 21, 1931. DRAWING #387-2.

Devine estate, plan, 1931. (SUNY ESF College Archives)

it, "rather loose growing but not untidy. It should get its harmony from similarity of foliage and color rather than uniformity of plant variety." His list of recommended plants reflects his broad horticultural knowledge: "For tall stuff I would use the Rosemary Willow (*Salix incana* which the botanists change from week to week to s. rosa rinifolia or s. eleagnus. The only sure, permanent name is always the common name). With it, perhaps every third plant, I would use *Eleagnus argentea* with an *Eleagnus umbellata* in front of it. The latter usually grows less high, though not always. The combination is interesting for color and fruit. Along the front edge I would use the dwarf *Salix purpurea nana,* which you can clip if you like."[128]

HYGHE CONTENTE
Mary Kenly
Manchester, Massachusetts
1933–1935

Steele was working on the North Shore again in 1933, at Hyghe Contente for Mary (Mrs. William Kennard) Kenly of Chicago.

Steele had already created gardens for Standish and Dorothy Backus's hillside home on School Street and for the Seyburns' more suburban residence in town. Mary Kenly and her granddaughter summered about a half mile west of the others at the end of a winding drive through woods—most of which would be preserved by Steele's design.

Hoover remembered the job as being one of the first where a good part of the design took place on-site. Even the pool was largely improvised as Henry Rice, Steele's rockwork specialist, labored to expose the ledge that would form one side. According to Hoover, plans were drawn afterward, to record what had been done.

Steele underscored the distant sea view by building a pool between viewer and vista. The frankly artificial pond acted as a visual prelude to the real thing. In case visitors missed the point, Neptune stood at one end, trident raised. Steele had bought the sculpture from the city of Watertown, Massachusetts, when the old water utilities building was razed.

Ten years earlier, Steele had successfully combined geometry and naturalistic rockwork in a swimming pool for Charles

Schweppe in Lake Forest, Illinois. He used the scheme again in 1931, in a Milton garden, and the Kenlys' pool was similarly designed. One side continued the wall that delineated the edge of the small lawn terrace near the house. The other edges of the pool were created by irregular rocks that merged with the existing landscape. The presence of Rice—draftsman, field supervisor, and geological wizard—was facilitating otherwise impossible designs. Steele's design effectively solved the problem of connecting the built landscape to the existing one.

The perimetal treatment of the Hyghe Contente pond boldly emphasized the dichotomy between the artificial and the natural. The railing along the straight edges gave visual support to the large figure and pedestal that sat at one of the right-angled intersections. The "natural," rocky side evoked Japan with bold plantings of Japanese iris, Japanese maple, and *Petasites*. Exotic, aggressive, and distinctive in large groups, *Petasites* (Japanese butterbur) was used often by Steele, although it was marginally hardy in most of his clients' growing zones. He used the plate-sized leaves in quantity a decade later in the Robert Stoddards' garden in Worcester. (The Stoddards were instructed to buy the plant from the owners of Hyghe Contente. The price was $1.30 at Steele's insistence: "My clients are not allowed to give plants to one another," he informed Helen Stoddard.[129])

Another of Steele's favorites, *Aralia spinosa*, Devil's walking stick, grew at the Manchester garden in small woodland clearings. Steele liked its distinctive, complex texture and its habit of reaching for the sun. Like *Petasites, Aralia* can be alarmingly

Hyghe Contente, pool, 1934. (SUNY ESF College Archives)

prolific in a happy environment but offers a dramatic show from spring through autumn. The leaves (composed of several dozen leaflets) grow to four feet, the creamy plumes of mid-summer flowers almost as long. Bright pink stems, black berries in August, and brilliant red foliage in October complete the performance.

Elsewhere on the Kenly property, lilacs, rhododendron, azaleas, and peonies were massed to provide year-round interest, the list probably reflecting the clients' specific requests. Twelve clematis vines on the house front, which appear in many of Steele's designs from the 1930s, may well have been his suggestion. The stone wall directly south of the house supported

roses, and the Italian-style pergola at the east end, wisteria.

A beech hedge and a stone retaining wall (continuing the architectural edge of the pool) delineated the north and south boundaries of a long, narrow lawn. Steele proposed an elaborate lattice structure for the end of the shady vista, but it was never built. A handsome pair of lights intended to mark the drive entry (whose design was also recommended to Mabel Choate for Naumkeag) were never realized either.

Steele's historical inspiration for the balcony and loggia that controlled the distant water view at the back of the house was Spanish. The pool and balcony had been situated to create the strong visual link to the ocean—a practice Steele identified as

Hyghe Contente, pool detail with Neptune sculpture, drawing. (SUNY ESF College Archives)

ESTATE OF MRS. WILLIAM K. KENLY
MANCHESTER MASSACHUSETTS
THE POOL

FLETCHER STEELE
BOSTON MASSACHUSETTS

MARCH 1934
DRAWING No. 395-11

Hyghe Contente, view to the pool and house. "The
garden is on a steep hillside, dominated by native woods.
Sophisticated lawns, pools and planting were all mixed
up with the wild. I like to mix formal and informal
features and have never found them out of keeping."
Steele to F. F. Rockwell, 10 June 1955. (SUNY ESF
College Archives)

Hyghe Contente, loggia. (LC. Photo by D. Jarvis)

characteristic of Moorish architecture. He also greatly admired Spanish ironwork, especially domestic designs, and often turned to *Hierros Artísticos*, by Luis Labarta, for information about household utensils, garden gates, hinges, and balconies. "It is an endless pleasure to study the amazing detail of a Spanish craftsman in iron."[130] Steele found great charm in small Spanish courtyards where flowerpots lined balconies and hung on walls. He imported the practice for use on the Kenlys' south-facing stucco houseback. The shady portico beneath the porch, of Spanish inspiration, provided refuge from the summer sun. Steele had been to Spain the year before he began Mary Kenly's garden and would return in 1935. Only China would haunt his memory in quite the same way.

China

In the spring of 1934 Steele realized a dream of his own: a trip to the Far East. The three-month tour to Japan and China was an adventure, taken in the company of friends and clients. "I don't travel," he once explained. "I just go places. It is fun to see and know foreigners and their gardens, their children and their animals and their sing song girls—every thing that means every day stuff, not politics nor economics nor art or anything that is news. I don't suppose I really learn much. But in this way I have become fond of many peoples, particularly the French, Chinese, Danes, Italians, Spanish, Turks and Haitiens. And I have found points to admire in Austrians, Russians, Norwegians, Swedes and English. There are other peoples whom I care nothing about and do not wish to visit again. With God's help, I shall never see Florida or California."[131]

Besides visiting the frequented tourist attractions, the group traveled to the temple at Wu T'ai Shan, far into the interior of China, several hundred miles from Peking, where Buddhism had taken on the exotic influence of Mongolia. "The whole place was alive, like a kicked ant's nest, with fierce [zealots]— sweeping around the prayer wheel walk, prostrating themselves on their faces all night long to the dull boom of a drum that has been beaten steadily now day and night. A glaring full moon made it more barbarous."[132] Steele kept copies of letters and journal notes and later collated them into a fifty-one-page travelogue. A few passages were reprinted in magazine articles, but most of it was never published. Steele's hierarchy of experience was idiosyncratic; above all, he was alive to visual stimuli. His account begins, characteristically, with color: "First impressions of Japan are confused somewhat by the admixture of the two perfect days of spring when leaf buds turn to pale yellow, pink and green before summer's deeper color. Never do I remember such vernal loveliness."[133]

He was intrigued by the fantastic shapes in the landscape: "the hills are sharp and the lowlands and valleys absolutely flat, all differences in grade being taken up by endless clever terracing." Odd bits of information captured his imagination: the cultivated fields "are planted with other things, some of which are just green, others of brilliant yellow mustard (from which they make the oil which keeps the women's hair in place in fearful and wonderful designs)."[134]

The "irregular symmetry" of the Japanese temple complexes reminded him of "old Mayan Yucatán," which he had visited the previous winter; he was deeply impressed by the powerful spaces created by the overhanging temple and pagoda roofs. "The proportions of width to height are so admirable that they have that sort of magic that I call the 4th dimension of space composition. It is one of the subjects of foremost interest with me—the main technical study of this trip. I know it is impossible to explain to anyone in words, but it must be mentioned in any account of my personal reactions to the trip."[135]

A more explicit description of the "occult" quality and its impact on the observer was formulated later:

Steele in Chieh Tai Ssu, 1934. "As is invariably the case in these complex groups of courtyards and terraces, built in the midst of grand scenery, the buildings are so arranged that one can see out only rarely and by chance." From "China Notes," 2, LC. (SUNY ESF College Archives)

Two images from Wu T'ai Shan, 1934. (SUNY ESF College Archives)

Never was it less expected than in the sand and stone court of the Ryoan-ji Temple in Kyoto. The place was ugly according to his standards. [Steele again refers to himself in the third person.] He stood in a small, rectangular plot, enclosed by walls and buildings. It was floored with sand, raked in patterns. Here and there a stone stuck up like rocks out of water at low tide. Not a sprig of grass, a bush or tree was inside the walls. Everything that made a garden, in his opinion, was not there. Yet he was suddenly yanked out of himself as if by magic.

The facts of stone and sand were forgotten. Length, breadth and thickness disappeared. Size no longer counted. He felt the suggestion of unmeasured space. He could only compare the effect in terms of sound with that of his village bell at home whose undertones and overtones multiplied in rich, vibrant harmony that almost hid the major note. The Ryoan-ji court captured the overtones and undertones of proportion so finely as to bemuse by interplay of form, mass and line.[136]

The emotional impact of the phenomenon intrigued him no less than the visual: "The Observer could not tell how it made other people feel to experience occult space. All he could do was to feel his own pulse . . . he found the effect bound up with the realization that, contrary to humdrum common sense, things clicked in a new way. He no longer remained a self-bounded unit to which came sight and sound from without—himself and the world two separate entities—subject and object—which were, by all the rules of arithmetic, impossible to add. What was outside was part of him, and the echo in him was surely part of it."[137] The evocation of self-transcending experiences constituted a new dimension to Steele's Beaux Arts spacemaking.

He wrote in admiration of the gardens of Kobori Ensyuu (circa 1600), who, at his best, "has never been approached by any other designer in the use of water, rocks, planting and earth sculpture." But he criticized Ensyuu's many followers: "Later Japanese gardens have become a bit fantastic and too overcrowded with plant material and gew-gaws for my taste."[138]

China held as many surprises as Japan. Steele compared the two: "In architecture and landscape architecture there are many matters in which now China, then Japan, is superior. In the arrangement and plan of buildings—and cities—China starts with a bigger, grander idea in almost every instance. The plan of Peking and the Forbidden City makes every other world capital seem tricky and childish. . . . Down through smaller cities and towns I was continually inspired by the splendor of idea and the singleness of purpose—the *inevitable* quality of Chinese design."[139]

In other respects, he thought Japan superior: "The temple interiors of Japan succeed where the Chinese fail. They are sparsely furnished with a few objects placed where by color or form they create good, sometimes admirable space compositions." Steele's interest in the emotional impact of environment was stirred: "The interiors of the buildings are evidently carefully studied in form and color to induce desired psychological moods, whether spacious and mysterious as at the Chion-in at Kyoto or the low, happily spaced anterooms and shrines at the Shoquu mausoleums in Tokio."[140]

In the end, the impact of China was more profound on Steele's work. He was, in fact, predisposed to appreciate certain aspects of Chinese gardens, having already developed, by 1934, a preference for walled gardens through his trips to Rome and Spain. Steele found many of his firmest ideas echoing through the ancient Chinese courtyards.

In 1946 Steele wrote an article, "China Teaches," for *Landscape Architecture*. There he presented Chinese prototypes as "propaganda for certain ideas and moods of gardens" and argued for the conscious development and preservation of empty space so characteristic of Chinese gardens. Steele also admired the privacy and the deliberateness of the Chinese garden.

Formalities hold strangers in the outer courts. Plants, too, must go through a careful novitiate. . . . They will have no plant that is not a friend, to be watched and tended as long as it lives, come good, come ill.

The Chinese would as easily say of his wife as of his garden: "You should have seen her last week when she was all dressed up." His pride in his wife and garden are too deep, too much part of his home, to wear on his sleeve for visitors to peek at. When the precious moment comes, when the moon is right and the peach tree is coming into flower next the pond, he will invite a close friend to share his pleasure without distraction of yesterday or tomorrow.[141]

Steele especially envied the respect for old gardens in China. "After seeing almost anything, from Newport mansions to Cape Cod cottages, torn down merely to try something else in their place, it is soothing to feel the timelessness of a design idea in China."[142] He had been in business long enough to see many of his gardens fade, others disappear altogether.

During the next ten years Steele crossed new aesthetic boundaries. His use of exotic motifs grew tangibly as a result of the Far East trip, but the more important impact was deeper, affecting his sense of garden space and freeing him from its more conventional manifestations.

Peking, Peony Temple, 1934. (SUNY ESF College Archives)

Summer Palace Garden, 1934. (SUNY ESF College Archives)

4 · Apex: Invention, 1936–1949

The experimentation that characterized Steele's work from the late 1930s was inspired by his travels, his interest in modern art, and his increasing skills. These explorations depended on trusting relationships with clients who were enthusiastic about the design process, but the contracting scale of projects during these years may also have served Steele's imaginative forces well. His work during the period tended to concentrate on individual features of larger gardens that were already substantially developed and on smaller gardens. Both were well suited to improvisation.

STANDISH BACKUS
Grosse Pointe Shores, Michigan
1934

By 1934 most of the fundamental design proposals for Standish Backus's estate had been approved and work was well under way. "This place is a bloody muddy mess," Backus wrote to Steele on 9 November. "I am home with a ptomaine attack in my ptummy. There are a steam shovel and two or three motor trucks engaged in transporting the East Mound to the South Stage. . . . As I wrote you before, we are following the contour lines on your blueprints just as closely as little steam shovel is able, and when we get it polished off by hand, it ought to look just as you have indicated."[1] Standish Backus was proving a good-natured and well-informed client. He liked the role of field superintendent and was capable of monitoring the disposition of soil according to Steele's grading plans.

Steele's sculpting of the front (east) lawn had a strong functional purpose as well as an aesthetic one: he was grading the

land so that it rose gently at its eastern end to hide the busy street but not the big lake. From the east house terrace, the street was invisible. On the street side, passersby saw only a retaining wall topped with a balustrade.

"We have found what appears to be a very nice stone for the dry walls [of the Stage area]," Backus continued in the same letter. "It is of rather a dark buff color, and is easily broken in three planes. Mr. Watt [the grounds superintendent] located it in a Junk Yard. It is from the old Moffet Building . . . in which my father once had an office. . . . It would seem more or less like re-assembling an old acquaintance in a new role." Steele often tried to locate and recycle old building materials—not only was it often cheaper this way, but old pieces had more character. Steele sometimes bought architectural remnants and then designed gardens around them. He also enjoyed working with well-established plants and encouraged Backus and his family to drive around "old Detroit" in search of ancient specimens on abandoned properties.

"I think it would be highly desirable for you to turn up on our front door step some morning in the not distant future," Backus went on. "I will be glad to see you." Steele had become a dear friend of the family. When he arrived, he would be set upon by the children, knocked to the floor, and tickled mercilessly.[2]

"P.S. #1," the letter continued, "The easterly end of the East lawn is now decorated with two tall piles of black and extremely fertile surface soil. We have named one of them Mt. Watt and the other Fletcher Heights." Backus's second postscript tackled the subject of the profile of the balusters that were to run on top of a curved wall in the Stage area. "To me, it looks a little bit 'effeminate' as compared to the other balusters around the place." He suggested instead a balustrade end post from Wollaton Hall.

The next day Backus sent a follow-up letter, ruminating about his previous choice of words. Steele had met his obsessive match, and the two perfectionists were having a field day.

Perhaps I can describe it better in this way: From the point of greatest diameter up, they remind me of the neck and shoulders of Marie Antoinette, and from about the middle down, they remind me of skirts with too many petticoats underneath, and I could think of nothing but lace-frilled pantalettes such as one sees when sitting in the front rows. . . . I again looked at the picture of the garden wall at Wollaton Hall. . . . I think it can be adapted very attractively by your delicate Italian hand to fit the locality under discussion. . . . If you would examine the picture carefully under a magnifying glass, I am confident you will see what I mean.[3]

The baluster was changed, and the letters, nearly five hundred in all, continued.

Steele wanted to plant the long drive with "a minimum of tall bushy stuff in order to avoid the pin cushion effect of solid shrubbery. Instead we should simply put in enough to modulate pleasantly into Mr. McCauley's planting [next door], with a considerably handsomer type of stuff. I would have a 3' border of grass next the drive proper. Otherwise overall ground cover material which would take a minimum of maintenance after it is in, out of which would grow occasional English hawthorns, broad-leaved evergreens, etc., in the English manner."[4] The other side of the drive, next to the big lawn, was to be bordered by a retaining wall and a close-clipped taxus hedge.

The estate's big forecourt was remarkable for its intricate Belgian block paving and a large obelisk that rose at its center, based on an eighteenth-century Scottish design reproduced in Gertrude Jekyll's *Garden Ornament.* Steele's ideas for the Forecourt underwent several changes before the final plan emerged. The obelisk replaced a tree that Steele had originally conceived for the island, and he changed the island's paving from pebbles to cobbles in an attempt to introduce a more robust, rustic quality to the area. Forecourt planting was limited to beds around the perimeter and at the four corners. *Clematis montana* softened the strong stone profile of one of the

Standish Backus and his daughters on the new wall of the entry drive, Grosse Pointe Shores, Mich., 1932. The house, upper right, is under construction. (SUNY ESF College Archives)

Backus estate, forecourt and view to Lake St. Clair. Clematis covers the forecourt balustrade, ca. 1939. (SUNY ESF College Archives)

ESTATE OF STANDISH BACKUS ESQ. GROSSE POINTE SHORES MICH.
THE SUNDIAL

Backus estate, forecourt sundial detail, 1933. The drawing was based on a 1630 design from Drummond Castle, Perthshire, featured in Gertrude Jekyll's *Garden Ornament.* (SUNY ESF College Archives)

garden's much disputed balustrades, while sweet bay magnolia was espaliered against one of the house walls. Baltic ivy was the predominant ground cover; clipped yews framed the entrance. Wisteria climbed against the massive stone house walls. The effect was traditional and elegant.

According to general guidelines, all materials used in the Forecourt repeated those in the house: "Walls shall be faced where exposed with limestone of the same kind and finish as that used in the ashlar stone work of the exterior house walls. It shall be cut to assemble with the same ashlar pattern as that used in the exterior house walls." Woodwork: "Any woodwork called for shall be of clear, seasoned oak and of the same kind as that used in house, half timber work." Hardware: "Where hardware is called for it shall be of best quality wrought iron, oil burned (no paint or shellac added)."[5]

Construction guidelines were extensive and specific. For example: "Under all coping, consoles and cap stones, lead flash

pans (to be of 16" sheet lead) shall be installed. All flash pans to be soldered to form one continuous unit from end to end, turned down ½" and fitted neatly to the wall top before cap stones or finials are put in place."[6]

A pair of matching lion's-head piers signaled the gateway to the Basecourt, roughly the same size as the Forecourt. Planting here was confined to a large herb garden, based on a design from *Gardeners Labrinthine* by Thomas Hyll (1584). The geometric layout also resembled modern French parterres. Backed with flowering peaches and old roses, the borders were edged in front with a lacy, scalloped design made with clumps of Artemisia, *Aubrieta,* yellow primula, and oenothera in a gray/purple/gray/yellow sequence. The nursery and apple orchard, primarily ornamental, lay just west of the service court.

The Wild Garden stretched along the south side of the lawn, serving as a buffer between it and the neighbor's, an inspired use for the narrow strip of land. In 1935 ferns were ordered in quantities of fifty or one hundred. Three hundred violets in four varieties, two hundred Virginia bluebells, two hundred bloodroot, and forty-seven other species of flowering plants were scattered to naturalize through the narrow tract. Seventeen varieties of primula clustered along the stream with six varieties of trout lily. Twelve species of botanical tulips and six kinds of narcissus, *Iris reticulata, Lilium canadense,* and *Camassia leichtlinii* re-created a rich, idealized Michigan woodland. An overstory of fragrant native and exotic trees shaded the forest floor; carpets of Baltic ivy and vinca softened transitions between planting clumps. A sinuous lead-bottom "stream" (with recirculating pump) formed the garden's backbone.

A ramp led from the Wild Garden to the South Lawn, past a small outdoor sitting room, first recorded in plan in 1932. A diminutive stone and leaded-window shelter designed shortly afterward did not win Backus's approval. The following year Steele proposed a tiny country cottage with stone chimney and porch, but this was not built either. Steele continued to design alternatives for the spot—presumably at Backus's request—but none were realized. Perhaps Backus liked the idea that there was perpetually one more garden feature to design because it gave him something to look forward to, something to argue about with his friend.

The Stage area on the South Lawn was originally planned as a bosquet and flower garden, but "developing a sense of vertical dimensions, even on apparently flat land," emerged as one of Steele's major goals in the new landscape. He later described how "all over the narrow lot—a couple of hundred feet in all, though more in depth—we raised walls, theatre stage and pool; sunk a wild garden and lead bottom stream; put in a long trick Lilac Garden; medieval grape arbor, etc; to make abundant the space which started out flat and cramped."[7] Steele had infused the East Lawn with vitality by scooping it into a new shape. The Stage area would be similarly enlivened by building up a small (about three-foot) terrace.

Two curving ramps led up to the turf terrace past a cast-stone and lead pool. Trumpet-blowing putti at both corners of

Backus estate, Wild Garden, view east from the ramp. Front lawn is on the left. (SUNY ESF College Archives)

PARAPET WALL IN THEATRE

ESTATE OF STANDISH BACKUS ESQ

AT GROSSE POINTE SHORES, MICHIGAN

FLETCHER STEELE
BOSTON MASSACHUSETTS

AUGUST 12, 1935
DRAWING No. 346-274

Backus estate, proposed Stage, drawing, 1935. (SUNY ESF College Archives)

the semicircular pool were designed by Archangelo Cascieri. Once drawings for the area had been approved, a model was made to work out problems of proportion—"I did the thing myself in plaster," Steele wrote.[8] Huge box, clipped into big cushions and overwintered in custom-made canvas tents, softened the transition from stone to lawn, amazing visitors because box of any size is unusual in Michigan. A beech hedge backed the Stage, and a clipped linden hedge defined the east end of the South Lawn; the west end opened onto the Long Shot.

Plans for the six two-sided bays reveal an approach ruled by geometry. The "walls" of the green room were arborvitae, trimmed, tied, and regularly replaced to maintain a firm architectural presence. Juniper was originally considered but re-

jected in favor of arborvitae's superior color and form. Within each bay evenly spaced lilacs backed the curving herbaceous borders. Plans drawn up in January 1935 specify one each of different lilac varieties; by April 1936 the scheme was calling for a homogeneous lilac hedge within each bay.

The borders were edged in gray-foliaged plants; artemisia, veronica, lambs' ear, and santolina were among the later recommendations. Each bay had its own distinct character. The planting plan for bay two included eight clumps of *Erianthus ravennae* and *Eulalia japonica*; ten clumps of delphinium; sixteen curving bands of *Veronica amethystina*; a three-foot band of blue violas; six clumps of *Iris orientalis* (white); and twenty-four *Thalictrum aquilegifolium*. The scheme was cool—blue, gray, and white—and dominated by the ten-foot clumps of ornamental grass. The third bay was largely white and pink. It included astilbe, foxglove, *Platycodon*, lupines, and six standard roses. Bay four was predominantly white: *Hosta grandiflora, althaea,* dahlias, *Caryopteris,* and *Speciosum* lilies. Bay five was coral, yellow, bronze, blue, and white. Bay six (only twenty-six feet long) was purple and pink. The planting scheme for each was parterre-like in its geometric divisions and repeating patterns. The bays were studies in color, texture, and shape.

The entrance to the Long Shot was eventually marked by two carved blocks, but Steele had earlier suggested red marble columns topped with car headlights shining "straight up to the heavens."[9] He also wanted to install a huge Gothic arch ruin, after Hubert Robert, at the end of the Long Shot and had a full-size maquette made that apparently satisfied no one.

When one reached the end of the Long Shot (probably before expected, given the false perspective), all that remained to do was to turn around and come back. The gardens appeared as distinct, abstract vignettes of color and fragrance, almost as though on exhibit in a gallery.*

*Planting plans for bay two of the Long Shot and the culinary herb garden in the Basecourt appear in appendix 2.

Backus estate, Long Shot, ca 1935. This photo shows the lengthening effect of the forced perspective. (SUNY ESF College Archives)

Steele had begun working for Edward Ellwanger and his family in 1923, but most of the development of their garden occurred during the mid- and late 1930s under the patronage of the Ellwangers' daughter Helen. Because the prominent Rochester family had figured so importantly in the city's horticultural history, the job had special meaning for Steele. In 1840 George Ellwanger, Edward's father, founded a nursery with Patrick Barry, which, Steele wrote, "made a great fruit garden of Western New York.... They realized ahead of others that the profitable wheat growing district had moved further west.... Now for hundreds of miles in that region the wanderer travels through orchards and vineyards and around every farmhouse and up and down the village streets he enjoys the sight of veteran trees and shrubs."[10]

Rochesterians were proud of their horticultural heritage. Highland Park—designed, in part, by Frederick Law Olmsted with plantings donated by Ellwanger and Barry—had dominated the city's heart since 1888. Mount Hope Cemetery was considered a national model in rural cemetery design. Besides its nurserymen and horticulturists, the area had produced many well-known designers, Bryant Fleming and Alling De Forest among them.

But it was Steele who had been hired to advise on the care and development of the original garden, a "rarely fine old place," dating to 1867.[11] Under his guidance, George Ellwanger's plantings (originally in an old pear orchard) continued to thrive—and so did George's horticultural acumen, in the figure of his granddaughter Helen, one of Fletcher and Esther Steele's closest friends. Steele wrote to Helen Ellwanger often about new botanical discoveries, appreciating both her horticultural sophistication and her quiet good taste. The friendship led to talk of more dramatic innovations on the Mount Hope Avenue estate.

In 1932 Steele began a series of projects that included improvements to the drive, conversion of a porte cochere to a "glass room" (for Helen's sister, Margaret, who had tuberculosis), the planting of an ornamental crab apple orchard, construction of a long wall to define the forecourt, and a modernistic rose garden.

For the forecourt wall, Steele reused the urn design for the Hopkins Memorial in 1925, setting the ornaments atop stucco posts joined by walls of traditional Spanish balustrade tile.

Evolution of the design from March to April 1936 shows a less pronounced bracket with gains in architectural strength.

The rose garden on the other side of the court was first proposed in a 1935 office memorandum as "a small terrace garden along irregular almost modernistic lines between the greenhouse and the old stable."[12] The concrete, multileveled abstraction provided beds for Helen's two hundred roses, many of them old and rare varieties. The layout was complex, jigsaw puzzle–like, but pragmatic too—paths, beds, stairs, and walls fit together to create maximum access to the plants.

The prominent diagonal path and two flights of steps split four tiers of concrete beds. Entry from the west came by a winding staircase emboldened by a sweep of curved wall. (A model of the staircase with a proposed fountain was featured on the cover of a 1937 exhibition catalogue at the San Francisco Museum of Art, *Contemporary Landscape Architecture and Its Sources.*) Despite Steele's "modern" label, the garden's geometry descended from Art Deco rather than modern (i.e., Bauhaus) prototypes. Other influences were present as well. The color—strong, dark pink—was exotic, and the plants were old-fashioned. Luxuriant shrub roses and ramblers, languid vines of clematis and grapes contradicted the deliberate clean, broad planes. The big pear tree that had inspired the spiral staircase and curving wall also evoked an earlier time.

Steele's pursuit of a modernist architectural vocabulary might have been more determined had more of his clients been interested in modern design, but on the whole they were conservative. Helen Ellwanger was no exception; the rose garden was Steele's idea. Steele's love of historical quotation and his taste for decorative surface also made it difficult for him to wholeheartedly embrace a sparer, clean-edged aesthetic.

In 1932 Steele presented a refinement of his ideas about modern gardens for *Landscape Architecture* in an essay titled "Landscape Design of the Future":

> In my opinion, the architect is primarily interested in the objects which he is designing; the landscape architect with the relation of things and the compositions of the spaces *between* them....
>
> ... I believe that successful space composition will be the next serious preoccupation of landscape architects.
>
> The difficulties of composing space are greater than the mere design of objects in and around its enclosed volumes, especially in our art which rarely offers us a more definite roof than the sky....
>
> Successful space composition has an entity of its own quite independent of the things around and in it. It is felt

Ellwanger estate, forecourt wall detail. "This wall was built up to invite the wanderer through and beyond, not to keep him out. On the far side are great trees, planted a hundred years ago. They dominate the garden and the wall which is there only to enframe them and emphasize their importance." Steele, *National Horticultural Magazine* (January 1945). (SUNY ESF College Archives)

Ellwanger estate, fore-
court wall, drawing,
1936. (SUNY ESF College
Archives)

Ellwanger estate, Rose
Garden, plan. (SUNY ESF
College Archives)

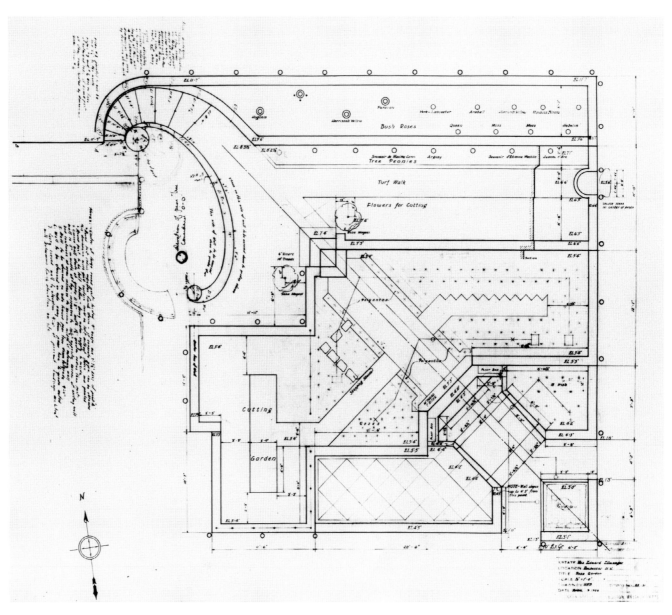

rather than seen. It houses the spirit and charm of a place. It is intangible yet continually felt. . . .

A good result depends on designing in three dimensions from the first. . . . The space must be conceived in volumes and the enclosures made to fit accordingly.[13]

Steele's subsequent articles on modern landscape design, for the 1937 *Contemporary Landscape Architecture and Its Sources* catalogue and for a 1936 entry in Norman Taylor's *The Garden Dictionary*, confirm an interest in the new movement based on concept rather than style. In the 1937 publication he wrote, "At bottom, the true aim of landscape architecture is one: by use of style, color and form, to create beauty in space composition."[14] A year before, he had written:

[The modern designer] designs in volumes rather than surfaces. He studies with far more care than used in the past not only size and proportions of his foliage and architectural masses, but also the shape of the air spaces between them. The modern designer of gardens is no longer satisfied with strictly static axial balance, nor with more lively but limited picturesqueness of park-like "natural" compositions. He groups so-called "formal" or architectural plans and masses with subtle irregularity around an axis that skips, turns and is sometimes lost. He grades land in frankly sculptural rather than natural forms. Does he not practice an art? Why should he shut his eyes to the possibility of sculpture on a grand scale?[15]

Steele had already begun to incorporate these concepts into his own work, at Camden Library and the South Lawn of Naumkeag. He developed them more extensively in a new garden for Harry Stoddard.

Ellwanger estate, curving staircase and greenhouse. (SUNY ESF College Archives)

Cover for the exhibition catalogue *Contemporary Landscape Architecture and Its Sources* (San Francisco Museum of Art, 1936), based on the Ellwanger design. (SUNY ESF College Archives)

Ellwanger estate, pear tree and curving staircase. (SUNY ESF
College Archives)

ROCKLAWN
Mr. and Mrs. Harry Stoddard
Bass Rocks, Gloucester, Massachusetts
1936–1953

Rocklawn was aptly named. The Gloucester summer home of Mr. and Mrs. Harry Stoddard was "perched," according Steele, "up on high grass banks which looked . . . like uneasy pin cushions. In the lawn below were big, medium and little rocks everywhere. . . . And the neighboring cottages in all directions exposed Mary Ann backs at their worst. So the problem posed itself at once as that of hiding the houses yet looking between them to see the water and planting out the huge ugly hotel."[16]

When Steele first saw the house in 1936 he felt immediately that most of the rocks would have to go. "They could not be filled over because the depth below the house was about right as it was. Moreover some of them were too big to cover."[17] The whole lawn would have to be blasted. The expense—and mess—would be enormous, and the Stoddards initially resisted the idea.

Rocklawn, Rose Garde, view toward the house. (SUNY ESF College Archives)

But Steele earned his clients' trust by solving some of their smaller problems. During the first year of work he created a "flower theater" at the front of the house by using existing rock ledges. He successfully moved large trees to screen the hotel and houses on either side. At the bottom of the lawn he laid out a rose garden whose lines enhanced those of the existing topography.

The blasting started the following year. "There was a lot of stone," Steele remembered. The granite was used first to build long curving retaining walls near the house. These defined a curved terrace that curled down to meet the lawn. At one end the passage was made via a ramp, at the other, by means of a spiral staircase with steps, "done to make one think of sea shells." A pyramidal planter was built of the same stone to provide a culminating accent to the stairs. The terraces and redesigned ledges related the house to its hilltop situation. The nautical theme of the step treads was continued by a rail of fish net and bamboo ("China had showed me that of all wood it is most truly 'natural'"[18]) and by a buoy-shaped fountain. White clematis twined through the fish net.

All the contours were worked out on the site. Steele's artistic goals here echoed those at Naumkeag's South Lawn: to relate foreground to background, to lead the eye through a dynamic landscape of curves. The logical organization of axis was rejected in favor of the immediate, kinetic impact of contour. At Rocklawn the problem was complicated somewhat by the small size of the place ("It was a real stunt making it seem unlimited," wrote Steele[19]) and by the ocean view, a natural focus for anyone on the house terrace. "I soon decided," Steele explained, "that my only hope on the small lot was to create a visual interest within strong enough so that one was satisfied to get an impression of sea without peering at it."[20] The curving walls, and eventually the unconventional planting scheme, were designed to compel—not with beauty, but with interest. Swirling terraces and ramps had transformed the Stoddards' lawn into a work of sculpture. Steele's specific inspiration for the scheme may have been a sixteenth-century sketch of fortifications by Michelangelo, a copy of which was in his library, but the impact was abstract.

In 1938 Steele suggested a second ledge, about halfway down

Rocklawn under construction. Planting has begun that will eventually screen the surrounding houses and frame the view to the ocean. (SUNY ESF College Archives)

Rocklawn, "The general scheme now is of a big pattern of brocade, let us say, formalized definitely yet leaving enough accidents to fool the average beholder into pulling his attention to details here and there while his major yet unconscious attention is firmly held in place by an integrated pattern." Steele, to *House and Garden* editor, 9 October 1952. (LC. Photo by Harry Stoddard)

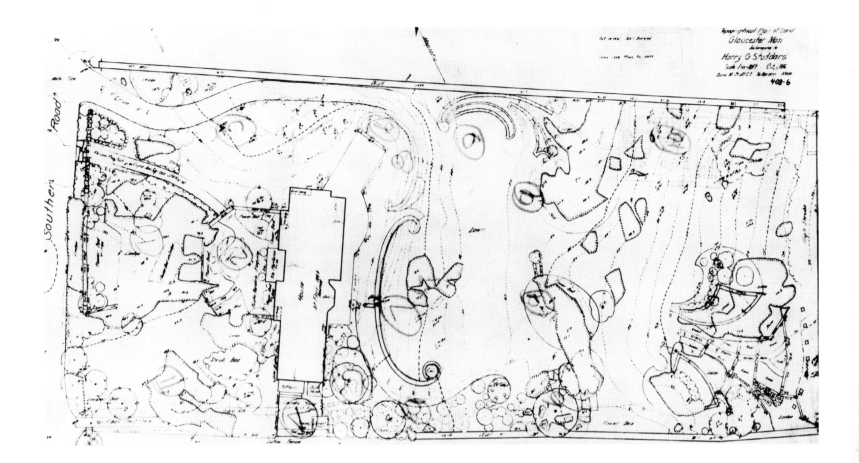

the lawn, to continue the motif begun at the house terrace. And then he took off for Europe. Upon returning, he discovered that the Stoddards' grounds superintendent, Robert Bolcome, had built in Steele's words, "the prettiest, boldest ledge imaginable—the first he had ever made." The second ledge considerably bolstered the south side of garden. It was planted as a desert garden "because we needed the barren relief from the indigestibly lush vegetation everywhere else."[21]

The garden picture from the house terrace was evolving into a comprehensive whole, but it lacked strength to the north. Steele decided he would use plants to repeat and elaborate the spiral forms he had begun with the first ledge. A tall yew hedge curled down the hill and into the lawn, decreasing in height along the way so as to form a spiral. The curl was stopped by a pyramidal arborvitae. The downward spiral and accent were repeating almost exactly the configuration of seashell steps and tiered planter at the north end of the terrace. Steele echoed the spiral motif in a low curving wall tucked inside the larger hedge. These two elements—hedge and wall—gave the bed its structure. Color and texture were provided by a planting scheme that reached a new level of boldness, even for Steele.

His plan for the area called for strong color and texture contrast in regular patterns. The plant list included *Erianthus*, *Festuca*, begonia (red and pink), ageratum, alyssum, and yellow canna lilies ("as you see them in France"). Strong, even, in Steele's words, "actually ugly" combinations of flower color that "would be instantly ripped out when they appeared on any other garden, are left to scream," he explained. "And I am pleased when scolded for making dreadful sights which attract the eye with violence. There is nothing like a bit of downright ugliness to attract attention away from what one does not want observed."[22]

The planting plan evolved from year to year. In 1940 Steele wrote to one seed supplier, "I want a bed of brown flowers. Not yellow nor apricot nor reddish, but brown. Bellperone looks brown. Papaver trinifolium is pretty brown. Last summer I saw a pure cafe au lait gaillardia but don't know the name. Diplocus is fairly brown. There is some brown in summer-flowering eremurus, but too much yellow to be right. Can you help me out with the names of more things?"[23]

In 1946 Stoddard and Steele decided that they wanted a "forthright burst of yellow in the color scheme," so Steele got to work researching plant possibilities for the same spot. He

Rocklawn, plan. The Atlantic Ocean lies to the east. (SUNY ESF College Archives)

Rocklawn, view to the house from the lawn.
(LC. Photo by Harry Stoddard)

wrote in detail to Kingsville Nurseries in Maryland, and several others: "I have a corner on one of my places that I want to have bright yellow all summer long with a minimum of green showing. This means that I must rely on yellow foliage not flowers. Last summer I got a pretty good start with yellow leafed Ligustrum vulgaris, Chamaecyparis pisifera filifera aurea and Thuya orientalis aurea conspicua."[24] He also inquired about bright yellow dwarf philadelphus, *Taxus baccata* Aurea, *Acer japonicum* Aureum, *Buxus sempervirens* Aurea, *Elaegnus pungens* Variegata, and several others. Hardiness was not essential; sensitive material was dug and overwintered in cold pits. Much of the rest of the garden was bedding plants anyway. The cluster of bright yellow plants was tucked into the curl of the yew hedge, glowing as if a ray of sun had pierced a cloud-covered sky. Over two decades earlier Steele had written about the use of unusual color in gardens.

In places fog shuts out the sun for days, even weeks at a time. In some such place I should like to see all the condemned summer yellows. Fog, sea and sand are found together. It would be sandy, barren soil. We would see much broom—detested weed now given a home—the Golden Marguerite, *Anthemis Kelwayi*; Yellow Vetch, *Astragalus* in variety; Wild Senna, *Cassia Marylandica*; Knapweed, *Centraurea Macrocephala* . . . the Yellow Day Lily, *Hemerocallis Thunbergii* would be best; the variegated White Day Lily, *Funkia Subcordata Variegata*, and every other flower that was coarse, yellow and despised. . . .

The subject of abnormal coloring in plants is not easy to handle. Anything strange was popular in the old carpet-bedding days. That is probably the reason why everything of the sort is now deprecated by connoisseurs. . . . In fact, there is no little challenge in universal condemnation. And in more than one case I have seen fit and pleasing uses of these more or less unusual objects.[25]

At the boundaries of the Stoddards' property, largely native overstory trees grew: black locusts, ash, and maples (and, later, birch). Year-round color and textural interest came from massed pine, rhododendron, laurel, and indigenous hemlock. *Koelreuteria*, in curving rows, defined the perimeter of the rose garden; large masses of *Hedera helix* provided ground cover. In the "garden theater" at the front of the house thousands of annuals blazed in their rock niches. A flat ledge was the foundation for a cubist checkerboard of blue and green factory flue tiles where herbs were grown. Steele based the design on a modernist garden by Gabriel Guevrekian in Neuilly.

Stoddard was a wealthy Worcester businessman who had never given much thought to landscape or "put his attention on the power and meaning of aesthetic details" before meeting Steele. But, as Steele saw it, "wherever he turns his mind it lights and clears his way." This was the kind of client relationship Steele had come to prize. "One of these days," Steele wrote to Harry after the garden was finished, "I am going to write an essay about the perfect client and you will be in the back of my mind. You are open-minded while being definite about what

Rocklawn, Herb Garden made from factory tiles. (SUNY ESF College Archives)

Rocklawn, Glorieta with ship ornament and bird-bath. The ocean can be glimpsed under the arch of the arbovitae. (SUNY ESF College Archives)

you like and do not like. You stimulate an effort to understand just what you want and then try to create it. When it works you get pleasure out of it. You have a strong appreciation for design and the beauty which comes with a fitting solution of a problem. You have forebearance for the workman's inevitable frustrations. In other words, you are a grand boss and an artist can ask for nothing better."[26]

Steele felt just as lucky to be working with Stoddard's groundskeeper, Robert Bolcome. "Naturally," he wrote to Stoddard, "you do not know the technical side the way I do and so I keep thinking that it is impossible for you to realize how truly remarkable he [Bolcome] has been from the first. He has been constantly alert to understand what was wanted and why far more than any superintendent I have ever worked with. In many things his ideas have been so good and fitted the need so well that they have become features of the place."[27]

The grounds superintendents of big, pre–World War II gardens figured importantly in Steele's work. The large crews assembled to construct garden features received direct supervision from the staff grounds superintendents, who were, in turn, supervised by Steele or members of his staff during site visits and, afterward, in reports. The arrangement—especially given Steele's high standards for meticulous craftsmanship—necessitated considerable patience on the part of the grounds-

keeper who stood at the middle of it all. Steele was harsh in his dealings with workers whose abilities he did not respect and generous in his praise for people like Robert Bolcome (or Ancrum House's Thomas Wallis) who valued quality work as much as he did. Often these men had no previous experience constructing the elaborate waterworks or summerhouses characteristic of Steele's designs. Neither were they master pruners or plant propagators. When Steele started, Bolcome did not know a fuchsia from a funkia. But all were expected to manage the crews during the garden building, run the greenhouses, and then keep the property in top shape after the design was fulfilled. Often Steele continued in an advisory capacity long after the garden was technically complete, communicating his observations and suggestions in the form of long formal reports that were turned over to grounds superintendents and their staffs to implement.

Work at Rocklawn continued for many years, as new ideas arose. "Only those who do not care leave things as they are," Steele later observed. "[The] one thing I want that I have not gotten [is] a big mirror pool to bring the ocean right up into the garden. It would be real delight. But I am the only one who wants it."[28]*

*A plant list for the drywall appears in appendix 2.

Money was a frequent topic in Steele's correspondence, and clients often disputed charges for time spent planning, cogitating, or "contemplating." Some of the disputes ended badly, but more often they were settled with slight reductions on Steele's side and grumbling on the client's. Steele was often teased, particularly by friends, about his high fees. He once received a book inscribed "Don't ever change." Misreading the handwriting, he began to sputter at the much-amused company. "'Don't ever charge, *DON'T EVER CHARGE'! What an idea!*"[29] Steele's tendency to mix business with pleasure contributed to the problem. More than once party guests who had cornered the well-known designer and pumped him for garden ideas found hefty bills on their desks the following day.

Joseph F. Taylor, whose Rochester garden Steele began in 1936, found his friend's high-priced methods especially exas-perating and wrote to object to a large bill. For $900 all Taylor had to show, he said, was a pink stone platform and plans for lattice to surround it. Steele's reply to Taylor's complaint managed to be conciliatory without yielding.

I do not know whether I told you or not, but certainly I should have, that while I never know exactly what would be the cost of the time which I and my assistants put in on a job, nevertheless, it works out in the long run to be approximately between 30% and 40% of the total cost of construction. That is one reason why I never charge on the commission basis as it would often be ridiculous. But a little reflection will show you that in many cases the cost of my work might be much more than the total cost of the work itself. For instance, it might take me several days to plan a garden of annuals for which all the materials would be seeds which could be bought for a dollar and a half. At the rate even charging on the commission basis of 35% all that I would get for my time would be 50 cents, and you know me well enough to realize that I would say to Hell with that.[30]

Taylor estate, Mrs. Joseph (Hilda) Taylor on the Terrace, 1947. (SUNY ESF College Archives)

Taylor estate, lawn with arborvitae arches.
(SUNY ESF College Archives)

Steele's courage under fire was extraordinary. His letter continued: "All this is leading up to the bitter fact that you still have coming a bill for professional services from me amounting to about ⅓ of what I estimate to be the actual cost of your work, to date about $800 rather than $900. I hope this won't be the straw to break the camel's back. At any rate you can say to yourself that you have got the use of the money instead of handing it all to the government."

Taylor replied:

Certain that it will be of value in our business, which, as you know, deals in both vision and collection, I have committed yours of the twelfth, which reached me this noon, to heart.

No! I still don't see why—etc. etc.

I am upset, annoyed, depressed, and in fact, completely furious, but the real hell of it is that I still like my blasted platform.

Think possibly it is just the old principle of prizing what we have to pay for dearly, but I find I love it.

Now planning to put up a tent and live there this winter. Maybe the pink stones will keep me warm when there aint no coal.

Check enclosed.

Yours,

Tom

P.S. And don't think for a minute that I will tell you when I put up the trellis. I am doing that myself in the dark of the moon. Then you can come and drink and admire, but not charge me any more.[31]

Steele's design included lattice trellises on either side of a bluestone terrace and the "pink platform" that defined a sunken lawn panel. Hilda Taylor reportedly spent hours, at Steele's instruction, weaving branches of tallhedge (*Rhannus columnaris*) through the tiny squares of lattice. A series of three arborvitae arches (inspired by Spain) formed the ends of the green room; the fourth side was open to a long view.

When the Taylors considered adding a new room to the back of the house in 1948, Steele was protective of the axes in his design. "Curiously enough," he wrote, "the relation of the proposed room to the Grass Panel is exactly like a problem I had at Lisburne Grange. So I am sure of the effect when I urge you to move the room out until it is on the same axis as the Panel. The result will be immeasurably better both indoors and out. Then the Panel will appear to have been made to fit the room which it will seem to be a part of. If you don't do that, things will look askew till the end of time."[32]

Seville, Spain, Steele's inspiration for the Taylor estate, 1926. Photograph in Steele's client files. (SUNY ESF College Archives)

Allen estate, shelter,
drawing, 1932. (SUNY ESF
College Archives)

ESTATE OF ATKINSON ALLEN ESQ.
AT ROCHESTER. NEW YORK.
SHELTER AT THE SWIMMING POOL.
FLETCHER STEELE   JUNE 20 1932
BOSTON MASSACHUSETTS   DRAWING NO. 40-97

CHARLOTTE WHITNEY ALLEN
Rochester, New York
1937

Every afternoon about 4:30, Charlotte Allen opened her door for what she called "the chilled-glass hour." A Rochester historian described the scene:

On a given afternoon one might meet the surviving friends of her youth; artists, writers, musicians, and other professional people; and neighbors. The categories overlapped, and the number and mixture of visitors varied daily, but the martinis were always very dry, the cheese had been flown up from Maison Glass in New York, and the talk was witty and fluent. The hostess observed certain ancient proprieties: she never addressed by his or her first name anyone she had not known most of her life, and she sometimes switched to French when a servant entered the room. . . . It could not

Allen estate, shelter, drawing, 1937. (SUNY ESF College Archives)

Charlotte Whitney Allen
and the pool shelter,
under construction,
1938. (SUNY ESF College
Archives)

rightly be called a salon. It was too homey, one may say too American for that. But it could sparkle and enchant.[33]

Weather permitting, Allen's parties took place in the "drinking pit" by the pool. (In winter the group gathered round the fireplace in the den, under the head of a stuffed lynx.) Steele had been designing little structures to better accommodate the high-spirited salons since 1932, but nothing concrete had materialized. Mid-decade, Allen's mother died and left her close to a million dollars, and plans for the new garden feature forged ahead.

Early sketches reveal that Steele had always envisioned a tentlike form for the structure. In fact, the final version resembles the original more than an intermittent Art Deco experiment that relied on a mesh curtain hung between metal columns and a big, shell-backed bench. The eventual design was less a backdrop than a little house based on the form of medieval campaign tents. The material was unconventional:

chain mail manufactured by the Whiting Davis Company in Plainville, Massachusetts, which made opera bags from it. Before committing himself to using it in the tent, Steele sent samples to a laboratory at Brown University for stress tests to see if the chain mail would hang without stretching. Harry Hoover reported to his boss in characteristic detail of "two samples 4 feet by 5 feet . . . made up for my inspection, one in aluminum and one in bronze."[34] The report, nearly three single-spaced typewritten pages, detailed strength, appearance, finish, possible installation techniques, and price (about two dollars a square foot).

All of the technical problems were eventually solved, elaborate finials designed for the supports, and the bronze tent was constructed shortly after. Over time the patina took on a dark blue-green cast. A tangled bower of hawthorn shrouded the tent, improbably but successfully evoking a medieval forest in the tiny space that had coalesced into a convincing vignette.

Allen estate, shelter, with furniture designed by Steele. (SUNY ESF College Archives)

NAUMKEAG
Mabel Choate
Stockbridge, Massachusetts
1937–1939

Two years elapsed before Steele designed the "Chinese House" that Ralph Cram had suggested after he visited Naumkeag in 1935. Mabel Choate's trip to China earlier that year—at Steele's urging—had fired her already considerable enthusiasm to the point that the garden could hold no more of the Chinese statues and sacred rocks that sat "dotted about the lawn." "I went with the Garden Club of America to its Annual Meeting in Tokio," she wrote, "where we had been invited by the Society of Japanese Cultural Relations. We had a wonderful time, and a friend and I were so enchanted that we left the Garden Club in Korea and went on to Pekin, where we took a house for a month. There things were even more thrilling, and I became so fascinated by the Oriental marble figures and carvings that I succumbed right and left."[35] "Without," Steele added, "guessing the shudders of her professional landscape advisor whose duty it was to make them feel at home on a New England hillside."[36]

"The Chinese Garden was built to bring a recollection of the atmosphere and appearance of places seen in China. . . . This is a Traveler's garden, bringing home to America the best of foreign life and habits to enrich our ways here."[37] Privately, Steele wrote to his sister, "Of course it is no more Chinese than an old parlor in Salem filled with Chinese objects."[38] The garden's major departure from authenticity was significant: the spectacular mountain view gained from the small temple. True Chinese courtyards focus inward.

Some elements of the temple were genuine artifacts: "The elaborate carved marble slab in the center of the staircase up to the building lies relatively in the same position that it formerly did in the Old Summer Palace outside Peking. Mortals walked up either side of it. Only the Emperor was carried over the sculptured dragon, pearl and peony." The temple's blue roof tiles "were made at the same factory which made the original tiles for the Temple of Heaven in Kublai Khan's day and still plods on, I guess, regardless of Japanese or Communists."[39]

The timbers came from a wrecking company in Brighton. All the construction details were worked out on the site,

Naumkeag, temple in the Chinese Garden, in construction, 1937. (SUNY ESF College Archives)

Naumkeag, temple in the Chinese Garden. (SUNY ESF College Archives)

Peking, Black Dragon
Pool Temple, 1934.
(SUNY ESF College
Archives)

Naumkeag, view from the temple in the Chinese Garden. (SUNY ESF College Archives)

Naumkeag, Chinese Garden. Marble water channels cross the garden floor of earth and moss. (SUNY ESF College Archives)

including the temple walls, steps, and the installation of the Spirit Walk. "The floor of earth, slightly covered with moss and continually swept, is carefully weeded of grass. There are no lawns in Chinese gardens. The marble boxes beside the walk, each guarding a Dianthus plant are a reminder of the same plant used the same way, in far off Tai Yuan Fu. The Peonies in the long narrow shelf at the foot of the Temple wall remind one of Tan Ch'ih Ssu and many another place. The stone rail-

ing on the terrace is a souvenir of a marvelous garden in Soochou."[40] *Petasites* evoked the large leaves of the lotus. A flo-wering peach, sacred in China, was included too.

Despite Choate's interest in plants, "there was no great talk of horticulture," wrote Steele. "One day she was bored by great argument about what to plant in the sixteen metal pots in the Chinese garden. She broke in. 'I know exactly what I am going to do,' and would say no more. When I went up again in a few weeks, all was finished. In each shining pot was a stalwart weed! She had spent her afternoons motoring about to find them."[41]

"Little streams of water trickle in marble channels across the floor," Mabel Choate later described, "and on one side is a group of nine (magic number) Gingko trees, amongst which we planted our best and tallest needle-rock on its Ming pedestal; on the other side is a marble table surrounded by marble stools. . . . Around the Chinese Garden we built a pink brick wall such as they have in the Forbidden City, and in the center of the wall a 'Devil Screen.' The lions were placed on the ground at the foot of the Temple steps. We found some bamboo chairs that looked suitable, and a Gloucester seaman's hammock."[42]

The color for the Chinese Garden's brick wall represented considerable effort on Steele's part. It was painted in six different shades of red, lightest toward the top, darkest near the ground. (Samples of these can still be found in one corner.) Over this a coat of whitewash was applied and then sprayed with a garden hose, while still wet, to make it seem as though "it had been raining since Confucius."[43]

The design for the marble checkers table and the surrounding "pin cushion" seats were based on a photograph of a Chinese tomb Steele purchased from the Philadelphia Commercial Museum. The Moon Gate (not built until 1955) was based on a prototype in one of Steele's own photographs, taken during his trip in the spring of 1934.

After Steele's client and friend Grahame ("Grady") Wood had seen the new garden during the annual birthday house party at Naumkeag, he told Mabel Choate that there was too much empty space in it, and she passed the criticism along to the designer. "As for the empty holes," Steele retorted, "nothing could be more Chinese. It is a purely western trick to put something down where there is a square inch of room. The fact that there is only one place where you and Grady thirst to put something strikes me with horror lest we already have altogether more objects in the place than should be there. Now we must hunt for things to throw out."[44]

Miss Choate was interested in India as well as China and traveled there in 1935, much to Steele's envy. It may have been on that trip that she met the Swami B. F. Bon from Calcutta, who later visited Naumkeag. "He fascinated us," wrote Choate's nephew Geoffrey Platt, who was visiting at the time, "by pacing up and down the stone step one morning . . . from 7:00 until about 10:00, reading a book intently. We assumed he was attending to his devotions. When he came in we asked

what the book was and he said it was *The Big Sleep* by Raymond Chandler."[45]

Naumkeag, Blue Steps, drawing, 1938. (SUNY ESF College Archives)

The Blue Steps

In October 1938 Steele wrote to his mother, "The season is about over. The official ending always seems to be the last weekend before Mabel Choate goes to Hot Springs. . . . She is building what I call the 'Back Stairs' down to the greenhouse, and they turn out to be rather interesting."[46] A steep, lilac-covered bank and Mabel Choate's fear of falling precipitated the design for what has become Steele's signature work: the Blue Steps.

In 1938 Choate announced that she was tired of risking her neck on her daily treks to the cutting garden. "I . . . told Mr. Steele he must make me some steps that would be both convenient and easy. . . . Little did I realize what I was in for."[47] Steele's design was presented to his client in June 1938 in the form of an elegant drawing by Hoover: it showed three arches (an alternate version showed four), no arched railings, and, significantly, no birches.

"She has been wanting [the steps] for years, and always said she didn't care how they looked, but they must be comfortable," Steele continued to his mother. "I figure that comfort in going up a steep hill depends on variety of leg action the lack of which makes a long flight of steps intolerable. . . . So I put up four 'divisions,' each one having a couple of steps and turns, two ramps of different steepness and a graduated flight of half a dozen steps to a platform. The latter go up over an arched opening in which is a dripping fountain and pool."[48]

Water for the concrete steps is supplied by a long, shallow brick channel inspired by memories of the Alhambra and other Moorish gardens in Spain. The runlet's strong linear

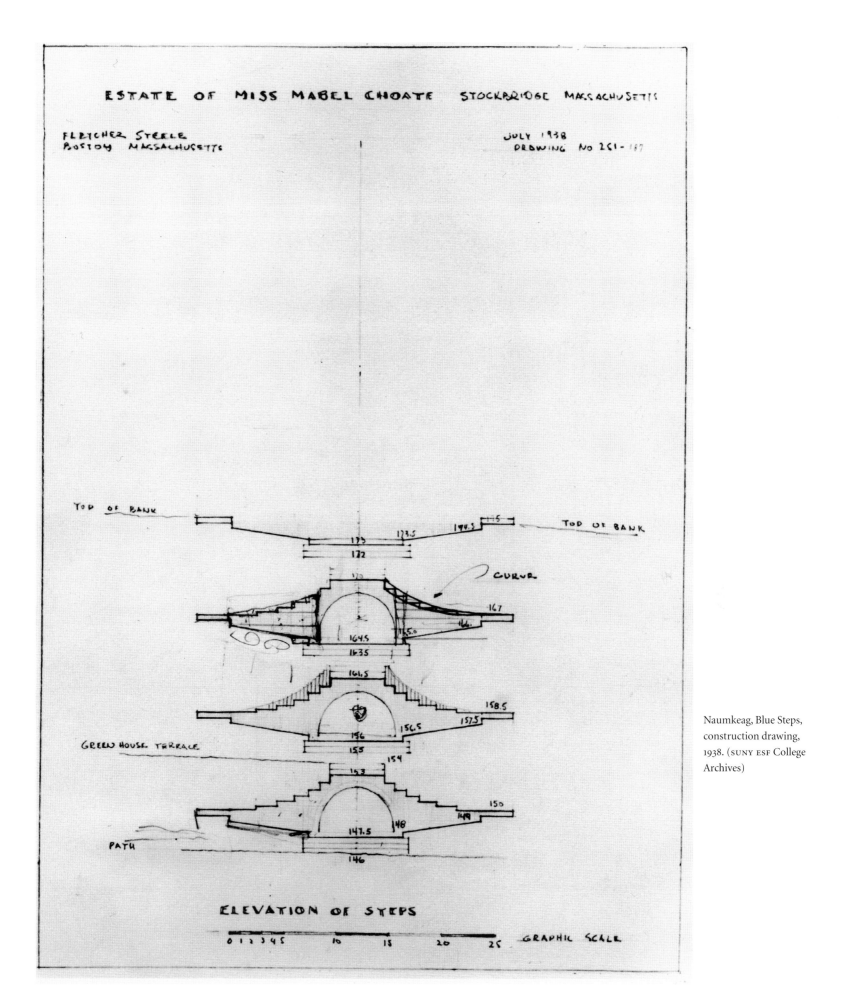

ESTATE OF MISS MABEL CHOATE   STOCKBRIDGE MASSACHUSETTS

FLETCHER STEELE
BOSTON MASSACHUSETTS

JULY 1938
DRAWING No 251-187

TOP OF BANK

TOP OF BANK

175

173.5

174.5

5

172

170

CURVE

167

164.5

5.0

166.

163.5

161.5

158.5

157.5

156

156.5

GREEN HOUSE TERRACE

155

154

153

150

149

148

147.5

PATH

146

ELEVATION OF STEPS

0 1 2 3 4 5   10   15   20   25   GRAPHIC SCALE

Naumkeag, Blue Steps,
construction drawing,
1938. (SUNY ESF College
Archives)

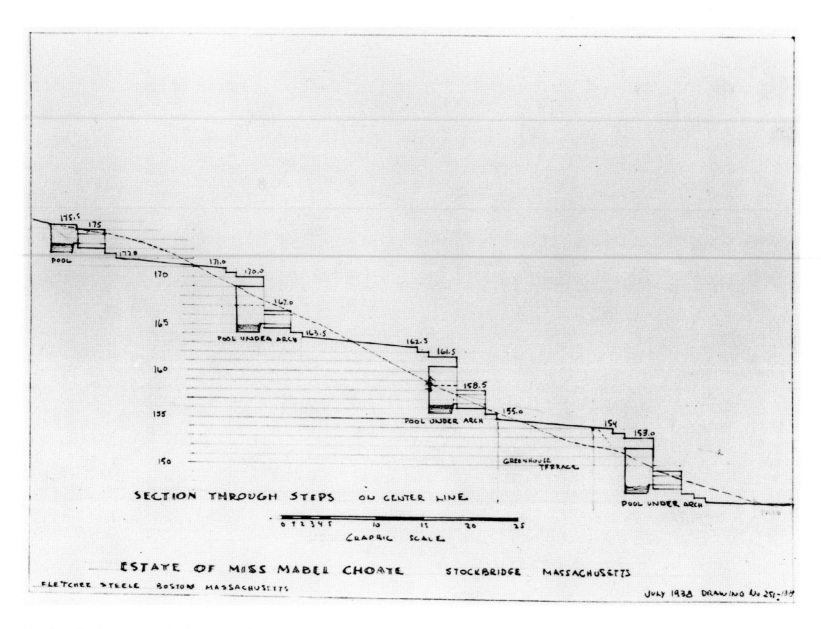

Naumkeag, Blue Steps, construction drawing, 1938. (SUNY ESF
College Archives)

Naumkeag, Blue Steps during construction, 1938. Cutting gardens are located at the bottom of the hill. (SUNY ESF College Archives)

presence is heightened by a rippling, quicksilver surface that attracts birds. The sound of water was important to both owner and artist.[49]

The idea of surrounding the water staircase with birch probably was inspired by the native trees on the site. The visual resonance between the white railing and birch trunks must have been immediately apparent; but also appealing, according to Steele, was the idea of using a native tree that occurred throughout the property and that would successfully integrate the new feature with it. He ordered the birches in several sizes and arranged them to resemble the diverse growth patterns that occur naturally.[50]

"Then," Choate remembered, "Mr. Steele had another idea: to paint the steps."[51] "We started painting it when the Dabneys & Iselins were there," Steele wrote to his mother. "You would have been amused to see them dash at it. O'Donnell would make a grand, careful house painter if he wanted to. Along the

top edge, outlining the steps is a broad band of bright blue. The arch is outlined with bright yellow & the body is barn red. Quite spectacular."[52] The wilder color scheme was eventually abandoned in favor of plain bright blue.

In 1938 Steele had just returned from the most extensive of his five trips to Italy. (He had taken his black Lincoln Zephyr to motor about the countryside on his own.) He was undoubtedly familiar with the water staircases in Italian villa gardens, but at Naumkeag he emphasized linear qualities with handrails of white piping, echoed by the birch trunks and branches. (Low yew hedges behind the curved railings increased their visibility.) The rail design was inspired by clean, modern lines and an Art Deco preference for machine-turned curves. In addition, Steele may have been influenced by Plâs Brondanw, a garden in Wales designed by the architect Sir Clough Williams-Ellis, circa 1908, that featured similarly curving handrails.

Steele cited utilitarian concerns for his clients' comfort as

Naumkeag, Blue Steps,
ca. 1939. (SUNY ESF
College Archives)

inspiration for the design, but the Blue Steps, like Williams-Ellis's feature, are also graphically striking. The best vantage point is at the bottom of the hill, from where the blue arches and white railings seem to disappear into the grove of birches. Wittily reversing identities, the railings imitate the lithe white birches and, conversely, the trees become sheer form.

Steele's intention was also sculptural. "Garden steps," he later wrote, "should be plastic. . . . It is pushing and pulling; hollowing and lumping; patting and scraping till something emerges which has length, breadth and thickness and a hint of more. A hint of movement, of grace promised, of beauty that hides or lies forgotten. It is the curve of the back of a leopard made clear in the rail of a stair."[53]

The brick walk flanking the channel catches visitors as they enter Naumberg's garden gate and coaxes them forward toward the birch grove over the crest of the hill. The cross axis begun at the garden's entrance is complete. Left, the South Lawn sweeps to a breathless, enigmatic conclusion. To the right, the Afternoon Garden's boy beckons with suggestions of a more intimate, garland-bedecked theater. Beyond, the Berkshires spread a blue-tinged backdrop to orchard, farm, and meadow. The evocative potential of design is fulfilled—and enhanced—by the "occult" power of space. This is Steele's success, the lesson he learned in Turkey and China and discovered again and again throughout the world.

The New Practitioners

Over the years Steele maintained occasional contact with Harvard's School of Landscape Architecture, as guest lecturer and critic. Between 1936 and 1938 he saw an impressive group of students arrive: James Rose, Daniel Kiley, and Garrett Eckbo

Opposite: Naumkeag, Blue Steps, ca. 1985. (Photo by Alan Ward)

Mabel Choate, her dog, and Steele on the South Lawn, Naumkeag. (SUNY ESF College Archives)

would soon change the appearance of American gardens for good. Kiley already knew Steele's work and was apprenticed to Warren Manning before entering Harvard. Garrett Eckbo met Steele for the first time at Harvard in 1936. He also visited Steele's office, where he studied project photographs and photostats and made lists of the designs he admired. Later he requested photographs of Naumkeag, Camden Library, both Backus gardens, Mary Schofield's Beside Still Waters, Wesson Seyburn's garden, Ancrum House (West Garden), and Samuel Sloan's swimming pool.

Eckbo sensed that Steele's gardens were offering a link between the Beaux Arts formalism that had dominated design in the first quarter of the century and the modernism that was transforming painting, sculpture, and architecture. Later Eckbo observed that it was Steele's experimental example as much as his designs that impressed him so deeply. He was also inspired by the talent and energy with which Steele wrought his work and by his frank questioning of the assumptions of his colleagues and predecessors. Steele's stylistic vocabulary (still heavily traditional) was of less interest to the young moderns.

Eckbo later wrote, "Our tendency to focus on periods and their assumed beginnings and endings often obscures the fact that design is a continuous stream, and that the smooth parts and rapids do not coincide in any particular way with the kinds of talents that pop up in it. Fifty years earlier Kiley, Rose, and I might have been talented traditionalists."[54]

WYNDMOOR
Randal and Frances Morgan
Chestnut Hill, Pennsylvania
1938–1940

Harry Hoover's last project with Steele took place in the wealthy Philadelphia suburb of Chestnut Hill where Mrs. Randal Morgan was considering a new glass room for Wyndmoor. Steele and Mrs. Morgan were old Garden Club of America buddies (she was president of the International Relations Committee for many years) and participated in the same social scene. A regular guest at Steele's annual birthday party at Naumkeag, she was also one of the Philadelphia crowd with

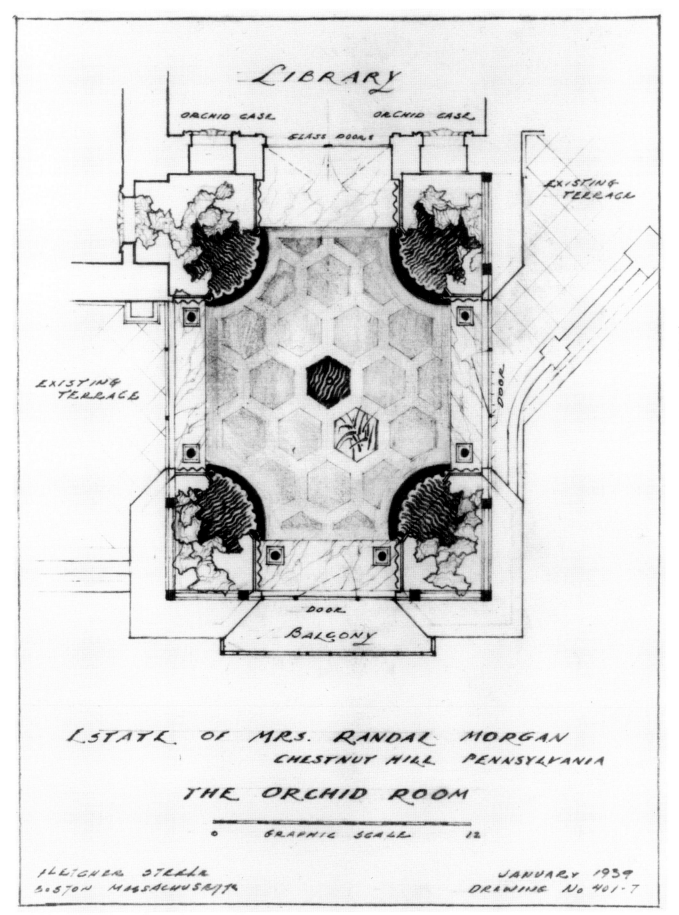

Wyndmoor, Orchid
Room plan, 1939. (SUNY
ESF College Archives)

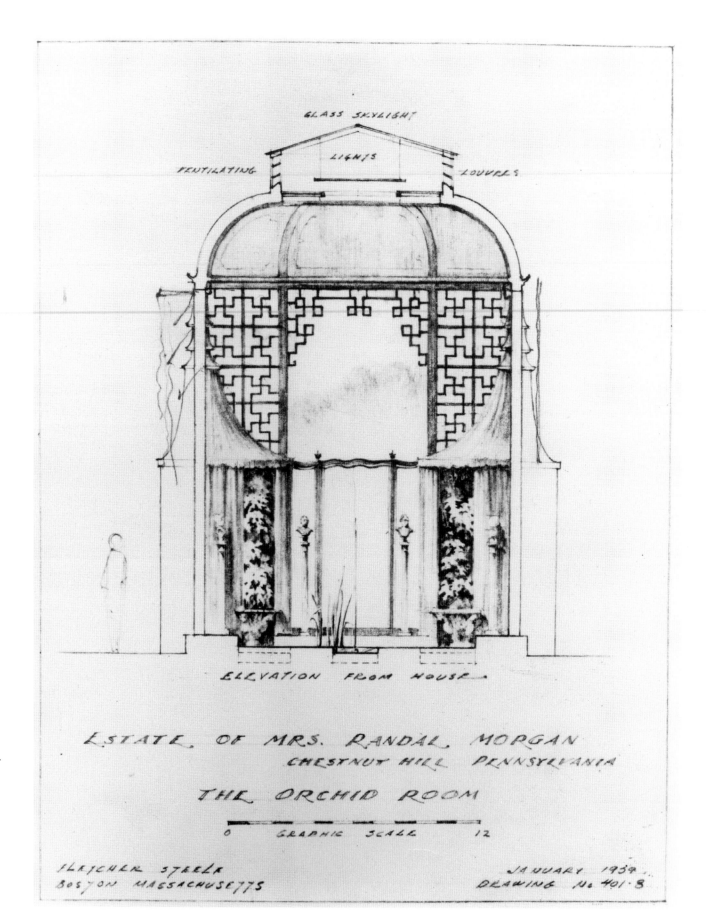

GLASS SKYLIGHT

VENTILATING   LIGHTS   LOUVERS

ELEVATION FROM HOUSE

ESTATE OF MRS. RANDAL MORGAN
CHESTNUT HILL PENNSYLVANIA

THE ORCHID ROOM

0   GRAPHIC SCALE   12

FLETCHER STEELE
BOSTON MASSACHUSETTS

JANUARY 1939
DRAWING No. 401·8

Wyndmoor, Orchid Room, drawing, 1939. (SUNY ESF College Archives)

whom he socialized. Drawings for the new feature from December 1938 show a large glass room (24 by 30 feet) dominated by one palm, one camellia, and a ten-sided orchid case in the corner. By January 1939 the scheme had become more elaborate.

In the final arrangement, the greenhouse had been abandoned in favor of an exotic fantasy reminiscent of both the cool seclusion of Spanish courtyards and the self-contained elegance of Chinese Chippendale. Three glass-front orchid cases (one in each corner plus a matching case for porcelain display) provided horticultural interest, while a small pool and jet enlivened the central space. Frances Morgan's bedroom overlooked the scene from a balcony of vermillion lacquer. Huge windows and doors filled three sides of the new room, and glass skylights and recessed lights were set into the ceiling. Ventilating louvres in the roof regulated temperature and humidity. The theatricality of the setting was heightened by a small flock of white doves that fluttered freely through the Orchid Room and roosted on the bedroom balcony. The maid, who cleaned up after the birds every morning, probably would have preferred a cat.

With its travertine floor and central fountain, the indoor courtyard recalled the Alhambra. But Philadelphia has neither the warmth nor the cloudless skies of Spain, and Steele's goal was not so much respite from the hot sun as finding enough light to keep the plants alive. Potted exotics bloomed throughout.

In the design of the orchid cases Steele stylized curving Chinese roof eaves into exaggerated scrolls atop curtains from the same chain mail in Charlotte Allen's "drinking pit" tent, also under construction at the time. The orchids grew in tufa, the porous rock Steele had used often for traditional rock gardens because its pockets and crevices supported lime-loving alpines. Period photographs show cascades of *Phalaenopsis*, looking rather uncannily like the white doves.

Light was conducted into the orchid cases via curved Lucite rods. The lamps were hidden so that the sparkles of light floated freely inside the cabinets. Steele's attraction to luxurious materials, such as Lucite or lacquer or chain mail, was in keeping with the Art Deco tastes that dominated American and European design during this period. His eclecticism and use of traditional motifs, however, were rooted in a quest for beauty that diverged markedly from Art Deco goals. Steele's near-complete avoidance of "primitive" art forms (which influenced most of the greatest painters, sculptors, and designers of the period) kept his work distinct from that of his contemporaries in other fields.

Frances Morgan's Orchid Room marked the end of an era for Fletcher Steele. Although small in comparison to the major

Wyndmoor, Orchid Room under construction, 1939. Workers are placing tufa in cases. (SUNY ESF College Archives)

Wyndmoor, Orchid Room. Small pools with tiny jets (at the bottom)
were set into the floor. (SUNY ESF College Archives)

estates, the opulent little courtyard expressed the essence and final purpose of so many of his gardens: a theater of luxury and imagination unrestrainedly serving wish fulfillment. White orchids, white doves, brilliant vermillion lacquer, gleaming travertine, green leaves kept lustrous by an attentive staff, water splashing and echoing through the marble and glass enclave— props that led to a sublime, physical contentment. Steele's vision had reached extremes of exoticism and sensuality. But American culture was about to change, and gardens would never be the same.

The gardens created by Steele in the late 1930s up to the onset of World War II were some of the most imaginative and lyrical of his career. Rocklawn, Harry Stoddard's Bass Rocks garden, marked an especially strong departure. There Steele abandoned the organizing Beaux Arts principle of axis altogether, relying instead on the force of view through the landscape for structure and cohesion. Other expressive designs followed. Naumkeag's Blue Steps, Charlotte Allen's Saracen Tent, the Sloans' Summer House, Standish Backus's (unbuilt) Stage Backdrops, and Frances Morgan's Orchid Room all burst forth in a Dionysian flurry of invention. Steele may have discovered new freedom in the gardens he knew his father, who had died in 1936, would never see. John Steele had been a loving but difficult father, and his son's letters to him invariably defended the career whose appeal the stern lawyer never quite understood.

Changes

In 1939 Steele and his colleague and former teacher Henry Vincent Hubbard were invited by the Boston Society of Landscape Architects to address the philosophical and aesthetic implications of the gradual but dramatic change in professional opportunities. Shrinking wealth was making it less and less practical to create big gardens and maintain them. Private commissions were becoming scarce for everyone, including Steele. As Steele's copresenter characterized the predicament: "In the good old days, only a little while ago . . . we could talk aesthetics to a client and not be obliged to ask, 'Will you have fifty cents worth of beauty, or can you afford only thirty-seven cents worth?'"[55] Steele maintained that work for the private client would survive, "as long as we think first in terms of beauty and only subordinately of ways and means." For Steele, the quest for beauty was still the driving force of all art. The next part of his address must have struck some listeners as a bit unrealistic: "The scale of his [the client's] enterprise is of no importance to us compared to his need and his cooperative dependence on our wits."[56]

Steele concluded his share of the address with the presentation of unexpectedly democratic ideas, particularly in the context of his own life's work. He thought the isolation of the modern artist "may not be the best way to good work and happiness. Great works of art have been by anonymous groups. . . . Artists have been happy in guilds. Very likely it can happen again."[57] Steele, of course, was speaking theoretically; his own professional experience had been very different from the one he was eulogizing.

As examples of "the common effort of equals," he cited the World's Columbian Exposition of 1893 and the McMillan plan for Washington, D.C. "These two alone are enough to prove how quickly able men, inspired by a common ideal rise above the thirst for individual personal applause. Perhaps that is the way that the Group movement will reach us and carry us to higher and better and happier achievements than have been reached before. That is my hope."[58]

Steele realized that opportunities to build monumental private gardens were fast dwindling and that the field's best chance for art lay in collaborative work for public spaces. History has borne out the insight; since the postwar period, teams of landscape architects, architects, and sculptors have worked to create public works of great distinction. But Steele would not—perhaps could not—alter the working style he had pursued for nearly three decades. Intense, often intimate relationships with private clients would continue to provide the context for his creativity.

Haiti

In 1939 Steele substituted a trip to Haiti for the usual one to Europe. He returned to Haiti the next winter, and again the following, bringing along several friends, including Ralph Cram, O'Donnell and Urhling Iselin, Mabel Choate, and the Backuses. At various other times—in 1947, 1948, 1949, 1955, 1965, and 1968—Steele would rendezvous there with other close friends and clients for "three weeks of constant chuckling."[59]

His favorite excursion was to the Vallée des Plaisances, whose prospect Steele considered was one of "the most beautiful on earth."[60] The trip involved a large entourage of locals and four spare tires, but he always included it in his stay and insisted that his friends did, too. "Adventure in Haiti has but little to do with physical experience," wrote Steele.

It is difficult to impart by words and quite impossible by pictures. Adventure there is visual and mental—perhaps at moments, spiritual. In Haiti there is nothing to do except

just live and know that you are alive. . . . Everybody and everything goes and comes before the eye, he thinks at first. Then his ear begins to catch what his eye is not quick enough to see. The underlying sounds and silences are strange—alien. Sweet at times and at night, foreboding.

The longer he stays the more it is borne in upon him that what he sees and hears is but a trifling part of what is there. In time his unease begins to tell him that the perpetual stream of human beings is as nothing to the mounting company of ghosts. . . .

They are not all happy. They do not forget that Sudden Death was there to meet the first arrival and ever since has been a busy spy among the natives.[61]

Elsewhere he wrote: "This place is an exhilaration. I feel like a small boy with a new toy. . . . Everything is more beautiful and fantastic than remembered. The only place I have ever been that was more new the third time than the first. . . . The tropics are sudden about everything. Perhaps that's why they suit my temperament so well."[62]

Haiti was entirely unlike Europe; it provided no new design ideas, travel was difficult, and good restaurants scarce. But the unpredictable strangeness compelled Steele. He delightedly repeated tales of local "savages" dressed in powdered wigs and ball gowns imitating the pretentious rituals of the French

Haitians pulling Steele's car through the mud, Haiti, 1939. (SUNY ESF College Archives)

THE SUMMER HOUSE
ESTATE OF STANDISH BACKUS ESQ.

FLETCHER STEELE
BOSTON MASSACHUSETTS

NOVEMBER 1940
DRAWING No. 346-369

noblemen they had overthrown. The designer who once spent his vacations admiring the flawless logic of Versailles and the Place Vendôme now slogged through the mud in search of ghost-inhabited ruins. The powerful cycle of work and travel had been broken by the force of world events. The appeal of Europe and Asia for Steele vanished as their inspirational design roles necessarily shrank. There would be no more projects to send the landscape architect steaming back and forth to Europe in search of just the right baluster profile, just the right urn.

STANDISH BACKUS
Grosse Pointe Shores, Michigan
1940–1942

Continuing deliberations about a "mosquito house" for Standish Backus were not leading anywhere. In 1940 Steele recommended a piece of chinoiserie based on a design from Sir William Chambers's classic *Gardens and Buildings*, accompanied by an exhaustive commentary.

Backus estate, Summerhouse, drawing, 1940, based on a design by Sir William Chambers. (SUNY ESF College Archives)

I selected the patterns shown as being (1) as nearly suitable to English chinoiserie; (2) of sizes and shapes that would best fit the Chambers plans and elevations; (3) as being susceptible to brilliant painted color in variety. For the triforium course under the upper roof, I have selected a different pattern, #88, as giving a little variety and being in tune with the Chinese character of the building.

We went far enough with the screen man to be definitely sure that the whole thing can be easily and properly screened in an inconspicuous ship-shape way.

This is all in line with what we had previously considered. In order to be sure that the roof would look right, I made a tiny model which I meant to show you but it is of no great importance.

. . . I don't see why the whole thing should not be extremely interesting and brilliant to look at as well as useful in case of sudden attack by mosquitoes. Last week-end I spent in Philadelphia where the Orchid House of Mrs. Morgan's was in full swing. In that I used a lot of chinoiserie of about the same period and if I do say so myself, it is rather brilliantly successful. So after doing that and the little Pagoda at Mabel Choate's in Stockbridge, I feel fairly sure of how the mosquito house would look and feel that it would be in scale and a most interesting finish for all that end of the place.[63]

Despite the pitch, Backus was not enthusiastic. Neither did some three dozen proposals for an architectural backdrop for the Stage area suit him, despite Steele's excitement over the dramatic potential for a big feature behind the pool. The subject had been under discussion for a decade. One of the most intriguing backdrop proposals had come in 1937, when Steele designed a monumental wall and arched niche that held a cascade of fluorescent stone, illuminated by ultraviolet. Although an office memorandum from 20 March 1937 claimed that "Mr. Backus approves in toto the arrangement for the central feature of the backdrop," the design was never realized. Steele's several proposals for the backdrop communicate a sharp urgency, perhaps a reflection of his interest in maintaining a working connection with Backus.

In 1940 Steele put forward yet another scheme.

Every time I have a brainstorm about the back-drop, I think it is the best yet. But I really do think this brings together all the various details that you and Dotty have spoken of.

1. It uses the pilasters similar to those at Cranborne which have already been full-sized and corrected by you.

2. It uses, in what I think is an improved form, the motifs that Dotty liked on top of one of the old sketches.

3. It gets much better than it has before what satisfies me, namely a strong vertical line, tying together the top of the arch reducing the curved ornaments to their proper place and scale. The whole thing seems to me to be much better tied together than it was but without any real change in ideas. . . .

The whole effect of this thing would be big enough but seem much less on the grand side than anything we have talked about before.[64]

Apparently the proposal was still too much on the grand (or perhaps, expensive) side for the Backuses, because the next scheme, which appeared about a year later, was to be constructed of lattice. "I got out the old English book, which was used when we made the original stage plans, and enclose the results," Steele wrote to Backus in October 1941. ". . . It gives you the three arches for which you have always clamored. It does away with all stonework which Dottie has never really liked. It is vigorous enough in form to give me the apex of the stage triangle, which I have always believed necessary."[65]

But Backus's worsening health prevented moving ahead with either new project. Steele was beginning to understand that the garden was finished despite unrealized plans. He wrote to his old friend, "Now I am about to start for Rochester again and have not yet written thanks for my stay with you. It did bring back to mind the necessarily frequent visits during the days when you were building the place, and what exceptional fun it all was. I imagine that in some ways you feel as I do— that the building and planning is almost better than the finished job with nothing much to do with it except enjoy the fruit of the work. It is harder for me to sit down and enjoy things than it is to work at them."[66]

Backus's health continued to decline. "I certainly am glad to get your letter," Steele wrote a year later, "and horrified to know what a mean time you have had! I only hope you won't try to get back in harness too quickly. . . . It would be fun to get out to Detroit the next time I am in Rochester. . . . Now that work is slack I don't throw money around so freely, and shall probably let two or three little jobs accumulate there before I go on again, probably in September."[67]

Standish died in July the following year, without having begun either the Stage backdrop or the mosquito house. Steele continued to advise Dottie on maintenance and renovation (the Long Shot was especially vulnerable to weather and age) but nothing new was built under her direction. It had always been her husband's project.

THE ESTATE OF STANDISH BACKUS ESQ.
GROSSE POINT SHORES, MICHIGAN
STUDY OF STAGE BACKDROP

FLETCHER STEELE
BOSTON MASSACHUSETTS

OCTOBER 9 1941
DRAWING NO. 346·375

End of an Era

As the American labor force went to war, those who depended on large gardening staffs were in tough straits. Even the most industrious homeowners could not keep pace with the mounting work. Growers were also hit hard. "We've been so short of gas," wrote Fairman Furness, one of Steele's oldest and most respected colleagues in the nursery business, "that I send the men out in one truck and I stay at home and try to keep this nursery from turning back into a jungle."[68] Steele cut his office "to the bone" and moved to smaller quarters down the hall at 7 Water Street. His work had been reduced to advising old clients how best to preserve the most important features of their gardens, writing, and lecturing. All construction stopped and plans on the drawing table were shelved.

"This last week," Steele wrote his sister Esther in March 1944, "I have given three talks and never want to give another. They take a lot of time and energy. This winter I have written them out and read them. It is really more satisfactory, as it makes no difference how you feel when the time comes and I may be able to use the papers later—some of them at any rate. . . . They seem to like best to hear things they don't agree with."[69]

Mabel Choate's shrinking garden staff was also struggling. It was impossible to "keep up with all the Victorian tasks of

Backus estate, Stage backdrop, drawing, 1941. (SUNY ESF College Archives)

raking graveled paths and mowing so much lawn," so the lawns had been converted first to rock gardens, and then terraces for her large collection of tree peonies. Male workers were scarce, so, on Steele's recommendation, Choate hired a female grounds supervisor, a "farmerette," who received periodic notes on maintenance from Steele.

"In view of the fact the season is to be one of curtailment and no expansion," Harry Stoddard wrote in a typical letter of the time, "I have a feeling that we might leave Robert [Bolcome] entirely 'on his own' and see how we get along." Stoddard's message reflected a twinge of guilt, no doubt, but his closing thought, "of hoping for a continuance when the emergency is over,"[70] was sincere. Steele did go on to develop new areas in the Stoddards' garden after the war. But times were fast changing.

Steele said that he told at least one millionaire client "to go to hell"[71] during the war, probably in response to unreasonable demands for perfection under trying circumstances. Charlotte Allen proved more resilient. She founded a "Sinking Ship Fund" to aid civilian victims of sea battles that raised $100,000. One afternoon, Allen, Tom Taylor, and a few other local patriots painted the bronze flowers in her Rochester garden red, white, and blue.

In 1944 Steele wrote a two-part article for the *Garden Club of America Bulletin* outlining the same suggestions for consolidation that he had been making to his wealthy private clients. The theme of Steele's article is that true culture and a refined way of life are not dependent on money.

Today it would be foolish to take the future surplus for granted. We must plan to make our demands fit the shrinking supply of worldly goods. Of true culture we shall have more, perhaps, than ever, based on a firmer foundation than in the past.

Anyone who can think farther than a labor union leader knows that a high standard of living, which depends solely on having more money to spend, is a mockery of true culture. At most that ends in running 'round Europe enjoying restaurants and churches between dates with the dressmaker....

The landscape architect hears this again and again. He is called in to be told about the place in the country. It was just right when filled with family and friends. Now they are scattered and it is too big to live in alone. Labor help has dwindled. Things cannot go on as they are. If it could only be simplified, it could be carried along—for the time being at any rate. He starts out by saying:

You might as well get it firmly in your head that you will pay for this work in three ways. Time, Labor and Money....

You say you want roses for cutting? If that is all, then move a few down to the vegetable garden.... Oh you want to enjoy them growing in their pretty beds? How many are there all told? You don't know? Well, if you don't know a simple thing like that, then no wonder the cost has gotten out of control. I'd say there were about five hundred and you are short on labor. Do you enjoy looking at five hundred roses covered with bugs and black spot? Are you willing to spray them yourself once a week all summer long? If not, then the flowers will be prettier on fifty plants well cared for than on more that are neglected.

... How about the flower garden and the borders which were a mess last year? ... The easiest border to maintain has splashes of color now and again between intervals when it quiets down. That can be arranged with perennials....

... Forget the favorite individual blooms and think of the garden picture in a broad way. Put more attention on good thrifty foliage than you used to do. Keep all that stays strong and green throughout the season, whether or not the flowers amount to much. Gas-plant, hosta, peonies, iris and hemerocallis are dependable greenery for months on end....

Lastly, to encourage vigor, which must be your chief consolation for a time, be more generous than usual with fertilizer and compost. I don't remember any restriction on manure and there is still some to be had.... Get any commercial fertilizer which will not make it necessary to commit perjury when used on ornamentals; balanced fertilizer if you can, unbalanced if you can't. Carry some of it around in your knitting bag and throw it about all summer long.[72]

The second installment of the article addressed vegetable gardens, fruit growing, house plants, and propagation.

If one wants to use quantities of groundcover in place of lawns, the greenhouse is a good place to increase plants either by seed cuttings or division during the winter. Mrs. Harold Pratt used to root hundreds of thousands of boxwood cuttings in the otherwise useless space under the benches of her greenhouse. But you don't need a greenhouse for that. I remember one house where the children cut yew twigs and pressed them in a bowl full of sand. They used it as a center piece all winter and had a grand time quarreling about how much water to put on during meals. In the spring they had a hundred little plants to set out and now they have a tall hedge.[73]

After the war, when vegetable "victory gardens" continued to threaten flowers altogether, Steele wrote in defense of floriculture.

Fortunately, Americans do not have to be told by their government what freedom is. For some hundreds of years each one has been making up his own mind about such matters. . . . The trouble is that food growing alone cannot make a complete garden. It lacks something. No ripening pumpkin can give the peculiar jerk of pleasure which never fails us in a rose. No fattening chicken can make us forget the hummingbird.

. . . We shall never forget that the war was fought and won to save the good life. It must go on! It is significant that letters from people in the bereft countries of Europe but seldom mention food. They long for their lost amenities and many of them miss most the beauty, charm and tranquility which once upon a time they knew in their gardens. The fact that we still nourish those virtues here is the best propaganda for our American way of life.[74]

In spite of Steele's plea, ornamental gardening was moving into an eclipse, and few of his postwar projects would be realized in the grand style, on a grand scale. But the issue was more than size or economics. Faced with the catastrophic reality of war, the idea of a garden as private theater seemed self-indulgent. By the time the war was over, the garden's potential as a fantasy world had dwindled, replaced by new kinds of socializing and more matter-of-fact concerns in residential landscape. Between Dunkirk and Nagasaki, the quest for play that had fueled garden extravagance and innocence had been lost.

Esther Steele

Mary Steele's death in 1943 marked a new intensity in Fletcher's relationship with his sister Esther—"Jupe" in the hundreds of letters that passed between them. Esther shared her brother's directness but not his highbrow tastes or exacting standards for order. (She quit the local garden club because it was too "highfalutin.") Fletcher liked her unpretentiousness. He tried to persuade his editor at the *Garden Club of America Bulletin* to pursue her for an article.

If she would take the trouble to write you might get something quite salty from her. She is a garden realist if ever there was one. She was bored with flowers this year and said they weren't even worth the trouble to plow up. So she turned to vegetables. Now she gets in a tantrum to find that all the things like gentians and queer Correvon plants that she

struggled for years to raise are fighting to drive out the quack grass and promise to turn into weeds, without getting any care whatever. . . . She spent a good many hours over the stove when I was home. Every once in a while she would mutter: "Thank heaven the strawberry crop was bad" or "I wish I hadn't planted the beans."[75]

Mary Steele in her garden. (SUNY ESF College Archives)

Despite (or perhaps because of) the siblings' closeness, Fletcher's Pittsford visits grew more tense. Sparks flew as Esther's relaxed housekeeping style and her brother's compulsivity collided. "Now I don't call common orderliness fastidious at all," wrote Fletcher.

It is just plain decency. And I have a definite bone to pick with you about that. . . . I am sure you do not want me to feel desperately uncomfortable all the time I am home nor to feel relief whenever I get away, which is now the case.

You forget sometimes that for many years I have trained

Esther Steele in the garden. (SUNY ESF College Archives)

myself to be exceptionally sensitive to the location of objects. My whole professional career depends on being more sensitive about such things than other people. When they are disorderly it gives me an actively nauseated sensation. Little as you will believe it, when I look into a disorderly spot filled with the dregs of life that [have] gone and will never return, I get precisely the same sensation that you would have if you found the cook tucking away garbage in the kitchen pots and pans. In a couple of days I am ready to burst.[76]

Fletcher's aesthetic nature again provoked conflict when it came time to place his parents' headstones at Mount Hope Cemetery; he had modeled them after those of John and Lucinda Adams. "My own choice," he wrote to his sister,

would be to have mother's stone set in exactly the same relation to father's that Mrs. Lucinda Adams is to her husband, John Adams.... It should be set snug against the other stone, that is, so that the carved surfaces are about an inch apart which will leave a small crack. . . . He [Mr. McMahon, the cemetery superintendent] will give you a thousand reasons for this being utterly impossible. All you have to do is to say that the stones are totally unlike anything in Mount Hope and they are done like old family stones and they must be set the same way regardless of the exact locations of the graves or whether anybody in Rochester ever did it before or will do it again. Lay great emphasis on our family sentiment and that we want it done precisely in the old fashioned way.[77]

Esther found the idea of landscaping with headstones unattractive, arguing that monuments should stand over the people whose names they bear. Her brother gave in without much of a fight.

Esther knew most of Steele's important clients and had visited their gardens through his arrangements. Sometimes he called on her to help with his social obligations. "Kitty Sloan writes she will be at Yeoman's Club near Charleston till the 25th. Do look her up. I think she is beginning to feel a bit old and forgotten. She . . . loves to talk about the place with people who have been there. She would be flattered if you called her up."[78]

In truth, Esther preferred the forest to the garden, and her own kitchen to expensive restaurants. One of her frequent companions was Marjorie Ward Seldon, a native Rochesterian (and distant relative of Clayla Ward, Charlotte Allen's friend) who also worked for many years as Steele's Rochester project manager, communicating with the Boston office about construction and planting details. (Steele was scrupulous about soil samples, which Mrs. Seldon collected and then sent for laboratory analysis.) Marjorie Seldon was a strong, well-built woman who bore an uncanny resemblance, one client claimed, to Margaret Rutherford. She spoke her mind, preferred overalls to hats and fur coats, and was building her house from bits and pieces of discarded architectural fragments gathered throughout the city. She was probably Esther and Fletcher's closest shared friend.

During the wartime business lull, Steele found time to compose most of his second book, *Gardens and People*. "The writing is going very well," he told his sister in 1942. "Quite a lot of people have volunteered that the most useful thing I could do would be to keep at it, thinking, I suppose, that it will serve a certain crowd to keep their minds on simple things. . . . I am now trying to finish up certain groups of the papers to be ready when the time comes to show them to some publisher, though I am not bothering about the end of things yet. Mr. Packer, the editor of our most influential paper here says that one of these days an editor will come to me, which will be more satisfactory than going to hunt for one. That seems likely enough."[79] In fact, Steele's book would fall victim to the same shift in attitude that was to so forcibly disrupt his garden-making. He would be two decades in finding a publisher to bring out a much-reduced, unillustrated version of the text.

As the end of the war approached, spirits lifted. "Dear Charlei," Steele wrote to Charlotte Allen, whom he had affectionately dubbed "Chuck" years before, "Do you think I have spelled my new nickname [for you] right? It looks odd somehow. Perhaps it is because I am sort of surprised to see it where it is. They always say that an author's characters run away with him and make him do the unexpected. Perhaps, after all, you are a character and I am a helpless author. Life is wonderful."[80]

That summer he wrote Esther: "Charlotte just sent one of her characteristic notes—thirty words all told. 'Douglas Gorsline was here yesterday afternoon. We were sitting in the garden with a few other people when Douglas suddenly said "This is the best garden in the whole United States." C.' Sometime you must take the trouble to go in and just sit around in it. On the whole I consider it going on twice as good as Naumkeag."[81]

When the war ended, Steele advertised for an assistant. To one hopeful applicant he explained, "During the war my office was cut down to nothing, though the work has kept coming in and I shall have to refuse more without some sort of assistance. It is only fair to let you know that I am primarily concerned with the fine art of landscape architecture rather than the engineering or business end. Wherever possible office plans are avoided. I need an assistant who is flexible and not easily frustrated."[82]

The winter after the war Steele took a long vacation in Rochester, avoiding New York, "a dreary place during the day —nothing to do and nothing that I care about going to see,"[83] in favor of spending time with the old crowd. The previous November he had had an unpleasant business confrontation with one of his best old clients, John Ellsworth, for whose farm estate in Connecticut Steele had been producing designs since 1925. Ellsworth had written to complain, convincingly, about a bill:

Frankly, I am not aware of any considerable amount of work that you have done for me this year. As a matter of fact, as I think I have previously indicated, my main job was to get somewhere with the Bog Garden and I had hoped that you would be able to give it your attention early in the Summer but you were very busy then and finally didn't get down here until after the place had frozen up and it was much too late to do anything about it. . . . As I have indicated to you before, I am much disappointed that the planting down there has not gotten going better, particularly where it shows the most on the hill slope. I have suggested to you that we are experimenting with material which is too delicate for this climate and though I have been willing to give these things a good trial, I am not satisfied to go on with bare ground year after year.[84]

Ellsworth continued, "I feel at this moment that I do not wish you to incur any further expenses for me until we decide just what direction it [the bill] shall take." He appears to have been losing faith in Steele's horticultural expertise, as a result of repeated plant failures in the area: "I might add that I am a little apprehensive as to the successful planting of Clematis in the spring judging from what your expert grower has to say about the advantage of planting in the Fall about September 15th." (Steele would later diagnose the chronic hillside planting failures as the result of deep-rooted meadow grass. His remedy was earthworms and striped corn, "most ornamental in an old fashioned way and also helps break up the ground pretty deep."[85])

Steele responded to Ellsworth's objections (over two months later) in a friendly but cautious note:

As for your bill, I don't see that you got an awful lot out of it myself, though I certainly worked the time charged for and odd evenings, too, looking up new material and stuff like that. Nothing of that sort seems to count, though it has to be done. . . .

Nevertheless, on thinking it over, I agree with you, at least fifty per cent. For I do think that I was able to give you a little advice about odd little things that will be useful to you.

Would you feel that a bill for fifty per cent of the bill sent—$161.00 instead of $322—was fair, or is that still too much? I really don't care what it is so long as you are happy about it.[86]

Ellsworth agreed, but unhappy clients would surface again, especially during the postwar years when expectations were changing and large-scale work was becoming scarce.

ROBERT AND HELEN STODDARD
Worcester, Massachusetts
1946–1949

The horizon brightened with a note from Harry Stoddard about a potential job for his son and daughter-in-law: "They have a rather unique place, and, in a weak moment, I told them that I would waive my commission if I could persuade you to give them a little help. They don't need anything very elaborate but the 'Fletcher Steele touch,' I am sure, will help a lot."[87] The casual offer does not hint at the extent of Steele's involvement with the young couple's garden or its importance in his work. He would soon write: "With the Robert Stoddard place my final convictions about the art of landscape architecture are being brought to fulfillment."[88]

"They have many traits like Rochesterians," Steele once confided to his sister. (He especially liked Helen Stoddard, whom he described admiringly as "a fearless young thing.") "It is not easy to explain why people from smaller cities are markedly different from villagers on one side & big city folk on the other. They have the same things—travel as much or more—read the same papers and books—go to the same shops. Nevertheless, they are a type by themselves."[89]

Helen and Robert had admired the senior Stoddards' garden at Bass Rocks in Gloucester while they struggled with their own Worcester property, a large lot in one of the city's most beautiful suburban neighborhoods. Their house sat atop a wooded hill that fell away gradually but unevenly to the back. There was no view and little hope of establishing a focal point to pull the topography into a meaningful pattern.

Steele conceptualized the design challenge in abstract terms: "The problem is working out . . . a relation of interlocking swirls derived from both the lay of the land and the form and mass of the house. The scheme is more subtle than at Naumkeag and depends on feeling the result of what is done rather than seeing the various steps, more or less as the average person feels the relations of forms and color in a good painting

without being able to analyze. As a matter of fact I am using the effects made on me by Titian's Bacchus and Ariadne at the Stoddards."[90] Titian's painting (which hung in the National Gallery in London) offered Steele more an intuitive than a specific visual solution to his spatial problem. The illusion of movement and downward spiral generated by Titian's gesturing central figures resembles Steele's grading configurations only in the broadest sense.

Steele tackled the project aware of the Stoddards' taste (based on their appreciation of the Gloucester place) and with two specific requests from the clients: they did not want to see "where the woods end and the gardens begin" and they wanted a bank of maidenhair fern like the ones they had seen in the New Hampshire woods.[91] Both requests reflected Robert Stoddard's love of native plants. Helen Stoddard was drawn to exotics. Steele would manage to satisfy the couple's divergent tastes by making the new garden and the surrounding woods equal parts of his design.

He worked without a paper plan, directing the bulldozer with hand signals to carve out the series of curves that he would later describe as resembling a cornucopia or giant lily. As Steele later described the process, probably in reference to his early (circa 1933) earth-sculpting experiment at Naumkeag, the prototype for the Worcester design,

> Since that morning there have been no more laborious grading plans made in my office. What good would they be when the bulldozer knows how to manage details with far more finesse and charm than I? Instead the driver and I meet on the ground, if possible with the client who should be in on the fun. We plan what we want. We tear up the land, then smooth it down again. The result is truly carved, like the work of a sculptor on a vast scale. The idea starts in the mind of the artist, who must be pliable and ready to change in detail according to what turns up in the earth—boulders or soft dirt. The machine forces its way in one place: is checked just beyond, as rocks and sand demand or it would be better to say, permit. Compromise is accepted. When the job is done it satisfies both man and nature because it fits the place. And the result is quite unexpected in detail since no preconceived studio plan could achieve such spontaneity tamed to human wants.[92]

The "calyx" of the giant lily sculpted by the bulldozer formed a triangular bed bordered by crushed blue stone and blue fescue grass. Steele's original planting scheme for the interior of the bed called for "tufts of plants, pink, white, purple and pale yellow over which would be a cloud of tiny red flowers of the

common Coral Bells. . . . On the whole, the colors will be very different from those in the flower border and yet the Coral Bells . . . will tie everything together."[93]

Steele also used blue fescue along the edge of the next bed where a long sweeping curve was graded to conceal a dry retaining wall and perennial border. From the house only the sweep of blue-green is visible. A band of thyme separates the fescue from the perennials. The planting scheme for the mixed border was largely left to Helen Stoddard, although Steele was adamant that it should be edged with the gray foliage of lamb's ear.

A similar scheme had been designed for the Backuses in Detroit, where each of the twelve Long Shot borders had gray edges. The uniformity was not only to give added strength and architectural presence to a mixed planting but also to ensure

high, intense color. "A quantity of silvery white will appreciably raise the color value of a large planting. The impressionist painters proved, among other things, that the use of exclusively high values, or in other words, light colors, omitting all darks, makes at times a very gay picture. Green foliage of most garden plants is notably darker than the light colored flowers. In order to get a sparkling effect, all that is needed is to hide the dark leaves behind white and light gray leaved plants so that the flowers rise from a bed of silver."[94] Steele had described this color technique in 1921.

It was not until visiting a garden in Bar Harbor that I realized how the thing should be done. It was a garden designed and planted by Beatrix Farrand, where high and intense color was wanted. Most of the color was insured by the use

Stoddard estate. "This place carries even further the uses of curves and walls of steps and grassy ramps as part of great swirls frankly introduced to drag the eye to similar more distant landscape shapes." Steele to book editor F. F. Rockwell, 10 June 1955, LC. (Photo by Marvin Richmond)

Stoddard estate. "The land, the clients' inclination and my own all led us to make a garden on a series of circular curves quite without obvious axes or a single straight line. Yet the whole is rigidly controlled on almost mathematical spirals." Steele to Mrs. Douglas, 1 February 1955, LC. (Photo by Marvin Richmond)

of the perennials we all know and plant. But in one respect her planting was more knowing than ours. In order to keep the color keyed up, Mrs. Farrand had hidden so far as possible, the green foliage of the perennials behind the whitish grey leaves of common and uncommon grey-foliage plants. Very little green could be seen in the beds. The flowers rose from grey and white borders. And the effect was as much gayer and brighter than the usual planting as a luminous Monet is more full of light than a Claude.[95]

The problem of a convincing transition between the frank artifice of the formal beds and the surrounding forest was solved by continuing the bedding plants into the woods. "My idea," wrote Steele to his client in 1947, "is that as you get more stuff than the border will hold, you will push it back up the bank around the laurels, so that garden and woods will be pulled together and gradually the strong things will look out for themselves without a lot of garden care. Some of the stuff is sure to naturalize itself if we give it a good start."[96] In principle,

it was the same technique he had employed years before at Wingfield, in Mount Kisco, New York.

About one-third the way down the hill, Steele laid out a big curve of 'Gruss en Aachen' perpetual shrub roses. These had a long season and would bloom in the high shade of the old elms, which few other roses would. A variety of low shrubs planted on the downward sloping side of this bed were invisible from the house, where the descending swirls coalesced into a funnel. At the bottom of the hill, the space was stopped by a great white pine.

As at Bass Rocks, Steele defined the area near the house by a curving terrace and dry rock wall. He brought the stone in from Castelia, Ohio. "It is a queer kind of light weight, very much pock marked material which is useful to me in certain kinds of work especially in fairly large sized chunks."[97] The stone, he described,

Stoddard estate. (Photo by Marvin Richmond)

holds moisture like a sponge. By dosing it continually with ground limestone and bonemeal, perhaps I can keep it on the sweet side, in part at any rate.

It [the wall] is some 150' long and varies in height from one to six feet. It faces west and north and lies in the shade of tall elms, though the roots will never be in the way. The wall curves up in the middle and down at both ends. There are endless crevices on the top as well as side to plant. The stone will be, in time, I hope, hidden under planting.

For the most part I shall depend on broad leaf evergreens, including Hedera Helix to do most of the work. But there should be also quantities of spreading and trailing rock plants.[98]

A wide, moss-carpeted stairway filled the same structural role, on a larger scale, as the seashell steps in the senior Stoddards' garden; both provided visual transition from the house terrace to the lawn as well as a way down the hill. The mossy staircase possessed a dreamlike, fairytale quality. Its banister of foam-flower (*Tiarella cordifolia*) was an inspired choice. A second mossy ramp leading straight down from the drive was actually an access for service vehicles. It was here that Steele made the maidenhair fern wall. An open, clay-pipe runlet carried the water to the end, where it dripped slowly onto the ferns.

A series of lead pools shaped to fit the irregular topography were designed on-site with Peter Moore of J. B. Lowell, Inc., and Garrow Brothers, roofing specialists who were experienced with lead burning. Helen Stoddard and her gardeners later designed another pool at the bottom of the hill where the old pine had originally stood.

The scale of the undertaking was huge. Steele had conceptualized and treated the garden space as a whole, carving it with broad, sculptural strokes. The result was deliberate, and highly artificial, yet retained (or perhaps achieved) the inevitable look of nature.

Steele felt the importance of abstraction, for his own work and for the art form generally. "Landscape architecture," he observed, "is turning away from architectural geometry and toward the forms which inspire abstract sculpture. More and more it struggles for plastic effects made possible by earth modeling without benefit of terraces, walls or other labels of architectural understanding." The idea of reshaping land certainly was not new. But what Steele goes on to propose in the undated essay amounts to a revised understanding of the landscape architect's role as interpreter rather than imitator of nature: "Modeling dirt for aesthetic purposes was begun by the English Landscape Gardeners two hundred years ago. They artificially piled up and carved out undulating meadows, valleys and hills, limiting themselves to imitations of natural scenery, aiming at the art which disguises art. There is a growing attempt to shape areas into forms that interpret nature without pretense of imitation."

Steele sensed great possibilities for landscape architects able to respond to the new aesthetic horizons opened through modern sculpture.

Making a good composition from the inside is a good deal like carving out a cave, and the landscape architect often feels that this is indeed what he is doing as he cuts vistas and gardens in the woods. When it is done, what one sees is the inner surface, or the reverse of the sculptor's figure hacked out of stone. One is inside his room, which can be enclosed by additional planting, or by cutting. More, a distant mountain range is as good a landscape wall as piled up brick. However he does it, the landscape architect moves with the freedom of modern sculpture rather than the rigid limitations of architecture which former landscape architects like Le Nôtre felt obliged to use.[99]

ANN AND MATTHIAS PLUM
Chatham, Cape Cod, Massachusetts
1946–1948

In the spring of 1946 Steele also started a job for Ann and Matthias Plum in Chatham on Cape Cod. Mrs. Plum, who found Steele through the Ellsworths, may have been warned by them about some of the recent fee controversies because she immediately asked for a definite plan and estimates. "Frankly," Steele replied, "estimates in this post-war period are not worth the money and time it costs to make them. We not only do not know what things will cost three months from now, we don't even know what they will be tomorrow."[100] He described his postwar gardenmaking method:

The client and I get together and go over the whole problem, for years to come as far as we can see ahead.

Then we consider what seems to be the first thing to do. It may be planting or a walk or terrace or garden. Then we try to get the labor and materials for one thing at a time, and do that. If it is question of planting, we go together to nurseries, when possible, and pick out the stuff wanted and know what it will cost. But even that is not done till the beds are properly prepared to plant in.

Done this way, the client can stop when he pleases at any time, after he has spent as much money as suits him for the moment. The only disadvantage is that things which are stopped that way, obviously look unfinished for the time being. I don't mind that myself, if something is clearly on the way. And if we use sense, everything can be complete up to a definite place.

Places done this way show the course of growth and development that ready made things never have. They show an acceptance of the limitations imposed on us by circumstances which we cannot control, and our power of making the most of them. In the long run, this spells charm.[101]

It also spelled reduced costs. The old process, which involved detailed presentation drawings, comprehensive schemes, and largely unlimited budgets, was no longer a viable alternative for Steele's clientele. Apparently his explanation satisfied the Plums. By August work was under way. "They will start cutting heavy stuff off the new drive line, which is necessary in order to save the topsoil without getting it messed up with shrubs, etc. Then he will go ahead bulldozing the new drive along the lines we staked it out. If all goes well in a couple of days your place will be in horrible condition and all Chatham showered with dust. Excellent."[102]

References to a new pine grove and a change in Mrs. Plum's mother's service and entrance drives indicated something of the scope of the project. Steele ordered fifteen tons of "Hyperhumus" to begin preparing planting sites, as had become his practice. His letter continued: "The whole picture is fast shaping up in my mind. I feel sure that the things we planned are on the right track and will lead to lots more things." He finished enthusiastically, "It was all great fun. Thank you for the hospitality. Your family are grand."

The ambitious start did lead to "lots more things," more, apparently, than Mrs. Plum, or her husband, had bargained for. The following summer Steele received a letter from Matthias Plum, a lawyer, informing him that Mrs. Plum did not "propose to incur any further expense in connection with the place at Chatham unless she has first been advised and approves of the proposed expenditure. I want you to know that we both think you have done a wonderful job on the place and the improvement is to say the least tremendous, but you will appreciate that it has been a very expensive proposition and these expenses must be stopped, unless, as above indicated, Mrs. Plum has first approved them before being incurred."[103]

It is likely that Steele had been overly zealous in ordering work. But underlying his behavior was a long-tested assumption that money would become available as the garden progressed and the beauty of the scheme became evident. It had happened reliably before. The conflict was eventually patched up. Years later Steele heard from a friend of the Plums, "Annie continually curses you as a high-priced robber; and in the next breath says what a wonderful job you did."[104]

Despite ongoing work at the Stoddards', a big job in New Brunswick, Canada, and several other smaller jobs, Steele's business had dwindled. He was in Rochester more often, and found new ways to amuse himself.

On the return from one visit to his sister, he stopped in Geneva, New York, to test fruit. "I never ate so many grapes in my life. We had to try every kind that is being hybridized and at least I got a list of the ones that seem best. . . . As for me, I

have never been fond of uncooked food of any sort, so fruit off the vine or tree means little to me, though I have learned to eat it because it is so hard to find cooked fruit or vegetables, for that matter, in our restaurants or on most people's tables. I really hate salad, as a matter of fact, but can get lettuce no other way. When I remember the purees and soups of lettuce in France it makes me long to go back to Paris. I still think that French cooking is so much better and more wholesome than American."[105]

Salad was only one aspect of the problem. In larger terms, it was a way of life that excluded lettuce soup, yearly trips to Paris, and, ultimately, even grape arbors. The seed catalogues and design volumes that had filled long winter evenings were no longer so compelling or so necessary.

The most amusing thing that has happened to me this autumn was to have a woman hire me to rearrange her parlor furniture, which I did for $100.00. It took me an hour going over her house from attic to cellar to find out what she owned and then an hour to move every single object out of it and three hours to put back a selected roomful of stuff. She kept saying: "Well, I never would have thought of that" or "What! You aren't going to use that old thing" or "Can't I have any of my treasures?"

When I got through we had tea in a corner where she said she never in her life had expected to sit. Now she writes: "They say it changes people to change their names, but it is nothing to what it does to have you change the furniture. I *feel* like somebody else and I *am* different, and I like it!"[106]

As Steele must have reflected, gardens changed lives just as dramatically.

In Haiti, he took up watercolors: "I do hope weaving is not so eternally frustrating as learning to do water colors," he wrote to his sister in 1947.

No matter how you work you never get any better. However, frustrating or not, it is lots of fun, though they continue to be dreadful. What is the use of having such nice high standards as I have, and getting nowhere?

Here is the one I did this Sunday morning. . . . For goodness sake don't let the connoisseurs see it! My artistic name would be mud. After all I only began the middle of January and did nothing the whole of March. Like all beginners I begin to defend myself.

Trees and shrubs are the hardest. They simply refuse to look like anything. It is easy to say that I am modern and don't care whether things look like anything or not. I find that when I start to paint a house I want it to look like a house, and a tree like a tree. Victorian at bottom, I fear.[107]

SEMINOLE
Catherine and John Bullard
Nonquitt, Dartmouth, Massachusetts
1948–1954

"Mrs. Bullard, like so many other people nowadays, expressed the opinion that she had no interest in flowers but wanted a layout that would be interesting at all times of the year; be suitable to entertain in for either large or small parties, be smart to look at, and never need weeding. I went down this weekend to a party of about 70, and it was most successful for that number, as well as for a normal house party of a dozen people. Some of the forms are really pretty good."[108] In fact, Mrs. Bullard's garden probably needed considerable weeding but not the intensive care that some of the old places required to look their best. In general, the landscape features at Seminole were broad and simple.

Soon after the start of the project, Steele wrote to Helen

Ellwanger: "Nonquitt is a good deal as though everybody we know in Rochester lived in one block and all fenced in together with the rest of the world kept strictly at bay. I had a very good time. Nevertheless, the place itself is simply unbelievable."[109] The exclusive section of Dartmouth, Massachusetts, sat on Buzzards Bay, not far from the great old whaling port of New Bedford. During the last quarter of the nineteenth century, wealthy residents of nearby cities discovered the idyllic setting and built large summer homes there. The appeal continued into the twentieth century; the Bullards' home was constructed in the 1930s.

Steele enjoyed the unpretentious couple, especially Mrs. Bullard, whom he thought Mabel Choate would like too. "Catherine," he wrote in 1949, "is refreshing. She keeps everything in good order because she likes it that way. Yet if painters are in the parlor, the garden half done and no new clothes home from the dressmaker, she can't see what that has to do with giving a party and goes ahead regardless."[110] In July he

arranged to meet Mrs. Bullard at Stockbridge. "I have some things to show her at Naumkeag which would help in the work at her place and it is much easier for people to understand what is needed when they see it."[111] Mabel Choate seemed happy enough to share her garden with curious visitors, budding professionals, and Steele's other clients.

Open fields and woods surrounded most of the house when Steele first began work in late 1948. His layout preserved much of this, in keeping with Bullard's request for low maintenance. Steele's plan identifies woods in four quadrants around the perimeter of the formally landscaped areas near the house. The meadow lay directly east of the house patio, a handsome middle ground to the wide ocean view. The rolling rhythm of long, indigenous grasses and wildflowers mimicked the movement of the ocean surf.

Two pools—one recreational, one ornamental—incorporated water into the formal landscape picture. The lily pool was lushly planted and enclosed within the patio terrace walls. The slightly larger swimming pool lay farther into the lawn, directly on axis with the living room, a rectangle of still water reflecting trees and sky. A path ran beside the swimming pool to two triangular cutting gardens, and eventually down through the meadow. A new wall and gate, built to abut the end of the house, provided the setting for yet another small garden.

Steele established a cross axis that began with a circle of juniper, big oaks, and azaleas and ended, to the south, in the apse of a long garden room cut into the woods. The "floor" of the room was a carpet of gold and orange and deep red primroses. Steele often found inspiration for landscape arrangements in

Seminole, view to the ocean. (SUNY ESF College Archives)

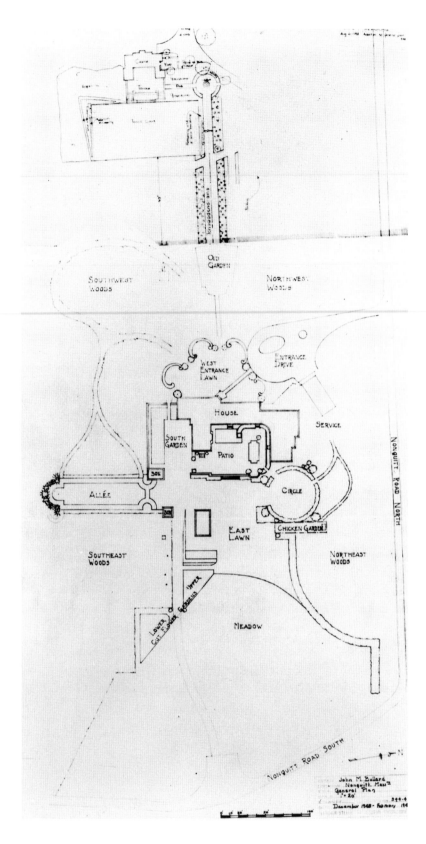

Seminole, general plan, 1948–49. (SUNY ESF College Archives)

other art forms, often painting. Here he had remembered the intricacy and boldness of ancient Persian rugs, which, appropriately enough, often depicted gardens, and acted as substitutes for them in marble-paved courtyards. Steele's bold abstraction was a far cry from carpet bedding schemes of Victorian gardens. The primrose garden was a painterly incident, as modern, surely, as the big curves of color defining the Stoddards' sloping lawn. The dimensions—100 by 25 feet, the proportions of a magnificent rug—contributed to the room's unforgettable impact.

Bullard found the fence and wrought-iron niche herself at a local antique shop; she already owned the marble angel that would serve as the focal point of the outdoor room. Steele's notes indicate that he completed the ironwork niche "on Golden Mean proportion" in 1949; this may refer to a horizontal element that appears to be located about 5/8 of the distance down to the pedestal. Ivy formed the carpet's border and eventually climbed to soften the white iron of fence and niche, as well as the trunks of the few indigenous trees that broke the expanse. From early May to early June, the clearing in the woods burned like a topaz.

Steele kept extensive notes on flower and foliage color under varying light conditions for his own use and argued publicly for the adoption of a standardized color chart for the field. In 1923 he wrote: "The sooner we can all agree,—nurserymen, plant societies, clients and landscape architects—about the names of colors, the better off we shall be."[112] Steele urged the American Society of Landscape Architects to form a committee to study the situation. He recommended adopting one standardized system, that of Dr. Robert Ridgeway, "Color Standards and Nomenclature."

Steele believed the color could play an increasingly strong role in landscape design.

A marked feature of modern appreciation and endeavor in the Fine Arts is the passion for brilliant color. Painters, architects, decorators and stage managers are all bestirring themselves with the problems of strong color arrangements. Gardeners are not behind in this movement. . . .

. . . In the spring one can have sheets of flat, daring color that leave the frantic cubist painter speechless. . . .

The possibilities of gardening, however, are to be differentiated from those of the graphic arts by the added element of time, which brings with it the power of dynamic climax, usually ascribed solely to music, poetry and the drama. . . .

. . . The progress of a symphony is counted in minutes; the movement of a play is confined to hours: but the action of our garden, the artistic conception of our minds as truly as the symphony or the play, is measured by the weeks, even the months, which life itself requires to give birth to a flower.

Steele also appreciated less dramatic climaxes.

> Spring's first moment should be felt rather than stamped on the consciousness. . . . To start the spring garden in this mood we have two flowers that best answer the purpose. First, the snowdrop, which should be planted near the corner where a patch of belated snow is apt to linger year by year. While snow remains, winter remains. Some fine morning the white patch looks somehow different. The snow has turned to snow drops. Second is the blue squill. At its culminating moment the squill sweeps the garden like a blue sword. But its first coming is gentle, almost imperceptible. . . . The hue of the budding flower exactly matches the tone of many a late winter shadow on snow.[113]

Steele's design for the Bullards' front lawn took the form of large scallops of *Teucrium* hedges that defined rose beds. Tall specimen arborvitae punctuated the ends of the curves and flanked the grass pathways that led to adjoining garden areas, woods, or walks. The low land was uncooperatively wet; even with a system of drains the roses never really took hold.

In 1953 Steele designed a long rhododendron allée as a path to the tennis court and casino. The rhododendron's time-limited show occurred about a month after the primrose garden's and occupied the other end of the color spectrum. As in the early garden for Ethan Allen at Rolling Ridge, Steele used a pale-pink-to-deep-purple scheme to enhance the illusion of distance.

LADY DAVIS
Saint Andrews, New Brunswick, Canada
1947

Yet a third big job dominating Steele's postwar business was that for Lady Davis of Saint Andrews, New Brunswick. Lady Davis did not fit Steele's model of the perfect client. "The job promises to be rather fine," he wrote Jupe shortly after getting under way. "Lady Davis has no idea how unusual it is as she has never stopped talking in any garden long enough to look around."[114]

Steele sensed that the new client was unsettled by the extent of the garden taking shape in her modest backyard. The price —"a couple thousand a week all summer"—does not seem to have been the issue; it was the bold scale of the emerging landscape that compelled her to remind Steele not to "do anything disproportionate." ("What do you suppose she meant?" he later asked.) In truth, the designer was also a little concerned about the discrepant impact of house and landscape: "While I tried hard to make it effective, and used every trick of proportion I could think of, yet I did not intend it to be quite so imposing, which it is to the point of grandeur. I fear that the result will be to make the insignificant stucco house at the top look like a matchbox. I did not count on that and am in a quandary as to what to do. This composition of space business might become an Old Man of the Sea let out of a jar."[115]

But Steele masked his uneasiness about the design in enthusiastic, excessively self-congratulatory letters home:

> The job is going to be superb, if I do say so as I shouldn't. As

Lady Davis estate, construction panorama, 1948. (SUNY ESF College Archives)

Lady Davis estate, model. (SUNY ESF College Archives)

you know, I care more for the composition of space than anything else, and this was my chance. In an area not much bigger than our front yard, if any, two stone walls curve around on either side, sloping down hill. The place is full of piles of dirt and holes and no planting done. It is a mess. Yet Lady Davis and two people I had never seen all rushed to meet me yelling, "It's marvellous! Come quick and look at it." I went to a cocktail party and all sorts of people asked to be introduced in order to say what a kick it gave them. And I agree. It is nothing short of astonishing how effective a couple of stone walls can be if they are in the right place and are the right shape. Even the workmen are agog about it. And there hasn't been a plan—just a tiny model to help

them when I am not there and [me] there once telling them to go higher and wider and curve it faster or slower according to a stick I had in my hand. It has been great fun.[116]

Steele's design approach at New Brunswick echoed that at the (much larger) Worcester Stoddards' place, where he had also carved a backyard into a cohesive picture. But the subsequent project relied on curved, terraced walls rather than beds to define contour and shape space. (No planting plans or orders survive for Lady Davis's garden, so it is difficult to compare the two in terms of design success.) The terrace scheme was adapted from a flight of steps at the Villa Corsini in Florence; the baluster profiles and massive posts with tufa insets are almost exact quotations of the baroque original.

Posterity

Mabel Choate and Steele had begun to think about Naum-keag's future. Steele's long-standing commitment to the Trustees of Reservations—as adviser and committee member—certainly influenced her decision to bequeath it and the Mission House to the Massachusetts organization. Steele described the Trustees' activities in a letter:

This society has been active for more than half a century in acquiring and preserving places of natural beauty and historic interest. It has been influential in the establishment of state and city parks, forests and reservations. It has materially assisted many public and private agencies in acquiring their own lands for conservation. It undertakes the education of our people in the use and importance of the conservation of land, flora and wild life.

It was the progenitor of the National Trust of England, with which it still maintains close affiliation. It has been active in helping to organize many other societies, such as the Landmark Society of Western New York.

After working a long time with both national and local organizations, I am convinced that local patriotism is most efficient, enthusiastic and understanding when it comes to the conservation and administration of local landmarks of natural beauty and historic interest. National control of such matters is remote and gets bureaucratic and impersonal. Privately organized bodies do best in preserving local monuments.[117]

Steele was also concerned about the future of Lisburne Grange, the Sloans' garden in Garrison, New York. In 1948 he was working out a plan to transform the private estate into a multidisciplinary center for the study of communal life after the owners' deaths. Unlike Beatrix Farrand, whose *Plant Book for Dumbarton Oaks* proved crucial to her masterwork's survival, Steele left no formal maintenance notes for any of his gardens. His work on the Lisburne Grange project was directed toward the development of the program rather than the physical landscape. "It is the consensus of opinion of the professors and practitioners with whom I have talked that there is a deplorable lack of reliable, collated information about problems relating to community life," wrote Steele in 1948.[118]

The key to workable communities, he predicted, would lie in a cross-disciplinary approach that encompassed the wide range of factors affecting life in that place. "A good presage has been the cooperation of the students of the Schools of Architecture, Landscape Architecture and City Planning of Harvard University who studied the local details of Economics and Industry, Land Use, Population Growth, Land Values, Income Groups, Taxation, Town Budget and the suitable number of schools, movie houses, etc., before making the Physical plan for the development of Framingham, Massachusetts. Yet even here many details of the problem were not touched upon."[119]

The center at Lisburne Grange was to be an American think tank, comprising a director, senior administrator, senior fellows or faculty, junior fellows, and librarian. Junior fellows would be invited on the merits of past work and supported during their tenure at the center, just as at the American Academy in Rome. Mrs. Sloan suggested Vassar as the parent institution for the new center. Aside from these broad, preliminary suggestions for organization, no other project documents survive. The proposal appears to have fizzled without a trace.

5 · Twilight: Frustration and Fulfillment, 1950–1971

Despite exceptional financial successes before the war, Steele arrived at age sixty-five with few assets. His exquisite tastes—in clothes, travel, books, food, and drink—were leaving him little choice. He was in good health. He would continue to work. "Now I am agreeably old," he wrote in 1952, "and still making mud-pies with friends. A good life."[1]

But Steele's artistic goals were increasingly at odds with general trends. The economic picture had changed, and so had tastes. A baroque water staircase—now a truly exorbitant expense—also seemed pretentious to most people. Why not a deck, or at most, a simple goldfish pool? But for Steele, there was little fun in simplicity.

The masons and carpenters who once trembled before the ferocious landscape maker now shook their heads in disbelief as he roared disapproval of a sloppy joint or skewed line. Perfection—Steele's creed—was scarcely attainable. The long downward spiral in quality of workmanship in America had gotten off to a fast postwar start. Sheer quantity of demand for new construction had made a virtue of the shortcut, and many traditional techniques were lost.

Steele's Edwardian manners and values became fiercer in the face of changing values. "I don't read newspapers nor go to the movies. I learned to hate the radio and gave it away. I see no reason to answer the telephone just because it rings. I like good general conversation and detest being in a room where lots of people are jabbering. I fear I am not a good member of the herd."[2] He was right.

In March 1951 Steele suffered a stroke. He recovered but decided—whether out of new caution about his health or a changed existential perspective—that he was doing too much, and promptly resigned from many organizations. His resignation from the American Society of Landscape Architects (which actually predated his stroke by a few months) was met with upset and protest by his colleagues: "If your indulgence will afford my personal honest response to this proposal, I was shocked by such an announcement," wrote past board member Edwin G. Thurlow. "I am particularly incensed about your proposal because I have long felt that the society needed more members of your calibre—i.e., members who considered and practiced landscape architecture as an art and actively contributed to the profession through their work, public utterances and student relationships."[3] The modesty in Steele's response was genuine: "To tell the truth it surprised me that anyone cared (save my old friends) whether I resigned or not from the a.s.l.a. And for the sake of them who care, I am willing to reconsider and stay in."[4]

In 1959 Steele would again tender his resignation to the asla, this time unequivocally. "Perhaps it is I who am wrong and instead of thinking the sense of beauty comes second, not first with most l.a.s, I would change my mind if I knew the young men. But then I look over the last few years of landscape architecture and see no signs of it in this country. Sweden is far ahead. They know what l.a. is and can do as an art. I don't think we do. I am tired of supporting a society that does not now and never did, support the importance of beauty in Fine Art, particularly its own art."[5]

He also wrote to the chairman of the asla Committee on Organization and Development.

Opposite: Turner estate, view through the orchard. (Photo by Carol Betsch)

I was instrumental in starting the chapter idea and in instituting the first chapter here in Boston many years ago. For a long time, I attended the meetings and followed the business closely. There was a period when the voice of the local chapter had influence in the community and always for worthwhile things but the intercourse between members for any other purpose was fruitless. The only thing they wanted to talk about was advertising the profession by which they hoped to get more work. But the subject of landscape architecture or any real consideration of the problems of the landscape architect in his own work were not mentioned and if ever they were brought up, they were responded to with the genial enthusiasm of a cow obviously thinking of other things.

This was either from lack of interest or from an unwholesome reticence, possibly the latter for there has been an underlying attempt on the part of certain individuals in the Society to tone down or omit all criticism of work on plans for the city or community. This prevented all live, active and stimulating criticism. For several years, as far as I was concerned, the business carried on by the chapter was flat, stale and unprofitable and I finally regretfully resigned to express my disappointment at the failure of the Boston chapter to think of anything else than its own advertisement."[6]

Whether a specific event precipitated Steele's condemnation of the professional society or the letters simply marked the culmination of mounting frustration, the theme was not new. Steele had been complaining for decades about his colleagues' indifference to art.

Nelson W. Aldrich, president of the Institute of Contemporary Art in Boston, wrote to ask Steele why he no longer was a museum member. "I get out now," Steele replied, "because the Institute no longer meets my personal wants; mind you, it is I who have changed. When the Institute started I was much younger. I was keenly curious about who the artists were as they came along and what they did. . . . All I want now is to see beautiful objects in a compatible environment because of the satisfaction they give. . . . And what I like I care intensely to see again and again as long as they live for me. So naturally I go to see objects and paintings that I am sure of rather than unknown things, which, frankly are more often than not on the dull side."[7] Some of Steele's other resignations, from the Association on American Indian Affairs and as a trustee of Boston's Children's Hospital, reflect the wide range of his previous interests and involvements.

He still enjoyed a night on the town, though, one of which, apparently, got out of hand. "Last Saturday evening my extensive stupidity caused some bother to several people at the hotel, which I sincerely regret. Please give my apologies to those concerned, most particularly to the hat check girl on the ground floor," he wrote to the manager of the Ritz-Carlton Hotel in Boston.[8]

Age was not dulling Steele's obsessive attention to detail, or his humor. He still made decisions, even small ones, with a degree of concern that would have drained a less energetic soul. "Please note," he wrote to the Massachusetts Audubon Society, "that I send my five dollars as a fee for membership. . . . I send this because I am interested in birds, just the same as I am interested in wild animals and the redwood trees of California, but frankly I am not particularly interested in birds any more than I am redwood trees. I consider that the voluntary gift of $3.00 added to the subscription would show an extraordinary interest in feathered creatures which I do not have and do not want to pretend to have."[9]

Correspondence with various merchants and organizations was voluminous. Purchases came after long and serious deliberation. He was particular about everything: his sheets, his handkerchiefs, his umbrella, his curtains. He wrote to one shop owner about some new curtains: "I am sending the native Haitian peasant's bag with bright blue green tassels of exactly the color I hope to get. . . . The main point is that they are extremely vivid with an aniline sharpness that would just suit me. . . . I would emphasize the point that what I want is bright color primarily and only get curtains because I can think of no other way of getting the color. . . . P.S. I don't want any soft refined color but something that shrieks."[10]

Steele continued to give garden club lectures at $100 apiece but adopted a new format, conducting the talks on-site at private homes. There he addressed "just how the land should be graded and where gardens, terrace, service, tool house, drives, garage etc. should be put and why."[11] These impromptu talks proved popular with his audiences. "Mr. Steele speaks most informally and with a fine sense of humor," one Bennington, Vermont, newspaper reported. "He began by saying that the most important thing to do in landscaping is to fit the land to the needs of the family . . . and to decide just what they want to look at."[12]

Aside from two book reviews for *Landscape Architecture* in 1950 and three articles for *House and Garden* (two about the Harry Stoddards' gardens and one about the Backuses'), Steele virtually stopped publishing. He may have been writing essays for his forthcoming book—he often wrote between 5:00 and 7:00 A.M.—but it is likely that he had more than enough mate-

rial for his text. He was well along in the work by 1947: "The thing that really interests me at the moment is carrying through the long series of little scraps that I have been writing about 'People and Gardens' [the final manuscript reversed the title]. . . . Before I die, I hope to do something about the gardener's eternal triangle—namely, the pull of the land itself and plants and climate at one corner, the pull of the client and owner and what he wants at another corner, and the pull of the designer and his sense of fine art at the third corner trying to pull everything together."[13]

Steele's gardens during the 1950s tended to be smaller than those of earlier years, in keeping with widespread preferences. Most were designed largely on-site, with few formal office plans or drawings. Some were charged with a frenetic quality that resulted in a compressed look (as though too much was occurring in a limited space, as was foreshadowed by the strug-

gle with scale at Lady Davis's garden in New Brunswick) or, more happily, in vital complexity.

The One-Hour Garden

Some of Steele's garden projects took the form of collaborative consultations that relied on his quick insightfulness and intensely visual, improvisatory gift. For $50 an hour he met his client on the grounds and shared every thought, every good possibility that occurred to him. No property was too small. After one such hour-long meeting, John Goetz, a Rochester friend, developed nearly all the ideas Steele had given him—scribbled on a napkin. Steele was delighted with the results: a spatially coherent green garden of terrace, lattice screen, clipped euonymus, vinca, and yew hedges. When insisted that the garden be included in a local tour of his Rochester work,

View from the Beacon Street apartment, pen-and-ink sketch by Steele, ca. 1948. (LC)

Goetz was reluctant. "But John," pleaded Steele, "this is the most important garden I've ever done."[14]

Steele had argued again and again that cost was not an important factor in good design, that an old shed and well-proportioned path might possess a kind of charm lacking in the most pretentious parterre. He also believed that sensitive people knew their own land more deeply than the visiting landscape architect ever could. Finally, Steele sensed the potential of the garden as a play space, not just in its final form, but as a creative, ongoing effort, a repository for invention and expression. The prospect of helping people discover and create their own dream gardens in this way did not, apparently, fill him with dread over lost opportunities for fame or fortune. The pleasure seemed deep and lasting; these consultations occupied much of his business during the last phase of his career.

HELEN GILBERT
Milton, Massachusetts
1953–1960

Helen Gilbert, no doubt, knew of Steele's many gardens in Milton; there had been twenty-five of them since the first in 1916. Certainly she knew the garden he had made for the Cliffords in 1926 just a half block away on School Street. Gilbert's Victorian, Italianate house (1855, with later additions) was less distinguished than the Cliffords' handsome colonial revival, and her narrow property was small and featureless by comparison. (At Steele's suggestion she would acquire additional woodland in 1957 to add to its depth.) Gilbert was not particularly sophisticated about matters of design, but she was enthusiastic about the increasingly complex project. And she liked Steele very much, enough to paint his portrait.

The garden would develop into a curious place, delightful in its individual features but jam-packed and extravagant. The design would have benefited from a few unwavering demands from the client, but in the small backyard, anything seemed possible—and ultimately proved to be. Work began in 1954.

Steele surrounded the front yard with a low white fence, inspired by Chinese Chippendale latticework. The size of the house and the front lot suggested caution, but there was nothing restrained about the design. The fence was both a reminiscence of the colonial treatment Steele so admired (in exotic rather than traditional garb) and a bold, volume-shaping gesture. It set the house apart from all the others on the street, but

it was so convincing, so right, that it was the neighboring houses that suddenly looked underdressed.

A brick path divided the enclosed front lawn almost exactly in two. "I drew the walk about as simply as I could," Steele wrote to his client in 1957. "It seemed much prettier to have it slightly vase-shaped than strictly parallel like ordinary old fashioned walks. It indicates better the flare out to the two openings in the fence." Rhododendrons were planted in a border around the front lawn panels. "I came across one nursery that will furnish Rhododendron racemosum, an unusual dwarf variety, pale pink, that is fine in a low flat mass. So I suggest that. They will be small for a year or two but that is how we get them for about 25 cts. each, which is low for any sort of rhododendrons."[15] Turf was replaced by two large beds of primroses and edged in ivy. Steele used 200 *Primula vulgaris* "all shades of true blue," and 850 "all color."[16] Presumably these were mixed so that the blue worked to provide occasional contrast to spark the abundant yellow and gold.

In the back, Steele laid out an upper, southern terrace of small, specialized gardens that included an alpine lawn and a "mosaic bed."* The alpine lawn (composed of six varieties of sempervivum, three veronicas, dianthus, *Phlox subulata*, campion, and *Armeria*) resembled a glaucous, hoary carpet with spots of white, pink, and blue emerging as various plants flowered throughout spring and summer. The mosaic bed had a similar pattern but was more deeply textured; it comprised many uncommon species including *Antennaria, Calluna, Draba*, gentians, *Houstonia*, and *Satureja*.

The lower house terrace was designed in relation and proportion to the living room from which it was visible. A towering Norway spruce near the house was saved and the geometric patterned beds laid out around it. The center beds were planted with ground covers (eventually blue rug juniper) and the six trefoil planters with floribunda roses. Birches were added to either side toward the bottom of the hill.

A crab allée (interplanted with other shrubs and trees) provided a visual corridor leading from the house terrace nearly to the back of the property. A pair of columns signaled the edge of the wooded buffer that visually isolated the house from the rest of the neighborhood; into this was cut a deep niche for a cast-stone sculpture of Persephone.

Gilbert appreciated the horticulturally rare and strange as much as Steele did. In 1957 he wrote to her: "I have just heard word from Fairman Furness's Nursery . . . that he has some little 6" Psendolaris Anabilis which sound ridiculously small

*A plant list for the mosaic bed appears in appendix 2.

but they grow very fast—they are golden yellow and especially beautiful large trees. What I hope you will do with them is to plant one on each side of your lower lawn so that they will frame the view through to the new land." He added, "They are not only very beautiful in themselves but you will have about the only ones in the Boston district certainly and that is always rather fun."[17]

The vista in Gilbert's garden reflected a design scheme that had served Steele well throughout his career, and did so here. In general terms, the feature consists of three elements: a house terrace, a middle ground that leads the eye outward, and a focal point—either a distant view or an object (sculpture, architecture, pool, or even plant) that holds the eye. Steele's careful management of these components frequently resulted in success.

Within the small garden space allotted, Steele had used a great many different materials. Brick, stone, Belgian blocks, wood pilings, gravel, arborvitae, and privet gave the house terraces their architectural structure, while a broad range of plants—including the big spruce, birches, roses, and various ground covers—contributed softer design interest. It almost seemed as though Steele were struggling to compress a garden of many acres into one.

Steele employed two draftsmen during the period but was coming to rely less on formal plans and drawings. Peter Hornbeck, who assisted him during the last stage of Naumkeag and other concurrent projects in 1951, reports being given hastily produced "smudges" and detailed instructions as the basis for construction drawings.[18] He found Steele formal, perfectionistic, and rigorous in his methods. Steele's library, a continuing source of design inspiration, was arranged according to the Library of Congress system. Old plans and drawings were retrieved from storage when needed, as space was small in the Park Street office where Steele had moved after the war. Steele had his draftsman tack the old plans to a wall and sketch modifications on tracing paper over them.

Much of the work during the 1950s consisted of alterations to existing gardens, but there was still much talk about client character and its role in guiding design. Hornbeck, who later taught at Harvard, was joined by a second draftsman, Kevin Rohrbah. He later wrote to Steele: "I must say I really enjoyed working for you this summer—I learned a great deal— patience, the necessity for being exact when dealing with clients in the office and all other people, that landscape architecture as you practice it, is truly a fine art, and your creative ability is really something to come in contact with."[19]

I. STUART AND MARY SMITH
Farmington, Connecticut
1954–1956

The fragmented complexity of Miss Gilbert's scheme did not characterize all Steele's work of the period. In fact, his concurrent designs for the Smiths (Farmington) and the Chapins (Detroit) represent two tightly organized plans. In both cases, Steele was able to combine European influence with powerful space-shaping.

Mary Smith met Fletcher Steele through her uncle, John Ellsworth, for whom he worked for many years. Steele met the Smiths in Farmington in 1954 and was entranced by their stately old home, built by Nehemiah Street in 1769, and they were intrigued by Steele.

He was quite a character. He used to bring his little tin trunk with all his instruments inside. He stayed in the upstairs bedroom where he spent long hours looking over the backyard. Every evening he had martinis. . . .

We called him in because I didn't like the way the lawn sloped away in the back. . . . That's about all I said to him. . . . He was interesting . . . we'd talk about all sorts of things. He thought the view out the back was awful, said it looked like Tobacco Road. So he decided to build a stage and put fountains all over the lawn. We said we didn't want to get that elaborate but he said "too bad, I've already put in the orders." We loved what he did even though it was much more involved than what we asked for.[20]

Steele's garden for the small, sloping backyard bore no stylistic relation to the colonial architecture of the house and workshop that bordered the property on two sides. The trappings—fourteen ram's head fountains—were fantastical.

Peter Moore of J. B. Lowell, Inc., who had worked with Steele elsewhere, also built the Smiths' garden. "As always,

Smith estate, view to the Stage. (Photo by M. Karson)

Smith estate, flower borders. (Photo by M. Karson)

Fletcher was very thorough, very exacting," said Moore. "We found a place in Boston specializing in nozzles for fountains and fire hoses and he went along with me to explain to the people there exactly what we were looking for. . . . The urns were sculpted and cast in Boston."[21]

Steele managed the sharp grade drop in the small backyard by creating a narrow lawn terrace defined by a stone retaining wall. This was echoed at the back of the property by a stage area. Both stage and terrace retaining walls were constructed of Connecticut brownstone, whose warm color was similar to that of the old wood workshop. The space between house terrace and stage was excavated and planting terraces added for vertical interest.

The center space was occupied by a *tapis vert* edged with anthracite, the shiny, hard coal that Steele had used in the Afternoon Garden at Naumkeag. Bordering the coal edging, a low tufa wall defined a narrow perennial bed. Then came a pink gravel walk, second tufa wall, flower bed, narrow turf walk, and shrub border—four levels altogether. The grade change, from central *tapis vert* to shrub border, was about four feet. Steele's plantings for the tufa walls included sedum, sempervivum, *Arabis,* and other low-maintenance rock plants. (The Smiths had only one gardener.)

Two flights of steps led directly into the sunken lawn from the house terrace; two flights of curving stairs (their spirals of the distinctive curl of a ram's horn) flanked the stage. The stage back was screened with arborvitae and surfaced with pink gravel, another memory from the Afternoon Garden. At the center of the stage was a cast-stone replica of an archaic statue of a water bearer. An ancient silver maple dominated one corner near the house, balanced on the drive side by a short flight of quarter-round steps with recessed lights. Each of the fourteen cast-stone ram's heads held a small basin and single jet, adjustable from a main valve. The design was incongruous and delightful, a product of Steele's memories of Italy and his sense of outrageous, good fun.

ROY AND INEZ CHAPIN
Grosse Pointe Farms, Michigan
1954–1967

The plan of Steele's Farmington project resembled that for a larger-scale job in Detroit. Dottie Backus had introduced Steele to her friend and neighbor Inez Chapin in the autumn of 1954. Mrs. Chapin wanted to change the grounds of her soon-to-be-purchased-house. The first conference was a success: "I enjoyed meeting you very much," she wrote to Steele afterward, "and think we had a lot of good laughs together."[22]

Then the Chapins suddenly decided to build rather than buy and hired Otto Eggers of Eggers and Higgins to design a large Georgian home on another property, on Provencal Road, not far from Dottie Backus on Lake Shore Drive. After a new series of discussions about the form the garden should take, Mrs. Chapin wrote to remind Steele: "Please keep in mind that I want a really small, formal, evergreen, cheap garden."[23] Like the Smiths, she would prove flexible.

"The Georgian house calls for a balanced garden plan and I propose to emphasize this by making it strictly symmetrical," Steele wrote to her. ". . . On paper it looks more fancy than it would in fact. It is 18th century in feeling. And by using metal curbing strips, fine gravel (which would be comfortable under foot), maintenance would be reduced to a minimum. You could even put small shrubs instead of flowers in the beds if you choose. I believe it would look best with half shrubs and half perennials."[24] Steele's inspiration for the design seems to have come from the Hotel L. Stern in Paris. A photograph in his records shows a similar fleur-de-lis design.

In April 1956 Steele criticized the house plans that Eggers had mailed to him. He liked the overall design but suggested moving two forecourt walls slightly (to provide more room for turning and maneuvering cars), and placing the house farther back on the site so that the neighbor's house would not be directly visible from the living room windows. All of these suggestions were implemented. He also recommended adding a narrow glass corridor that would run along the outside of the library and living room windows for a row of camellia trees. This contribution—not particularly Georgian in spirit—was never realized. Steele wanted a big forecourt: "By pushing the house 150' back from Provencal Road, you would give yourself

room for an adequate automobile court in an area which in most houses is an inadequate lawn spoiled by curving drives right on the public street. You could wall it in as they do abroad, surround it with a row of clipped trees, and generally have it in fine, generous Georgian scale such as is all too little seen in America."[25]

Not only scale but cost had become a point of contention. Mrs. Chapin was worried about Steele's method, which still did not include estimates. He explained:

As to my bills, the only thing I can say is that they depend on the amount of time that any problem requires. I wish I could be more definite but if I were I would be depending on speculative profit, like a business man rather than an artist. Invariably that tends toward plans seeming ready-made by the yard rather than fitted to the place and owner. The situation is quite different from that of a house architect. Before he begins he knows pretty nearly what is wanted and goes ahead accordingly. A landscape architect can have only the foggiest notion because any good landscape plan is worked out as it goes along. Your safeguard lies in the fact that it is clearly understood that the service of the landscape architect can be had for as much or as little work as you please and terminated at any time. If you are not happy then surely he will not be and parting will be no pain on either side.[26]

The architect wrote to Steele that he thought the forecourt scheme too bold: "Is it possible that the large expanse of what I assume to be gravel will, it being toward the south, produce an uncomfortable glare from the summer sun? Would not a central patch of grass be desirable?"[27] Mrs. Chapin's groundskeeper, Lewis Garred, agreed with Eggers. Steele responded impatiently, "If Mrs. Chapin really wants a smaller Forecourt and Garden, then a smaller one I will try to draw up. But I warn her and you that every inch it is made smaller makes it more, what I call, provincial American. That has been the out about American gardens. All on the 'cottage' scale rather than the Manor House which she plans for a residence. A great many American houses suffer because generous scale in architecture is set in timidly small surroundings."[28]

Mrs. Chapin was convinced. Almost. "In your last letter," she wrote, "you seemed so discouraged, so depressed that I should send along a letter to tell you things are not that bad. From the start, I have been crazy about your concept of this problem—and solution—i.e. house far back—spacious courtyard. I think your first plan [April 1956] showed a court 60' x 95'. . . . That is what I would like to go back to." (Steele had expanded the

courtyard to 110' and incorporated the neighbor's wall into the scheme to gain space; Mrs. Chapin said it made her feel like an "unattached Siamese twin.") "As for the garden. I think your design is beautiful—formal & green & white. I love the fat hedge coming out of the gravel. Can't say I'm sold on the fleur-de-lis. It's on the fancy side. Without losing the proportions could the whole thing be compressed—or reduced? . . . I am crazy about the whole thing, really."[29]

By the following year, Mrs. Chapin had become Steele's partner in the new design: "I am offering an idea—which might possibly be completely unacceptable—but it appeals to me. A TINY little walled garden off the library, where in the early spring we could have all those adorable little blossoms and where it would be so cozy to sit in the sun out of the wind."[30] She enclosed a snapshot of the country-club terrace at Baden-Baden where hopes of improved health had recently

Chapin/Higbie estate, parterre. (SUNY ESF College Archives)

lured her. Steele took up her suggestion and designed a narrow serpentine terrace of brick and Belgian block edging. The new garden offered an intimate alternative to the grand space under construction in the back, which was developed almost exactly as Steele had proposed originally.

Mrs. Chapin died suddenly in 1957 and construction stopped. But her daughter and son-in-law decided to take over the house and proceed with Steele's plan, which was realized about 1967. The garden was finished with a large pair of wrought-iron gates adapted from a design at Brampford Speke, Exeter (later adapted again for Charlotte Whitney Allen's garden).

In 1958 Steele was commissioned to design a memorial for Frank E. Gannett, prominent Rochesterian and founder of the national newspaper chain of the same name. Steele's records list seventeen such commissions, not including war memorials; there was a preponderance of cemetery work during the 1950s, which reflected both the lack of garden work and the death of several clients. Mrs. Gannett hired Steele to design her garden immediately after her husband's headstone was under way.

The Mount Hope Cemetery gravesite was not far from that of the Steele family where John and Mary's headstones had finally been placed. The larger, more centrally located Gannett setting called for a design of strength and originality. Steele's choice was a large sculpture relief based on an "endless knot" motif (in Quincy pink granite) surrounded by a field of black mosaic tiles. The big stone would lie flat against the ground, surrounded by a simple yew hedge. According to Peter Moore, Steele was fastidious about the exact shade of tile and about solving the technical problems of cementing tile to stone. To assure permanency, he prepared several samples of adhesives, which were subjected to five hundred freeze-thaw cycles, on the advice of engineers at the Worcester Polytechnic Institute.[31]

NAUMKEAG
Mabel Choate
Stockbridge, Massachusetts
1947–1959

"I have been at Naumkeag so often that the usual trials of visiting have rather worn off. Margaret keeps us all—including Mabel—so well in our place that the machinery creaks very little. But then, the tricks of staying in people's houses had to be learned by me many years ago. The other night at St. Andrews I heard myself saying right after dinner 'Well, it's been a long day. I guess I'll go to bed.' For a moment Lady Davis, who is almost frantically conventional, looked as if I'd hit her on the head. Then for the only time, she relaxed and beamed: 'Good! I'll put my feet up and read the papers. I haven't seen them for a week.' I am convinced that the only rule when visiting is to feel and act 100% at home. With the reasonable advantages of being decently brought up, all goes well."[32]

Steele now slept in his own room in Stockbridge. The water pipe that Mabel Choate had brought him from Turkey sat on one of the antique dressers. A bell connected the honored guest to Margaret and her headquarters in the kitchen downstairs. But apart from the sunsets on the terrace, the best part of the visits, even for Choate, was the work. After one of his annual birthday house parties at Naumkeag (which typically included the "Philadelphia crowd"—Frances Morgan and Grady Wood), Steele described the business part of his trip: "Sunday was clear again and we all tore about doctoring plants, taking notes on peonies, weeding and what not. I think one reason we have such a good time is that I keep them all at work from morning till night."[33]

"So [in] my mind," Mabel Choate wrote Steele in 1950, "Naumkeag is now a work of art. Thanks to you. I am more interested in it and excited about it all the time … for you know, I have always wanted to make it a complete whole, like a picture in its frame."[34] Steele, too, felt that the garden had reached resolution, which could only come with age. "Nothing looks right until Time gets in its work," he had written of Naumkeag six years before.[35]

Much of the estate was kept as a working farm: meadows, barns, dairy herd, and orchard evoked the estate's nineteenth-century origins and provided rich foreground scenery for the gardens above. Mary Dabney, a frequent visitor, told her daughter that Mabel Choate would cue the farmer to prod the cows so that they would walk across the pasture and become part of the picture from the terrace.

In 1952 Steele proposed a rose garden for the lawn south of the arborvitae allée. The area was defined by a recessed tool house and storage bins that had been added a decade before. (The large bins were filled with "(A) Humus, (B) Sand and (C) loam" and the smaller ones with cocoa shells, charcoal, English Fuchsia fertilizer, and cottonseed meal.[36]) The columns of the wood bins and the swag chain of the rail above were painted purple—a hue, Steele had often remarked, that seemed particularly undisruptive outdoors.

Steele made the rose garden a parterre. His search for a motif that would relate the design to the Chinese Garden and

Naumkeag. (Photo by Clemens Kalischer)

Naumkeag, Rose Garden. (SUNY ESF College Archives)

Opposite: Naumkeag, detail of plantings in the Evergreen Garden, site of the old garden by Nathan Barrett. (SUNY ESF College Archives)

Naumkeag, Chinese Garden wall, before construction of final section. (SUNY ESF College Archives)

the hills beyond led him to a stylized curve based on a traditional Chinese scepter, or, in Peter Hornbeck's memory, the sacred mushroom. Floribunda roses were planted in eleven scalloped beds located along the abstracted waves defined by lead edges and filled with the same pink gravel used in the Afternoon Garden. A large elm anchored the first wave and provided high canopy.

Piecemeal design and construction at Naumkeag had resulted in complexity and richness rare in any garden, but it had also exaggerated Steele's tendency to conceptualize garden areas separately. In truth, he rarely considered the aesthetic experience of movement in a garden, or the effect of areas on one another when experienced sequentially. (A brilliant though early exception was Rolling Ridge.) Concern with circulation was particularly lacking at Naumkeag in favor of an emphasis on a Victorian love of diversity.

The last big project on the Stockbridge estate was the completion of the final section of the Chinese Garden wall in 1955. Steele had anticipated the importance of the feature five years before: "When the south side of that wall is completed, the secret of the whole valley and surrounding hills as seen from this place will be clarified and reduced to one continuous curve. All of Naumkeag and the landscape beyond will be like the unfolding of a seashell whose nucleus is the Chinese Garden itself."[37]

Steele was well satisfied by its effect. "The one thing that seems to have made most difference to everybody [was] the building of the Chinese Wall. It settled everything down."[38] The wall provided a sense of enclosure for the Chinese Garden by separating it from the arborvitae allée to the west. Its curve was reiterated within by two hedges (originally box, later yew) flanking the Temple, echoing the curves that had been intro-

Mabel Choate in the Afternoon Garden, Naumkeag, ca. 1947. (SUNY ESF College Archives)

Moon gate, China, 1934. (SUNY ESF College Archives)

duced throughout the property during the 1930s: the swirling conclusion of the South Lawn and its crescentic terrace edge; the rounded form of the southwest corner of the house terrace; the Rond Pointe; the bowed railings and concentric arches of the Blue Steps. The contour of the new wall also paralleled exactly the curve in the winding back road, which was, and is today, the estate's most spectacular approach. For more than thirty years, Steele's work at Naumkeag had focused on the task of introducing curves to Nathan Barrett's rectilinear plan, largely in response to the challenge of relating the designed landscape to its mountain context. Inspiration for the new designs for Naumkeag, Steele cryptically explained to Esther in 1950, had come from "the effect made on me by a cock pheasant."[39]

The new wall was pierced with a moon gate, a reminiscence of Chieh Tai Ssu, which Steele had visited twenty years before. The circular opening offered visitors a glimpse into the exotic interior of the sequestered garden, but it was also a passageway, a shortcut to the Chinese Garden from the house and a conduit for those engaged in "touring" the grounds. By 1955 Naumkeag was truly finished. Steele was seventy, Choate eighty-six.

The circle of emptiness cut into the Chinese wall was an almost mystical climax to a design partnership that had spanned three decades.

"Going in search of happiness gets to be a rare trait in older people," Steele once wrote to his sister. "Mabel is one of the few I know who uses all the strength she can muster to work for it. She gets a lot of it in consequence and at the same time gives a lot to others. I don't know but I suppose she is ten and perhaps fifteen years older than we are. All her life she has never known good health. In fact, she is physically weak. Yet her spirit revives after every period of exhaustion. . . . The one thing she will not do to conserve her failing strength is to give up the quest of active happiness. She is a constant inspiration."[40]

There is no doubt that Choate sustained Steele in his own long quest for pleasure—her patronage facilitated a lifestyle that would have been otherwise beyond reach. But Naumkeag's landscape expresses more than money, or station, or elegance, or even artistic brilliance. Laughter, "the quest of active happiness," lies at the heart of this garden. An almost audible chuckle still rolls across its broad green lawns, the echo of an amused affirmation of life born of broad and deeply felt expe-

rience. It was this that its designers shared, and that empowered them to create what they did.

Death finally signaled the end of most of Steele's gardening projects, and so it was with Naumkeag. In October 1958 Steele lost his great design partner, patron, and friend. There would be new partners and patrons, even new friends, but none of them would inspire him as Mabel Choate had.

Return to Pittsford

In September 1962 Steele moved from Boston back to Pittsford, where he lived with Esther in the old farmhouse. He was preparing the final draft of his book for Houghton-Mifflin with the help of a friend and client from Manchester, Gertrude Munroe Smith Goodhue. *Gardens and People* appeared two years later, compiled from the hundreds of short essays Steele had written since he began the project years before. In the final version, the book's 221 pages assume a long perspective on its subject, addressing the fundamental questions of the art form. From the first chapter, "What Makes a Good Garden?" to the last, "What Makes Charm in Gardens?" Steele's voice is feisty, direct, sometimes funny, unequivocal. The publisher's decision not to illustrate the text likely undermined its sales, which were very modest—Steele's frequent references to famous European gardens probably did not mean much to a general audience. The book was remaindered almost immediately but received strong critical praise from within the profession. Stanley White reviewed it for *Landscape Architecture*.

The choice was fitting since White had been one of Steele's first draftsmen. In the half century since his short apprenticeship, White had also become an important teacher at the University of Illinois and a strong theoretical voice in the field. He characterized Steele as "a talented designer of unique experience and wide travel over broad lands" and the book as a "treasure house of knowledge."

"The sense of beauty of the land in all its cultural urgency, and the insistent and various habits of people in moulding their gardens are all there. . . . But," White continued, "it is also fun to read, as he intended it to be. It can be sober as a judge, but it is clear as a bell and lively as a cricket. Indeed it is a rare privilege for the reader to go to see the great landscapes through the eyes of Steele, the keen observer, ingenious critic,

Naumkeag, Moon Gate. (Photo by Robin Karson)

Steele, 1967. (SUNY ESF
College Archives.
Photographer un-
known)

Opposite: Larch Farm,
house terrace. (Photo by
Felice Frankel)

ally brought Steele to "human motives" and to "the old village homestead where he was raised." It is a surprising and moving perspective from one who spent his life mastering the technical complexities of his craft. He felt the deep warm appeal as he remembered "watching his father plant a peach tree for scorn of the market fruit" and "his sister down on her stomach, shaking seeds off a living trillium," and family and friends "picking grapes and flowers in the twilight."[44]

His childhood garden had no parterres or pergolas. But it had charm: "Here and everywhere, now and always, charm in gardens grows out of love of the land so deep that it hurts to leave home for a day; so natural that it is part and parcel of children's play, men's work, and old folk's leisure."[45]

Most of the projects that now came Steele's way were small, local jobs. These and planting advice, design consultations, and stock investments kept him in comfortable but not lavish circumstances. He maintained a driver for a time, but the man (whom he had helped emigrate from Haiti) disappeared. Someone came in to clean the house, but he cooked his own meals. Neighbors wondered about the old man who dressed so formally, even for a trip to the grocery store. As they stopped to chat, they noticed that his old-fashioned clothes, very fine in their day, were worn.

LARCH FARM
James and Elizabeth Reynolds
Wenham, Massachusetts
1963–1968

and interpret of meanings of life in the scene and of the poetry behind the scene."[41]

Particularly intriguing are the distillations that occur in the book's final chapter where Steele's broad commentary contracts to illuminate the heart of his knowledge: the secret of charm. It was a word he used often in speech, in reference to places, people, and objects, always to convey a peculiar and treasured quality, "a sense of deep, warm appeal which affected him like sympathy."[42]

Steele could not offer a formula for charm—which he clearly valued above "studied design"—and did not hesitate to acknowledge its unpredictability. "When he meets charm in a garden . . . his faculties weaken and his standards of design, space, composition, and common sense wobble helplessly. Though sometimes the garden with charm is built according to rule, quite as often it flies in the face of every precept."[43]

The search for the answer to "the enigma of charm" eventu-

Steele started what would be his last colonial garden in the spring of 1963. The setting was distinguished. Larch Farm had once belonged to Timothy Pickering, postmaster general to Washington, secretary of war to Adams, and member of Congress. The English larches Pickering had planted in front of the house and along the drive were majestic in their maturity when Steele first saw the house. The stand of English lindens on the front lawn were placed there, legend has it, by Pickering's friend Alexander Hamilton. There were originally thirteen, one for each colony, planted to form a P.

Steele was impressed by the fine house (parts of which date to 1699) and the bucolic setting that suited it well. Ancient apple trees sheltered the property to the south; a pond lay at the bottom of the hill, and a long stone wall curved through open meadow nearby. The length of the area at the back of the house, where Steele sited the new garden, was limited to about fifty yards by a train track and old spruce hedgerow. ("Otherwise, we might have gone on forever," his clients later commented.[46])

Larch Farm, view to the garden and armillary sphere. (Photo by Felice Frankel)

In spite of general intentions to cut back, Steele, then seventy-eight, did not hesitate when the Reynoldses offered him the job. "Do you have anyone who can use a chain saw?" he asked, literally minutes after meeting his new clients. They were dumbfounded—and intrigued—as a worker was instructed to cut six of their fifteen-foot lilacs nearly to the ground. "They'll move better this way," explained Steele. "You'd better start looking around for a good contractor."[47]

Steele liked the Reynoldses very much. They were gracious, clear-minded, and sensitive to beauty. And they loved their old home and had invested dearly in restoring and improving it. At their first meeting, all agreed that while the character of the garden must reflect the historical roots of the house, it need not imitate an actual colonial layout or include only seventeenth-century plants. The main garden would be based on a traditional mix of fruits and flowers. Maintenance demands would be low since the clients had only one gardener.

Steele, characteristically, responded to the house axes in determining placement of major features, and to the larger picture of rolling hills, pond, and wide meadows in establishing relationships between the main areas. He considered the existing Norway spruces at the back of the lawn both an advantage and a liability. They would help establish an "old" character in the new garden, but their height (close to a hundred feet) would dwarf the new plantings of small trees and shrubs—the limited area dictated a small scale. So Steele ordered twenty feet topped from the big trees, warning his clients that the expensive task would have to be undertaken periodically to preserve the intimate scale of the new garden.

The lilacs were moved to form pairs along a new axis leading from the back door of the house into the center of the proposed formal garden. The grade change was negotiated via two short flights of steps made of local granite. Along the same axis, extending through the formal garden, Steele planted a crab apple allée, reaching to the Norway spruce hedgerow and a gate marking the back boundary of the garden.

A shorter cross axis was made through the center of the formal garden beginning in the east with a grape trellis and ending, to the west, at a gate (matching the first) that opened to the meadow and pond. The intersection of the axes was marked by an armillary sphere (a present from the client's brother) atop a Chelmsford granite pedestal designed by Steele. "I think that the top of the sphere should be about as high as your armpit," he wrote. "That may not make the sphere quite as high as you prefer but it fits the garden better—and remember, an armillary sphere is to be studied just as a terrestrial globe is. Whoever heard of putting a globe so high that you could not look down on the north pole?"[48] The sphere was the garden's centerpiece and sole piece of statuary.

Steele suggested doing away altogether with the old flower garden at the southwest of the house and changing the course of the stone wall along which it had been planted. The curve of the wall would then echo, in reverse, the curve of the house terrace he was planning. It would be a relationship more felt than distinctly seen.

The most significant part of the design came in the shaping of the terrace that tied house to garden. The handsome fence that marked the terrace edge and two ornamental gates provided the major architectural elements in the garden.

Fruits and flowers were grown in geometrically interlocking beds. Four pear trees were planted in the corners of the central gravel square and armillary sphere; large boxwood specimens finished the curve of the raspberry hedge. (Large box also flanked the entry to the garden inside the house terrace fence.) Four white dogwoods marked the rectangular outer limits of the planting. Spring bulbs, strawberries, iris, and other perennials grew in the lavender-edged beds. Two rows of blueberries were planted to take the view from within the square, west, to the pond. Inside a low stone wall laid out at the area's south edge, Steele planted a small perennial border.

Yet one more garden was laid out on the new terrace adjacent to the west (rear) side of the house, wrapping around it

Larch Farm, fence detail and terrace. (Photo by Felice Frankel)

to the south. The small graveled area would be a sun trap on cool days, an intimate spot for enjoying early pinks or late asters. The Reynoldses could not quite bring themselves to paint the garden benches the purple that Steele suggested. But they saved the can of paint, just in case.

It is arguable that Steele had arrived at a true late style at Larch Farm. The decorative intensity and extensive details that characterized his gardens of the 1950s (including those for Helen Gilbert, the Smiths, and the Chapins) were here supplanted by broader concerns. In Wenham, Steele's handling of the spatial relationships between garden features and the larger landscape appeared almost inevitable. The big garden picture was notable for its simple strength; the artist's view seemed large again, as though he had taken a step back and let fine, seductive details disappear.

"Well designed landscape has continuity of interest," wrote Steele. "Rhythm swings close as night turns to day and day to twilight; spring to summer and year to year. The landscape architect can bring rhythm to focus by his selection and location of materials. His work lacks the tense drama and climax of great poetry and music. But it has one precious advantage over them. Landscape architecture is part of nature itself. The story does not end. On it goes, getting more and more interesting as we get old and have time to understand."[49]*

NANCY AND RICHARD TURNER
Pittsford, New York
1963–1968

Steele's last big garden was a distillation of a life's work. Its calm spoke of absolutes. The new clients lived only a few miles from Pittsford center where Steele now made his home, as his parents had before him. Steele knew this land better than any other.

Nancy and Richard Turner contacted the retired landscape architect four years after moving their 1840 Greek revival–style house from its original site in Henrietta, where filling stations and convenience stores had steadily encroached upon the elegant old structure. The new country plot was a large, rolling cornfield, devoid of even the most rudimentary plantings except an allée of red maples along the drive that had been designed by Katherine Wilson Rahn. The Elihu Kirby house had special meaning for Steele beyond its distinguished architectural and historical presence: his father had boarded there as a schoolboy many years before.

The Turners approached Steele about a job. He agreed, but

warned them that his working methods had changed. He had no office help and no idea where he might find stone and mason contractors of the caliber he required. The Turners were very pleased that the venerable Mr. Steele was willing to tackle their project at all. They would work piecemeal as their budget and Steele's fading health and stamina permitted. He would supervise the workmen from the field, as had become his custom, with a cane. (Many years before, when asked what was the best grading method, Steele replied, "Oh, I do all my grading with a cane." The eager students were perplexed. "Like this," Steele demonstrated. "You point at a pile of dirt, and tell your workman move that," he redirected his pointer, "over there. It works every time."[50])

Steele made the most of the handsome house by organizing the long terrace garden directly on axis with it. The structure's dramatic front and back facades would figure prominently in views within the garden. This was not Steele's characteristic approach, but rarely had he worked with architecture that lent itself so forcefully—or so abstractly—to picturemaking.

The initial view of the powerful white facade was framed by piers and short fence sections. The long drive through the maple allée led to a turnaround with an island, which Steele replaced with an immense gravel forecourt (over 7,500 square feet) bounded by a white fence. He kept the forecourt planting uncharacteristically austere, to handsome effect. Two big maples were placed at the house corners; the gravel expanse was relieved only by ivy beds flanking the generous front porch. The veteran designer's sense of proportion had served him well. The massive proportions of the white picket fence were taken from pilasters on the rear house facade; their tops were derived from the architectural detail at the top of the pilasters. The fence was backplanted with tallhedge (*Rhamnus columnaris*) to further bolster the feeling of enclosure. The grand space was truly monumental.

Steele's plan was a classical, French scheme: *cours d'honneur* (forecourt), *corps de logis* (principal building), garden. The large, formal landscape areas were biaxially symmetrical and the movement, or procession, unidirectional. The formal allée found fulfillment in the court, which reflected and amplified the grandeur of the facade. All was consummated in the grand vista of the garden behind. Steele made forceful use of the existing drop in grade—it became one of the most tangible and exciting characteristics of the long vista.

Richard Turner was an involved and enthusiastic partner. Turner's passion had begun with his house, but it extended to the setting, and he participated in the design dialogue with sophistication and authority. His letters, like those of Standish Backus three decades before, were filled with sketches, questions, suggestions. As in the old days, Steele's letters al-

*A planting plan for the terrace borders appears in appendix 2.

Turner estate, forecourt and house, front facade.
(Photo by David Broda)

so contained recommendations for travel itineraries—what to see in Japan, where to stay in Spain. But unlike the Backuses, who were Steele's seniors, the Turners were Steele's students. He was teaching them about gardens, about beauty, even about life, and they were attentive and appreciative.

West of the forecourt Steele laid out an apple orchard, which quickly grew to form a windbreak. An antique lattice well house—relocated from yet another site—provided a terminus for the path through the orchard's center, a cross axis to the main approach. The crab allée was planted symmetrically in a repeating pattern of Hyslop, Dolgo, and Young American. Altogether the orchard contained seventy-three trees in almost as many varieties. A path within the orchard led to a tiny green room defined by sassafras, *Clethra,* Washington hawthorn, three varieties of ornamental cherry, yellow root, and

Bradford pear trees. Beds on either side of the short path were planted with tree peonies, *Cytisus,* and *Anemone japonica.*

To the east of the forecourt Steele planted a richly textured woods. Among the first trees to thrust over the horizon were shimmering pairs of Lombardy poplars, valued for their architectural contribution in spite of their short-livedness. Native sugar maple and hemlock grew at a more moderate pace alongside Katsura trees and silverbell; *Aralia elata* and Japanese tree lilacs lent their strange flowers beside indigenous viburnum and winter honeysuckle. Firs, green ash, American holly, Amur corktree, Colorado spruce, and American plane trees were planted for large interest and small, winter through summer. Steele planted the woods densely, experimentally, expecting a high mortality rate and interesting results—he got both.

Turner estate, view to the Orchard from the forecourt. (Photo by Carol Betsch)

Opposite: Turner estate, approach to the forecourt. (Photo by Carol Betsch)

Turner estate, vista.
(Photo by David Broda)

While the accidents and fortunes of nature were called upon to help design the woods, Steele left little to chance on the north side of the house. Here he sculpted a series of terraces into a vista that rivaled his greatest past work. The "room" was shaped by two walls of trees that met in a curve of arborvitae and blue spruce. A circular pool of deepest blue reflected light and shadow and patches of sky. From house to apse, the vista was two hundred feet, but it looked twice that long as a result of the gradual narrowing of the perimeter plantings and the drop in grade.

Steele found inspiration for the garden's character in the Turners' upcoming trip to Spain; he instructed them to bring back oil jars for which he would make wrought-iron stands to sit at the entries to the house terrace. At either side of the narrow lawn, Steele shaped two semicircular seating areas, paved "like antimacassars" with cobbles and medina stone from a

nearby quarry. Each was backed by a curving yew hedge, both ends of which terminated in specimen giant arborvitae (*Thuja plicata fastigata*).

Steele also took cues from Spain for the long baluster that stretched across the edge of the house terrace. The post finials were cast iron; the delicate wrought-iron loops were based on a motif adapted from the handsome house grilles. Each section of the baluster held seven pots, filled with whatever plants Nancy Turner (fast becoming a sophisticated gardener) wished. Rarely had Steele integrated pots into a garden so formally. They allowed Mrs. Turner to interact with her garden in a creative and evolving way, without changing the basic design structure.

The chain baluster solved the problem of enclosing the ter-

Turner estate, steps from house terrace to the grotto. (Photo by Carol Betsch)

Turner estate, grotto
detail. (Photo by Carol
Betsch)

race without obstructing the complementary view. It was the same problem, and roughly the same solution, as at Naumkeag's Afternoon Garden, where the contrast between the intimacy of the terrace and grand vista also gave rise to a distinctive experience: the pleasure of confronting the largeness of nature from a safely bounded vantage point.

Steele worked on-site with local masons ("put on this earth," he confided to Nancy Turner, "only to plague me"[51]). They constructed a double flight of steps leading beside the terrace retaining wall to an ivy-covered grotto at its center. Steele used six tiny supply pipes hidden in the stonework cave to keep the surface dripping. A runnel carried overflow from the small grotto pool to clay pipe channels on either side. The terrace perimeter was planted with roses, largely old varieties, and other flowering shrubs.

The trees and shrubs on either side and at the terminus of the terraces were a giant hedge, a tapestry of changing color and texture reflecting the seasons as it defined an immense volume of space. The variety of conifers and deciduous trees (many flowering) used in the hedge were vast; nearly all of them were uncommon, selected for their distinctive show of flower, foliage, and branch structure.

Throughout his long career, Steele's big landscape gestures were successful largely because they were powerful and convincing. But the Turners' vista sounded an even deeper chord, one uncommon in Steele's work: the harmony between strength and peace, between grandness and quiescence. The result, in this case, was a meditative, numinous space.

Steele might have scoffed at a psychological interpretation of his gardens. He thought as a designer; he solved problems as an artist. But the aging, failing Mr. Steele certainly might have assumed that this would be his last garden. The Turners had given him an opportunity to end his gardenmaking on the scale he had begun it. Fifty years before, Steele had thrilled Ethan Allen and his guests with a show of thrust and white water. But nothing broke the still surface of the last, midnight-blue pool.*

*A plant list for the vista appears in appendix 2.

Turner estate, view to the rear facade of the house.
(Photo by David Broda)

Last Years

Esther Steele's death in 1964 made the old (and shrinking) circle of Rochester friends more dear than ever. Development continued at Charlotte Allen's place. Since the war Steele had worked on retainer, the garden budget varying from $1,500 to $3,000 annually. The money underwrote maintenance as well as new design experiments. One of these was a fleur-de-lis in the turf panel, edged with metal curbing strips and filled with a contrasting variety of grass. Another was a chamomile border for the small lawn. (Both proved transitory.) Steele added a small pool and fountain to the terrace and, in 1967, he designed a large wrought-iron gate to the drive. He adapted the delicate tracery from a similar design in the Higbie's Grosse Pointe garden forecourt. The gates were supported by Tudor octagonal piers. Charlotte and Fletcher placed a ceremonial magnum of champagne within as construction began.

The little Oliver Street garden, begun in 1915, was complete. The drawing-room ambience extended down the brick drive to the curb. There a small paving area had been set into the outlawn to receive guests arriving by car. Charlotte Allen continued her salons. Near the end of her life, when she was too ill to do otherwise, she took her martinis in bed—through a straw—enjoying the garden from a second-story window, her fingernails Chinese lacquer red, her dark hair still piled high on her head.

In March 1966 Stanley Schuler, author and photographer, queried Steele for possible projects to include in his book *America's Great Private Gardens*. Steele responded:

It is hard to tell which gardens are good today. I have not heard from a lot of people for years—I am almost eighty one—and have outlived a great many of my clients whose places have gone to pot, I fancy.

So I nominate the Robert W. Stoddards' place in Worcester, Massachusetts for the east. . . . And Mrs. Standish Backus' place in Detroit for another. . . . And as a third, Mrs. Whitney Allen's garden . . . which I have been working on continuously since 1915 though it is little bigger than a postage stamp. The Stoddard place is large. The Backus place is pretentious though the Detroit grounds are restricted. The Allen place is tiny.[52]

Steele did not know, even as he wrote, that negotiations were under way to sell the Backus estate for development. Schuler's photographs, taken the summer of 1966, were the last ever of the garden.

It took a wrecking crew three weeks to tear apart the house and level the garden. The parcel was sold to a developer who built a cluster of large homes; in front of each a grand and highly visible front lawn was planted, exactly as Steele would have hated. When Angelica Gerry died in 1960, her estate met a

Allen estate, fountain on the house terrace. (Photo by Carol Betsch)

similar fate. Stripped and then razed to avoid taxes, the house vanished abruptly; the abandoned garden faded slowly. Parts of it are there still.

In 1962 the Garden Club of America awarded Steele the Mrs. Oakleigh Thorne Medal, its highest design commendation. Steele had known Mrs. Thorne and many of her colleagues before they were names on medals, and worked with them to help shape the goals of gardeners and, eventually, environmental activists. He had often written *Bulletin* articles about the importance of the larger picture:

> A true-hearted gardener's composition of daisies and buttercups from the field can be more beautiful than one stiff stalk of the most gorgeous larkspur ever brought to perfection by a horticulturist. . . . Its truth is tested by the hope and encouragement that it offers. For it reveals to the village cottager that she can create beauty with weeds from the meadow and it rebukes the purseproud for supposing that they can buy beauty by paying for a greenhouse and the services of a corps of inartistic "Gardeners."[53]

The inscription on the medal read: "To a distinguished landscape architect, whose many works reflect his fine discri-

mination, artistry, insight, and creative skill." That same year the Massachusetts Horticultural Society bestowed on Steele the George Robert White Medal of Honor. The citation stated that he would long be remembered for his "imaginative quality of design, perfection of craftsmanship and freedom from conventions."

In 1968 Steele met two young psychiatrists who soon became frequent companions. G. Porter Perham and David Mactye delighted in Steele's quick wit and his wild reminiscences—of China, Russia during the First World War, Haiti during the Second, a woman named Mabel Choate who had a summer place in the mountains. They appreciated his dignity, his opinionated approach to life, and the care with which he cooked vegetables and mixed drinks. He was a character distinct from anybody they had ever met, a man from another time.

Mactye, who had a large farm in the country outside Rochester, asked Steele to look it over with an eye toward doing some work there. The not very distinguished farmhouse sat wearily among old trees and a rusty house trailer. "If I were you I'd junk the house and live in the trailer," snorted Steele as they approached. At the wheel of his tractor, Mactye pointed

Allen estate. (SUNY ESF College Archives)

out the trees and shrubs he had already planted. After the tour, he turned around and asked Steele, who was being pulled on a wagon and old Chevy seat, "Well, what do you think of what I've done so far?" Steele looked over the beautiful pasture and woodland its owner had spruced up. He shouted over the tractor engine: "You've gilded the lily, and gilded the lily, and gilded the lily. Now stop gilding the lily!"[54]

Nearer the house, Steele was less adamant about natural beauty. He suggested a terrace adjacent to the little farmhouse with a metal-pipe trellis covering. "It has to be at least twelve feet high," he explained, "so that the wisteria racemes don't get tangled in the women's hats." Mactye discreetly adjusted the proportions of the trellis so as not to further overwhelm the little house, as he rarely entertained women in hats.[55]

The three traveled to Haiti together in 1968—it would be Steele's last trip, a replacement for a canceled tour of Egypt his health would not permit. Time was taking its toll, but not on Steele's humor. He told Mactye and Perham that he was annoyed with a client who was always pumping him for free landscape ideas, so he had told the man that a small stand of corn would be just the thing for his new dooryard garden. Much to his delight, the man took his advice.

One of Steele's last jobs was for the recently completed wing of Rochester's Memorial Art Gallery, which fronted on University Avenue. The simple scheme involved a linden allée which ran parallel to the new facade, establishing a clean con-

temporary line. For a small courtyard at the rear of the building, Steele was faced with the problem of finding a tree that would survive despite almost impossibly shallow root space. He wrote to Donald Wyman at the Arnold Arboretum for advice. Steele's practice of consulting horticultural experts when faced with unusual circumstances had begun decades ago; he enjoyed a collegiality with top-notch horticulturists which he seemed rarely to feel with members of his own profession. Wyman somewhat mischievously suggested *Ailanthus altissima,* the ubiquitous weed tree known as Tree-of-Heaven, for the difficult spot. Steele took his advice, and the tree flourishes there today.

Steele's last years were peaceful and unhurried. Gardens in progress were visited, and workmen praised or terrorized. Letters were answered with the same formality and charm as ever. Steele's garden was left to its own devices. Snowdrops spread to form a glistening mat by the front door under an ancient oak. To Peter Hornbeck he confided, "all goes by minutes when you are 84."[56]

Steele suddenly decided to re-wallpaper his office, and moved all his files out to the barn in the process. "I put on some Chinese hand done paper that I brought from China 45 years ago and kept in the attic all this time. The result was worth waiting for," he wrote to Betty Reynolds.[57]

Steele, with David Mactye, Rochester, N.Y., 1968. (Photo by G. Porter Perham)

Steele, at the country estate of David Mactye. (Photo by David Mactye)

Four decades earlier he had told an audience at Williams College, "Perhaps sometime I shall honestly believe that even for me the highest [value] is spiritual, which I already believe for others."[58] He had never been a churchgoer (despite claiming, "I just feel that Republicans and Presbyterians are a little better"[59]) nor did he subscribe to any formal religion, but he was a reflective man, and the final years of his life undoubtedly gave him more opportunity to ponder deeper questions.

In July 1971 Steele was a guest at a small dinner party given by Mactye and Perham. The undiagnosed lung cancer that would shortly claim his life was causing him to cough violently, but Steele was still able to socialize and he still enjoyed a good drink. The conversation turned toward Japan, as one of the guests had recently traveled there. Her admiration for the country seemed to annoy Steele, who announced that he found China more interesting and civilized, and he told a story, which was recorded on audiotape.

"We were on a trip through the mountains when we saw a man, off to one side, and he was evidently dying. So I stopped and said to my boy, 'Give that man some water.' He stood perfectly still. He didn't even pretend to do what I'd told him to. So I said, 'Can't you give that man some water, please?' He just stood there. Then after a minute he said, 'You Americans will not leave us in peace. Even when we're dying you cannot leave us alone.' I was wrong. He was right. But it seemed very strange to me—you couldn't even bring water to a man who was dying."

"You mean," asked the guest, "to let him have his dignity, in death?"

"No." Steele was emphatic. "He was in it alone. He should have been. A very proper way to die. I see that now."[60]

A few nights later Marjorie Seldon called Perham and Mactye to say that Steele was gravely ill and she needed their help getting him to the hospital. They came immediately and realized that, in spite of severe pain, Steele was very much himself and able, with assistance, to walk out to the car. Halfway down the front walk, he suddenly refused to continue. The little group stopped, first worried and then perplexed over what was happening. Slowly they understood. Poised motionless over Esther's daylilies, Fletcher Steele was taking his leave of the moonlight and the dew gathering on the new buds. He knew he would not see them again.

THE LAST DEEP PLEASURE of the spirit to be learned from a garden will lie in its permanence. It is rational to desire to link those things which we see and know with what we have learned through history, science, and tradition. A good garden abounds in suggestions of the past. If it is old it is alive with that flavor of the long-gone designer's care and forethought. If it be new, it is nonetheless a tribute to the past in its expression of the traditions, the likes, and interests that we have inherited from our fathers. . . .

As we relish the past, so should we prepare for the future and other coming lovers of gardens yet unborn. The true gardener has abiding faith and must express it, if only by planting an acorn where the "Genius loci" calls for an oak. Better still is some imprint of ourselves in imperishable wall, in steps of stone, in a terrace that will be but more beautiful if the neglect of centuries overtakes it perchance. Then will our sound satisfaction lie not in showy flowers, not in exquisite details of the moment, but in knowledge that the charm which has been discovered, the genius of the place which has been revealed and adorned, is safe for all time, a gift to the future more lovely then than even we can now dream. For of all the works of man the garden alone, the garden that graces the site, becomes more beautiful as the generations pass through it, as lichens gather on the ancient weathered rocks, as the seedling which we have nourished grows to spread great branches over the undreamed children of tomorrow.

FLETCHER STEELE, "The Appeal to the Intelligence"

Afterword

Fletcher Steele's will directed that his father's law office, the "Little House," be given to the Landmark Society of Western New York State and fifty-five acres of land in Penfield Swamp go to the Nature Conservancy. Fossilized pollen sequences obtained from this unusual land, now known as "The Thousand Acre Swamp," have been determined to date from the last ice age.

Steele bequeathed his voluminous professional papers to the American Society of Landscape Architects. Having no resources for storing or administering these, the ASLA donated the paper documents (100,000 items of correspondence, inter-office memorandums, plant orders, notes, and essays) to the Library of Congress, in Washington, D.C., and thirty-two bound albums of photographs to the F. Franklin Moon Library, State University of New York College of Environmental Science and Forestry, in Syracuse. SUNY also received Steele's library, photographic negatives, slides, and several volumes of client plant orders, a total of 42 linear feet of material. The collection, since that time, has acquired an additional 30 feet of documentation relating to Steele's professional career. SUNY has also created a 1,000 print study collection of Steele's photographs of his work and circulates a sizable touring exhibition, *The Gardens of Fletcher Steele*. Students and researchers are encouraged to explore this rich repository of documents.

Mr. and Mrs. Stuart Bolger, who purchased Steele's Pittsford home after his death, discovered several hundred professional documents in Steele's barn, which they donated to Rush Rhees Library, University of Rochester, where they are still housed. Family correspondence—letters from Steele to his father, mother, and sister—and other personal documents relating to Steele's life, including his apprenticeship with Warren Manning, are housed at the Rochester Historical Society.

Appendix 1 · Client List

1914–1968

This list has been compiled from information in Steele's client files, Fletcher Steele Papers, Manuscript Division, Library of Congress, Washington, D.C. Projects are listed according to starting dates. Spelling and locations have been corrected whenever possible. In some cases, location is unknown.

1914

St. Anthony Hall, Williamstown, Mass.
Century of Progress Lumberyard
Herbert Pells Ward, Bushnell's Basin, N.Y.
Miss Allierta Houghton, Cambridge, Mass.
Rev. William H. Deward, Milton, Mass.
Arapaho Indian Mission (Bishop V. S. Thomas),
    Laramie, Wyo.
Bishop Randall Hospital
Warren H. Manning
Ethan Allen Cemetery Lot
Warren Manning Confederate Memorial
St. Anthony Club, Boston, Mass.
Mrs. William Byers
Grahame Wood, Esq., Wawa, Pa.
Josiah Waxey
Mrs. E. L. Osgood, Hopedale, Mass.
Warren H. Manning, State sketches
Austin B. Mason, Noble & Greenough School,
    Boston, Mass.

1915

Miss Charlotte R. Vose, Milton, Mass.
Ethan Allen, North Andover, Mass.
Mrs. H. H. Fay
Mrs. Grahame Wood
W. S. R. Wake, Esq., Waterbury, Conn.
Mrs. A. L. Dodge
Mrs. Charles Linzee Tilden, Milton, Mass.
Mrs. Edwin Allen Stebbins, Rochester, N.Y.
Mrs. George C. Buell
Harper Sibley, Rochester, N.Y.
E. J. Frost
Jesse Philyer Symon
E. H. Palmer
Henry G. Palmer
Atkinson Allen, Rochester, N.Y.

1916

Mrs. Sylvester McKeen, Marion, Mass.
Mrs. A. Lawrence Hopkins
Harrison Mifflin, North Andover, Mass.
Rufus A. Sibley, Rochester, N.Y.
William Chattem, Wetherill
Mrs. Herbert H. White
Mrs. Anna L. Prichard, Peterborough, N.H.
Mrs. Warham Whitney, Rochester, N.Y.
Miss Helen Ellwanger, Rochester, N.Y.

Mrs. Thomas Motley Jr., Nahant, N.Y.
Edward G. Miner Jr., Rochester, N.Y.
John H. Rose
Freeman Allen, Rochester, N.Y.
Richard D. Wood Sr.
S. G. Etherington, Esq., Biddeford, Me.
Richard Thorndike, Esq., Millis, Mass.
Mrs. Gibson McCall
A. G. Lewis, Geneva, N.Y.
Walter Howard, Geneva, N.Y.
Dr. Lambeth, University of Virginia

1917

Dr. Arthur D. Little, North Andover, Mass.
Robert S. Bradley, Beverly Farms, Mass.
McKinney Etherington, Woodlawn Cemetery,
    New York, N.Y.
Ethan Allen Farm, North Andover, Mass.
O. J. C. Rose, Geneva, N.Y.
George C. Thomas, Chestnut Hill, Pa.
Mrs. William Byers, North Andover, Mass.
Judge W. H. Cabot, Brookline, Mass.
G. Willard Bigelow, Esq., Brookline, Mass.

1920

Mr. E. B. Richardson
Mrs. C. Minot Weld, Milton, Mass.
J. Sherlock Andrews, North Andover, Mass.
George E. Kunhardt, North Andover, Mass.
North Andover Community Pine Blister Rust,
    North Andover, Mass.
Boston St. Anthony Club, Boston, Mass.
Mrs. Roy H. Beattie, Tiverton, R.I.
Mr. George H. Waring, Tiverton, R.I.
Mr. Courtney Crocker, Wayland, Mass.

1921

John H. Towne, Mount Kisco, N.Y.
Mrs. Lewis S. Bigelow, North Andover, Mass.
Horace Allen
Andrew Wheeler, Esq., Ardmore, Pa.
S. G. Etherington, Esq., New York, N.Y.
Harper Sibley, Esq., Rochester, N.Y.
Mrs. William Forbes, Milton, Mass.

James Russell, Esq., Milton, Mass.
S. B. Parker, Esq., Newmarket Village, N.H.
S. B. Parker, Esq. (house), Newmarket, N.H.
Ralph Erksine, Esq., Stamford, Conn.
Mrs. Walter Jackson, Milton, Mass.
W. A. Harvey, Esq., Dover, Mass.
William B. Thurber, Esq., Milton, Mass.
Lawrence YWCA
Stephen Child, Esq.
Samuel Bennett Jr., Milton, Mass.
Bentley Warren, Esq., Williamstown, Mass.
Samuel Sloan, Garrison, N.Y.
Charles Kellog, Boston, Mass.
J. P. Stevens Co., North Andover, Mass.
Mrs. F. L. Gay
Mrs. J. H. Towne (camp), Adirondacks, N.Y.

1922

Mrs. A. L. Jackson, Cambridge, Mass.
Bishop N. S. Thomas, Laramie, Wyo.
John M. Steele, Esq., Pittsford, N.Y.
Mrs. John A. Frye, Marlborough, Mass.
Miss Elizabeth Thurber, Milton, Mass.
Tiger Inn, Princeton, N.J.
Miss Edith Hale, Rochester, N.Y.
Mr. F. S. Kershaw, Cambridge, Mass.
Mrs. Dudley Dupingnac
John W. and Frederick H. Scott, Hubbard Woods, Ill.
Howard Chapman, Stamford, Conn.
Seth L. Pierrepont, Ridgefield Town Hall, Ridgefield, Conn.
C. Milton Fessenden, Stamford, Conn.
S. D. Cushing, Stamford, Conn.

1923

Miss J. A. Maxwell, Rockville, Conn.
Clement Scott, Hartford, Conn.
Marlborough Hospital (John A. Frye), Marlborough, Mass.
John W. Wood, Stoughton, Mass.
Miss Eugenia B. Frothingham, Cambridge, Mass.
Seth Low Pierrepont, Ridgefield, Conn.
Frederick W. Eaton, Concord, Mass.
Miss Dora Spalding, Peterborough, N.H.
Mrs. Charles P. Ford, Rochester, N.Y.
National Society of the Daughters of American Colonists
    (Plymouth Bench)

Miss Ethel Noyes, Milford, Pa.

Michael Cadigan, American Legion, Beverly Farms, Mass.

All Saints Chapel, Mrs. William H. Schofield,
    Peterborough, N.H.

Mrs. Hawley Ward, Rochester, N.Y.

Henry S. Dennison, Framingham, Mass.

Williams College, Williamstown, Mass.

Charles B. Pike, Lake Forest, Ill.

Charles B. Schweppe, Lake Forest, Ill.

Francis G. Farwell, Lake Forest, Ill.

Mrs. Robert Amory, Readville, Mass.

Henry W. Channing, Wareham, Mass.

G. L. Curtis, Clinton, Iowa

Miss Sophie Moen, Woods Hole, Mass.

John Thayer, Lancaster, Mass.

Mrs. Bayard Thayer, South Lancaster, Mass.

Miss S. S. Hopkins, Williamstown, Mass.

Miss Mary Wheelwright, Northeast Harbor, Me.

George B. Dabney, Wareham, Mass.

Danforth Geer, Short Hills, N.J.

Mrs. John Reynolds, Milton, Mass.

Oliver J. Schoonmaker, Ashburnham, Mass.

Robert Mallory Jr., Rye, N.Y.

David S. Cowles Sr., Rye, N.Y.

David S. Cowles Jr., Rye, N.Y.

William D. Miller, Ashburnham, Mass.

1924

Samuel Fuller, White Plains, N.Y.

Clement S. Houghton, Chestnut Hill, Mass.

William T. Barbour, Subdivision (Bloomfield Hills),
    Detroit, Mich.

Russell B. Lowe, Fitchburg, Mass.

Mrs. Matthew Luce, Cohasset, Mass.

George B. Dabney, Medfield, Mass.

George C. Roeding, Piedmont, Calif.

J. W. Taussig, Englewood, N.J.

Charles G. Loring, Boston, Mass.

Dr. Sylvester McKeen

Mrs. Theodore Little, Cohasset, Mass.

Philip L. Spalding, Milton, Mass.

Downing P. Brown, Berlin, N.H.

William T. Barbour, Bloomfield Hills, Mich.

Provident Mutual Life Insurance Co., Philadelphia, Pa.

Charles F. Wallace, Chestnut Hill, Mass.

Gustavos D. Pope, Detroit, Mich.

1925

J. Edward Newton, Little Compton, R.I.

Joseph Balch, Westwood, Mass.

Daughters of the American Revolution Memorial

Alfred Curtis, Concord, Mass.

George Hedges

Mrs. James G. Stewart, Cincinnati, Ohio

Lowthorpe School, Groton, Mass.

Bradley Palmer

Herbert Brown, Cumberland Subdivision

State Street Congregational Church

Herbert J. Brown, Falmouth Foreside House,
    Portland, Me.

James C. Howe

Levi S. Ward, Canandaigua, N.Y.

Henry L. Hopewell

Paul B. Morgan, Worcester, Mass.

Charles P. Clifford, Milton, Mass.

Williams College, Williamstown, Mass.

William Hanford Curtiss

John S. Ellsworth, Simsbury, Conn.

Gerry Delaware Park

Dr. Francis W. Peabody, Northeast Harbor, Me.

Cold Spring Hospital

The Southmayd Home, Waterbury, Conn.

Miss Angelica L. Gerry, Ancrum House, Lake
    Delaware, N.Y.

The Brown Company, Berlin, N.H.

Mrs. Wayland Minot, Milton, Mass.

Mr. George F. Shephard, Milton, Mass.

Charles S. French, Framingham, Mass.

Charles B. Russell

Dr. Jason Mixter, Brookline, Mass.

1926

William A. Parker, North Easton, Mass.

Maine General Hospital

Norman Brown

Phillips Payson

Harry Little, Wianno, Mass.

Gerry, changes in road near church, Delhi, N.Y.

Mrs. Peter Geolet Gerry, Biltmore, N.C.

Thomas Motley, Milton, Mass.

Henry H. Fay, Concord, Mass.

Richard D. Wood

Mr. G. D. B. Bonbright, Rochester, N.Y.

Miss Margery Hayden, Waterbury, Conn.

Berkeley Wheeler, Concord, Mass.

Ralph Adams Cram, Sudbury Center, Mass.

Mabel Choate, Naumkeag, Stockbridge, Mass.

Memorial for First American Railroad (Mr. Spalding)

Gerry-Warwick

Dr. Henry Lyman, Sutton's Island, Me.

The Waterfall Terrace, Peterborough, N.H.

Stockbridge Mission House, Stockbridge, Mass.

W. W. Tracy, Williamstown, Mass.

Dr. A. M. Murray

Dr. Charles G. Mixter, Brookline, Mass.

1927

Hopkins Memorial, Williams College, Williamstown, Mass.

Clifford Cemetery

Peterborough Railroad Station, Peterborough, N.H.

Sisters of Saint Anne, Cambridge, Mass.

Samuel H. Wolcott, Milton, Mass.

J. Brooks B. Parker

Beth Israel Hospital, Boston, Mass.

Medfield Church, Medfield, Mass.

Second Congregational Church

Chase Park

Mrs. A. M. Dodge, Wheatogue, Conn.

Mrs. George H. Ingals

Mrs. Sarah D. Reed

Woodberey Forest School, Woodberey Forest, Va.

Mrs. William H. Schofield, East Hill, Peterborough, N.H.

Quincy Bent

Danvers High School, Danvers, Mass.

John Coe, Waterbury, Conn.

John A. Fry, Detroit, Mich.

Medfield School, Medfield, Mass.

1928

Ferris Greenslet

Livingston Davis, Brookline, Mass.

Henry W. Marsh

Charles H. Stuart

Concord Street House Site, Peterborough, N.H.

C. M. Dick

R. P. Snelling, Beverly Farms, Mass.

Miss Lucy Crehore, Jamaica Plain, Mass.

Mr. Quincy A. Shaw Jr., Jamaica Plain, Mass.

Camden Library, Camden, Me.

William E. Schrafft, Winchester, Mass.

Fields Park, Williamstown, Mass.

Dr. Sidney A. Lord, Concord, Mass.

James Smithwick, East Gloucester, Mass.

Swimming pool of Schofield, Peterborough, N.H.

St. Anthony Hall, Chapel Hill, N.C.

Teachers Lodge, Peterborough, N.H.

Wawa Dairy Farms, Wawa, Pa.

B. S. Cortrell, Jamestown, R.I.

Mr. Everst D. Haight, Litchfield, Conn.

Mrs. George A. LaMonte, Bound Brook, N.J.

Henry de la B. Carpender, Somerville, N.J.

Warren K. Emerson, Chestnut Hill, Mass.

Gorham Brooks, Brookline, Mass.

Schrafft Cemetery Lot, Mt. Auburn Cemetery, Cambridge, Mass.

Claude R. Branch, Seekonk, Mass.

Mrs. F. H. Stone, South Dartmouth, Mass.

George A. Lyon, Brookline, Mass.

Russell Tyson (Rolling Ridge), North Andover, Mass.

1929

Independent Presbyterian Church, Savannah, Ga.

Thomas Spencer, Rochester, N.Y.

Sibley Cemetery Lot, Rochester, N.Y.

Mrs. William H. Schofield, The Manoir Dorval, Dorval, Quebec

E. R. Kittredge, Dedham, Mass.

Mrs. Mortimer J. Fox, Peekskill, N.Y.

William Bancroft, Harrisville, R.I.

Porter Farrell, Westport, Conn.

New England Telephone and Telegraph Exchange, Worcester, Mass.

Schofield Factory

Charles D. Rockwell, Bristol, R.I.

Miss Louis Hood, Marblehead, Mass.

C. Griggs Plant, Cohasset, Mass.

Standish Backus, Manchester, Mass.

Allan Shelden, Manchester, Mass.

First Church of Boston, Unitarian, Boston, Mass.

George Doubleday, Ridgefield, Conn.

Wesson Seyburn, Manchester, Mass.

Standish Backus, Grosse Pointe Farms, Mich.

Dr. J. Henry Lancashire, Manchester, Mass.

1930

Miss Alberta Houghton, Marlborough, N.H.
Lawrence Buhl, Grosse Pointe Farms, Mich.
Paul Hammond, Syosset, Long Island, N.Y.
Mrs. Robert P. Bass, Peterborough, N.H.
Richard Bentley, Lake Forest, Ill.
Josiah Wheelwright
Schofield New Land, Peterborough, N.H.
Dr. John W. Bartol, Milton, Mass.
Mrs. E. Dimon Bird, Greenwich, Conn.
Frederick Bagley, High Westwood, Mass.
Arthur B. Lisle, East Greenwich, R.I.
Henry Warren, Weston, Mass.
The Hanson Town Hall, Hanson, Mass.
Hon. Peter G. Gerry, Providence, R.I.
Charles Sterns, Providence, R.I.
Samuel Mixter, Brookline, Mass.
W. G. Nickerson, Dedham, Mass.
Marshall Prentiss, Litchfield, Conn.
Camden Common, Camden, Me.

1931

Father Burton, St. Francis House, Cambridge, Mass.
William H. White Jr., Washington, D.C.
Mrs. Frederick T. Pierson, Pittsford, N.Y.
Augustin H. Parker, Charles River Village, Mass.
John H. Pierce Park, Lincoln, Mass.
Mrs. Emily B. Swindells, Rockville, Conn.
Frederick L. Dabney, Dover, Mass.
Mrs. Samuel A. Welldon, Hamilton, Mass.
Mrs. W. M. Crane, Dalton, Mass.
Mrs. S. Parker Bremer, Dublin, N.H.
Mrs. Hobart Ames, North Easton, Mass.
Adrian G. Devine, Brighton, N.Y.

1932

G. C. Tarbell, Lincoln, Mass.
Austin Levy, Harrisville, R.I.
Raymond Bentley, Rochester, N.Y.
W. Brewster Lee, Rochester, N.Y.
Mary C. Wheelwright, Alcalde, N.M.
Richard Cameron, Concord, Mass.
Mrs. William Kenley, Manchester, Mass.

1934

Edward P. Curtis, Rochester, N.Y.
Mrs. Rudolph H. Hofheinz, Rochester, N.Y.
St. Agnes School, Albany, N.Y.
Palmer Cosslet Putnam, South Harwich, Mass.
Longwood Cricket Club, Newton, Mass.

1935

Mrs. Randal Morgan, Chestnut Hill, Pa.
Miss Marion Hague, Stockbridge, Mass.
Mr. Henry R. Guild, Needham, Mass.
Mrs. Arthur Allen, Boxford, Mass.
John M. Elliot, Needham, Mass.
Mrs. Charles W. Dodge, Rochester, N.Y.

1936

Mrs. Henry H. Selden, Avon, N.Y.
Harry G. Stoddard, Gloucester, Mass.
Joseph F. Taylor, Rochester, N.Y.
Miss M. Louis Kelley, Rochester, N.Y.
Dover Town Hall, Dover, Mass.
Mrs. Alan Cunningham, Sherborn, Mass.
Mrs. George P. McLean, Simsbury, Conn.
Mr. Robert Darling, Simsbury, Conn.
Simsbury Garden Club, Simsbury, Conn.
Mrs. John W. Headman
G. O. B. Bonbright, Nantucket, Mass.
Mrs. Harry Ellsworth, Simsbury, Conn.
The Warner House, Dartmouth, N.H.
James J. Gilbert, Gloucester, Mass.
Mr. William G. Foulke, Wawa, Pa.

1937

Gilliat G. Schroeder, Wawa, Pa.
Campbell House, Rochester, N.Y.
Bjarne Ursin, Weston, Mass.
Mr. Edwin Allen Stebbins, Webster, N.Y.
Susan Ellsworth, West Hartford, Conn.
John J. Ellsworth Jr., Simsbury, Conn.
Alan Valentine, Rochester, N.Y.
Henry E. Ellsworth, Simsbury, Conn.
University of Rochester, Rochester, N.Y.

Christ Church Parish House (Leslie Glenn),
    Cambridge, Mass.
Mrs. Kenneth Field, Rochester, N.Y.
Mrs. Charles L. Riker, Dublin, N.H.
Charles B. Rockwell, Bristol, R.I.

1938

Frederick C. Church, Beverly Farms, Mass.
J. Abrams
Martin Mower, Cambridge, Mass.
John M. Steele Cemetery Lot, Rochester, N.Y.
Burroughs Company Plymouth Plant, Plymouth, Mich.

1939

Louis H. Hamel, Haverhill, Mass.
J. D. Cameron Bradley, Wolfpen Farm, Southborough, Mass.
John W. Higgins, Worcester, Mass.
Mrs. Emily B. Swindells, Groton, Conn.
Mrs. Roy Bates, Cambridge, Mass.
W. P. Wolcott, Milton, Mass.

1940

Choate Cemetery Lot, Stockbridge, Mass.
Industrial School for Girls, Dorchester, Mass.
William D. MacColl, North Farm, Bristol, R.I.
Mrs. John H. Cunningham Jr., Brookline, Mass.
John E. Ellsworth, Simsbury, Conn.

1941

Mr. Homer Strong, Rochester, N.Y.
John S. Howe, Milton, Mass.
Senator Walsh, St. John's Cemetery, Clinton, N.Y.
Museum of Natural History, Boston, Mass.

1942

Richard D. Wood Jr., Wawa, Pa.

1943

Mrs. Chester N. Greenough, Belmont, Mass.
Trinity Church, New Rochelle, N.Y.
Mrs. Kingsley Porter

Drescher Cemetery Lot, Mt. Hope Cemetery, Rochester, N.Y.
Mr. and Mrs. Robert F. Taylor
Warner Cemetery Lot, Mt. Hope Cemetery, Rochester, N.Y.
Theodore Drescher, Pittsford, N.Y.
Mrs. Charles P. Clifford, Milton, Mass.
George E. Norton
Mrs. William A. E. Drucher, Rochester, N.Y.
Tavern (Choate), South Lee, Mass.
Mrs. W. E. Sedgwick, Cemetery Lot

1944

Mr. and Mrs. W. I. Williams, Wellesley Hills, Mass.
Chelsea Naval Hospital, Cushing General Hospital
Miss Mary L. Ronald, Old Lyme, Conn.
O'Donnell Iselin, New Rochelle, N.Y.
Colonel Hugh Bullock, Royalston, Mass.
Mr. and Mrs. Stewart S. Hatheway, Rye, N.Y.
John Henry Towne Cemetery Lot
J. Roy Allen, Rye, N.Y.
Edward H. Jewett, Lapeer, Mich.
Mrs. James Roberts, Milton, Mass.

1945

Alfred E. Smith Estate Cemetery Lot, Calvary Cemetery
Mr. and Mrs. Halfdon Lee, Osterville, Mass.
Watson Cemetery Lot, Rochester, N.Y.
Mr. and Mrs. Ellery Sedgwick, Beverly, Mass.
Mrs. John W. Higgins Cemetery Lot
First Congregational Church Memorial, Methuen, Mass.
Miss Lewllyn Parsons, Crescent Surf, Kennebunk, Me.
Hovey
Albert Spalding, Great Barrington, Mass.

1946

Miss Elizabeth Weld, Brookline, Mass.
Mrs. Ralph Manny, Rye, N.Y.
Mr. and Mrs. W. H. Robinson Jr., Gloucester, Mass.
Lincoln Library War Memorial, George G. Tarbell,
    Lincoln, Mass.
Mr. and Mrs. Robert W. Stoddard, Worcester, Mass.
Mt. Vernon Town Club, Baltimore, Md.
Mrs. R. Boyer Miller, Beverly, Mass.
De Cordova Museum, Lincoln, Mass.
Methuen Music Building, Methuen, Mass.

Frank Ross, Milton, Mass.

Mr. and Mrs. Ward French, Westport, Conn.

Mr. and Mrs. Hollister Spencer, Rochester, N.Y.

Mr. and Mrs. George H. Taber Jr., Rye, N.Y.

Mr. and Mrs. Matthias Plum, Chatham, Mass.

Mrs. Roy A. Rainey, Chatham, Mass.

Miss Mary L. Ronald, Newport, R.I.

Mr. and Mrs. Dunbar Lockwood, Topsfield, Mass.

Mrs. W. H. Taylor, Gloucester, Mass.

Mrs. Barrett Wendell, Hamilton, Mass.

Mrs. Lawrence Black

1947

Lady Davis, St. Andrews, New Brunswick, Canada

Mrs. John O. Stubbs, Westwood

Mrs. Edwin A. Land, Cambridge, Mass.

Mrs. Robert Perkins Bass, Peterborough, N.H.

George Lewis Jr.

Northeast Harbor Library, Northeast Harbor, Me.

J. W. Farley

Dr. and Mrs. Gavin Miller, Cloverly, St. Andrews,
    New Brunswick, Canada

1948

Dr. Claude M. Fuess, Andover, Mass.

J. Linzee Weld

Trustees of Public Reservations, Ipswich, Mass.

Mrs. George W. Bunnell, Herring Brook Farm,
    Norwell, Mass.

Ms. and Mrs. Russell Burrage, Beverly Farms, Mass.

Mr. and Mrs. Wellington B. Hay, Mendham, N.J.

Mrs. John M. Bullard, Nonquitt, Dartmouth, Mass.

Mr. and Mrs. Standish Bradford, Hamilton, Mass.

1949

Old North Church plan for Beacon Hill Garden Club,
    Boston, Mass.

Mr. and Mrs. E. B. Badger, Osterville, Mass.

Mrs. John Gardner Coolidge, North Andover, Mass.

Thomas Motley, Woods Hole, Mass.

Mrs. George B. Dabney, Woods Hole, Mass.

Mrs. E. Clarence Hovey, Prides Crossing, Mass.

Mrs. John M. Bullard, New Bedford, Mass.

Mr. and Mrs. William Cone, Bennington, Vt.

Mr. and Mrs. L. G. Graves, Old Bennington, Vt.

Mr. and Mrs. Caleb E. Elliott, Old Bennington, Vt.

Dr. and Mrs. William Jason Mixter, Woods Hole, Mass.

Mr. and Mrs. Roger Hallowell, Westwood, Mass.

Mr. and Mrs. Edmund P. Lumken, Cincinnati, Ohio

Mrs. Frances Crane, Woods Hole, Mass.

Miss S. Frances Marden, Milton, Mass.

1950

Mr. and Mrs. L. Cushing Goodhue, Manchester, Mass.

Mr. and Mrs. Seabury Stanton, Padanaram Village
    (New Bedford), Mass.

Mr. and Mrs. John C. Case, Morristown, N.J.

Brooks School, Garden of Memory, Richard S. Russell

Mr. and Mrs. Wirt Thompson Jr., Wawa, Pa.

Mr. and Mrs. David Wood, Wawa, Pa.

Mr. and Mrs. Andrew D. Wolfe, Rochester, N.Y.

Miss Elizabeth G. Holahan, Rochester, N.Y.

Mrs. James Sibley Watson, Rochester, N.Y.

Mr. and Mrs. Nathanial Sage, Brookline, Mass.

Mrs. James Chapman, Cambridge, Mass.

Mrs. Grace Hall Booth, Prides Crossing, Mass.

Brown University, Mrs. Henry D. Sharpe (Elizabeth),
    Providence, R.I.

Jackson Memorial, Mrs. Henry D. Sharpe

C. Clement Costello, Lowell, Mass.

Mr. and Mrs. H. Blake Bent, Farmington, Conn.

Mr. and Mrs. Loring P. Jordan, Manchester, Mass.

Mrs. John M. Elliot, Manchester, Mass.

Mr. and Mrs. William Parsons, Cold Springs Harbor, N.Y.

1951

Simsbury Cemetery, Simsbury, Conn.

Lowell Stadium

Mr. and Mrs. Philip C. Barney, Farmington, Conn.

Mr. and Mrs. Reginald Jenney, Chestnut Hill, Mass.

C. C. Costello, Magnolia Cottage, Lowell, Mass.

Mr. and Mrs. John L. Senior, Lenox, Mass.

Mrs. William Kenly, New London, N.H.

Mrs. Frank S. White, Milton, Mass.

Mrs. John Bryant, Brookline, Mass.

Mr. and Mrs. Milton I. Morse, Jaffrey, N.H.

Mr. and Mrs. John E. Goetz, Rochester, N.Y.

Wigglesworth Cemetery Lot, Milton Cemetery

Mrs. Edward Watkins, Manchester, Mass.

Mr. and Mrs. Gordon Whelpley
Dr. and Mrs. H. Thomas Ballentine Jr., Dedham, Mass.

1952

Mr. and Mrs. Robert Lee Hale, New Canaan, Conn.
Mrs. John Sutcliffe, Norwood, Mass.
Mr. and Mrs. James Lawrence, Brookline, Mass.
Mr. and Mrs. Thomas N. Dabney, Dedham, Mass.
Miss Ellen D. Sharpe, Providence, R.I.
Mrs. Henry D. Sharpe, Providence, R.I.
Mr. and Mrs. Mortimer A. Seabury
Mr. and Mrs. Michael Watson, Rochester, N.Y.
Mr. John M. Bullard, Dartmouth, Mass.
David Jewett, Pittsford, N.Y.
General and Mrs. W. C. Crane, Woods Hole, Mass.

1953

Mrs. George Putnam, Manchester, Mass.
Mrs. Henry G. Powning, Manchester, Mass.
Mrs. Bacon, Manchester, Mass.

1954

Mrs. George P. Denny, Milton, Mass.
Mr. and Mrs. John C. Trahey, Webster, N.Y.
Mrs. Carl J. Gilbert, Strawberry Hill, Dover, Mass.
Mrs. George B. Dabney, Dedham, Mass.
Mr. and Mrs. Lewis S. Dabney, Medfield, Mass.
Wellesley College Chapel, Wellesley, Mass.
Knights of Columbus Monument, Waterbury, Conn.
Morton P. Prince, Boston, Mass.
Mr. and Mrs. Albert C. Burrage, Candlewood Farm,
  Ipswich, Mass.
Mrs. Francis D'Amanda, Putneyville, N.Y.
I. Stuart Smith, Farmington, Conn.
Mrs. W. O. Schock, North Hampton, N.H.
Mrs. George A. Bushec, Newburyport, Mass.
Miss Helen C. Gilbert, Milton, Mass.
Bennington Historical and Art Museum, Bennington, Vt.
Mrs. Roy D. Chapin, Grosse Pointe, Mich.
Mrs. L. M. Strong, Deep River, Conn.
Mrs. Kingsley Swan
Mrs. Ruby Boyer-Miller

1955

Mortimer A. Seabury Jr. Inn, Lexington, Mass.
Thomas D. Spencer, New Canaan, Conn.
Mrs. John Alden Carpenter, Beverly, Mass.
Mr. and Mrs. Thomas B. Card, Fairhaven, Mass.
The Country Club, Farmington, Conn.
Harold C. Townson, Rochester, N.Y.
Mr. and Mrs. Kenneth House, Rochester, N.Y.
Mrs. Allyn B. Forbes, Cambridge, Mass.
Spencer Field, Milton, Mass.

1956

Mrs. Roy D. Chapin, Grosse Pointe Farms, Mich.
Mr. John Swing, Lakeville, Conn.
Mr. and Mrs. Irving Levy, Cambridge, Mass.

1957

Mrs. William P. Allis, Cambridge, Mass.
Mr. and Mrs. Herman M. Cohn, Pittsford, N.Y.
Cambridge Red Cross
Mrs. Nathan Hayward, Manchester, Mass.
Mr. and Mrs. Arthur Stern Jr., Rochester, N.Y.
Rochester Historical Society, Rochester, N.Y.

1958

Mr. and Mrs. Sherman Selden, Pittsford, N.Y.
Mrs. Dabney, Beech
Mr. and Mrs. Edward L. Gates, Manchester, Mass.
Richard Hart, Brookline, Mass.
Dr. and Mrs. Philip Bachelder, Rumford, R.I.
Mr. and Mrs. James B. Mabon Jr., Canaan, Conn.
General and Mrs. William J. Blake, Boston, Mass.
Cambridge Red Cross
Frank E. Gannett Cemetery Lot, Rochester, N.Y.
Mrs. Frank E. Gannett, Rochester, N.Y.
John S. Ellsworth Jr., Guilford, Conn.

1959

Mr. and Mrs. Norman Samuel, Andover, Mass.
Dr. and Mrs. Robert J. Calihan, Rochester, N.Y.
Mr. and Mrs. John Buffington, Milton, Mass.

1960

Mrs. Richard Wood, Philadelphia, Pa.
Mr. and Mrs. John S. Howe, Prides Crossing, Mass.
Mr. and Mrs. T. S. Ross, Manchester, Mass.
Mr. and Mrs. Gilliat Schroeder, Wawa, Pa.

1961

Mr. and Mrs. Robert P. Tibolt, Cohasset, Mass.
Mr. and Mrs. Randall Thompson, Cambridge, Mass.
Mr. L. Cushing Goodhue, Manchester, Mass.

1962

Louis D. D'Amanda, Rochester, N.Y.
The Ensign Bickford Co., Simsbury, Conn.

1963

Eastman House, Rochester, N.Y.
William Selden, Pittsford, N.Y.
The Connecticut Society of Colonial Dames of America,
    Wethersfield, Conn.
Little House, Pittsford, N.Y.
The B'rith Kodush Congregation, Rochester, N.Y.
Spencer Memorial, Rochester, N.Y.
Richard L. Turner, Pittsford, N.Y.
Mr. and Mrs. James R. Reynolds, Wenham, Mass.

1964

Mrs. Frances Weld, Manchester, Mass.
Mr. Wilbur L. Coon, Fairport, N.Y.
Robert B. Frame

1965

Dr. and Mrs. William Alfred Sawyer, Pittsford, N.Y.
Worcester Science Museums, Worcester, Mass.
McQuilken, Rochester, N.Y.
Mr. and Mrs. Daniel H. Robbins, Brighton, N.Y.
H. H. Fay Memorial Planting, Woods Hole, Mass.

1966

Dr. and Mrs. Martha Bentley, Brookline, Mass.
Dr. and Mrs. M. J. Hancher, Rochester, N.Y.

1967

Memorial Art Gallery, Rochester, N.Y.
Werner Cemetery Lot, Mt. Hope Cemetery, Rochester, N.Y.
Dr. G. Porter Perham and Dr. David Mactye, Pittsford, N.Y.
Mr. and Mrs. Henry White, Waterford, Conn.
Mr. and Mrs. John E. Ellsworth, Waterford, Conn.
Mr. and Mrs. William P. Boswell, Cincinnati, Ohio

1968

Mr. and Mrs. Henry M. Hamlin, Fairport, N.Y.
Mr. and Mrs. Edward F. Macnickol, South Hamilton, Mass.

No Date

Mr. and Mrs. George A. Richter, Pittsford, N.Y.
Mrs. Walter Dabney (Mary Fay), Rochester, N.Y.
Mrs. Chester F. Carlson (Dorris), Pittsford, N.Y.
Mr. and Mrs. Michael Watson, Rochester, N.Y.
Mr. Orrin Harschman, Pittsford, N.Y.

Appendix 2 · Planting Plans and Lists

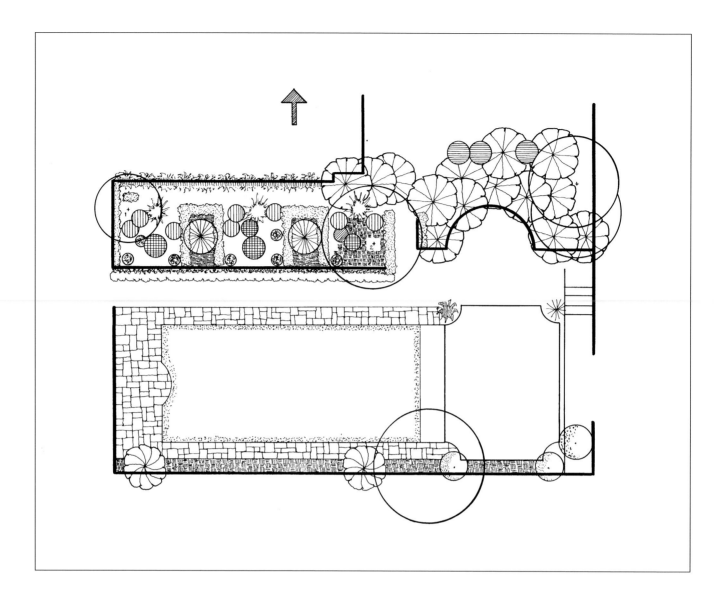

Botanical names in Latin form have been added or corrected wherever omissions or errors in Steele's lists occurred. Current identifications for obsolete forms have been supplied from *Hortus Third* (New York: Macmillan, 1976). It was Steele's usual practice to give his clients lists with both Latin and common names.

CHARLOTTE WHITNEY ALLEN *Rochester, N.Y.*

Plan for formal garden, based on a 1978 plan created by Wilbur Wright, horticultural consultant for the University of Rochester.

KEY

Cornus florida 'Pendula' (weeping dogwood)
Robinia pseudoacacia (black locust)
Acer pseudoplantanus (sycamore maple)
Crataegus phaenopyrum (Washington hawthorn)

Crataegus monogyna (English hawthorn)

Crataegus succulenta (fleshy hawthorn)

Crataegus monogyna 'Compacta' (globe hawthorn)

Syringa vulgaris (common lilac)

Philadelphus coronarius (sweet mock orange)

 Pyracantha coccinea 'Lalandei' (Laland firethorn)

Taxus cuspidata (Japanese yew)

Euonymus alatus 'Compactus' (dwarf burning bush)

Ilex crenata f. *microphylla* (Japanese holly)

Pieris floribunda (fetterbush)

Mahonia aquifolium (Oregon grape)

Prunus laurocerasus 'Schipkaensis' (Schipka cherry laurel)

 Wisteria floribunda (Japanese wisteria)

 Taxus x *media* 'Hicksii' (Hicks yew)

 Buxus sempervirens (common boxwood)

 Heuchera sanguinea (coralbells)

 Hedera helix 'Baltica' (English ivy)

 Ajuga reptans 'Burgundy Lace' (carpet bugle)

STANDISH BACKUS *Grosse Pointe Shores, Mich., April 1936*
Bay #2, Long Shot.

KEY

  Syringa vulgaris (Ludwig Spaeth)

  24 *Erianthus ravennae* (Ravenna grass) and 24 *Miscan-thus sinensis* 'Gracillimus' (eulalia), 8 clumps of 3 each

  52 *Iris orientalis,* 3 in each clump, 8 feet apart

  50 *Delphinium* × Belladonna, 10 clumps of 5 each, 3 feet apart

  16 lines of 6 *Veronica spuria*

600 blue *Viola grandiflora* in 3-foot band

  Thuja occidentalis

Added September 1936:

24   *Erianthus ravennae*
24   *Miscanthus sinensis* 'Gracillimus'
50   *Delphinium* (Watkin Samuel's Wrekham hybrids)
100 *Delphinium* × Belladonna
26   *Thalictrum aquilegifolium*

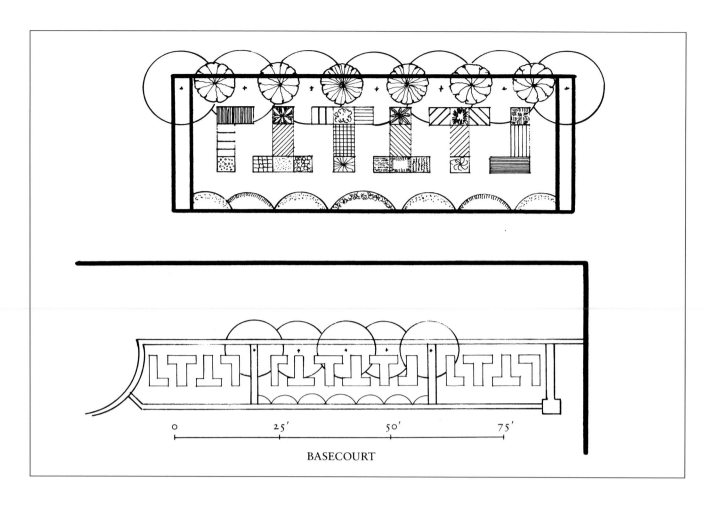

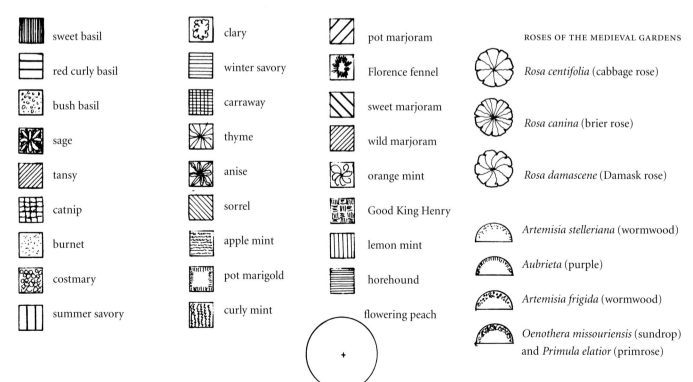

BASECOURT

STANDISH BACKUS *Grosse Pointe Shores, Mich.*
Planting plan for Culinary Herb Garden, Basecourt.

KEY

sweet basil	clary	pot marjoram
red curly basil	winter savory	Florence fennel
bush basil	carraway	sweet marjoram
sage	thyme	wild marjoram
tansy	anise	orange mint
catnip	sorrel	Good King Henry
burnet	apple mint	lemon mint
costmary	pot marigold	horehound
summer savory	curly mint	flowering peach

ROSES OF THE MEDIEVAL GARDENS

Rosa centifolia (cabbage rose)

Rosa canina (brier rose)

Rosa damascene (Damask rose)

Artemisia stelleriana (wormwood)

Aubrieta (purple)

Artemisia frigida (wormwood)

Oenothera missouriensis (sundrop)
and *Primula elatior* (primrose)

ROCKLAWN   *Harry Stoddard, Gloucester, Mass., 1937–1938*
Drywall Planting.

Cerastium tomentosum (snow in summer)

Chrysanthemum 'White Swan'

Dianthus deltoides 'Nana Erecta' (maiden pink)

Gypsophila repens (creeping gypsophila)

Saxifraga cordifolia (heartleaf saxifrage)

Saxifraga paniculata 'Rosea'

Saxifraga macnabiana (McNab saxifrage)

Sedum ewersii (Ewers' stonecrop)

Sedum sieboldi (Siebold stonecrop)

Potentilla tridentata (three-toothed cinquefoil)

Thymus vulgaris (thyme)

Dianthus deltoides 'Brilliant' (maiden pink)

Aubrieta deltoidea

Pinus mugo (Mugo pine)

Saxifraga (white saxifrage)

Ajuga (bugleweed)

Petrorhagia saxifraga (coat flower)

Veronica pectinata (speedwell)

Nepeta mussinii (catmint)

Mazus reptans

HELEN GILBERT   *Milton, Mass., May 1956*

Mosaic Bed, a small, rectangular bed on the upper terrace.
12 each of:

Antennaria neodioica (everlasting)

Arabis sturii (rockcress)

Arenaria verna (sandwort)

Dianthus myrtinervius (pink)

Draba aspera

Gentiana acaulis (gentian)

Globularia meridionalis

Hedyotis michauxii (creeping bluets)

Satureja montana (winter savory)

Saxifraga paniculata

Saxifraga × *macnabiana*

Sempervivum ruthenicum (houseleek)

Sempervivum tectorum var. *violaceum* (houseleek)

Aquilegia flabellata 'Nana' (columbine)

2 each of:

Calluna vulgaris 'Foxii' (heather)

Calluna vulgaris 'Nana' (heather)

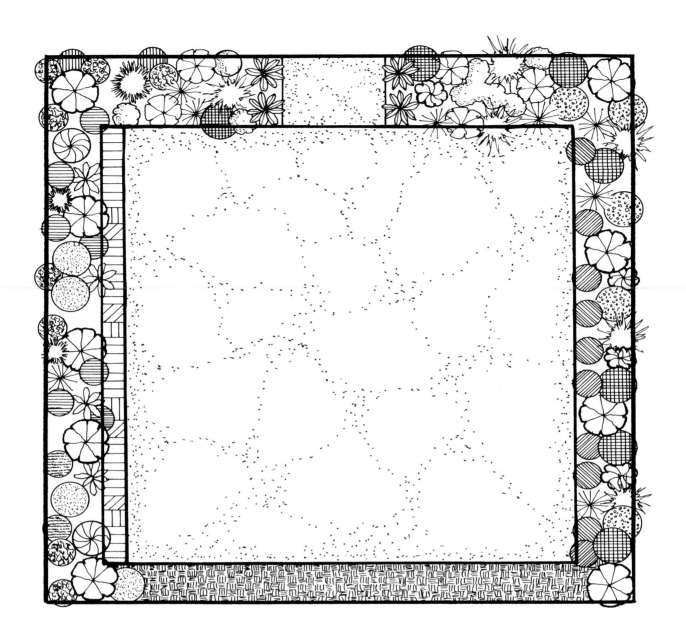

JAMES R. AND ELIZABETH REYNOLDS
Larch Farm, Wenham, Mass., 1965

The small, gravel terrace at the south end of the house was
edged on three sides by perennial borders.

KEY

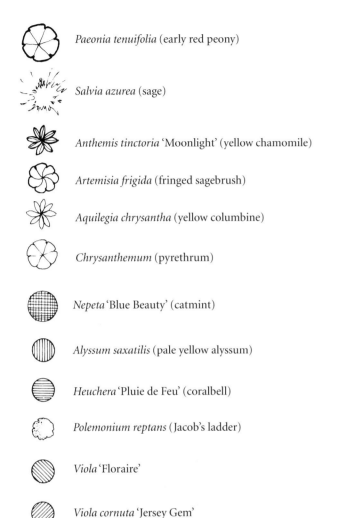

Paeonia tenuifolia (early red peony)

Salvia azurea (sage)

Anthemis tinctoria 'Moonlight' (yellow chamomile)

Artemisia frigida (fringed sagebrush)

Aquilegia chrysantha (yellow columbine)

Chrysanthemum (pyrethrum)

Nepeta 'Blue Beauty' (catmint)

Alyssum saxatilis (pale yellow alyssum)

Heuchera 'Pluie de Feu' (coralbell)

Polemonium reptans (Jacob's ladder)

Viola 'Floraire'

Viola cornuta 'Jersey Gem'

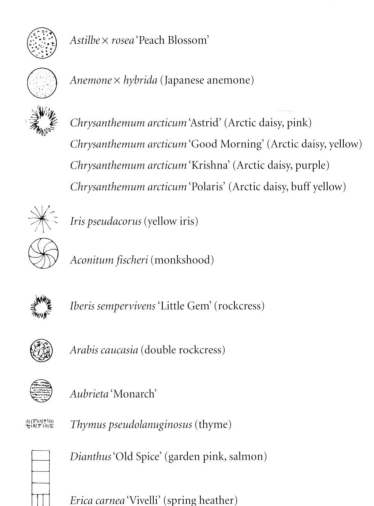

Astilbe × rosea 'Peach Blossom'

Anemone × hybrida (Japanese anemone)

Chrysanthemum arcticum 'Astrid' (Arctic daisy, pink)
Chrysanthemum arcticum 'Good Morning' (Arctic daisy, yellow)
Chrysanthemum arcticum 'Krishna' (Arctic daisy, purple)
Chrysanthemum arcticum 'Polaris' (Arctic daisy, buff yellow)

Iris pseudacorus (yellow iris)

Aconitum fischeri (monkshood)

Iberis sempervivens 'Little Gem' (rockcress)

Arabis caucasia (double rockcress)

Aubrieta 'Monarch'

Thymus pseudolanuginosus (thyme)

Dianthus 'Old Spice' (garden pink, salmon)

Erica carnea 'Vivelli' (spring heather)
Gypsophila 'Pink Star'

RICHARD AND NANCY TURNER   *Pittsford, N.Y., 1966*

North Vista plant list.

Abies concolor (white fir)

Acer ginnala (amur maple)

Acer rubrum (red maple)

Aesculus pavia (red buckeye)

Amelanchier × *grandiflora* (serviceberry)

Berberis × *mentorensis* (barberry)

Buddleia alternifolia (butterfly bush)

Chaenomeles × *californica* (flowering quince)

Chamaecyparis nootkatensis (Nootka cypress)

Chionanthus virginicus (fringe tree)

Cornus florida var. *rubra* (pink flowering dogwood)

Crataegus laevigata 'Paulii' (English hawthorn)

Elaeagnus angustifolia (oleaster)

Euonymus europaeus 'Aldenhamensis' (European spindle tree)

Fagus sylvatica 'Riversii' (European beech)

Franklinia alatamaha (Franklin tree)

Ginkgo biloba (maidenhair tree)

Halesia monticola (silver-bell tree)

Hamamelis mollis (Chinese witch hazel)

Ilex opaca (American holly)

Ilex verticillata (sparkleberry)

Laburnum × *watereri* (golden-chain tree)

Liquidambar styraciflua (sweet gum tree)

Magnolia stellata (star magnolia)

Malus spp. (apple)

Picea abies 'Aurea' (Norway spruce)

Picea glauca (white spruce)

Picea omorika (Serbian spruce)

Picea pungens var. *glauca* (Colorado spruce)

Platanus × *acerifolia* (London plane tree)

Prunus cerasifera 'Thundercloud' (cherry plum)

Pseudotsuga menziesii (Douglas fir)

Salix caprea (pussy willow)

Sophora japonica (Japanese pagoda tree)

Sorbus aucuparia (rowan)

Syringa vulgaris (lilac)

Thuja plicata 'Fastigiata' (giant arborvitae)

Tilia cordata (small-leaved European linden)

Xanthorhiza simplicissima (yellow-root)

Notes

Manuscript collections are identified by the following abbreviations:

LC   Fletcher Steele Papers
Manuscript Division
Library of Congress, Washington, D.C.

RHS   Fletcher Steele Papers
Rochester Historical Society
Rochester, N.Y.

RRL   Fletcher Steele Papers
Department of Rare Books and Special Collections
Rush Rhees Library, University of Rochester, Rochester, N.Y.

ML/SUNY Fletcher Steele Manuscript Collection
Terence J. Hoverter College Archives
F. Franklin Moon Library
State University of New York College of Environmental
Science and Forestry, Syracuse, N.Y.

Introduction

1. Garrett Eckbo, telephone interview by author, 19 April 1988.
2. Daniel Kiley, telephone interview by author, 8 April 1988.
3. George B. Tobey to Marlene Salon, 30 October 1978 (ML/SUNY).
4. Peter H. Hornbeck to author, 14 May 1988.
5. Steele to F. F. Rockwell, 10 June 1955 (LC).
6. Fletcher Steele, "Naumkeag Gardens Develop" (unpublished essay, May 1947, LC), 6.
7. Andrew D. Wolfe, "Fletcher Steele, Individualist," *Brighton-Pittsford Post*, 6 June 1963.
8. Steele, *Gardens and People* (Boston: Houghton Mifflin, 1964), 2
9. Ibid., 75.
10. Steele to Stanley Schuler, 30 March 1966 (LC).
11. Steele to F. F. Rockwell, 10 June 1955 (LC).

1   Origins, 1885–1914

1. Steele to Mrs. Marshall, 8 May 1947 (LC).
2. Fletcher Steele, "Rochester Yesterday and the Day Before" (lecture manuscript, n.d., LC), 10.
3. Steele to Mary Steele, 17 December 1920 (RHS).
4. Steele, "Rochester Yesterday," 18–19.
5. Ibid., 13.
6. Fletcher Steele, "Let Us Go to Cultivate Our Garden" (unpublished essay, n.d., RHS), 1–2.
7. Steele to Miss Engel, 10 October 1952 (LC).
8. Steele to George Yarwood, March 1955 (LC).
9. Fletcher Steele, *Gardens and People* (Boston: Houghton Mifflin, 1964), ix.
10. Ibid.
11. Steele to Miss Engel, 10 October 1952 (LC).
12. Steele to Mrs. Marshall, 8 May 1947 (LC).
13. Steele to Mary Steele, 25 November 1907 (RHS).
14. James Sturgis Pray, "The Department of Landscape Architecture in Harvard University," *Landscape Architecture* 1 (January 1911): 57.
15. Ibid., 57–58.
16. Ibid., 55–56.
17. Ibid., 59.
18. Arthur Drexler, ed., *The Architecture of the Ecole des Beaux-Arts* (New York: Museum of Modern Art, 1977), 112.
19. Fletcher Steele, "Where Art and Nature Overlap" (unpublished essay, n.d., RHS), 11.
20. Steele to Mary Steele, 2 March 1908 (RHS).
21. Steele to Mary Steele, 8 April 1908 (RHS).
22. Steele to Mary Steele, 2 September 1908 (RHS).
23. Warren Manning, "The Field of Landscape Architecture," *Landscape Architecture* 2 (April 1912): 108.
24. Steele to John Steele, 19 December 1908 (RHS).
25. Steele to Mary Steele, 22 February 1909 (RHS).

26. Steele to Mary Steele, 23 July 1909 (RHS).

27. Steele to Mary Steele, 9 August 1909 (RHS).

28. Steele to Mary Steele, 4 September 1909 (RHS).

29. Steele to Mary Steele, 10 September 1909 (RHS).

30. Steele to Mary Steele, 10 February 1910 (RHS).

31. Steele to Mary Steele, 24 May 1910 (RHS).

32. Steele to Mary Steele, 17 June 1910 (RHS).

33. Steele to Mary Steele, 5 October 1910 (RHS).

34. Steele to John Steele, 27 January 1912 (RHS).

35. Ibid.

36. Fletcher Steele, "Europe, 1913" (travel diary prepared for Warren Manning, 1913, ML/SUNY, 1.

37. Ibid., 106.

38. Ibid., 5.

39. Ibid., 10.

40. Ibid., 14–15.

41. Ibid., 20.

42. Ibid., 52.

43. Ibid., 64, 82.

44. Steele to John Steele, 24 March 1914 (RHS).

45. Steele to John Steele, 2 April 1914 (RHS).

46. This information comes from a letter from Maria M. Thompson to Catha Grace Rambusch, 20 January 1993. Thompson lists the other Wood family clients and their estates as George Wood (Red Roof); Mrs. Richard D. Wood (Red Roof and Burnbank); Mrs. Richard D. Wood Jr. (Hurricane Hollow); Mr. and Mrs. Gilliat Schroeder (White Oak); Miss Dorothea Wood (Forge Hill); Mrs. Mary W. Wiltsie (Burnbank).

    An article from the *Philadelphia Inquirer*, "Descendant of Wawa Founder Retains Family Mansion in Auction," 2 August 1993, reports that Frederick Wood, grandson of Grahame Wood, purchased Blossom Hill at auction from his mother's estate and intended to continue to live there.

47. Steele to John Steele, 4 June 1914 (RHS).

48. See Doris Cole, *Eleanor Raymond, Architect* (Philadelphia: Art Alliance Press, 1981), 18.

49. Fletcher Steele, "The Landscaping of Peridot," *Garden Magazine*, February 1915, 12.

50. Ibid., 14.

2 First Flowering: Tradition and Experiment, 1915–1926

1. Fletcher Steele, "A Garden Constructed before the House," *House Beautiful*, August 1930, 141–44.

2. Fletcher Steele, "Caption for Paris Exhibition" (Notes, March 1930, LC).

3. Steele, "Garden Constructed," 142.

4. Steele to Mary Steele, 30 October 1922 (RHS).

5. Ibid.

6. Fletcher Steele, *Gardens and People* (Boston: Houghton Mifflin, 1964), 9.

7. Charlotte Whitney Allen to Steele, n.d. (LC).

8. Charles Cares, interview by author, Ann Arbor, Mich., 26 June 1988. Cares and other students from the graduate program in Landscape Architecture at Cornell University visited Charlotte Allen's garden (and Fletcher Steele's in Pittsford) on a circa 1946 field trip.

9. Steele to Mr. Jackson B. Hester, Agricultural Research Laboratories, 15 July 1958 (LC).

10. Charlotte Allen to Fletcher Steele, 21 March 1945 (LC).

11. Steele to Betty Blossom, 21 July 1953 (LC).

12. James Rieger, "Dear Hearts: Clara Louise Werner Ward (1889–1973) and Charlotte Whitney Allen (1891–1978)," *University of Rochester Library Bulletin* 32 (Winter 1979): 6.

13. Alexander Calder, *Calder, An Autobiography with Pictures*, 2d ed. (New York: Pantheon, 1977), 154.

14. Steele to Mary Steele, 27 May 1917 (RHS).

15. *Macmillan Encyclopedia of Architects*, s.v. "Cram, Ralph Adams."

16. Fletcher Steele, untitled essay, 1910 (LC), 1.

17. Steele to Mary Fay, 4 August 1915, private collection, Boston.

18. Caroline Runner, telephone interview by author, 11 September 1988.

19. Bremer Pond, "Fifty Years in Retrospect," *Landscape Architecture* 40 (January 1950): 63.

20. Steele to Mary Steele, 13 September 1918 (RHS).

21. Steele to Mary Steele, 10 July 1918 (RHS).

22. Fletcher Steele, "Lecture Delivered at Williams College" (manuscript, 20 January 1925, LC), 1.

23. Steele, letter to the Editor, *Boston Transcript*, 8 August 1918.

24. Steele, letter to the Editor, *Rochester Democrat and Chronicle*, 28 November 1919.

25. Steele to Esther Steele, n.d. (RHS).

26. Steele, "Caption for Paris Exhibition."

27. *New York Sun*, 20 June 1931.

28. Garden Club of America, *The Garden Club of America History, 1913–1938* (Boston, 1938), 33.

29. Fletcher Steele, "Lisburne Grange," *Garden Club of America Bulletin*, September 1935, 112.

30. Ibid., 115.

31. Ibid.

32. Ibid., 115–16.

33. Ibid., 115.

34. Ibid., 116.

35. Ibid.

36. Ibid.

37. Ibid., 116–17.

38. Fletcher Steele, "French Gardens and Their Racial Characteristics," *Landscape Architecture* 12 (July 1922): 212.

39. Ibid., 214, 213.

40. J. C. N. Forestier, *Gardens: A Note-book of Plans and Sketches*, trans. Helen Morgenthau Fox (New York: Charles Scribner's Sons, 1928), 7–8.

41. Steele, "French Gardens," 222.

42. Steele to Mary Steele, 18 March 1923 (RHS).

43. *Cincinnati Enquirer*, 8 January 1925.

44. Fletcher Steele, "Plant Material," *Garden Club of America Bulletin*, September 1921, 41.

45. Ibid., 43.

46. Leslie Rose Close, *Portrait of an Era in Landscape Architecture: The Photographs of Mattie Edwards Hewitt*, exhibition catalogue (New York: Wave Hill, 1983).

47. Steele to Mary Steele, 18 March 1923 (RHS).

48. This quote is taken from a newspaper clipping in one of Steele's note-

books (ML/SUNY). No title, author, date, or page appears, nor is the publication identified.

49. Review of *Design in the Little Garden* by Fletcher Steele, *Horticulture*, 15 April 1924, 313.

50. George B. Tobey, *A History of Landscape Architecture: The Relation of People to Environment* (New York: American Elsevier Publishing, 1973), 198–99.

51. George B. Tobey, telephone interview by author, 16 August 1988.

52. Fletcher Steele, *Design in the Little Garden* (Boston: Atlantic Monthly Press, 1924), 13–14.

53. Ibid., 12.

54. Ibid., 34.

55. Ibid., 3, 4.

56. Ibid., 8, 9.

57. Ibid., 25.

58. Ibid., 26, 27.

59. Ibid., 42, 43.

60. Ibid., 31, 32.

61. Ibid., 41.

62. Fletcher Steele, "Your Own . . . Your Neighbor's Land," *House Beautiful*, September 1934, 38.

63. Ibid., 80.

64. Fletcher Steele, "When Trees Turn into Problems," *Horticulture*, 15 September 1946, 415.

65. Steele, "Your Neighbor's Land," 40.

66. Steele to Bay State Nurseries, North Abington, Mass., plant order, 6 October 1926 (LC).

67. Steele, "Your Neighbor's Land," 39, 40.

68. Henry Hoover, interview by author, Lincoln, Mass., 4 March 1987. Hoover, Steele's assistant during the project, remembers Clifford as being among the husbands who expressed concern about the size—and budget—of Steele's proposals.

69. Steele to George Yarwood, 4 March 1955 (LC).

70. Steele to Esther Steele, 18 April 1950 (RHS).

71. Steele, *Little Garden*, 21–22.

72. Fletcher Steele, "A Dooryard Garden with Intimate Planting," *House Beautiful*, March 1931, 275.

73. R. N., "Interview with Fletcher Steele," *Town and Country*, December 1926.

74. Steele, *Gardens and People*, 15.

75. Steele to Angelica Gerry, 1 August 1927 (RRL).

76. Steele reproduced a large number of garden images from various books and photographic services as source material for his own designs. Many references in his correspondence confirm that these images were shared with clients; in fact, client names appear on a small percentage of them. (Steele catalogued most of these images in the "H" series notebooks, ML/SUNY, although a few appear in the "L" series as well.) The pond overlook at Lake Ancrum was based on photograph no. 10.326, mounted in vol. 20, "L" series.

77. Steele, *Gardens and People*, 119.

78. Steele to Angelica Gerry, 1 August 1927 (RRL).

79. Ibid.

80. "Miss Gerry Hostess to Large Garden Party," *Delaware Republican* (Delhi, N.Y.), 24 August 1932.

81. Steele, *Gardens and People*, 167.

82. Ibid.

83. Steele to Esther Steele, 23 January 1926 (RHS).

3   Deeper Dreams, 1926–1935

1. Fletcher Steele, "Westport, Connecticut" (lecture manuscript, n.d., LC), 1–2.

2. Fletcher Steele, "New Pioneering in Garden Design," *Landscape Architecture* 20 (1930): 167.

3. Ibid., 166.

4. See Robin Karson, "Spheres, Cones, and Other Least Common Denominators: Modern French Gardens through the Eyes of Fletcher Steele," *Masters of American Garden Design III: The Modern Garden in Europe and the United States* (Cold Spring, N.Y.: Garden Conservancy, 1993).

5. Fletcher Steele, "Dublin Club" (lecture manuscript, 1923, LC), 1.

6. Steele to Mary Steele, 8 July 1926 (RHS).

7. Steele to Charles D. Webster, 25 June 1968 (LC).

8. Mabel Choate, "Naumkeag Notes" (Memoirs, Naumkeag Archives, 1952–1954), XIX, 1. Mabel Choate recorded sixty-nine typewritten pages of memoirs. These were organized into short sections (usually two to three pages each), identified by roman numerals. The memoirs begin with Ruluff's death in 1885 and end with that of Joseph Choate in 1917.

9. Morgan Bulkeley, "The Choates at Naumkeag" (Lecture Notes, Naumkeag Archives, 4 July 1968), 7.

10. Choate, "Naumkeag Notes," I, 2.

11. Mabel Choate quoted in *Naumkeag* (Milton, Mass.: Trustees of Reservations, 1965), 2.

12. Bulkeley, "Choates at Naumkeag," 6.

13. Choate, "Naumkeag Notes," I, 2.

14. Fletcher Steele, "Naumkeag Gardens Develop" (unpublished essay, May 1947, LC), 1.

15. Choate, "Naumkeag Notes," II, 1.

16. Ibid.

17. Ibid., 2.

18. Steele, "Naumkeag Gardens Develop," 2.

19. Daniel Kiley, telephone interview by author, 8 April 1988. This story was told to Kiley by Fletcher Steele when Kiley visited Naumkeag in 1932.

20. Mabel Choate, "Naumkeag Garden" (tourbook of the garden, Stockbridge, Mass., Summer 1956), 2.

21. Fletcher Steele, untitled essay describing work at Naumkeag, n.d. (LC), 9.

22. Ibid., 12.

23. Steele, "Naumkeag Gardens Develop," 3.

24. Duane A. Dietz to author, 17 April 1990 and 21 June 1990. According to Dietz's letters, this information came from Sturtevant's 1935 résumé; according to Sturtevant's 1926–32 client list, he also worked for Steele's clients the Gerrys in Asheville, N.C., and Providence, R.I.

25. Fletcher Steele, "The Temple Garden," *House Beautiful*, July 1933, 21.

26. Steele, untitled essay describing work at Naumkeag, 11–14.

27. A complete account of the coal experiment is related by Mabel Choate in "Coal in the Garden," *Bulletin of the Garden Club of America*, July 1939, 79–80.

28. Steele, "Naumkeag Gardens Develop," 4

29. "Four Scenes from the Work of Mr. Fletcher Steele," *National Horticulture Magazine*, January 1945, 40.

30. Peter H. Hornbeck to author, 8 July 1988.

31. Henry Hoover, interview by author, Lincoln, Mass., 4 March, 1987.

32. Fletcher Steele, untitled essay on style, n.d. (LC), 1.

33. Steele to Mr. Butler, 31 October 1946 (LC).

34. Steele to Mr. Nettleton, 6 February 1930 (LC).

35. Between 4 March 1987 and 17 January 1988, the author interviewed Henry Hoover five times in Lincoln, Mass. Much of the information concerning Steele's working methods, certain client information, some details about designs, and the physical description of the office comes from these interviews.

36. Fletcher Steele, "Where Art and Nature Overlap," section titled "Pattern a Shallow Boon" (unpublished essay, n.d., RHS), 8.

37. See Fletcher Steele, "A Landscape Architect's Kit," *Landscape Architecture* 11 (January 1921): 63–65.

38. Hoover interview, 4 March 1987.

39. Henry Hoover, interview by author, Lincoln, Mass., 17 January 1988.

40. Fletcher Steele, "Mission House," *House Beautiful*, July 1930, 32

41. Ibid.

42. Hoover interview, 17 January 1988.

43. Fletcher Steele, "The Colonial Garden Today," in American Society of Landscape Architects, *Colonial Gardens* (Washington, D.C.: U.S. George Washington Bicentennial Commission, 1932), 60.

44. Steele, "Mission House," 30.

45. Steele, *Colonial Gardens*, 64.

46. Fletcher Steele, *Design in the Little Garden* (Boston: Atlantic Monthly Press, 1924), 15.

47. Steele, *Colonial Gardens*, 66.

48. Steele, "Mission House," 33.

49. Alice Page Pickman, telephone interview by author, 14 July 1987. Pickman could recall no other projects on which her father and Steele had worked together.

50. Fletcher Steele to William Marquis, 25 January 1969 (LC).

51. Hoover interview, 17 January 1988.

52. Steele to William Marquis, 25 January 1969 (LC).

53. Frederick Law Olmsted Jr., office memorandum, 31 October 1928 (National Park Service, Frederick Law Olmsted National Historic Site), 1, 5. The author is indebted to Eleanor G. Ames, of Portland, Me., for informing her about the existence of the documents that chronicle the conflict. See also Robin Karson, "Fletcher Steele and the Camden Public Library Amphitheatre," in *Maine Olmsted Alliance for Parks and Landscapes Journal*, Spring 1992, 1, 3–6; and "Historic Landscape Preservation Treatment Plan for Camden Library Grounds, Camden Amphitheater and Harbor Park," prepared by Landscapes, Charlotte, Vt., August 1997.

54. Fletcher Steele, conference memorandum, 31 October 1928 (National Park Service, Frederick Law Olmsted National Historic Site).

55. Mr. Zach to Fletcher Steele, 28 August 1929 (National Park Service, Frederick Law Olmsted National Historic Site).

56. Nellie A. Hart to author, 9 December 1986.

57. Fletcher Steele, "New Styles in Gardening," *House Beautiful*, March 1929, 317.

58. Ibid., 353.

59. Fletcher Steele, "The Effective Use of Planting," *The Garden*, March 1949, 23.

60. Steele to Mrs. Edward Bok, 19 December 1941 (LC).

61. Steele, "Naumkeag Gardens Develop," 4–5.

62. Steele to Charlotte Whitney Allen, 10 August 1944 (LC).

63. Geoffrey Platt, "Narration—Garden Party, Naumkeag" (audiotape transcription, Naumkeag Archives, 21 July 1983), 1.

64. Amy Bess Miller, interview by author, Pittsfield, Mass., 5 July 1988.

65. Platt, "Narration," 2.

66. Steele to Esther Steele, 24 September 1950 (RHS).

67. Steele, "Naumkeag Gardens Develop," 8.

68. Ibid.

69. Ibid., 8–9.

70. Ibid., 7, 8.

71. Ibid., 1

72. Steele to H. O. Whittemore, 17 March 1930 (RRL).

73. Standish Backus to Fletcher Steele, 5 August 1932 (RRL). Backus writes: "I know that you think we are running the danger of keeping too much to one era, and in this I have no doubt that you may be right."

74. Hoover interview, 4 March 1987.

75. Butler Sturtevant to Fletcher Steele, 14 September 1943 (LC).

76. Virginia Cavendish, office memorandum, 9 September 1931 (LC), 4.

77. Ibid.

78. Steele to Standish Backus, 31 December 1931 (RRL).

79. Standish Backus to Fletcher Steele, 5 August 1932 (RRL).

80. Steele to "Harry" Hoover, 19 August 1932 (RRL).

81. Steele to Standish Backus, 13 July 1932 (RRL).

82. Steele to Standish Backus, 30 September 1932 (RRL).

83. Steele to Standish Backus, 15 December 1931 (RRL).

84. Steele to Standish Backus, 18 December 1931 (RRL).

85. Steele to Standish Backus, 21 December 1931 (RRL).

86. Standish Backus to Fletcher Steele, 7 March 1932 (RRL).

87. George B. Tobey, telephone interview by author, 16 August 1988. According to Tobey, who researched the matter while teaching at Ohio State University, about half of the profession worked for private clients during the Depression. The results of this research are not published.

88. Steele to John Steele, 16 June 1930 (LC).

89. Sidney Shurcliff, "Memories of Fletcher Steele" (Notes, n.d., ML/SUNY), 1.

90. Andrew D. Wolfe, "Fletcher Steele, Individualist," *Brighton-Pittsford Post*, 6 June 1963.

91. George Yarwood, letter to author, 11 December 1986. "[A]s I recall Steele's design it was the most interesting, but did not place first."

92. Fletcher Steele, "Fine Art in Landscape Architecture," *Landscape Architecture* 24 (July 1934): 177.

93. Mrs. George (Mary) Doubleday, "A Patio Greenhouse," *Garden Club of America Bulletin*, November 1941, 23–24.

94. Ibid., 25.

95. Ibid.

96. Ibid., 26–27.

97. Fletcher Steele, "Enlightened Laziness," *Horticulture*, February 1943, 46.

98. Fletcher Steele, "New Styles in Gardening," *House Beautiful*, March 1929, 317, 354

99. Fletcher Steele, "New Pioneering in Garden Design," *Landscape Architecture* 20 (April 1930): 163, 164.

100. Ibid., 161. Barr's remarks are quoted from the foreword to the first catalogue of the Museum of Modern Art.

101. Ibid., 162.

102. Kiley interview, 8 April 1988.

103. See Joachim Wolsche-Bulmahn, "The Peculiar Garden—The Advent and the Destruction of Modernism in German Garden Design," *Masters of American Garden Design III: The Modern Garden in Europe and the United States* (Cold Spring, N. Y.: Garden Conservancy, 1993).

104. Steele to F. F. Rockwell, 10 June 1955 (LC).

105. Fletcher Steele, Planting Plan, No. 342-12, 17 February 1930 (ML/SUNY).

106. Steele to Esther Steele, 26 January 1932 (RHS).

107. Henry Hoover, interview by author, Lincoln, Mass., 4 April 1987.

108. Arthur Sylvester, telephone interview by author, 16 November 1986.

109. Kiley interview, 8 April 1988.

110. Steele to Mary Steele, 1 June 1932 (RHS).

111. Steele to Esther Steele, 13 July 1932 (RHS).

112. Steele to Henry Frost, 12 February 1942 (LC).

113. Steele to Emily Swindells, 21 August 1931, Private papers, Rockville, Conn.

114. Steele to Emily Swindells, 11 March 1932, Private papers, Rockville, Conn.

115. Peter H. Hornbeck, interview by author, North Andover, Mass., 7 January 1987.

116. Fletcher Steele, "Report on Mr. Steele's Visit to Rockville, March 27, 1934" (office memorandum, Private papers, Rockville, Conn., 28 March 1934), 1.

117. Steele to Emily Swindells, August 1934, Private papers, Rockville, Conn.

118. Steele to Emily Swindells, 26 November 1934, Private papers, Rockville, Conn.

119. Steele to Emily Swindells, 7 December 1934, Private papers, Rockville, Conn.

120. Steele to Emily Swindells, 1 April 1935, Private papers, Rockville, Conn.

121. Steele to Emily Swindells, 14 April 1936, Private papers, Rockville, Conn.

122. Emily Swindells to Fletcher Steele, 21 October 1948, Private papers, Rockville, Conn.

123. Alexander Calder to Fletcher Steele, December 1934 (LC).

124. Alexander Calder, *Calder, An Autobiography with Pictures*, 2d ed. (New York: Pantheon, 1977), 153–54.

125. James Rieger, "Dear Hearts: Clara Louise Werner Ward (1889–1973) and Charlotte Whitney Allen (1891–1978)," *University of Rochester Library Bulletin* 32 (Winter 1979): 33.

126. Barbara Vancheri, "Charlotte Whitney Allen," *Democrat and Chronicle*, 15 January 1984.

127. Steele to Charlotte Devine, 19 April 1933 (LC).

128. Steele to Charlotte Devine, 6 April 1943 (LC).

129. Helen Stoddard, interview by author, Worcester, Mass., 9 May 1987.

130. Fletcher Steele, "Spain," *Landscape Architecture* 19 (January 1929): 65.

131. Steele to Mrs. Marshall, 8 May 1947 (LC).

132. Fletcher Steele, "Notes on Trip to China" (unpublished essay, 1934, LC), 6.

133. Ibid., 39.

134. Ibid.

135. Ibid.

136. Steele, "Where Art and Nature Overlap," 15–16.

137. Ibid., 16.

138. Steele, "Notes on Trip to China," 24.

139. Ibid., 22.

140. Ibid., 23.

141. Fletcher Steele, "China Teaches," *Landscape Architecture* 37 (April 1947):

88. Based on a talk before the Boston Society of Landscape Architects, 6 November 1946.

142. Ibid., 92.

4   Apex: Invention, 1936–1949

1. Standish Backus to Fletcher Steele, November 1934 (RRL).

2. Virginia (Backus) Caulkins, interview by author, Grosse Pointe Farms, Mich., August 1986.

3. Standish Backus to Fletcher Steele, 10 November 1934 (RRL).

4. Steele to Standish Backus, 18 December 1931 (RRL).

5. Fletcher Steele, "Forecourt Specifications for Backus Garden" (construction guidelines, 16 August 1932, LC).

6. Ibid.

7. Steele to F. F. Rockwell, 10 June 1955 (LC).

8. Steele to Standish Backus, November 1934 (RRL).

9. Steele to Standish Backus, 8 November 1934 (RRL).

10. Fletcher Steele, letter to the Editor, *Horticulture*, 1 December 1943.

11. George Ellwanger's garden still exists at 625 Mount Hope Avenue, Rochester. It is owned and maintained by the Landmark Society of Western New York State and open to the public.

12. Fletcher Steele, memorandum, 2 November 1935 (Helen C. Ellwanger Papers, Landmark Society of Western New York State, Rochester), 2.

13. Fletcher Steele, "Landscape Design of the Future," *Landscape Architecture* 22 (July 1932): 299–300.

14. Fletcher Steele, "Modern Landscape Architecture," in *Contemporary Landscape Architecture and Its Sources*, exhibition catalogue (San Francisco: San Francisco Museum of Art, 1937), 25.

15. Fletcher Steele, "Modern Garden Design," in *The Garden Dictionary*, ed. Norman Taylor (Boston: Houghton Mifflin, 1936), 506.

16. Steele to Betty Blossom, 9 October 1952 (LC).

17. Ibid.

18. Ibid.

19. Steele to F. F. Rockwell, 10 June 1955 (LC).

20. Steele to Betty Blossom, 9 October 1952 (LC).

21. Ibid.

22. Ibid.

23. Steele to Carl Cropp, 10 December 1940 (LC).

24. Steele to Mr. H. J. Hohman, 2 December 1947 (LC).

25. Fletcher Steele, "Plant Material," *Garden Club of America Bulletin*, September 1921, 40.

26. Steele to Harry Stoddard, 22 February 1949 (LC).

27. Ibid.

28. Steele to Betty Blossom, 9 October 1952 (LC).

29. G. Porter Perham, interview by author, Rochester, N.Y., 7 October 1986.

30. Steele to Joseph Taylor, 12 August 1936 (LC).

31. Joseph Taylor to Fletcher Steele, 17 August 1936 (LC).

32. Steele to Joseph Taylor, 11 March 1948 (LC).

33. James Rieger, "Dear Hearts: Clara Louise Werner Ward (1899–1973) and Charlotte Whitney Allen (1891–1978)," *University of Rochester Library Bulletin* 32 (Winter 1979): 36.

34. Henry Hoover, office memorandum, 21 July 1937 (LC), 1.

35. Mabel Choate, "Naumkeag Garden" (tour book of the garden, Stockbridge, Mass., Summer 1956), 5.

36. Steele, "Naumkeag Gardens Develop," 7.

37. Fletcher Steele, "The Chinese Garden at Naumkeag" (unpublished essay, n.d., LC), 1.

38. Steele to Esther Steele, 1949 (RHS).

39. Steele, "Chinese Garden," 2.

40. Ibid.

41. Steele to Charles D. Webster, 25 June 1968 (LC).

42. Choate, "Naumkeag," 7.

43. Henry Hoover, interview by author, Lincoln, Mass., 17 January 1988.

44. Steele to Mabel Choate, 13 June 1949 (LC).

45. Geoffrey Platt, "Narration—Garden Party, Naumkeag" (audiotape transcription, Naumkeag Archives, 21 July 1983), 5.

46. Steele to Mary Steele, 23 October 1938 (RHS).

47. Choate, "Naumkeag," 4.

48. Steele to Mary Steele, 23 October 1938 (RHS).

49. Amy Bess Miller, interview by author, Pittsfield, Mass., 5 July 1988.

50. Michael Van Valkenburgh, "Naumkeag," in *Built Landscapes: Gardens of the Northeast*, exhibition catalogue (Brattleboro, Vt.: Brattleboro Museum and Art Center, 1984), 34.

51. Choate, "Naumkeag," 5.

52. Steele to Mary Steele, 23 October 1938 (RHS).

53. Fletcher Steele, *Gardens and People* (Boston: Houghton Mifflin, 1964), 3.

54. Garrett Eckbo to author, 26 July 1988.

55. Henry Hubbard, "The Bureau and the Landscape Designer," in "The Landscape Architect in the Present Situation" by H. Hubbard and F. Steele, *Landscape Architecture* 31 (January 1941): 68.

56. Fletcher Steele, "Private Delight and the Communal Ideal" in "The Landscape Architect in the Present Situation," 70.

57. Ibid.

58. Ibid., 71.

59. Steele to Elizabeth Reynolds, 14 March 1965, Private papers, Wenham, Mass.

60. G. Porter Perham, interview by author, Rochester, N.Y., 26 June 1987.

61. Fletcher Steele, "Adventure in Haiti" (slide lecture, n.d., RHS), 2.

62. Steele to Esther Steele, 14 January 1947 (RHS).

63. Steele to Standish Backus, 12 December 1940 (LC).

64. Steele to Standish Backus, 22 April 1940 (LC).

65. Steele to Standish Backus, 11 October 1941 (LC).

66. Steele to Standish Backus, 15 November 1941 (LC).

67. Steele to Standish Backus, 20 August 1942 (LC).

68. Fairman Furness to Fletcher Steele, 29 June 1943 (LC).

69. Steele to Esther Steele, 24 March 1944 (RHS).

70. Harry Stoddard to Fletcher Steele, 15 March 1942 (LC).

71. Fairman Furness to Fletcher Steele, 29 June 1943 (LC). "[I] have thought many times of your telling the millionaire to go to hell, & have been tempted to follow your example."

72. Fletcher Steele, "Private Post-War Planning" (part 1), *Garden Club of America Bulletin*, June 1944, 11.

73. Fletcher Steele, "Private Post-War Planning" (part 2), *Garden Club of America Bulletin*, September 1944, 17–18.

74. Fletcher Steele, "Food Alone Is Not Enough, Flowers for Freedom, Too," *Horticulture*, March 1948, 87.

75. Steele to Mrs. McKnight, 19 July 1943 (LC).

76. Steele to Esther Steele, 24 March 1942 (RHS).

77. Steele to Esther Steele, 14 May 1947 (RHS).

78. Steele to Esther Steele, 17 March 1947 (RHS).

79. Steele to Esther Steele, 24 March 1942 (RHS).

80. Steele to Charlotte Whitney Allen, 20 April 1945 (LC).

81. Steele to Esther Steele, 28 August 1945 (RHS).

82. Steele to Mr. Shumsky, 1 February 1946 (LC).

83. Steele to John Ellsworth, 2 February 1946 (LC).

84. John Ellsworth to Fletcher Steele, 26 November 1946 (LC).

85. Steele to John Ellsworth, 4 May 1946 (LC).

86. Steele to John Ellsworth, 2 February 1946 (LC).

87. Harry Stoddard to Fletcher Steele, 5 February 1946 (LC).

88. Steele to Esther Steele, 24 September 1950 (RHS).

89. Steele to Esther Steele, 22 July 1948 (RHS).

90. Steele to Esther Steele, 24 September 1950 (RHS).

91. Helen Stoddard, interview by author, Worcester, Mass., 9 May 1987.

92. Fletcher Steele, "New Forms and Dimensions in Landscape Design" (lecture delivered at Williamsburg Garden Symposium, 1953, LC), 18.

93. Steele to Helen Stoddard, 29 July 1948 (LC).

94. Fletcher Steele, "Gray-Leaved Plants," *House Beautiful*, November 1922, 428.

95. Steele, "Plant Material," 43.

96. Steele to Helen Stoddard, 11 March 1947 (LC).

97. Steele to Mr. Charles Eggert, 12 June 1947 (LC).

98. Steele to Mrs. DeBevoise, 8 November 1947 (LC).

99. Fletcher Steele, "Landscape Architecture" (unpublished essay, 4 March 1942, RHS), 1–2.

100. Steele to Mrs. Plum, 6 May 1946 (LC).

101. Steele to Mrs. Plum, 6 June 1946 (LC).

102. Steele to Mrs. Plum, 19 August 1946 (LC).

103. Matthias Plum to Fletcher Steele, 21 July 1947 (LC).

104. A. H. Alexander to Fletcher Steele, 5 October 1958 (LC).

105. Steele to Esther Steele, 1 November 1946 (RHS).

106. Ibid.

107. Steele to Esther Steele, 4 May 1947 (RHS).

108. Steele to Betty Blossom, 21 July 1953 (LC).

109. Steele to Helen Ellwanger, 11 July 1949 (LC).

110. Steele to Esther Steele, 24 June 1949 (LC).

111. Ibid.

112. Fletcher Steele, "Color Charts and Their Use in Gardening," *Landscape Architecture* 13 (January 1923): 97.

113. Fletcher Steele, "Aesthetic Principles in the Spring Flower Garden," *House Beautiful*, March 1922, 197.

114. Steele to Esther Steele, 22 June 1947 (RHS).

115. Ibid.

116. Steele to Esther Steele, 20 July 1947 (RHS).

117. Steele to Mrs. Livermore, 27 March 1948 (LC).

118. Steele to Mrs. Morris Hadley, 4 March 1948 (LC).

119. Ibid.

5 Twilight: Frustration and Fulfillment, 1950–1971

1. Steele to Miss Engel, 10 October 1952 (LC).

2. Steele to Mrs. Marshall, 8 May 1947 (LC).

3. Edwin G. Thurlow to Fletcher Steele, 22 February 1951 (LC).

4. Steele to Bradford Williams, 2 October 1951 (LC).

5. Steele to Bradford Williams, 24 March 1959 (LC).

6. Steele to Stuart M. Mertz, 12 November 1959 (LC).

7. Steele to Nelson W. Aldrich, 2 November 1953 (LC).

8. Steele to the Manager, Ritz-Carlton Hotel, Boston, 27 January 1953 (LC).

9. Steele to C. Russell Mason, 22 May 1954 (LC).

10. Steele to P. A. Snelling, January 1948 (LC).

11. Steele to Mrs. Richard Worrell, February 1950.

12. *The Banner* (Bennington, Vt.), 9 August 1950.

13. Steele to Mrs. Roy Hunt, 27 February 1947 (LC).

14. John Goetz, interview by author, Rochester, N.Y., 15 May 1986.

15. Steele to Helen Gilbert, 13 August 1955 (LC).

16. Fletcher Steele, plant order to Barnhaven Garden, 8 August 1957 (LC).

17. Steele to Helen Gilbert, 16 August 1957 (LC).

18. Peter H. Hornbeck, interview by author, North Andover, Mass., 7 January 1987.

19. Kevin Rohrbah to Fletcher Steele, 14 October 1951 (LC).

20. Mary Smith, telephone interview by author, 23 April 1987.

21. Peter Moore, interview by author, West Townshend, Vt., 12 January 1987.

22. Inez Chapin to Fletcher Steele, 24 November 1954 (LC).

23. Inez Chapin to Fletcher Steele, 6 February 1956 (LC).

24. Steele to Inez Chapin, 21 September 1956 (LC).

25. Steele to Inez Chapin, 10 April 1956 (LC).

26. Ibid.

27. Otto Eggers to Fletcher Steele, 2 October 1956 (LC).

28. Steele to Lewis Garred, 20 November 1956 (LC).

29. Inez Chapin to Fletcher Steele, 5 December 1956 (LC).

30. Inez Chapin to Fletcher Steele, n.d. (LC).

31. Moore interview, 12 January 1987.

32. Steele to Esther Steele, 25 January 1947 (RHS).

33. Steele to Esther Steele, 13 June 1944 (RHS).

34. Mabel Choate to Fletcher Steele, 21 August 1950 (LC).

35. Steele to Esther Steele, 13 June 1944 (RHS).

36. Fletcher Steele, "Notes for Miss Renshaw" (Notes, 13 June 1949, LC), 1.

37. Steele to Esther Steele, 24 September 1950 (RHS).

38. Steele to Esther Steele, 15 August 1948 (RHS).

39. Steele to Esther Steele, 24 September 1950 (RHS).

40. Steele to Esther Steele, 18 October 1950 (RHS).

41. Stanley White, review of *Gardens and People* by Fletcher Steele, *Landscape Architecture* 55 (October 1964): 71.

42. Steele, *Gardens and People*, 218.

43. Ibid., 220.

44. Ibid., 220, 221.

45. Ibid., 231.

46. Elizabeth Reynolds and James R. Reynolds, interview by author, Wenham, Mass., 15 April 1987.

47. Ibid.

48. Steele to James R. Reynolds, 20 November 1968, Private papers, Wenham, Mass.

49. Fletcher Steele, "Landscape Architecture" (manuscript marked "A-3," 4 March 1942, LC), 3.

50. Vincent Merrill, interview by author, Lincoln, Mass., 4 March 1987.

51. Nancy Turner, interview by author, Pittsford, N.Y., 6 October 1986.

52. Steele to Stanley Schuler, 30 March 1966 (LC).

53. Fletcher Steele, "Plant Material," *Garden Club of America Bulletin*, September 1921, 43.

54. David Mactye, interview by author, Rochester, N.Y., 20 January 1987.

55. Ibid.

56. Steele to Peter Hornbeck, 9 June 1969, Private papers, North Andover, Mass.

57. Steele to Elizabeth Reynolds, 9 June 1969, Private papers, Wenham, Mass.

58. Fletcher Steele, "Lecture Delivered at Williams College" (manuscript, 20 January 1925, LC), 1.

59. Andrew Wolfe, "Fletcher Steele, Individualist," *Brighton-Pittsford Post*, 6 June 1963.

60. Audiocassette of dinner party, July 1971, Private papers, Rochester, N.Y.

Glossary

AERIAL HEDGE A hedge produced by pleaching (see *pleaching*).

ALLÉE A walk cut through a mass of trees; any formally landscaped walk with trees on either side, arranged regularly.

ARBOR A small garden shelter, usually of trellis with climbing plants.

AXIS An imaginary line of direction, vision, or motion through architecture or landscape.

BALCONY A narrow outdoor platform attached to the upper stories of a house and enclosed with a rail.

BALUSTER A pillar or column supporting a handrail or coping; a series of these is a balustrade.

BASECOURT A service court, often accessed via a service road.

BELVEDERE A roofed but open-sided structure affording an extensive view, often located on an eminence. Also called a *gazebo*.

BOSQUET A thick grove of trees, often geometrically planted. In Italian, *bosco*.

BOWER A shelter of tree boughs, an arbor.

BOWLING GREEN A rectangular, perfectly flat length of lawn used for a game popular in the early twentieth century.

CAPSTONE A coping stone (see *coping*).

CASCADE A waterfall in which the water runs over a stepped slope rather than dropping straight down. A favorite of Italian garden designers, it was adopted and formalized by the French.

COLONNADE A series of columns set at regular intervals, supporting a roof.

CONSOLE A projecting member to support a weight, generally formed with scrolls or volutes.

COPING The covering course of a wall, usually sloping.

CORDON A tree (often a fruit tree) trained by removing all lateral branches to form one main stem.

CROSS-AXIS A secondary line of direction that lies at right angles to the major organizing line or axis.

CUBISM An early twentieth-century movement in painting and sculpture characterized by an exploration of form through simultaneous perspectives. Cubist gardens exhibited similarly faceted appearances.

DRYWALL A stone wall, laid without mortar, with crevices suitable for growing alpine plants.

ENTABLATURE The upper section of a wall, supported by columns or pilasters.

EXEDRA A semicircular or rectangular recess with benches.

FINIAL A crowning ornament or detail on an architectural element.

FOCAL POINT An object or place that attracts the eye.

FORCED PERSPECTIVE A view that has been altered to appear longer than it actually is.

FORECOURT A formal automobile court, adjacent to the house entrance and reached via a formal approach.

GAZEBO See *belvedere*.

GLORIETA A Spanish word for any summerhouse, bower, or arbor. Steele used it specifically to mean a structure of evergreen trees planted in a circle and joined at the top. In French, *gloriette*.

GRAPESTAKE An informal wooden fencing material, found throughout Europe in country gardens.

GROTTO A natural, or more often, artificial, cave, often used as a retreat from the sun.

JET D'EAU Water jet.

LATTICE Thin, wooden strips joined at right angles, used for trellises and garden houses.

LOGGIA A gallery behind a colonnade.

PALAZZO A palace or grand home.

PARAPET A low wall or railing to protect the edge of a platform.

PARTERRE A level space ornamented with flower beds of elaborate shapes, intended to be viewed from above.

PAVILION A temporary, tentlike structure; almost any open-sided shelter in gardens and parks.

PERGOLA A walk of pillars and cross members, often covered with vines.

PIAZZA An open space or square surrounded by buildings.

PLEACHING A technique for forming a dense aerial hedge by interweaving the branches of trees (often lime or hornbeam).

PORTE COCHÈRE A roofed structure extending from the entrance of a building over an adjacent driveway, to shelter arriving visitors.

PORTICO A colonnaded space forming an entrance or vestibule.

RADIAL CIRCULATION A raylike pattern of walks or drives by which a landscape is explored.

TAPIS VERT French for "green carpet;" a small lawn, ornamental in impact.

TERMINUS The end of a view or a walk.

TERRACE A paved surface adjacent to the back or side of the house, for seating.

TORCHÈRE Torch.

TREILLAGE Trelliswork; a pattern of wooden laths used as a screen to support climbing plants and to form elaborate architectural features.

TRELLIS A support for climbing plants, made of treillage.

TUFA A porous rock formed from deposits in springs or streams; especially valuable in rock gardens.

VERANDA A roofed porch.

VISTA A view, particularly a long narrow one, as opposed to a panorama (a wide sweeping view).

Select Bibliography

I Publications by Fletcher Steele

"An Emergency Report for Bangor, Maine." *Landscape Architecture* 2 (October 1911): 1–15.

"Civic Improvement." *The Survey*, 23 March 1912.

"The New Richmond College." *Landscape Architecture* 3 (January 1913): 59–67.

"Wall Gardens for America." *Garden Magazine*, September 1914.

"Some Good and Bad Cases of Garden Design." *Garden Magazine*, November 1914.

"The Landscaping of Peridot." *Garden Magazine*, February 1915.

"The Lombardy Poplar." *House Beautiful*, March 1915.

"The Secrets of Garden Furnishings." *Vogue*, 1 May 1915.

"The Construction of Walks." *Country Life in America*, July 1915.

"Tying Together House and Garden." *Garden Magazine*, August 1915.

"How Wide Is a Walk?" *Country Life in America*, September 1915.

"Robert Fleming Gourlay, City Planner." *Landscape Architecture* 6 (October 1915): 1–14.

"What I Want and What I Can Afford: A Few Questions That Must Be Decided by Everyone before the Garden Is Attempted." *Garden Magazine*, January 1916.

"Irrigation, Watering, Sprinkling: A Review of the Main Advantage Points of the Various Artificial Systems of Supplying Water to the Garden and Grounds." *Garden Magazine*, June 1916.

"Better Bridges on the Country Place." *Country Life in America*, April 1917.

"The Use of Trees." *Country Life in America*, August 1917.

"Worthy Memorials of the Great War." *Landscape Architecture* 10 (January 1920): 57–64.

"Vines That Differ for Different Places." *Garden Magazine*, March 1920.

"Sculpture in Landscape Architecture." *Architecture*, May 1920.

"Models for Suburban Lot Design and Planting." *House Beautiful*, June 1920.

"Billboard Legislation." *Garden Club of America Bulletin*, December 1920.

"Circles Give Arapaho Indian Village Racial Appeal." *Popular Mechanics*, December 1920.

"Color Charts." *Garden Club of America Bulletin*, December 1920.

"A Landscape Architect's Kit." *Landscape Architecture* 11 (January 1921): 63–65.

"Color Charts for Gardeners." *Garden Magazine*, May 1921.

"Plant Material." *Garden Club of America Bulletin*, September 1921.

"The Stotesbury Place." *Garden Club of America Bulletin*, November 1921.

"Use and Beauty Go Hand in Hand." *House Beautiful*, February 1922.

"Aesthetic Principles of the Spring Flower Garden." *House Beautiful*, March 1922.

"Evergreen Euonymus Vines and Shrubs." *Garden Club of America Bulletin*, March 1922.

"Is Beauty Practical around the Farm House?" *Farm & Garden*, April 1922.

"French Gardens and Their Racial Characteristics." *Landscape Architecture* 12 (July 1922): 211–23

"Sample Color Chart Cards." *Garden Club of America Bulletin*, September 1922.

"Gray-Leaved Plants." *House Beautiful*, November 1922.

"Color Charts and Their Use in Gardening." *Landscape Architecture* 13 (January 1923): 97–105.

"A Connecticut Rock Garden." *House Beautiful*, March 1923.

Review of *Lists of Plant Types for Landscape Planting: The Materials of Planting for Ornament Listed According to Their Various Uses*, by Stephen F. Hamblin. *Landscape Architecture* 13 (April 1923): 278.

Review of *Modern Color*, by Carl Gordon Cutler and Stephen C. Pepper. *Landscape Architecture* 13 (April 1923): 278–79.

"Cutting Garden Costs." *Country Life in America*, April 1923.

"The Charm of Gardens, the Appeal to the Intelligence." *Arts*, May 1923.

"Models for Suburban Lot Design and Planting." *House Beautiful*, June 1923.

Design in the Little Garden. Boston: Atlantic Monthly Press, 1924.

Review of *Standardized Plant Names,* by the American Joint Committee on Horticultural Nomenclature. *Garden Club of America Bulletin*, March 1924.

"Water for the Country House, for both Practical and Ornamental Purposes." *House Beautiful*, April 1924.

"Constructing a Rock Garden." *Country Life in America*, October 1924.

"City Gardens." *Garden Club of America Bulletin*, January 1925.

"Design of the Small Place." In *The House Beautiful Gardening Manual.* Boston: Atlantic Monthly Company, 1926.

"Color Chart Notes." *Garden Club of America Bulletin*, July 1926.

"Birds-eye Perspective of the Dooryard Garden of Mrs. Wallace D. Barkley." *House Beautiful*, February 1927.

"A Criticism of Mr. Rehder's New Book." *Horticulture*, 15 March 1927.

"Edgings for Paths and Garden Beds." *Garden and Home Builder*, April 1927.

Review of *The Art and Craft of Garden Making,* by Thomas Mawson. *House Beautiful*, October 1927.

"A Timely Protest from Fletcher Steele." *Horticulture*, 15 December 1927.

"Outmoded Rules of Thumb in Landscape Architecture." *The Vista*, Spring 1928.

"Landscaping a Continual Task." In *Boston Herald Book of Gardens,* edited by Bremer Pond. Boston: Boston Herald, 1929.

"Spain." *Landscape Architecture* 19 (January 1929): 6–66.

"New Styles in Gardening: Will Landscape Architecture Reflect the Modernistic Tendencies Seen in the Other Arts?" *House Beautiful*, March 1929.

"A Group of Books on French Garden Design." *Garden Club of America Bulletin*, May 1929.

"Lighting the Grounds." *House Beautiful*, June 1929.

"A Colonial Garden Home." *Ladies' Home Journal*, October 1929.

"New Pioneering in Garden Design." *Landscape Architecture* 20 (April 1930): 159–77.

"Planning the Small Place." *Horticulture*, April 1930.

"Mission House." *House Beautiful*, July 1930.

"A Garden Constructed before the House." *House Beautiful*, August 1930.

"Modern Gardens." *Country Life*, November 1930.

"Swedish Horticulture Society, Model Garden." *Garden Club of America Bulletin*, January 1931.

"A Groups of Books on Spanish Garden Design." *Garden Club of America Bulletin*, March 1931.

"Garden Patterns #151 & 152, New England Area," *Ladies' Home Journal*, June 1931.

"The Colonial Garden Today." In *Colonial Gardens.* American Society of Landscape Architects, 1932.

"Landscape Design of the Future." *Landscape Architecture* 22 (July 1932): 299–302.

"Space Design." *Parks & Recreation*, September 1932.

"Garden Comfort." *Home Acres*, January/February 1933.

"Hopkins Memorial Steps." *New England Architect and Builder*, April/May 1933.

"The Gardener's Mystery Chemical." *Horticulture*, 1 June 1933.

"Why Is Not the Modern Park a Work of Art?" *Parks & Recreations*, June 1933.

"The Temple Garden; the Garden of M. Choate, Stockbridge, Mass." *House Beautiful*, July 1933.

"Theatre Out of Doors." *Country Life in America*, September 1933.

"Tender Plants in a Cold Climate." *Horticulture*, 1 December 1933.

"Comfort in a Garden." *Decorator's Digest*, February 1934.

"Summer in an Old Quebec Farmhouse, Schofield Garden, Dorval." *House Beautiful*, May 1934.

Review of *The Art of Japanese Flower Arrangement,* by Alfred Doehn. *Garden Club of America Bulletin*, May 1934.

"Fine Art in Landscape Architecture." *Landscape Architecture* 24 (July 1934): 177–79.

"Your Own . . . Your Neighbor's Land." *House Beautiful*, September 1934.

"For Listening to the Sighing Pines." *Country Life in America*, March 1935.

"Lisburne Grange." *Garden Club of America Bulletin*, September 1935.

"Modern Garden Design." In *The Garden Dictionary,* edited by Norman Taylor. Boston: Houghton Mifflin, 1936.

"Modern Landscape Architecture." In *Contemporary Landscape Architecture and Its Sources.* San Francisco: San Francisco Museum of Art, 1936.

"Chinese Exhibition, Burlington House." *Garden Club of America Bulletin*, March 1936.

Review of *The Garden Dictionary,* edited by Norman Taylor. *Landscape Architecture* 26 (July 1936): 218–19.

Review of *Chinese Influence on European Garden Structures,* by Eleanor Von Erdberg. *Garden Club of America Bulletin*, May 1937.

Review of *Jardins Modernes. Exposition Internationale de 1937,* by Jacques Gréber. *Landscape Architecture* 28 (January 1938): 117–18.

"A New Colour Chart for Flowers." *Garden Club of America Bulletin*, January 1938.

"Look Here upon This Picture, and on This. . . ." *Landscape Architecture* 28 (July 1938): 205–7.

Review of *William Shenstone: An Eighteenth Century Portrait,* by A. R. Humphreys. *Landscape Architecture* 28 (July 1938): 216.

Review of "Horticultural Colour Chart." *Landscape Architecture* 29 (April 1939): 148.

Review of *Garden Club of America History 1913–1938,* by the Garden Club of America. *Landscape Architecture* 30 (July 1939): 196.

"Is American Garden Tradition Worth Preserving?" *Garden Club of America Bulletin*, March 1940.

Review of *The American Colorist,* by Faber Birren. *Landscape Architecture* 30 (July 1940): 199.

"Private Delight and the Communal Ideal." In "The Landscape Architect and the Present Situation" by Henry Vincent Hubbard and Fletcher Steele. *Landscape Architecture* 31 (January 1941): 69–71.

"Background of Culture and Horticulture in the Genesee Valley." *Garden Club of America Bulletin*, July 1941.

"The Scenery of Central Massachusetts and the Elliott Reservation at

Phillipston."Milton, Mass.: Trustees of Reservations, 1941.

"The Voice Is Jacob's Voice, but the Hands. . . ." *Landscape Architecture* 32 (January 1942): 64–65.

"Modern Gardens for Modern Houses." *Landscape Architecture* 32 (January 1942): 64–65.

"Enlightened Laziness." *Horticulture*, February 1943.

"A Leaf from Nature's Notebook." *Horticulture*, October 1943.

Review of *New Designs of Small Properties: A Book for the Homeowner in City and Country,* by M. E. Bottomly. *Landscape Architecture* 39 (October 1943): 39–40.

"Mr. Steele Is Reminiscent." *Horticulture*, December 1943.

"Prejudice in Rock Garden Design." *Bulletin of the American Rock Garden Society,* May/June 1944.

"The Vegetable Garden and the Greenhouse." *Garden Club of America Bulletin,* June 1944.

"Private Post-War Planning," *Garden Club of America Bulletin,* June and September 1944.

"Tree Virtues." *Horticulture,* March 1945.

"Forest Memorials." *Forest and Park News,* January 1946.

"When Trees Turn into Problems." *Horticulture,* September 1946.

"Beech and Hemlock: Of Time and Trees." *Horticulture,* February 1947.

"Appeal for the Conservation of Our National Historical Records." *Old Time New England,* April 1947.

"China Teaches: Ideas and Moods from the Landscape of the Celestial Empire." *Landscape Architecture* 3 (April 1947): 88–93.

"Naumkeag: Miss Mabel Choate's Place in Stockbridge, Massachusetts, Has Been Shaped by Two Generations of Changing Taste." *House and Garden,* July 1947.

"Needed: A San Francisco Charter, Education and Concerted Action among the Professions." *Landscape Architecture* 38 (October 1947): 19–20.

"Food Alone Is Not Enough, Flowers for Freedom, Too." *Horticulture,* March 1948.

"The Effective Use of Planting in Landscape Architecture and Gardening." *The Garden,* March and June 1949.

Review of *Jardins Français Classiques des XVII et XVIII Siècles,* by Alfred Marie. *Landscape Architecture* 40 (October 1949): 39–40.

Review of *Plant Buyers Guide to Seed and Plant Materials in the Trade,* edited by Edwin F. Steffek. *Landscape Architecture* 40 (April 1950): 141–42.

"Lilacs Grow Green in a Michigan Garden Cut to an English Pattern." *House and Garden,* September 1950.

Review of *Les Jardins de France et Leur Decor,* by Ernest de Ganay. *Landscape Architecture* 41 (October 1950): 37–38.

"A Ten Year Plan Gave This Garden New Personality." *House and Garden,* January 1953.

Gardens and People. Boston: Houghton Mifflin, 1964.

II   Works about Fletcher Steele

Adams, William Howard. *Grounds for Change: Major Gardens of the Twentieth Century.* Boston: Little, Brown, 1993.

Beck, JoAnn Dietz. "Fletcher Steele: His Contributions to American Landscape Architecture." Master's thesis, SUNY/Syracuse, 1980.

Beck, JoAnn Dietz, and M. C. K. Doell. "Fletcher Steele: Landscape Architect and Garden Maker." *Newsletter/Preservation League of New York State,* Summer 1987.

Better Homes & Gardens. *America's Gardens.* Des Moines, Iowa, and New York: Meredith Press, 1964.

Calkins, Carroll C. *Great Gardens of America.* New York: Coward-McCann, 1969.

Close, Leslie Rose. Review of *Fletcher Steele, Landscape Architect,* by Robin Karson. *Journal of the Society of Architectural Historians* 49 (December 1990): 452–53.

Current Architecture: Published in Connection with a Joint Exhibition Held in Boston November 1916. Boston: Boston Architectural Club, 1916.

Doubleday, Mrs. George. "A Patio Greenhouse." *Garden Club of America Bulletin,* November 1941.

"Estate of Mr. and Mrs. Samuel Sloan." *Town and Country,* July 1925.

Figley, Marty. Review of *Fletcher Steele, Landscape Architect,* by Robin Karson. *Observer and Eccentric Newspapers,* 12 July 1990.

Fitch, James M., and F. F. Rockwell. *Treasury of American Gardens.* New York: Harper & Brothers, 1956.

Griswold, Mac. "Gardens of Steele." Review of *Fletcher Steele, Landscape Architect,* by Robin Karson. *Garden Design,* Autumn 1989.

———. Review of *Fletcher Steele, Landscape Architect,* by Robin Karson. *Landscape Architecture* 79 (October 1989): 139+.

———. Review of *Fletcher Steele, Landscape Architect* exhibition. *House and Garden,* March 1990.

Griswold, Mac, and Eleanor Weller. *The Golden Age of American Gardens.* New York: Harry N. Abrams, 1991.

Harlow, Nora. Review of *Fletcher Steele, Landscape Architect,* by Robin Karson. *Pacific Horticulture,* Fall 1990.

Henderson, Anne Hoover. Review of *Fletcher Steele: Landscape Architect,* by Robin Karson. *Landscape Journal* 10 (Fall 1991): 187–88.

"Honor Award in Communication." *Landscape Architecture* 80 (November 1990): 60–61.

"Hyghe Contente." *North Shore Breeze,* August 1936.

"Inspiration." *Santa Barbara (California) Gardener,* August 1933.

Karson, Robin. "Of Consequence and Caprice." *Garden Design,* Spring 1984.

———. "Naumkeag, Stockbridge, Mass." *Art in America,* August 1985.

———. "Fletcher Steele's Last Vista." *Garden Design,* Spring 1988.

———. "The Designer as Artist." *American Horticulturist,* October 1988.

———. "Fletcher Steele's Places to Dream." *Landscape Architecture* 78 (December 1988): 108–13.

———. "Clarity and Elegance: Fletcher Steele's Masterpiece of Design, a Garden Room, in Rochester, New York." *Garden Design,* Spring 1989.

———. "The Blue Steps of Naumkeag." *Art New England,* July/August 1990.

———. "Gardens of Glory: Recapturing America's Heritage." *Garden Design,* January/February 1991.

———. "Masters of American Garden Design II: The Country Place Era—A Symposium." *Land and History: A Newsletter of the ASLA Historic Preservation Open Committee,* Spring 1991.

———. "Gardens of the Country Place Era." *Hortus,* Autumn 1991.

———. "The Camden Public Library Theater, 1928: Fletcher Steele and F. L. Olmsted, Jr." *Maine Olmsted Alliance for Parks and Landscapes Newsletter*, Spring 1992.

———. "Spheres, Cones, and Other Least Common Denominators: Modern French Gardens through the Eyes of Fletcher Steele." In *Masters of American Garden Design III: The Modern Garden in Europe and the United States.* Cold Spring, N.Y.: The Garden Conservancy, 1994.

———. "Library of American Landscape History." In *Land and History: A Newsletter of the ASLA Historic Preservation Open Committee,* Winter 1998.

———. "Fletcher Steele." In *Pioneers of American Landscape Design,* edited by Charles A. Birnbaum and Robin Karson. Boston: McGraw-Hill, 2000.

———. "The Age of the American Country Place." *The Magazine Antiques,* October 2000.

Kay, Jane Holtz. "A Modernist Whose Landscape Artistry Redefined Gardens." *The New York Times,* 24 August 1989.

McCormick, Kathleen. "Steele's Magic; Landscape Architects: Fletcher Steele." *Historic Preservation,* September/October 1991.

McKutcheon, Kathryn. Review of *Fletcher Steele, Landscape Architect,* by Robin Karson. *American Horticulturist,* October 1989.

Mercer, F. A., ed. *Gardens and Gardening 1936.* New York: The Studio Publications, 1936.

Messervy, Julie Moir. "Seeing Things." *Garden Design,* August/September 1994.

"Mr. Fletcher Steele." *Town and Country,* 15 December 1926.

"Mr. and Mrs. Charles H. Schweppe's Home." *The Spur,* November 1926.

"Naumkeag, Stockbridge, MA." *Art in America* 73 (August 1985): 116.

North, Tim. Review of *Fletcher Steele, Landscape Architect,* by Robin Karson. *The Australian Garden,* August/September 1991.

Otis, Denise. *Grounds for Pleasure: Four Centuries of the American Garden.* New York: Harry N. Abrams, 2002.

Plumptre, George. *Great Gardens, Great Designers.* London: Ward Lock, 1994.

"Portrait." *House Beautiful,* July 1930.

"Portraits of Gardens in the Bay State." *The Spur,* March 1934.

Reed, Christopher. Review of *Fletcher Steele, Landscape Architect,* by Robin Karson. *Horticulture,* November 1990.

———. "Enduring Steele." *Horticulture,* January 1998.

Review of *Design in the Little Garden,* by Fletcher Steele. *Horticulture,* April 1924.

Review of *Fletcher Steele, Landscape Architect,* by Robin Karson. *Publishers Weekly,* 18 August 1989.

Review of *The Gardens of Fletcher Steele* exhibition. *Landscape Architecture* 80 (July 1990): 20.

Rogers, Elizabeth Barlow. *Landscape Design: A Cultural and Architectural History.* New York: Harry N. Abrams, 2001.

Schuler, Stanley. *America's Great Private Gardens.* New York: Macmillan, 1967.

Shurcliff, Sidney. "The Formal Versus the Naturalistic Swimming Pool." *The Sportsman,* May 1934.

Stebbins, Doris. "Herb Gardens." *House and Garden,* April 1953.

Tobey, George B. *A History of Landscape Architecture: The Relation of People to Environment.* New York: American Elsevier Publishing, 1973.

Treib, Marc. Review of *Fletcher Steele, Landscape Architect,* by Robin Karson. *Journal of Garden History* 11 (July–September 1991): 177–81.

Trexler, John. "The Gift of a Garden." *Garden Design,* Spring 1985.

Trowbridge, Peter. Review of *Fletcher Steele, Landscape Architect,* by Robin Karson. *The Public Garden: The Journal of the American Association of Botanical Gardens and Arboreta* 5 (January 1990): 37.

Van Valkenburgh, Michael. "Naumkeag." In *Built Landscapes: Gardens in the Northeast.* Brattleboro, Vt.: Brattleboro Museum and Art Center, 1984.

White, Stanley. Review of *Gardens and People,* by Fletcher Steele. *Landscape Architecture* 55 (October 1964): 71.

Wolfe, Andrew D. "Fletcher Steele, Individualist." *Brighton-Pittsford (New York) Post,* 6 June 1963.

Acknowledgments

I owe thanks to many people, over many years, for their help and encouragement during the two phases of working on this book. Ngaere Macray believed in this project and supported it from the first, for which I remain grateful. I am also grateful to Flora Nyland, archivist of the Fletcher Steele papers at F. Franklin Moon Library, State University of New York, Syracuse, who has been unfailingly kind and generous with her time and has become a close friend. Nancy R. Turner, one of Steele's last clients, has also been a source of incalculable support, and she, too, has become a dear friend as well as a highly regarded adviser. I owe her more than I can express on this page or, perhaps, anywhere.

Peter Hornbeck, who learned his art from Fletcher Steele, died since the first edition was published. Peter was kind and enthusiastic, and he is missed. Among others who offered great help during the course of this project who are now gone is Henry Hoover, Steele's assistant for many years. My thanks for early support also go to Susan Maney O'Leary, formerly horticulturist for the Landmark Society of Western New York State; to Gordon Clark and Will Garrison, of the Trustees of Reservations; and to Steve McMahon, for many years of collegiality and shared projects. Carolyn Marsh Lindsay was enthusiastic and helpful in ways too numerous to count.

I am also grateful to the many clients who shared their homes and reminiscences with me: Willard and Barbara Bunney; James and Elizabeth Reynolds; Martha Weissberger; Virginia (Backus) Caulkins; Mrs. Hugo Higbie; Susie and Alan Spencer; Mr. and Mrs. John Parke; Mr. and Mrs. Joseph Taylor; Dr. and Mrs. Grinols; Mrs. Edith Clifford; Mrs. Nathaniel Lord; Mrs. Charles F. Barrett; Mrs. Louis P. Hoffman; Mrs. Pamela Lowry; Mrs. John Bartlett; Slim Proctor; Mr. and Mrs. Anthony Bolland; Mrs. William Eberle; Admiral and Mrs. Harry Hull; Mrs. George Putnam Jr.; Mr. and Mrs. Denison Hall; and Mr. and Mrs. Agnello.

I am also grateful to Mr. and Mrs. Alex Bass, Mrs. John C. Bullard, Caryl Haskins, Mrs. Kathryn Moss, Mr. and Mrs. Mehta, Mrs. Merle Rimler, Mrs. Lewis Preston, and to Steele's former employees, Arthur Sylvester and Edward Orlando, both of whom contributed new information, as did Peter Moore. I thank the staff of the Rochester Historical Society and Rush Rhees Library, University of Rochester, and Nellie Hart, of the Camden Public Library. I am grateful to Eleanor Ames and Patricia O'Donnell, who offered additional information and fresh insights about the amphitheater there.

Many Rochesterians contributed information and hospitality to this project over the years. I am grateful to Jean Czerkas, Jean Ferris, and I fondly remember Mrs. William Webber, Steele's neighbor in Pittsford. I also have fond memories of Basil Megna, who I met through Porter Perham, one of Steele's closest friends at the end of his life. Porter and David Mactye offered invaluable personal recollections of Steele and are both are now dear friends. There were several others who knew Steele and kindly added insight: Fay Dabney, Lewis Dabney, Carol Runner, Amy Bess Miller, and Alice Page Pickman. Daniel Kiley, Garrett Eckbo, and George Tobey contributed both words and ideas to this manuscript. Others who reviewed portions of it include Reuben Rainey, Susan Rademacher, Vincent Merrill, Leslie Close, Catha Grace Rambusch, Diana

Balmori, John Scruggs, George Yarwood, Mac Griswold, and Michael Van Valkenburgh. JoAnn Beck's master's thesis on Steele offered a strong point of departure for my work. Patrick Chassé generously sent me slides from Steele's trip to China and Japan.

I thank Felice Frankel for her patience, support, and her beautiful photographs in both editions and David Broda, who not only took many wonderful new photographs but made several hundred prints from Steele's highly variable negatives for both editions. I thank Helen Rollins and the Garden Club of America for lending glass slides for reproduction; Mr. and Mrs. William Oles of Delhi, New York, who generously facilitated my borrowing irreplaceable historical photographs; the National Endowment for the Arts for an individual research grant in 1986; and the Hubbard Educational Foundation for underwriting the substantial costs of reprinting photographs from Steele's collection. My parents, Jean and Robert Robinson, were a great source of support during the years I spent writing this book in the 1980s when my children were very young.

I thank my sons, too, as I do their father, Michael Karson.

Over the past year, a host of new people have helped bring the current edition to print. Foremost among these are Michael and Evelyn Jefcoat, who contributed generously to its production. I am also grateful to LALH trustees Charles D. Warren and Nancy R. Turner, and our Pittsford friends, Nancy and Stuart Bolger, who helped raise awareness and funds for this project.

I thank Christina J. Selvek, who generously shared information compiled for her SUNY master's thesis, Nancy Howard, Tina Hummel, and Tanya Cushman, who keeps all on track. I thank Bruce Wilcox, director of University of Massachusetts Press for his interest in this project; Julia Gaviria, who worked with speed and aplomb, as always; and Mary Mendell, who created this elegant new design. My deepest thanks go to Carol Betsch—editor, photographer, friend, and partner—and to the board of the Library of American Landscape History for continuing to believe in the organization *Fletcher Steele* engendered fourteen years ago.

I also thank the following individuals who have generously helped underwrite costs of the revised edition:

Jack Ahern, FASLA
Carol Betsch
Carol Booth and Linda Fidnick
    in honor of Robin Karson and Carol Betsch
Jane Roy Brown
George W. Curry, FASLA
Tanya Cushman
Mary Dewart
W. Lake Douglas
William H. Frederick Jr., ASLA
Bradford M. Greene, ASLA
Maurine S. Hausser
Mary H. H. Hayden
    in honor of Nancy R. Turner
Mr. and Mrs. John Fitzpatrick
Grant and Siobahn Holcomb
Mr. and Mrs. Michael Jefcoat
    in honor of Robin Karson
Susan L. Klaus
    in honor of Robin Karson
Dr. David Mactye
Madison Cox Design, Inc.
Charles C. McLaughlin

Mrs. James T. McMillan II
Eleanor McQuilken
John K. Notz Jr.
Frances A. Numrich
Flora May and Ralph D. Nyland
Dr. G. Porter Perham
Marion E. Pressley, FASLA
Doris Rindler
Mr. and Mrs. Robert Robinson
Mr. and Mrs. Douglas Roby Jr.
Elizabeth Barlow Rogers
Mrs. Douglas Rollins
Mrs. Peter G. Smith
Walter and Nesta Spink
Mrs. Katherine S. Taylor
Ted Collins Associates, Ltd.
James R. Turner and Dede Delaney
Nancy R. Turner
James van Sweden, FASLA
Charles D. Warren
Mr. and Mrs. William C. Warren III
William Webber
Mrs. Arnold Weissberger
Perry Carpenter Wheelock, ASLA
Carolyn S. Wolfe
    in honor of Nancy R. Turner

Index

Client names are in **boldface** type.
Illustrations are in *italics*.

and unity with surrounding landscape, x, 38, 40, 108, 125, 130, 234–35, 260, 272
    See also landscape design; modernism; planting design; space composition
garden maintenance. *See* maintenance, garden
garden ornament. *See* ornament, garden
Garden Ornament (Jekyll), 38, 178, 180
gardens
    purposes of, ix, 10, 14–15, 46, 103–4, 149, 229, 248
    recreation in, 58–59
    and travel, 32. *See also* travel
Gardens and People, 234, 246–47, 261–62
Garnier, Tony, *147*, 148
Garred, Lewis, 252
Generalife (Granada, Spain), 25, 28, *100* (plan), 110
genius loci, x, 29, 40, 113, 184, 187, 279
Germany, 30, 156. *See also* May, Ernst
Gerry, Angelica, 83
Gerry, Angelica, estate (Ancrum House)
    construction of, 83–89, *86*
    demolition of, 274–75
    general plan, *84, 85*
    major features
        Drury Seat, 89, *90*, 94, 96
        Flower Garden, 83, 93–94
        Gallop, *86*
        Lilac Garden, 89
        Octagon seat, *92* (plan), *93, 94*
        Overlook, 96, *97*
        pergola, 93–94, *95*
Gerry, Edith and Peter, estate (Frith House), 98–100, *98, 99*
Gerry, Elbridge, 83
Gerry, Peter, 83
Gilbert, Helen, estate *248*, 248–49, 266, 295
Goetz, John, garden, 247–48
Goodhue, Gertrude Munroe Smith, 261
grading. *See* space composition: and land sculpting
Great Depression, 133, 142, 163
grounds superintendents, 196. *See also* Bolcome, Robert; Wallis, Thomas
Guevrekian, Gabriel, *104*, 104, 148, 195

Hagia Sophia, 156–57
Haiti, *224*, 224–25, 237, 276
Hamilton, Alexander, 262
Harvard University graduate program in landscape architecture, 7–10, 56, 114, 217–18, 243
    Steele on, 11
hedges, *50, 51, 53*, 152, 164, *192*, 275
Hepburn, Andrew, 21
herb gardens. *See* **Backus, Standish,** estate; **Stoddard, Harry,** estate
Hewitt, Mattie Edwards, 38, *41–45*
Higbie, Mr. and Mrs. Hugo. *See* **Chapin, Roy and Inez,** estate
Highland Park (Rochester, N.Y.), 184
Hoover, Henry, 114–17, 120, 139, 157, 168, 203, 210, 218

Hopkins Memorial. *See* **Williams College**
Hornbeck, Peter, ix, 249, 259, 276
Hubbard, Henry Vincent, 8, 223
Hyghe Contente. *See* **Kenly, Mary,** estate
Hyll, Thomas, 180

Illinois, Lake Forest, 57–59
India, 209
Ireland, *89*
ironwork, 53, *54*, 76–78, *144*, 146, 172
Iselin, O'Donnell, 33, 34, 214, 224
Istanbul, 156–57
Italy
    influence of, 25, 29, 46–51, 113, 127, 143, 214, 242
    travel to, 12–15, 57, 77, 214

Japan, 172–75, 204, 277
Jekyll, Gertrude, 38, 178, 180

Kenly, Mary, estate (Hyghe Contente), 21, 168–72, *169–72*
Kiley, Daniel, ix, 149, 157, 217–18
King, Louisa Yeomans, Little Garden Series, 63
Kirby, Elihu, 266

labor
    during Great Depression, 133, 142
    effect of World War II on, 227–29, 245
Lachaise, Gaston, 81–83, *81, 82, 164*, 164–65
landscape architecture
    as a fine art, x, 56, 97, 103, 114–15, 142, 148–49, 157, 231, 245
    profession of, 97, 245–46
    Steele's definition of, 7, 187
    Steele's origins in, 6–7
    women and, 56, 157–58
    See also American Society of Landscape Architects; garden design; landscape design
landscape design
    composition in, 8–9, 184–87, 236, 241–42
    and functionalism, 19, 62, 117–18
    rhythm in, 27, 67, 266
    and time, 240–41, 254, 266, 279
    See also garden design; landscape architecture; space composition
"Landscaping of Peridot," 18–19, 63
Laprade, Albert, 148
Larch Farm. *See* **Reynolds, James and Elizabeth,** estate
Lausanne (Switzerland), 57
lawns, 63–64, 133, 135, 166, 208, 227–28
Le Nôtre, 54, 236
Lenox (Mass.) Garden Club, 105
Lisburne Grange. *See* **Sloan, Samuel and Katherine,** estate
Loring, Charles, 115, 120
Lorrain, Claude, 113, 234
Lowthorpe School of Landscape Architecture, Gardening and Horticulture for Women, 56, 157–58

Lurçat, André, 148, *149*

McKim, Charles, 106
McKinley, President William, 105–6
MacMonnies, Frederick, 108
    Boy with Heron, 102, 106, 112, 113
Mactye, David, estate, 275–77, *276, 277*
Maine, Camden, 120–25
maintenance, garden, 56, 63, 227–28, 238
Mallet-Stevens, Robert, 104, 148
Manning, Warren H., *9*
    and ASLA, 7
    apprenticeship of Steele with, 9–12, 15
    and genius loci, 40
    Kiley's opinion of, 157
Manship, Paul, 81
Massachusetts projects
    Chatham, Cape Cod, 236–37
    Gloucester, 149, 190–96, 295
    Manchester, 145–47, 152–56, 168–72
    Milton, 61–62, 64–70, 248–49, 295
    Nonquitt, Dartmouth, 238–41
    North Andover, 20–29
    Seekonk, 149
    Stockbridge. *See* **Choate, Mabel,** estate (Naumkeag)
    Sudbury Center, 101
    Wenham, 262–66, 296–97
    Williamstown, 76–77
    Worcester, 232–36
Maxwell, Miss J. A., estate, 57, 159
May, Ernst, 149, *149*
Memorial Art Gallery (Rochester, N.Y.), 276
memorials, 76–77, 230, 254
Mexico, Steele's travel to, 156, 173
Michigan projects
    Bloomfield Hills, 59–61
    Grosse Pointe Shores, 133–42, 177–83, 225–27, 252–54, 293–94
Milles, Carl. *See* Sweden
Mission House. *See* **Choate, Mabel** (Mission House)
mobiles, 164–66, *165, 166*
model village, 59–61
modernism, and landscape design, ix, 34, 62, 104, 146, 148–51, *149*, 184–89, 218, 236,
modernist gardens, European, *104, 148, 149*
Moore, Peter, 236, 250–51, 254
Morgan, Frances, 254
Morgan, Randal and Frances, estate (Wyndmoor), Orchid Room, 218–23, *218, 219* (plan), *220–22*, 226, 254
Mount Hope Cemetery (Rochester, N.Y.), 184, 230, 254
Mount Vernon (Va.), 117
Munich School of landscape design, 30

Naples, Bay of, 13–14
National Park Service, 142
National Trust (England), 243
native plants, 122, 195, 214, 232

231, 236–37, 247–49, 276
and religion, 9, 277
travel. *See* China; England; European tour of
    1913; France; Haiti; Italy; Japan; Portugal;
    Russia; Spain; Sweden; Turkey
views on
    abstraction, 33–34, 154. *See also* modernism
    architectural spaces, 156. *See also* Hagia
        Sophia; Ryoan-ji Temple
    imagination, 63–64
    invention, 167–68, 223
    landscape preservation, 243
    originality, 33
    pure design, 33
    wealth, 223, 228, 275
    See also garden design; gardens; landscape
        design; space composition; women and
        society
vocational roots, of, 6, 7, 10–11
World War I and, 34–36
World War II and, 223, 227–29
writings by, 18–19, 36, 54–55, 63, 146, 148, 175,
    184, 187–88, 231, 246–47, 261–62
Steele, John, 3–4, 5, 223, *223*
Steele, Mary, 3–4, *5*, 229
steps. *See* stair designs
stock market. *See* Great Depression
Stoddard, Harry, 195–96, 232
Stoddard, Harry, estate (Rocklawn), 187, 190–96,
    190–93 (plan), *194–96*, 228, 295
Stoddard, Robert and Helen, estate, 169, 232–36,
    233–35, 242, 274
Sturtevant, Butler S., 108, 135
Sweden, 156
    and Milles, Carl, influence on Steele, 146–47
Swindells, Emily and Stephen, estate, 158–63,
    160–62 (plan)

Sylvester, Arthur, 157

Taylor, Hilda, *197*, 199
Taylor, Joseph "Tom" F., estate, 165, 197–99, *197,
    198*, 228
Tennessee Valley Authority, 142
Thurlow, Edwin G., 245
Titian, 232
Tobey, George, ix, 63
Town and Country (Steele interview), 77, 279
Towne, John and Nora, estate (Wingfield), 36–45,
    37–45, 234–35
trees, 64, 67, 108, 123–25, 127, 264. *See also* planting
    design: general discussions of
Trustees of Reservations, 243
Turkey, 156–57
Turner, Nancy and Richard, estate, *244*, 266–73,
    267–73, *278*, 300
Tyson, Russell, 21

Utility. *See* landscape design: functionalism

Vallée des Plaisances. *See* Haiti
Vaux, Calvert, 6
Venice. *See* European tour of 1913
Vera, André, 55, *55*, 148
Vera, Paul, *55*, 148
Versailles, Steele on, 54–55, 149
Victorian design, 64, 108, 122, 259
Villa Aldobrandini, Steele on, 15
Villa d'Este, *13*, *49*, 51
Villa Lante, *13*, 15
village improvement, 56

Wake, W. S. R., estate, *18* (plan), 19
wall plantings: **Clifford, Charles and Edith,** es-
    tate; **Devine, Charlotte and Adrian,**

estate; **Smith, I. Stuart and Mary,** estate;
    Stoddard, Harry, estate (Rocklawn);
    Stoddard, Robert and Helen, estate;
    Swindells, Emily and Stephen, estate
Wallis, Thomas, 87, 196
Ward, Clayla, 32–33
Washington, George, 119, 262
Watteau, (Jean) Antoine, 37
Westmoreland. *See* **Doubleday, George and
    Mary,** estate
White, Henry, 58
White, Stanford. *See* **Choate, Mabel,** estate
    (Naumkeag): house
White, Stanley, 30, 261–62
Williams College, 7, 277
Williams College (Hopkins Memorial), 76–77, *76,
    77*, 123, 184
Williams-Ellis, Sir Clough, 214, 217
Windclyffe. *See* **Backus, Standish,** estate
Wingfield. *See* **Towne, John and Nora,** estate
women and society, Steele's views on, 103–4. *See
    also* landscape architecture: and women;
    Cambridge School of Architecture and
    Landscape Architecture
Wood, Grahame "Grady," 7, 15, 18, 209, 254,
    302n.46
Wood, Grahame "Grady," estate (Blossom Hill),
    15–18, *16*, *17* (plan)
World War I, 34–36, *35*
World War II, impact of, on Steele's gardens,
    227–28, 231
World's Columbian Exposition (Chicago), 8, 223
Wyman, Donald, 276
Wyndmoor. *See* **Morgan, Randal and Frances,**
    estate

Yugoslavia, Steele's travel to, 156